THE NEW REAL

THE NEW REAL

MEDIA AND MIMESIS IN JAPAN FROM STEREOGRAPHS TO EMOJI

Jonathan E. Abel

University of Minnesota Press
Minneapolis
London

The University of Minnesota Press gratefully acknowledges support for the open-access publication of this book from the Department of Asian Studies at Penn State University, with help from the Janssen Family Fund in Asian Studies.

Portions of chapter 4 are adapted from "Masked Justice: Allegories of the Superhero in Cold War Japan," *Japan Forum* 26, no. 2 (2014): 187–208; reprinted by permission of Taylor & Francis Ltd., http://www.tandfonline.com. Portions of the Conclusion are adapted from "Not Everyone 🗿s; or, The Question of Emoji as 'Universal' Expression," in *Emoticons,* Kaomoji, *and Emoji: The Transformation of Communication in the Digital Age,* ed. Elena Giannoulis and Lukas R. A. Wilde, 25–43 (New York: Routledge, 2019); reprinted by permission of Taylor & Francis Group, LLC, a division of Informa PLC; permission conveyed through Copyright Clearance Center Inc.

Published by the University of Minnesota Press
111 Third Avenue South, Suite 290
Minneapolis, MN 55401-2520
http://www.upress.umn.edu

🖿 Available as a Manifold edition at manifold.umn.edu

ISBN 978-1-5179-1066-2 (hc)
ISBN 978-1-5179-1391-5 (pb)

A Cataloging-in-Publication record for this book is available from the Library of Congress.

Printed in the United States of America on acid-free paper

The University of Minnesota is an equal-opportunity educator and employer.

Contents

Introduction

Two origin myths have long founded the history of film as a new medium—one from France, and the other from Japan. Legend has it that when the Lumière brothers first screened the film *Arrival of a Train at Ciotat Station* (*L'arrivée d'un train en gare de La Ciotat*) in 1895, the Parisian audience panicked because it seemed to them that the train threatened to burst through the screen.[1] In another tale, when businessman Inabata Katsutarō first brought the Lumière brothers' motion pictures to Osaka, Kyoto, and Tokyo in 1897, audiences sat down in front of both the screen at stage right and the cinematograph camera-cum-projector at stage left; so rather than hiding the magic of the technology behind a wall at the back of the theater, early Japanese screeners supposedly displayed the projection and the projecting simultaneously.[2] In the first story, the new technology makes a spectacle because the audience confuses the representation for reality as the apparatus is screened from view; in the second, the reality of the new technology itself is staged as a spectacle of equal importance to the representation. These two spurious, yet foundational narratives about the dawn of film reveal a fundamental desire about the advent of new media: people want new media to produce new spectacles; but these expectations are continually disappointed by what is delivered by the media, even as the media themselves remain desired spectacles.

This book examines the shared core of these two stories of film's introduction as a new medium through consideration of the promotion, use, and presence of various forms of new media over the course of 150 years in Japan. It articulates a commonality between the desire for a heightened sense of reality to be found in productions of new media and the mundane ways in which the world is actually transformed by them. *The New Real* juxtaposes the sensational claim that accompanies every new medium that comes along—that it can deliver more direct and intense access to reality, that it creates "immediacy"—with the perpetual desire to develop, acquire, and consume new technologies for such delivery.[3] Newspapers, translations, photographs, phonographs, televisions, video games, mobile phones, and even emoji: whenever new media appear, they are accompanied by a discourse about unprecedented access to (and often a counterintuitive and equally disquieting disconnection from) the real world. Since this discourse appears cyclically with the advent of each new medium, claims for newness on these grounds are themselves quite old. The situation described by these advertised advances is a recurring, well-marketed, mythical desire in which users of a new medium are captivated, but only until the new becomes old and settles into the comfortable routine of ordinary life. "The new real" names both the marketing hype about media's transformation of the world through closer connection and higher fidelity (representation) and the actual everyday transformations of human behavior realized by the presence of media (mimicry).

Beyond the marketing rhetoric, new media are accompanied by another (often concurrent) narrative of such technological cultural products. This narrative posits a "new normal" of living with the new medium. This quieter, alternative discourse is particularly evident in moments of "hypermediacy," when media present images of themselves or of other media.[4] For instance, in 1904, the photographer Enami Nobukuni included a stereoscopic image of three geisha looking through a Holmes stereoscope viewer in the set of five hundred images he sold to the Keystone View Company and later to Sears, Roebuck and Company for their "Views of Japan" series. In 1940, prima donna Miura Tamaki, known worldwide as the embodiment of Puccini's Madame Butterfly, composed and recorded her own song about the tragic heroine in order to avoid copyright fees for using Puccini's music. In 1958, the *Moonlight Mask* (*Gekkō kamen*) television superhero series included fictional newscasts reporting threats to the nation that only the masked hero of justice could prevent. In 2009, when the main character in the video game *Steins;Gate* stares at the fictional Alpacaman video game, he also stares out at the players of the game he inhabits. Such moments, spotlighting their own mediation, are not merely representations that reflect "intermedia consciousness" of the producers.[5] They do not simply snap the audience out of their "suspension of disbelief," weakening the sense of realism by drawing attention to the scene of their own user-level consumption. Nor are they simply instances of gazing into a constructed abyss, as theories of representation through a *mise en abyme* would have it.[6] Rather, they are origin points for an inverted or reverse mimesis that jumps the divide between the mediated world and the media in the world. Instead of the medium acting to reflect our world (as does the mirror of traditional mimesis), hypermediacy around new media, like mirrors reflecting mirrors, provides us with alternative self-reflective discourses on our new media and fundamentally alters what media are and can be.

Such self-reflexive discourse contradicts the mainstream marketing that hypes better representations, closer connections, and more immediate delivery. In moments when mediated images show consumers how to behave with and use a new medium, media impact and change the world through their presence in it. In each of these cases, it is not solely the operation of the new medium (its mediation) that brings about this reimagination of its place in the everyday world but rather the mediated "content" that reshapes the image of media and mediation. This suggests an important characteristic of media: that media themselves are always already mediated and remediated by the content they transmit. Even before media begin to function as conduits, discourse around the work of mediation prefigures the reception of a new medium. Just as no content arrives unmediated, no medium can be perceived independent of such content or of the mediation of media.

Media theory has shown the necessity of questioning the relation between the media and the mediated, between the system of a message transfer and the content of the message.[7] In information and communication studies, a strictly definable border between communicated content or a message and the system that carries it is cast in doubt.[8] But this doubt placed on distinguishing the message from the communication system—not so much the signal from the noise, but the canvas, frame, and wall from the painting itself—is bracketed by the problem of the message-communication system's relation to everything else: namely, to the real world. If post-structural and media-ecological troubling of the border between the picture and frame extends our thinking outward so that we must talk also about a border between the picture–frame amalgam and the real or the picture–frame–world divisions, then what is new about a new medium is not actually its degree of transparency or the clarity of its mediation of the world but rather the way it mediates this question of immediacy or transparency itself.[9] When a new medium has become quotidian and unremarkable, even boring, and we are ready for yet another "next new thing," the new real arrives, our lives having been transformed through the social absorption of the no-longer-new medium.

Even if technological innovation and growth of digital cultures allow the transmission of reality in a manner that feels fundamentally different from older analog methods, the concepts with which those differences have been assessed remain unchanged.[10] Derived from seventeenth-century Cartesian mathematics and proliferating in gadgets of the nineteenth century, graphical perspective continues to organize principles in popular media such as virtual reality and multiplanar formats like animation.[11] Similarly, with digital music reproduction and simulation, questions of mimicry and simulation return through terms like *sampling* and *synthesization.* Today's mass online shooter games raise fears of normalizing violence through interactivity, but real-world violence resulting from televisual representation has been a concern since the dawn of that medium. Video games restage a mode of passive relation with our media in relation to visions of the apocalypse that began perhaps with masks and the invocation of gods. And emoji simply mark the latest version of pictographic communication as old as cave paintings. Despite the change in modes of expression, capture, storage, and transmission, representation and mimicry persist as key factors in the sale and evaluation of new cultural forms and technologies.

Furthermore, it is remarkable how marketing rhetoric and academic talk about media change parallel one another: for one of the most recent versions of this, compare the following claim by media theorist Neil Postman in 1993 to the pithier marketing slogan touted by Steve Jobs on the advent of the iPhone in 2007. Postman wrote: "Technological change is neither additive nor subtractive. It is ecological. . . . One significant change generates total change. . . . It changes everything."[12] Jobs quipped: "This changes everything." But the fact that Jobs was back at it again (in 2010 with the release of iPhone 4 and its slogan "This changes everything. Again.") as much as admits the rhetoric was empty. Despite such bombastic claims ricocheting through the echo chamber of media ecology that includes marketers and media scholars, there are no great rifts separating the media of the old and that of the new that withstand historical inquiry.[13]

This book questions the subtle but stubborn penetration of the marketing rhetoric of "new" into technical, semantic, aesthetic, ethical, and academic discussions of media. Japanese cultural and technological products provide an ultimate test case for this rhetoric of the "new" not only because the idea of the "new release" (*shinhatsubai*, a phenomenon whereby new products enjoy a phantasmagorically deceptive sales pitch, akin to the "new and improved" marketing label in the United States) pervades advertising in Japan today but also because the nation has figured so prominently in the arguments that founded new media studies historically and globally. Since Marshall McLuhan argued that the "medium is the message" in 1964, Japan has consistently been one of the small handful of countries to be considered a leader, with many "firsts" in new media ideas, technologies of circulation, and cultures that thrive on and within them.[14] And, as Yoshimoto Mitsuhiro persuasively argues, Japan has been used as a test case to prove the supposed universal applicability of media theory.[15] Part of the reason for this has to do with Japan's history as a leader in the fields of communication and information technologies. Japan, then, is not so much a test case for the new as a compelling place for evaluating the efficacy of the concept.

While discussing the self-projected images of innovation and newness embedded in Japanese new media, this book also recognizes a perceived threat of a technological Japan from the outside (techno-orientalism), arising as early as 1897 with the introduction of the Arisaka rifle, the design of which was emulated by the British navy until 1921, and perhaps even earlier with Jonathan Swift's spoof of European images of Japan in *Gulliver's Travels* (1726). Swift portrays a partly real but highly fictionalized Japan (based on scant factual sources) as a politically and technologically superior nation in order to ground the even more fanciful places to which he sends his roving protagonist and connect them to the real world of readers. This tendency to muse about Japan as a real place in the present through which to philosophize and fantasize about other possible worlds and futures is echoed in much more recent cyberpunk visions, the locus classicus of which is William Gibson's *Neuromancer*. In that 1984

English-language novel, Gibson imagines an information-connected center in futuristic Ono-Sendai, Japan, where one could "jack in" to an information hub that he names "cyberspace." From Swift to Gibson, Japan has been represented and constructed as a kind of virtual space or heterotopia that is both here in the world and elsewhere, a conduit through which to imagine other places, as well as an exceptional other place itself.[16] That is to say, a medium.

This book shows that, although many recent innovations in media technology have come from Japan, the role of Japanese industry is entirely contingent and historicizable: little about these innovations is specific to Japan or inherently Japanese. Though nothing essential about Japan or Japanese culture warrants a special position as a center of "new media" discourse, it has often been placed there by culture creators, media scholars, pundits, and marketers both within and outside of Japan. In the late nineteenth and early twentieth centuries, Japan was a temporal medium for connecting a modernizing present with a premodern past. During the Cold War, Japan became more of a spatial medium that bridged the divide between East and West, communist and capitalist regimes, acting as a node for U.S. hegemony in Asia.[17] Japan's role as a medium was not simply thrust upon it from the outside but carefully maintained and cultivated from within.

This book directly intervenes in two major, reinforcing discourses around Japan's role in media studies. On the one hand, the techno-orientalist discourse fetishizes Japan in terms of technology (for instance, in representations from the fictional worlds of Gibson to those of Kon Satoshi, in sensationalist news coverage of Japanese robot animal companions, and through viral videos of synthetic humanoid vocalization robots as the pinnacle of innovation).[18] On the other hand, self-exoticizing "theories of Japaneseness" consider Japanese technology—especially Japanese-developed consumer technologies, like Sony VAIO netbooks (the world's first mass-marketed computers with fingerprint security), Canon digital 3D cameras, and Capcom's fighting video games like *Street Fighter* and *Sengoku Basara*—as uniquely positioned to dominate the global techno- and mediascapes.[19] These two discourses depict Japan as a real place that, even as it exists in the present day, somehow also represents a future not yet realized in the rest of the world. Beyond its own borders, Japan's mythical status as a tech nation appears real because consumers continue to prize "made in Japan" as a label indicating precise, well-designed, cutting-edge technology. As such, the case of Japan is essential to the study of new media. If new media are not new in the supposedly futuristic Japan, then they were never new at all.

Chapter 1 explains the main argument and interventions in media studies and theories of mimesis. The following chapters present case studies of four particular "new" media. Each case highlights different keywords in the recent glorification of "new media" as a radical break from the past. And each navigates seemingly different notions of mimesis. By connecting the histories of analog and digital "new media," this approach ultimately reveals the limits and value of the continued use of the term *new media*. The book identifies both what is specific to our current moment and what is shared across time in our contemporary usage of jargon like *virtuality, immersive, intellectual property, copycat violence,* and *embodiment.*

Chapter 2, on stereomimesis, contrasts Japan's role in the global stereoscopic trade of the early twentieth century with recent claims about the connections between high-tech Japanese televisions (widescreen, high-definition, or 3D) and superflat animation. Echoing the production of stereoscopy, which produces its 3D effect by pairing two nearly identical two-dimensional images, this chapter juxtaposes "what was represented" with "the presentation of the apparatus."[20] This history of stereoscopy and its relation to the visual exhibits (*misemono*) that were popular in the Meiji period connects recent multiplanar criticism of cel animation to a longer history of philosophical notions of parallax and stereographic viewing. Rather than toggling between two perspectives to enhance a worldview, the products of three-dimensional photography project themselves into and thereby transform our world, whether through images that seem to grant better perspectives, machines that provide views of those images, or 3D-printed statues manufactured from those images.

Chapter 3 examines the lasting impact of the collision between expanding international copyright regulations and the new media of records and radio in Japan of the 1930s. The interactions and litigation between Miura Tamaki, who played Madame Butterfly in over two thousand performances around the globe, and Wilhelm Plage, the notorious copyright hound advocating for European copyright conglomerates throughout Asia, led to the promulgation of a new series of Japanese copyright laws that established the current system for rights-holding. The recording history of Puccini's *Madama Butterfly* in Japan provides a stark example of the ways in which new media are caught up in long-standing issues of cultural production and appropriation, originality and copying, and body and identity, or what Steven Feld terms, in reference to recorded music, "schizophonic mimesis."[21]

Chapter 4 considers the role of the television in Japanese homes through examples of copycat play and copycat violence, focusing on one case that resulted in the cancellation of the first Japanese super-hero program in the 1950s. This case study reveals how forms of violent mimicry relate to the contemporary practice of cosplay (costume play) and to the ongoing discourse on education and moral panic around new media. Restaging René Girard's notion of "mimetic rivalry," this chapter explains why masked television superheroes became a genre in Japan and illuminates the reception of that specific genre and of television as a medium. Girard's mimetic theories, though couched as ahistorical truths about Judeo-Christian culture, are products of the television age. Thus, the idea that television promotes violent mimetic rivalries explains as much about the medium as it exhibits the very symptoms of the rivalry it purports to find there.

Chapter 5 examines the hopes and fears around video games as either bringing families together or driving society apart. The chapter begins with a deep history of early gaming theory through the remediation of video games in the older media of films and novels. It then focuses on a case study of a particularly Japanese form of video gaming known as the "visual novel game." In *Steins;Gate* (2009), the place of the player in the game and the game in the player's world is revealed through the insertion of metagame effects into the gameplay. Between the end-of-the-world games that were popular in the last years of the Cold War and the connected disconnect of post–web 2.0 (post–social media) gaming, this medium built a world of fan communities and connections, best captured in the recent trend of posting video playthroughs of games online. Contemporary ideas of ecomimesis inform the description of the world-building and world-destroying power of games.

Chapter 6 turns to the question of the body that is present in all the chapters through an archaeology, genealogy, and mimetology of emoji. Japanese digital youth cultures transcend the marketing and consumption of mobile phone novels, light novels, visual novel games, and alternate history fiction through appeals to the seemingly universal body. If mimesis marks a kind of real-world metaphor (standing in for others and becoming others), it is in the body that we can see how copying, substitution, and emerging mimesis function. For this reason, every chapter begins with an external medium (stereoscopy, records, television, video games, emoji) but ends with the body. From a standard smiley face to the strangely cute poop emoji, the pictogram characters attempt to reinsert the body into linguistic communication, but their failure to do so reveals a different form of embodied connection beyond the screen.

The concluding reprise brings back several themes of the case studies to think again about Japan as a medium, stereotyped as a copycat nation, prized for its technological products and carefully cultivated media contents.

Though the case studies of the chapters are arranged roughly chronologically, each covering about four decades of media history in Japan, the movement through the chapters should not suggest a narrative of historical progress. The Marxian notion (from the *Eighteenth Brumaire of Louis Bonaparte*) that history repeats itself first as tragedy then as farce contains his familiar three-part dialectic tension. But it gives us no guide to know within which moment of history we might happen to be dwelling: the original, the second (farce), or the third (tragedy). Recognizing that even Napoleon I (whom Marx positioned as the first) was not an original, this book assumes that the first movement presents simply the myth of origins and that, rather, we dwell in a world in which copies toggle between the farcical and tragic. This is not to suggest a faith in cyclical history or ahistorical truths but rather to recognize that our contingent use of particular media (in this case, the medium of language and its concepts of media) ground and imply the use of other terms such as *mimesis*.

Rather than telling media history through failed projects, as does Siegfried Zielinski, or arcana, as does Friedrich Kittler, this book provides a series of media archaeologies and genealogies through mainstream and popular Japanese new media in order to suggest that concepts of media themselves are imbricated with the multifarious concepts of mimesis.[22] Following the lead of media historians such as Charles R. Acland, Lisa Gitelman, and Wendy Chun, the chapters successively contextualize major current keywords of media studies within earlier modes of representation. Rather than a teleology of technological progress or even a widespread historical arc of the development or cultivation of mimesis over time (from, say, representation to mimicry), readers will find repeating patterns revealing how new media teach their users how to be used through a dialectic tension between representation and mimicry: the stories mime one another, echoing themes with differences and variations that speak to the distinct historical circumstances and conceptual frameworks of the case studies. This repetition displays in structure what is argued through the content—that is, that re-presentation and copying are only one aspect of mediation. Therefore, the repetitions can be read as the patterns we are programmed to see in history, as well as the transhistorical nature of change. This cyclical expansion of what we had before differs from progress; though it will create something new through mimicry, it is not necessarily radically new. Any claims for the radical newness of media have been greatly exaggerated: Welcome to the new real; same as the old real.

1

Welcome to the New Real!

What Media? Which Mimesis? Why Japan?

This first chapter lays out the theoretical stakes for the arguments of the book—that media studies can benefit from a regrounding outside of media systems; that mimetic theory continues to be vital for thinking about how we live with(in) media; that Japan is an instrumental (if not necessary) case for developing this mimetic understanding of media. As such, the chapter can be usefully read either before the case studies as a foundation upon which those chapters can be understood or afterward as a theoretical explication.

Japan as Cyberspace

Especially in the age of cyberspace, Japan has become a medium for thinking about mediation. To understand this assertion, it will help to recount some recent histories of the concept of media and theories of cyberspace.

John Guillory's excavation of many historical concepts of media reveals how "media" have tended to presuppose a distance between worlds, dimensions, realms, or layers to be mediated: "The enabling condition of mediation is the interposition of *distance* (spatial, temporal, or even notional) between the terminal poles of the communication process (these can be persons but also now machines, even persons and machines)."[1] As connectors in a communication model around the advent of information studies, media were often positioned as lines in the distance or space between nodes, often reduced to wires. This narrow vision of *medium* has not been its primary conception through its long and expansive history. According to Guillory, the pivotal moment in the history of *media* came in the wake of World War I, when the term became associated with conjuring spirits from the other world. In that moment, media came to be seen primarily as a means of communication. Previously, medium had been thought of simply as the material on or in which art had been brought into existence or made manifest.[2] But it was the advent of a person acting as an embodied conjurer of the dead (indeed, in many cases an actor) that the question of media and mediation as a connector of two otherwise separate worlds, dimensions, or levels became well known.

Guillory's notion of "distantiation" incorporates and exceeds the basic concept of distance posited in the information studies communicative models, where it is simply the space between two points: sender and receiver, writer and reader, artist and audience, creator and consumer. Rethought to include instances when the sender is also a receiver and vice versa, when both sender and receiver themselves are media, or when the message has less to do with a substance or content delivered than the biographical details or identities of the poles, the grander concept of media (including both information studies models and spiritualists conjuring other planes of existence) allows for a wider sense of what is at stake in contemporary uses of the term. With the human embodiment of the bridge in the distantiation, the gadgetry, mechanism, trick, or cheat of the media concept comes into high relief, embodied as an active, subjective agent rather than as a transparent window. In this sense, media are necessarily relational and often liminal, on the edge between this world and that, but not completely here or there. They are more than conduits or bridges; they can be virtual—both here and elsewhere, as well as the form that connects the notion of the here with the elsewhere. As originally conceived, cyberspace was just such a space. And the "here" or proper place of cyberspace was Japan.

Since the 1990s, the perspective of Japan as a medium that conjures or channels another place of pure artifice has been vividly theorized through the ideas of cyberspace. William Gibson's notion of cyberspace was anchored in the real world—in some sense "Japan" was necessary or proper to his neologism. Subsequent ideas about cyberspace bore the taint of this imagined exotic Japaneseness even when they did not ever make those connections explicit. Such exoticism is a willful "blindness" that is ontologically productive; as Karatani Kōjin argues, such Kantian "bracketing [of] other concerns" is the origin of aesthetics as such.[3] Slavoj Žižek's attempts to conceptualize the social importance of cyberspace beginning in the late 1990s relate a particular kind of aestheticized blindness to the world that creates the aesthetics of the new medium. In "Cyberspace, or The Unbearable Closure of Being," Žižek begins with the example of J. G. Ballard's short story "The Gioconda of the Twilight Noon," in which the main character willingly chooses to blind himself in order to enjoy his continued dreamlike visions.[4] Žižek's reading lines up this fiction with that of Plato's cave, Saki's "The Open Window," Roland Emmerich's *Stargate,* and Orson Welles's *The Trial* to highlight willful play with phantasmatic media (such as dreams, cave walls, windows, gates, and doors) that provide vantage points to connect with other spaces that seem more desirable than either the reality embodied in the (corporeal, social) world (of labor, scarcity, irrationality) or the directly inaccessible infinite (Lacanian) real. For Žižek, it is the preference for the virtual or simulacrum that reproduces the structures of desire apparent in the mass participatory behaviors of the internet.[5] In this sense, Žižek is less interested in the medium per se than in how cyberspace provides a real-world instantiation of long-running human psychological concerns about the ontological status of being and reality. What happens when a country itself takes the place of that threshold or medium?

Critic Azuma Hiroki picks up Žižek's thread dealing with cyberspace as a simulacrum in a series of essays published in *Intercommunication* between 1997 and 2000. There, Azuma fixates on computer graphics (CG) in films and video games as the visual instantiation of the absent presence of simulacra.[6] Mindful of Walter Benjamin's notion of the optical unconscious in the spatial and temporal magnification and expansion that media can produce, Azuma recognizes that media can capture aspects of the otherwise imperceptible real, resulting in a consequent lack or loss of what Benjamin would term "aura." Azuma parallels this form of simulacrum based on a distortion of reality with Lacan's notion that the Other "does not exist." For Azuma, the notion that CG can create spaces, people, and things that do not exist outside of the media is an almost perfect analogue for what he, following Žižek, terms a degradation of the Symbolic register or an end of the Symbolic era. This supposition about postmodern loss of meaning relies, of course, on the assumption of the existence of an earlier time when media supposedly had a more direct relation to reality.[7] Azuma claims that CG, the internet, and, implicitly, all such virtualizing media require new metaphors to help us understand them. In his view, the old visual and spatial metaphors and representations (such as mirrors) no longer suffice to help us grasp our state of mediation.

For his explication of cyberspace, Azuma lands on the thinking of science fiction writer Bruce Sterling and others, who propose "mirrorshades" as the appropriate metaphor for the literary form of cyberpunk.[8] At a key moment in his essay, Azuma quotes Samuel Delany from an interview with critic Takayuki Tatsumi, elaborating on the aviator sunglasses popular in the 1970s and 1980s as the exemplary metaphor for cyberspace:

> What are mirrorshades, after all? They're a thin film of reflective mylar. They cut off your gaze—at any rate, darken what you see. At the same time, they mask the gaze's source. Someone looking at you cannot tell whether you're looking at them or looking away. Thus, they both mask the gaze and distort the gaze. They protect us against a painful light. At the same time, they displace the gaze of the reader, who must always look at himself or herself any time she or he seeks to find the origin of the gaze. All you can find is yourself. . . . Well, they constitute the structure of a particular displacement of the notion of vision—and since the whole notion of the gaze comes from Lacan, and from Lacan's emphasis on the mirror stage, the text becomes someplace where you look to see what's going on, only what you see is yourself looking at the text to see what's going on—while at the same time, the text presents a gaze that is somehow darkened, distorted, and reflected. . . . It's not quite clear whether you're the one wearing the mirrorshades or whether the text is wearing them. I think in cyberpunk the text is wearing them—the mirrorshades.[9]

In this statement, Delany explains how "mirrorshades" work to capture the cyberpunk aesthetic, as well as how they function in society. Azuma takes this notion of the mirrorshades as being emblematic not only of cyberpunk but also of cyberspace itself. He aligns the metaphor with Derrida's notion of a visor effect ("effet de visière") in his reading of the ghost of the father in *Hamlet,* who wears armor and a helmet with the beaver up, essentially giving Hamlet and the audience a sense of being watched by a faceless spirit.[10] For Azuma, whether mirrorshades or the ghost's visor, the weight of the idea of the absent presence falls more significantly on the absence side, in his paralleling of the two forms of headgear with cyberspace. This is because for him, it is the ability to dwell in cyberspace as an anonymous participator that enables a kind of free subjectivity. This cyber-utopian idea that we can participate in without a trace leading back to an individual outside of the network is key and later led Azuma to reconceive cyberspace as Rousseau's participative democracy—precisely this sort of anonymous participatory space.[11] But this notion of cyberspace as virtual simulacrum that disconnects users from the world by transitioning them into virtual selves or avatars is a core problem with Azuma's thinking of cyberspace and media in general.[12]

The notion that anonymity holds in cyberspace (or behind the mirrorshades of a 1970s California highway patrolman, for that matter) is but an imaginary fantasy.[13] And although Azuma acknowledges that the internet relies on the material infrastructure of "telephone lines, antennas, modems, tuners and computers," ultimately he argues that "'media space' and 'cyberspace' do not physically exist."[14] His argument amounts to a willful ignorance of its own, a dismissal of work like Lev Manovich's that places cyberspace squarely as a product of the Cold War military-industrial complex.[15] This is because Azuma fundamentally believes the postmodern hype that we have now drifted away from traditional meaning-making structures (like the Symbolic), when in fact new media simply present another moment of having to rediscover how meanings are made (a new occasion or context for understanding the Symbolic). In short, Azuma emphasizes the power of hiding identity behind the mask or screen, the anonymity of the web, as being the sum total of agency itself.[16] And, of course, even in today's cyberspace that always already seeks to hide its origins and technical apparatus in favor of smooth, frictionless consumer experience, there is also a more distributed form of power, a force that accumulates through peeking behind the mirrorshades, in reading code, in calculating the carbon footprint of its servers, in understanding algorithms, and in reconnecting IP addresses to actual people in order, for instance, to assign blame for cybercrime or responsibility for cyberparticipation.[17] We have reached a moment in history when our recognition of new symbols may be lacking because we have yet to develop a dynamic sense of the new media.

In a way, the postmodern (to which Azuma too often clings) describes not the real as such, not an actually new crisis in signification, but a bubble in signification, one pumped up like a bubble economy on hype. And like an economic bubble, this bubble in signification marks a precarity of presentism that ignores the inevitable futurity when such bubbles pop and the real returns with force. Just as the bursting of a bubble economy indicates a time when our debts will have to be paid and real values will be reassigned to the formerly inflated ones, so too will behaviors in cyberspace have real-world effects when people are directly identified with their online avatars. To understand the importance of cyberspace as a useful example and metaphor for thinking about media, to reground its importance as today's medium par excellence, it is not enough to recognize, as Azuma does, that the shared symbolic and material ground for the internet does not simply reside in the infrastructure of its servers and networks. Rather, the quasi-reality of a Japan imagined by techno-orientalists from Gibson to NTT DoCoMo (the corporation that was Japan's primary internet provider and published *Intercommunication*, the journal in which Azuma launched his ideas on cyberspace), the neither-past-nor-future, neither-here-nor-there-like reality of Japan is the ontological reality that founds the media concept today as such. In other words, cyberspace is like mirrorshades—not because we cannot see the person behind the glasses, but because it makes a performance of not being able to see behind them. It is a performance in which the wearer appears to be unknowable but is either knowable or theoretically discoverable. If cyberspace can be read through the metaphor of mirrorshades, Japan is the name behind the japanning veneer of the internet.

Further developing Azuma's thoughts on cyberspace in the provocative book *Media Do Not Exist* (*Media wa sonzai shinai*), Lacanian psychoanalyst and occasional media theorist Saitō Tamaki complicates notions of the real and virtual in productive ways. For Azuma, as we have seen, the essence of cyberspace is its virtuality (extant nonexistence). But for Saitō, who draws more deeply on Lacan, the insubstantiality of CG and their relation to the Lacanian Other must be considered in a different way. Ultimately, Saitō understands the notion of "does not exist" in the vein of Lacan's notion that "the Woman does not exist" ("la Femme n'existe pas"). Individual women exist, the stereotype exists, but the stereotypical woman does not.[18] So too with Saitō's titular homage to Lacan, where he substitutes "the media" for Lacan's "the Woman": though Media writ large does not exist, we have uncountable instances or examples of media. We cannot study Media per se, but we can study its examples—for instance, a given medium.

To make this argument, Saitō connects questions of virtuality and cyberspace with the psychosociological prison experiment conducted at Stanford University in 1971. The human subject simulations in that experiment became, for the participants, the real thing. The experiment was canceled early when participants role-playing as guards and inmates began to exhibit all too real and violent prison-like behaviors. To Saitō, this experiment is an example of cyberspace, meaning that, if given enough time and pressure, virtual behaviors in cyberspace become real.[19] At a certain point, the simulation ceases to simulate and simply becomes our lived reality. The primary point of difference between Saitō's view of cyberspace and Azuma's comes down to this having-become-real quality of the virtual: for Azuma mirrorshades present a dark bar beyond which the gaze cannot penetrate; for Saitō the virtual performance in the cyberspace will necessarily bleed into the real.

Saitō views cyberspace as part of the world of information. To explain our informatization, he deems "rendering" (as in CG) to be a primary function of digital media. That is, as he defines it, media render data so that data can be perceivable or understandable by humans. Rendering is thus a metaphor for thinking about data or information processing, though for Saitō it never rises to the level of an interpretation of data. Rather, he sees rendering or mediation as a conversion or transformation (*henkan*), a reworking in different terms, or what other media theorists might call a remediation of data. Saitō is then proposing something like a rigid distinction or difference between a passive transliteration and a creative translation. Like Azuma, Saitō is interested in the problem of what rendering means when it creates an actor without a body in our world. Not exactly creating a virtual body out of thin air but out of digitized data. What does it mean that media can create a reality? Here again there is an echo of the notion that media do not exist. But Saitō recognizes that, once rendered, the rendered image has a substance; it exists not in a generalizable way but in a very specific mode that can act in and on the world.

Cyberspace and media in a sense create or name the dichotomy between the real and the simulacra they purport to bridge. Tracking the history of new media from photography to computing, Lev Manovich notes a return of computing to the original function of media "as information carrier, nothing less, nothing more," that accompanied the birth of the Zuse computer that used discarded film as the medium for programming, thus abandoning the "pretense" of new media's "simulations of sensible reality."[20] Yet with the increased connectivity of networked systems, size of informational storage potential, and speed of computing power, the rendering of the particular new medium of cyberspace has brought the digital full circle back to a medium that promises precisely the delivery of such simulacra. Wendy Hui Kyong Chun narrates a similar disillusionment with cyberspace itself over the course of the nineties that began with utopian dreams over anonymity and ended with dystopian nightmares of surveillance:

> The image of the Internet has shifted radically from the mid to late 1990s, when it was seen as "cyberspace," an anonymous and empowering space of freedom in which no one knew if you were a dog, to the mid to late 2010s, when the Internet was commonly conceived of as a space of total surveillance or as a privatized space of social media. In both cases, knowing who was a dog and who was not was key.[21]

The confusion of humans and dogs before new media will compose a portion of the end of this chapter and so will be left alone here. But the transition from the initial utopian rhetoric of a free place of play to the system of control functioning around the identity of the sender is key to the functioning of the new media system. Or as Chun puts it elsewhere: "If online communications threaten to submerge users in representation—if they threaten to turn users into media spectacles—high-tech Orientalism allows people to turn a blind eye to their own vulnerability and to enjoy themselves while doing so, to enjoy one's emasculation."[22] Cyberspace enables two modes of mimesis: representation of identity (that either comports with a body or does not) as well as disguise through mimicry.

In sum, the concept of media at once presents a distance and the bridging of the distance. Media are neither quite entirely here nor completely elsewhere. In other words, the concept of media is so troubling that it forces us to search for other words, to repeat it in different ways, represent it in smaller, more tangible modes—modes that are more ready-to-hand than not, more here than there. Digital media of recent years (CG and cyberspace) have provided some key examples with which to think through these problems of media. And yet they, too, have been explications or metaphors that require still other examples and analogues for understanding (such as mirrorshades, the Stanford prison experiments, and many other possibilities). As such, the concept of media is thoroughly imbricated with mimesis.

Mimesis in Japan

Thus far, mimesis has played a minor role in both media studies and Japanese studies. This probably has as much to do with the way the disciplines draw their borders as it does with the historical concerns of these disciplines. Media studies tends to emphasize the technological system of the medium as a means of communicating information. In such work, the focus is on the quality or fidelity of message transfer within the system, often regardless of fidelity of the input to the real world outside of the system.[23] And oddly, in focusing on the affordances of the technological apparatus, media studies tends to ignore technique (despite the recent spate of treatises using the word *technê*), drawing less on the skills of the human beings and bodies involved in the cultivation of the external (to body) media.[24] Mimetic theory has long considered the representation of the world in art, or the art of mimicry by human beings and their bodies, as a skill that has a transformative role in the world. This is why it can be mutually beneficial to bring communication and media studies together with disciplines such as anthropology and literature that are traditionally more interested in questions of mimesis. In addition, both media and mimetic studies have largely remained Western and even anglophone in orientation, despite anomalous and stochastic use of non-Western examples, and even though so much of our audio, video, and digital media equipment have been produced in Asia since the dawn of the discipline. This is one reason why bringing a study of Japanese media into this discussion can be fruitful.

The intertwining and problematic concepts of media and mimesis are the spine that runs through and binds the case studies of this book together. The expansion of media studies beyond the press and mass media to book history, screen studies, and information systems over the past several decades and the trendiness of the term *media* have raised questions about its precision and continued utility.[25] Yet despite doubts about the term, it remains useful not only because it is a valuable ontological category in mainstream discourse but also because it pinpoints a conundrum in the age-old text/context or content/frame distinctions. The conundrum is this: there is no clear way to determine how the content of any media directly affects the world (there is no clear line connecting what happens within cultural products and their various receptions); yet, at the same time, this lack of direct and determinable impact does not mean that content is entirely disconnected from the world or without world-changing possibilities. The concept of media directly labels this problem. As a bridge (or connection between inside and outside), media continue to provide a useful rubric for considering the problem of relating what is in the system and what is outside of it. In short, attention to media and mediation helps articulate the paths connecting content and frame, text and context, culture (from art and information to criticism and knowledge) and the objective real world. And it is in this final connection to the real world that mimetic theories can be helpful.

If, as Akira Lippit, Marc Steinberg, and Alexander Zahlten argue, the media concept is a problematic import in the Japanese instance, then the same critique can be made even more strongly for *mimesis*, a Western term of ancient Greek origin.[26] To study Japanese media in the terms of mimesis could seem like yet another example of the colonial technique of mining non-Western sources for the service and application of Western theory. This book is an effort to generate a broad and deep understanding of how the multiple concepts of mimesis could help media studies; how media history might add nuance to theories of mimesis; how mimesis continues to have relevance as a product of convergent evolution of thought and homogenization of cultures via globalization and modernization and the accompanying homogenization and diversification of new media technologies. If theories of mimesis have been seen by many as a Western form of representation, it is because the rise of the printed word (*logos*) in modernity itself has displaced one of the aspects of mimesis already present in the ancient Greek notion—mimicry (*mimos*).[27] To put it another way, theories of mimesis written in the print era are already transformed by print media and, therefore, tend to overemphasize its representational aspects while neglecting the mimicry embedded in the original term.[28] Consideration of Japan's alternative modernity within the variegated global modernity allows us to see the global modern as multifaceted, creative, multipolar, unevenly distributed, and asynchronous.²⁹

To some degree, attention to mimesis and mimetic theory is already present in Japanese culture and Japanese studies, as there are at least three native Japanese concepts that correspond roughly to the three major strains of mimesis examined here. The Japanese aesthetic tradition of *ari no mama* (things as they are), the Noh drama principle of *monomane* (imitation of things), and the Japanese visual arts concept of *mitate* (resemblance) all resemble ideas encompassed in the term *mimesis*. But they do not correspond perfectly: unlike traditional views of mimesis as representation in the West, the desire to present things ari no mama is not simply a representational realism.³⁰ And unlike standard views of mimicry as mimesis, the concept of monomane, for instance, is not a mirror or perfect copy but, according to Noh drama theorist Zeami Motokiyo, when done best, a distortion that gestures ironically toward its own imitation.³¹ Likewise, beyond metaphorical understandings of visual mimesis, mitate does not simply implore viewers to see one thing as another but to see the one thing through the other, to see how such a metaphor or re-presentation transforms or bends the thing itself—noting the critique and irony that accrue through repetition with differences.³² These historical terms might provide the beginnings of a traditional Japanese mode of considering mimesis. More recently, there have been other specific ways in which *mimesis* has been used in Japanese studies. Japanese linguists rely on the concept of mimesis today to explain the proliferation of Japanese onomatopoeias as a technical term for sound symbolism.³³ And occasionally Japanese art history and history use mimesis as a foil to the role of originality and creativity.³⁴ But such historical reverse translations of native terms or current-day applications to Japanese culture of a predefined notion of mimesis are not the subject of this book.

Rather, this book takes as a starting point the modern moment, in which the globe directly matters as much for culture on the Japanese archipelago as it does elsewhere. Mimesis is considered not simply as a universal, human faculty but also as a useful way to understand long-running concerns about media that remain with us today. Since the contemporary study of media is itself a conceptual product of global and alternative modernities, this approach makes sense. The study of something like "Japanese media" is imbricated in the modern moment, in which the concepts of mimesis and media are already active and too often assumed or neglected. This book attempts to challenge the disciplinary inclinations of both media studies and Japanese studies to disregard the importance of the mimesis concept, in both senses of representation and mimicry.

Even when we are holding in our hands what is sold as a sign of the future that will connect us more immediately to the world, we resort to comparisons with the media of the past. Even as it sells the novelty of the new, the marketing and remediation of new media tacitly acknowledge their connections to the past. This explains why, for the debut of the camera function on mobile phones in 2001, a television commercial by Japanese telecom company au by KDDI contrived a convoluted explanation of why anyone would want a camera on their phone. The commercial depicted a man (played by charismatic star Asano Tadanobu) bumping into an old acquaintance. Sucked into conversation, Asano's character is at a loss for how he knows the apparent acquaintance. The acquaintance recalls the wedding of a mutual friend, Okamoto. Asano snaps a photo and sends it to the mutual friend with the message: "What's this guy's name?"[35] In doing so au by KDDI draws on the late nineteenth-century discourse of the photograph as a form of portable identity that had been solidified soon after the arrival of photography as a mass medium.[36] Here we have a very old problem (identity and recognition) being solved through the marriage of photography with the new tools of the mobile phone camera and its high-speed connection.

This issue is widespread; for instance, the rampant use of skeuomorphic design, as when digital media interfaces reference the analog world, exemplifies such remediating tendencies. One way to measure a new medium's connection to the past would be by tracking the ornamental leftovers from a previous era still lingering in the new media, as when a narrative film changes scene by the contrivance of a page turn, or when television is referred to as the electric *kamishibai* (paper theater), or when mobile phones' buttons seem to emit tones (which had in the previous era actually started the connection signal), or how keyboards today maintain the QWERTY layout despite the fact that it was developed to slow typing so as to prevent key jams endemic on typewriters with speedier keyboard layouts. Such taking stock of media nostalgia through remediation is one measure of traditional mimesis (in which media represent the world as given, to the point of representing media within that world), keeping the newness at bay, translating the known and acceptable and now seemingly natural through the supposedly new, or even the reverse—translating the putatively new through the known.

What is old seems real, so through remediation, the new media seem to connect us to the real by bringing such old media effects into updated forms. Long after the disappearance of analog filing cabinets and folders from physical office spaces, they linger on in digital environments, shaping our ability to conceive of alternative hierarchical structures for organizing information. But the success or failure of skeuomorphic design features is dependent on the fact that the media (like mirrors) exist as objects in our world and so play a role in its slow transformation through successive mediations. The media's secondary function as a mirror of our world is well articulated in Michel Foucault's notion of heterotopia, which helps us recognize the ways in which clear access to reality, often fetishized by the marketing of new media, neglects the presence of the media in reality.[37] Marketed as both an "other space" and as an access point to reality, new media can be a portal opening into "other spaces" of reality that occupy space here in our hands or at our fingertips. The notion that the space being represented through media is truly other to the here and now is mythological. It is not another space that can be accessed through the media, because it is already ready to hand. To grasp represented space as other denies the material objective reality of its mediated existence. Recognizing this dual structure of media as both the conveyor of the message and part of the message is another way of understanding hyperreality, a meta-real that encompasses all others, such that there can be no other reality to the real. Rather than in their representative claims on immediacy, it is in the way media occupy space that they become transformative, making human beings behave in accordance with their affordances (mimicry) because of their presence in the world.

Mimesis and the New Real

There are numerous definitions for the obscure yet foundational word *mimesis*. In some renderings, mimesis forms a basis for the concept of media. John Guillory understands the development of the media concept as a historical pivot away from mimesis because he sees mimesis primarily in its representational mode. For him, the media concept resolves problems in the consideration of art in the world by focusing on the systemic issues defined in communication studies.[38] But Stephen Halliwell resuscitates the term *mimesis* by showing the complexity of the multifarious early recorded uses of the term. According to Halliwell, the discourse on the word has been divided since its various meanings appeared in ancient Greece. He identifies five subcategories of definitions within conceptual families of mimetic ideas: resemblance, imitation, impersonation, expressive sound, and metaphysical conformity.[39] Halliwell then distills these various definitions of *mimesis* into largely two categories, identifying a tension present in the term from Aristotle through Goethe and continuing today, between representation and mimicry. These two major modes of mimesis (art imitating life and life imitating art) inform the histories of the media presented in this book, even as they clear a path for other considerations: life imitates life; art imitates art; everything is imitation; nothing imitates anything. In all of these possibilities, media as a means for imitation can facilitate and impede, and as the manifestation of mimesis in the world, media are one link between the mediated world and the world in which media dwells.

The major poles of mimesis (representation and mimicry) are overlapping and intertwined rather than mutually exclusive. In its representational mode the medium is said to reflect the world and in its miming mode the medium is said to affect or change the world directly or indirectly by inspiring its users, consumers, or audiences to change their behavior. The two modes have been studied in separate quarters in academia: generally, philosophy, literary studies, and art history have held on to the representational meanings of the term, while dramaturgical, anthropological, psychological, and sociological studies have been more concerned with questions of mimicry. From Erich Auerbach and Clement Greenberg through Luce Irigaray and Richard Rorty, the central role of representationality in cultural products has been studied through historical, hermeneutical, analytical, and philosophical lenses.[40] In contrast, thinkers such as Michael Taussig, René Girard, and Roger Caillois, who work on less print-mediated areas of study, such as performance or anthropology of rituals, have focused on definitions of *mimesis* that emphasize embodied mimicry.[41]

The history of mimesis in the Platonic tradition presumes an inside and outside to art, artifice, or the manufactured. This assumed distinction (between that which was built and that which simply is given) provides the foundation for concepts of representation and mimicry and is paralleled within the concept of media itself.[42] If media bridge a border, they also demarcate it. If you want to find such a border, look at the media. Mediation itself may even be the means by which such borders come into being, providing the very situation in which an objective reality would need to be reflected or represented. In this sense, media and mimesis are deeply entwined.

This entanglement explains why there is a perpetual fetish for better, more transparent mediation—a desire for a better mirror or even clearer window onto what feels like an "other world." When attention to media reframes debate about how meanings are made, content is being redefined. What was previously considered content was shown to be lacking explanatory power in and of itself; media held the answer to how meaning was made. So now content and its media are said to be the drivers of meaning, and when those meanings become tired and lose their explanatory force a different medium beyond the frame of the old one will have to be sought. Attention to media then creates or mediates a conflation of content and media and thus produces a new outside that will be mediated by a different medium. What we may hope to find in this continual search for a new way of framing meaning at best is simply a recognition of the problem of fidelity, correctness, or truth of the mediated. This does not mean a better fidelity of the medium; it means more consciousness about the issue of fidelity. When content draws attention to media, when content becomes its own media critique or theory, or when the mediated reflects upon mediation as such, the interlacing of mimesis and media is palpable. Media especially afford glimpses of truth about mimesis when they pay attention to or reflect on mediation.

The entwinement of media and mimesis can be illustrated through some of the most frequently referenced concepts in media studies of recent years—Jay David Bolter and Richard Grusin's terms developed for describing how new media relate to older media. They develop three key terms for describing how new media, old media, and the real world interact. *Remediation,* according to their theory, is the "formal logic by which new media refashion" or reform and improve on older media.[43] They then identify two ways in which this is accomplished—immediacy and hypermediacy. *Immediacy* is a transparency and speed of connection that makes the world seem real, up close, clear, present, and unfiltered. Marking when media refer to media, *hypermediacy* might seem at first an inversion of immediacy, putting us at greater distance from the real. But of course, since media are part the world, hypermediacy is but a form of immediacy—better reflecting a world in which the real is always already mediated.

The intertwining of media and mimesis resides in a tension over an old binary notion of copying: either art (artifice) imitates life (nature) or life imitates art. These two notions present two modes that are more or less salient in all instances of human creation. Imitations are not only framed by media but also materialized there, and it is in this materialization itself that life affects art and art transforms the world. One way to give more nuance to this dichotomy is to think more carefully about the conceptual binary between the mediated and the unmediated. Halliwell and Martin Jay point out that, over the course of the twentieth century, the two major strains of mimetic conceptualization have more and more been thought together.[44] This book participates in this tradition of the reunification of the dichotomies of mimesis. These two forms or modalities of mimesis—the representational (copying recorded on external media) and the anthropological (how realities are copied by the bodies of living beings)—were reunited in twentieth-century philosophy.[45] Media themselves manifest the link between representation and mimicry.

Meditations on Mediation: Nipper in Three Modes of Mimesis

Mimesis I. Representation: Imitating the Real

The famous dog stands before the new medium of the phonograph, tilting his head as though fooled by the representational mimesis of the media in its replay of his dead master's voice.

Jacques Lacan's distinction between the real and realities clarifies a link between media and mimesis. For Lacan, "the Real" is infinite, while "realities" are finite. The Real comprises all realities. It can never be represented in its totality and, therefore, must be forfeited for representation to take place. Realities, by contrast, are always already representations and projections (the Symbolic and the Imaginary).

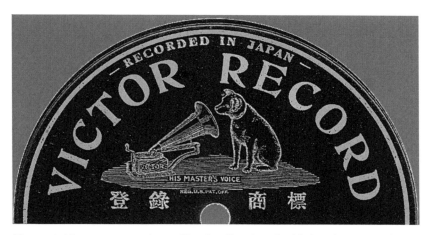

Figure 1. Nipper goes to Japan: The familiar dog tilts his head on an early twentieth-century Victor Japan record label. Photograph from the author's collection.

All that can be represented is a reality. Newspaper accounts, histories, dreams, films, songs, and novels all fall into the category of realities, as do the actual, though finite, life experiences of sentient beings.[46] In a sense, the real is both "objective reality" and all "subjective realities" combined.

The media concept grows from distinctions like this Lacanian one. In other words, to say that something is mediated is to say that it is limited, frameable, or finite. It is but one reality among others. Therefore, in calling something mediated, we also acknowledge a break between the mediated and the real. In a sense, Lacan's real—as an amalgam of the Symbolic and the Imaginary registers, of the objective reality and all subjective realities (including virtual ones)—resembles Timothy J. Welsh's idea of "mixed realism" that has fidelity to both real and virtual realities.[47] However, in Lacan's schema there is neither a categorical distinction between objective reality and subjective ones nor a historical moment when virtuality became more salient: simply put, reality and virtuality together have always already composed the Real. So if we understand Lacan's notion of the Real as all realities combined—a meta-, mixed, or hyperreality that encompasses all others—we can see its relation to media studies through, for instance, Bolton and Grusin's idea of hypermediation that refers to the process of mediation and, thereby, seems not only more self-conscious but also more real. We might find increasingly bigger realities through increases in immediacy and hypermediacy (ones that feel fleetingly more realistic), but this perception of increase is relative to the finitude of the previous media regime and only approaches without ever arriving at the always already infinite real.[48]

Lacan's distinction between the Real and realities (both Symbolic and Imaginary) provides some of the basis for this book's elaboration of the bifurcated concept of "the new real." On the one hand, the phenomenon of thinking that our media can grasp the real is clearly hype for a new real that never comes. Media can present nothing more than realities, even though again and again they make us think we are drawing closer to the real, evoking the impossibility of immediate contact with the real; this false sense of approaching the real through media is a part of what I am calling the new real. On the other hand, there is another aspect to this new real (akin to the cliché term "the new normal") that names the seemingly new situation in which the hype no longer holds and the new media become part of our lived landscape, subtly transforming our everyday existence.[49]

The false sense of a new real arises when one more layer, one more medium, one more reality is added to the numerous realities through which we already perceive the real. For a moment (which in practice can be anything from a quick flash to a decades-long era), it may seem as though the new medium (and the finite reality it provides) has connected us to the real. As users inevitably learn the limits of the new reality or medium (the next false new real in the chain of new reals), the real is transformed, remade, or expanded. This simple dynamic historical structure of media explains the cyclical desire for and inevitable frustration with technologies of immediacy. It also explains the need for a history of realism as an aesthetic as much as it does the history of media.

This fundamental modal relation between media, reality, and the real is clear when viewed through one of the most well-known and overused examples of an encounter with new media. The famous painting of the dog Nipper tilting his head toward the sound horn on a phonograph depicts an instance of the most basic form of representational mimesis brought through new media: a record seems to fool the animal because of its fidelity to the original human master's voice. First painted by Francis Barraud, the brother of Nipper's deceased master Mark Henry Barraud, the image was acquired by

William Barry Owen in 1899 for the Gramophone Company because it captured something more general and potentially universal about the encounter with new media than the personal memorialization evoked by the painting. After it had been adopted as the logo of the Victor Talking Machine Company in the early 1900s, the image soon spread with the technology around the world, becoming one of the first global corporate logos. And Japan, as we will see, became one of the more fecund places for the dissemination of this advertising meme.[50]

Let us tilt our heads, too, for a moment as we ponder the image: Why do human beings around the world continue to relate to the image? What gives it such sustained resonance and what Lisa Gitelman calls "the apparent power of mechanical reproduction to appeal and entrance"?[51] Nipper's expression is cute because we see our naive selves in him, even as we safely maintain our distance from his position as one duped by the medium.[52] We recognize his situation even though we are not experiencing it in the same instance in which he is. As Nipper tilts his head standing before the record player, we may smile or even tilt our heads as we gaze upon the image of Nipper. In this instance, the old medium of oil painting (or its copies) has conveyed something true about the new one to us. The old medium has become part of the new real, mediating what the new medium is supposed to do—trick us. Thinking about the social place of Barraud's painting, anthropologist Michael Taussig writes that "mimesis is of a piece with primitivism," meaning that when our experience of the world is transformed by media, we share something with magical, talismanic, and shamanistic cultures.[53] Here Nipper is the primitive and human viewers are the sophisticates. In a kind of translation of folklorist James George Frazer's distinction between the "imitative" and the "contagious" around magic, Taussig notes how this mimesis teeters between "imitation and sensuousness."[54] Today we might recognize these split tendencies as imitation and viral circulation, or the differences between attempts to copy the real and copying a copy (a particular reality).[55]

Nipper's situation of being fooled by the media recalls, of course, the previously mentioned issue of virtuality and confusion occasioned around the advent of computer graphics. So having considered both Lacan's terminology and a bit about Nipper, we may return to Azuma's and Saitō's views on CG with renewed understanding.

Though both theorists are concerned with CG's ability to fool our senses, they assume that, because a given consciousness can be fooled by a reality (for instance, CG or a gramophone record), such a media-created reality is real. In fact, the inverse is true. The fact that a medium can fool us temporarily means only that it is a medium, that it can be recognized as one. The medium is doing what media do—creating a reality that, in turn, composes but an infinitesimal portion of the real. In media studies, the importance of paying attention to the canvas, frame, wall, or medium is precisely to reveal the perceived reality on or within it to be (not so much a false reality but) an incomplete one. So it should be no surprise that a medium creates a reality in which we may be subsumed for a more or less lengthy period. That is all they ever do. What they never do is create or transmit the real. They only create multiple and varied components of the real. And in this case, the medium's affordance to the represented is less meaningful than what it affords to the world.

Lacan's distinction between realities and the real is useful precisely because it gives a background terminology to explain our continual confusion of realms when confronted with (especially new) media. If *psychosis* in traditional psychoanalysis is defined by losing touch with the real, Lacan's distinction reveals how we are all suffering from differing degrees of psychosis because there will always remain a bar between our realities and the real. This is because we can never quite see the world for what it is. We only see it filtered through its composite realities; the world comes to us as always already mediated. Yet despite this premediated state in which we apprehend the world, our continual confusion can itself become part of our daily lived experience composing a new aspect to the real. How do we talk about the enduring commodity fetish for gadgets of mediation in a world in which faith in objective reality has been utterly lost? The answer is that it has not been lost at all. Indeed, the Lacanian schema presupposes, requires, and reifies the objective world, placing ultimate faith in an infinite real that exceeds the possibility of any human or media grasping it in its totality. Our only hope for reconciling our psychosis is recognizing the dynamic relation with our media, admitting our continually being duped by them, or empathizing with the dog.

To put this mimesis and media nexus in Lacanian terms, the Symbolic register produces signifiers (the mediated) that signify the Real, providing flashes or glimpses refracting it, without capturing it in its entirety, without opening access to it. This means that the Imaginary propels subjects (users, consumers, etc.) to demand more from their media because their demand (by its nature) will never be satisfied. Yet it is in this register of the Imaginary where the Symbolic is mis-recognized for the Real. In other words, when we become frustrated with mediations for not providing us some satisfaction at having de-livered the Real or when we are satisfied with them for doing so, the tension is happening within us (in the Imaginary register) and not in the mediated (Symbolic) or the Real as such. But there is a more grounded history to these mis/recognitions when they happen at a societal level—that is, when everyone seems to grow frustrated with a medium at the same time. In moments of great critical introspection, radical world upheaval, and media shift, for a time we might see our mediated reality for what it is—finite. For instance, in the aftermath of the Fukushima disasters many Japanese people turned to Twitter out of frustration with the traditional news media of press, radio, and television, because the new medium seemed to open another, more immediate access to the real. Before such turns, when we dwell within a particular finite reality, like an older medium, it seems like that is all there is. In other words, what we encounter through media is the limit of our ability to grasp the real. We can only impute the vastness of the real from our coming to terms with the failure of media to access it. The mirror stage (a developmental psychosis around recognition of a reality) is precisely that fun—ultimately infantile—infatuation that we shall need to get beyond when the next new medium (mirror-shades, perhaps) comes along to reveal the lack within the mirror. In this view, Lacanian psychoanalytic critique (because it points out mirrors) is but one subset of media studies.

If media studies reveals the mediation/limitations of realities, then it also exposes something of the limitlessness of human desire for the real. For Azuma, there is no objective, infinite real beyond finite, medi-ated realities.[56] And so, in contrast to Azuma, Saitō argues that media have an impact on the psyche, but that ultimately this is because of their representational function. If media (multiple mediums) reveal anything, it is that we are doomed to know nothing about the real other than through such various virtualizations. It is not simply that we are, as Saitō argues, deceived by our media, but we are necessarily deceived because we cannot receive the infinite in any direct sense. We rely on realities because the real does not—nor will it ever—

compute. And this knowledge cannot provide an inoculation against the false consciousness of any given media. But through understanding of this dynamic, our knowledge about the real is expanded. As Achilles remains always at least a step behind the tortoise in Zeno's paradox, the real will always necessarily recede into the distance. Or, to put it in terms of Nipper, though his master's voice will seem to reverberate through the medium again and again, the dog will never hear his master's voice again.

Mimesis II. Mimicry: Imitating Realities

The omnipresence of the dog logo transforms how we live with and think about the medium.

Representation is concerned with transparently copying the world. Mimicry is concerned with copying copies or simulacra and, thereby, with conforming to or evoking established norms or genres. If fidelity to the real world (representation) comprises the function of mediation captured in the concept of immediacy, fidelity to yet another mediated reality (mimicry) corresponds to the concept of remediation. This alternative form of mimetic copying (copying copies) may seem to derive from copying the real, but it is probably better to consider neither form to have a hierarchical primacy or privilege over the other, because as we have seen, all mediated representations are finite. It is better to conceive of both forms of copying (representation and mimicry) as two antipodal modes of copying that are often concurrent. If we deem the real to be barred from contact and foreclosed from capture, the former mode of copying is simply a pose, while the latter is in some sense acknowledgment of the bar.

The stakes of copying other copies can probably best be gleaned from thinking about those styles of particular cultural products that bear little resemblance to the world (e.g., surreal, abstract, fantastic art, or genre fiction). To give an example, all genre fiction mobilizes some tropes unique to the genre. Consider the brilliant detective or mad scientist: though such figures may have once been based on specific historical persons, their appearance in mystery stories or science fiction now is a product less of representational mimesis than of mimicry of those genres. In his explication of some of the most common fantasies expressed in the media of manga and anime representing

infantile desires for a fighting girl who can save the world, Saitō compares the space of the Japanese fictive world to that of the West:

> In Japanese space . . . it is permissible for all sorts of fictions to
> have their own autonomous reality [*riariti*]. In other words, actual
> [*riaru*] fictions do not necessarily require *the security of the real*
> [*genjitsu*]. There is absolutely no need in this space for fiction to
> imitate the real. Fiction is able to clear a space around itself for its
> own reality.[57]

Though, of course, he essentializes a wider phenomenon to a Japanese space, Saitō recognizes a fact long since theorized about the cultivation and vanishing of various realisms in aesthetic and symbolic
realms: namely, that realisms must adhere to a truth of the medium
or genre almost more than the real itself. Here Saitō uses the term
the "reality of fiction" (*kyokō no riariti*) to designate what Michael
Riffaterre labeled "fictional truth."[58] This is also the same kind of truth
that Azuma Hiroki is concerned with in his discussion of the "game-
like realism" (gēmu-teki riarizumu) of games (or manga, anime, or
novels) that adhere to the experience of other games (intra-reality
reference) rather than to the real itself.[59] And, indeed, this is also what
Marshall McLuhan means when he writes, "The 'content' of any medium is always another medium."[60] Clement Greenberg argues that a
mimesis that turns to mediated content rather than to external reality
as its source for imitation pervades modernist art.[61] So for McLuhan
the phenomenon is media-bound, for Greenberg it is historical and
an aesthetic, and for Saitō it is all of these. Nevertheless, it seems clear
that in all of these cases, the media and mimesis concepts themselves
tacitly rely on structures similar to the Lacanian distinction between
realities and the real—whether the dichotomies of art and the world,
inside and outside of the frame, or other binary schema. Such concepts produce the situation in which copying is recognizable as representing the real, realities, or some combination of both.

Such concepts make explicit the fact that the source for a reality
need not be the real. The source cannot be the real directly apprehended. Rather, since the real itself is sensed through media and is
composed of the net sum of all realities, the source is to be found in
realities. Such concepts, thereby, sidestep another important aspect

of copying. Regardless of it being expressed in terms of Azuma's game-like realism or Oscar Wilde's art for art's sake, the argument that the realities of cultural production must comply with rules of their communication systems (media or genre) elides the fact that such rules also affect and are part of our real world. In a way, the argument that art exists only for the sake of art contradicts the ability for such injunctions to remain bound within media alone; this is because to argue that art need not wrestle with the real is an argument already wrestling with art in the world.[62]

The division between representation of the world and mimicry of cultural forms can be seen by contrasting the Nipper image showing the dog's confusion at representation with the viral meme-like circulation of that image around the world through numerous products and companies—copying within the world of the image as opposed to copies of the image in the world. One lineage of the global circulation, reproduction, and reception of the logo—the Japanese one—can be instructive for elaborating the difference between the dog's fidelity to his master and the advertised fidelity of the goods sold. The first versions of the logo that circulated in Japan were directly transplanted from the British and American sources—even including the untranslated English phrase "His Master's Voice." Later Japanese iterations of the meme would drift from the sense of fidelity contained in that slogan.[63]

Nipper was a major presence in the Japanese mediascape of the phonograph age. In thinking about the way that one new medium (film) became the opportunity and cause not for merely remediation but also for what he terms "transcultural mimesis," Japanese film scholar Michael Raine reworks Taussig's notions of mimesis for the circulation of the new global medium, showing the effects from copying of Hollywood generic memes into early Japanese cinema where the opportunities for misprision and reinvention abound. So Raine quotes one 1930s critic's praise of director Ozu Yasujirō's "portrait of gangsters who are so natural in their actions that it's as if a gang of ruffians from New York's East Side red light district had immigrated to Japan."[64] This kind of adherence to the norms of the medium produces a surreality that is quickly naturalized and, in so doing, the media transform reality. Scenes that take place in a Victor Talking Machine shop in Tokyo in Ozu's silent gangster classic *Dragnet Girl* (*Hijōsen no Onna,* 1933) illustrate how a new medium interpellates

Figure 2. Direct encounter: A student boxes with a big Nipper. Screengrab from Ozu Yasujirō's *Dragnet Girl* (1933).

subjects and how this subjugation becomes part of lived reality.[65] Two-dimensional Nipper logos and three-dimensional statuettes of the dog adorn the shop's space and fill the filmic frame. In an early scene, a student bumps into one of the larger-than-life-size figures of Nipper, then, after nearly knocking it over, jokingly boxes Chaplin-style with it. Here the statue about media literally gets in the way.

Of course, meanings drift as a copy inspires other copies. At least one other dog-based mythos stood in relation to the fidelity of Nipper in Japan—the story of Hachikō, the dog who famously waited every day at Shibuya Station after his master died suddenly at work in 1925. When Nipper was incorporated in Japan with the Japan Victor Talking Machine Company in 1927, Hachikō presumably had already waited. But it would be seven years before that faithful dog would become the stuff of mythic legend when a newspaper told his story, and it soon became nationalist lore. It does not particularly matter whether Hachikō paved the way for Nipper or drew on Nipper's popularity, since both stories stem from a fascination with a dog that exhibits intense fidelity to its human master. Historian Aaron Skabelund argues, "Hachikō both shaped and reflected Imperial Japan."[66] Nipper (and the global-capital-produced corporate media world in which he circulated), in turn, shaped and reflected Hachikō. Whether Nipper in Japan was then a completely foreign import or received into a native tradition does not really matter, because with each new copy or mediation comes a potentially radically new moment of articulation with radically new possibilities.[67] These instances of mediation of dog-based fidelity mark the always present modalities of mimesis that are more or less salient at one time. The two instances (the press media carry the story of an actual dog and the logo bounces around the media echo chamber of the marketplace of our commodity-infused world) exemplify the one-two punch of the new media—fidelity to the real and fidelity to other realities.

The ideas of art-for-art's-sake or game-like realism seem like the inverse of immediacy, as they reject connections to the real in favor of reference to other cultural products. These notions that all we copy are copies find an echo in Richard Rorty's claim that Western philosophy is a prisoner to representationality.[68] We (artists, gamers, philosophers) are compelled to copy nature, but we can never do so successfully, a bind that Derek Brewer calls the "mimetic fallacy."[69] In Brewer's understanding, the fallacy is a historical one, connected to the modern notion that culture must reflect the world. These ideas around the failures of copies of copies (whether Azuma's, Rorty's, or Brewer's) are all limited by the representational definition of *mimesis*. In their willful turn from nature to artifice because at least artifice can be true to artifice, these ideas appear to work against Walter Benjamin's notion of a "mimetic faculty"—that we human beings are inherently copiers of nature.[70] But the tension between our ability to copy copies and our compulsion to copy nature can be resolved by understanding that Benjamin's notion of mimesis blends both representation and mimicry; one of his clearest examples is dancers moving to the beat of a drum, miming the sound reverberations with their bodies (see discussion of dancing in chapter 6 and the Conclusion). The fact that the insularity of art and philosophy is a common trope suggests the degree to which representationality alone is a limited way of thinking about copying in the world (see ecomimesis discussed in chapter 5). In addition, because art and philosophy are among the finite realities that compose the infinite real, even being a mirror of other realities is also connecting with the real.

Mimesis III. Hypermediation as Homomediation: Imitating the Self

The dog speaks.

The forms of mimesis discussed above—art imitating life (representation) and its corollary, art imitating art (mimicry)—capture much of the way art can be understood as copying, but neither explains the role of such copying when manifest in the world. What at first seems to connect directly to the real may later be revealed as a tropological style that simply copied from other mediations rather than from the world. What may seem as confined entirely within genre norms, too, may be found to present the truth of a given situation in the world. To be sure, sometimes art imitates life, sometimes art imitates art, and occasionally life repeats art.

This seems to be precisely what media theorist and activist Nakai Masakazu was gesturing toward when, only a few months after the debut of Ozu's film, he published an article titled "The Needle of the Gramophone":

> No matter what needle you use, Victor records are Victor records. In fact each needle itself may differ, but a Victor record is still a Victor record. Each one of them is just a "type."
>
> The emergence of a "type" is something that has been demanded by marketing which is to say the system.
>
> Nowadays, human beings too are finally commodified and instrumentalized in the form of employment which is to say policies. In other words, we are being molded into a possible form of "type."[71]

Here it is not only the medium of records that is filtered through the needle but also human beings, who become a kind of cog in the talking machine market entanglement. What the uniformity of the commodity suggests is a wider homogenization of the human.

Thus far we have considered two aspects of mimesis: copying of the real (mediation) and copying of a reality (remediation). Another

Figure 3. Framed by the open phonograph lid in the foreground, Jōji flirts, as a decal of the dog on the window mediates. Screengrab from Ozu Yasujirō's *Dragnet Girl* (1933).

aspect of the new real is the way in which these copies, in turn, affect the real world through media in what has sometimes been called reverse mimesis. Studying media helps us track this imitation, because media capture, carry, and project mimesis in action. Such study can help elaborate whether the real drives representation or representation transforms the real, or whether such drive emanates from elsewhere in our desires for media to create spectacles or to be transformative.

In a later scene in Ozu's *Dragnet Girl*, we see the gangster Jōji listening intently to a record with his head cocked toward the player in a listening room in the Victor Talking Machine shop. The shopgirl Tokiko asks, through a window emblazoned with the Nipper logo, if he likes what he hears, to which he jokingly responds that such music is "too good for him." Later in the scene, another woman is surprised to see that such a man is listening to high-class music, and Jōji gestures to the iconic image of Nipper and says, "Even the dog is listening."

Here in the world of the film, the dog listening is directly paralleled or at least comparable to the uncivilized gangster listening. Gone is the representational reference of the dog to the master's voice, and with it the notion that the medium's fidelity to the real is represented by the dog's fidelity to the master. Here the medium and the dog conjure not an image of the absent, dead master but music appreciation by the masses. And in Jōji's comment, we find a confusion of the borders of the human and the animal occasioned by the medium.[72] The Nipper meme provides an active and malleable theory for understanding the medium.

This inevitable drift from Nipper's original meanings is most obvious in postwar Japanese versions. For instance, a 1952 children's book and record vividly display reverse mimesis in Japanese cultural materializations of Nipper. The twenty-six-page children's picture book by psychologist Hatano Isoko, titled *Victor's Famous Dog Story: Little Nipper,* tells the canine's life story. The book brings the young dog to life with the anecdote that he not only responded to the recorded voice of his master on phonograph but even begged with a bark for more as soon as the record stopped.[73] The representational immediacy of the voice is not simply recognized but actively desired.

But it is in the 1952 song "Little Puppy, Nipper" performed by Hattori Junko with the Victor Children's Orchestra where this particular legacy of the Nipper mythology is revealed.[74] Beginning and ending with the recording of an actual dog bark, the song is sung from Nipper's point of view:

I am Nipper; I am Nipper;
I am the little dog Nipper.
Nice to meet you, bow wow (*wan wan wan*).
Good little boy and girl
Let's be friends and play
Please, please.

I am Nipper; I am Nipper;
I am the little dog Nipper.
I really like songs, bow wow.
When I'm happy, I wag my tail
My nose goes sniff sniff.[75]

ビクター名犬物語

ニッパーちゃん

監修 波多野 勤子

VICTOR

小学館製作

Figure 4. Cover of Hatano Isoko's *Nippā-chan* repaints the classic image with a younger Nipper. Hatano Isoko, *Bikutā meiken monogatari: Nippā-chan* (Tokyo: Shōgakukan, 1952).

Here the cute dog likes music (not the voice of his master). Nipper's recorded voice takes the place of his master's. The song begins with a recording of an actual dog's bark, but that is followed immediately by an imagined translation of those barks sung in Japanese. The fiction of this implicit translation comes in the contrast between the opening recorded barks and the sung onomatopoetic ideophone for barks (*wan wan*) when Nipper slips from human (Japanese) language back into his own putatively dog language. In fact, he fails to entirely become animal again but only emits the human-sounding mimetic words. Representation and mimicry both fail to capture or connect with the real, but in this failure they reveal the affordances of the medium.

Though he speaks Japanese, this example of a talking Nipper is not specifically Japanese. Taussig too identifies a general tendency of Nipper fans around the world to call him the "Talking Dog" when, in fact, he does no such thing in the original painting. In this drift from "Victor's Talking Machine" to the "Talking Dog," Taussig sees a slippage between machine and animal or media and dog, "the dog now being the civilized man's servant in the detection, and hence selling, of good copy." Taussig continues later:

> To refer to this as "the talking dog" is not only to reverse the talking machine from a player into a recorder, or to see the dog as entering into a conversation with the player, but also to magically endow—with effortless ease—the hound with the human faculties of the talking machine.[76]

In Taussig's telling, the animal as machine or animal-machine-as-media nexus bridges the distantiation between the human and the primitive or the individual and the universal. We do not need to reinvent the wheel in new materialist terms when the old ones do just fine at explaining what Jane Bennett calls "thing-power," or the way things transform and enact "the curious ability . . . to animate, to act, to produce effects dramatic and subtle."[77] Rather, in the Nipper nexus, the representation caught on record and the movement of the animal in front of the machine reveal the continuum between things, animals, and humans obscured by questions of subjectivity and language. And we can see in the 1952 song that almost magically brings Nipper's voice to life an instantiation of the desire for such erasing of distinctions. The initial story, painting, and title prioritized the dog's fidelity to his master and thus implied the fidelity of the record itself to the real. The later iteration that created the dog's voice, a copy of that earlier copy, showed fidelity to the association of a dog with recordings.

The adaptation and drift of the logo's meanings became starker when the label itself became the intellectual property of a Japanese corporation. The logo was so successful in Japan that even after the subsidiary Japan Victor Talking Machine Company split from the multinational corporation Victor Talking Machine Company during World War II, it retained the rights to the Nipper logo in Japan, such that even today, HMV (His Master's Voice, the namesake British corporation) cannot display Nipper in Japan in competition with the contemporary Japan Victor Corporation (JVC). Whether or not this shift in local ownership caused the drift in meanings of the logo, it attests to the role of mimesis in remaking the marketplace.

Today Nipper remains remarkably popular in Japan: in April 2020, a new picture book by Ishimura Masaru retells the origin story of the logo, and the Japanese Victor Entertainment store website sells goods emblazoned with the image, including t-shirts, bags, hats, mugs, keychains, stickers, coasters, cell phone holders, statuettes, and "puppy on board" signs.[78] In 2015, one fan even tried to commemorate the dog's contribution to Japanese society with a Memorial Nipper Day on February 8, because the Japanese approximation of the English Nipper, Nippā, sounds similar to ni-ha or "two-eight." Since then, the corporation has appropriated that date for the release of new songs, including a 2020 song about Nipper by the comedy band Sūshinchū (Fourth Planet) titled "Famed Dog Nipper's Dog 'N' Roll" ("Meiken Nippā doggunrōru").[79] This sort of viral appropriation of the logo is part of the mimetic marketing strategy much discussed by Theodor W. Adorno and Max Horkheimer, but it also might be thought of as one way in which the media is assimilated into the world, transforming it in various ways, creating a new real.[80]

The frame for Nipper is that he is an animal and we are not. The image of Nipper is cute because even as we recognize ourselves in the dog, we can feel comfortable that we ourselves are not quite so foolish. We are superior. We are not fooled by the media. But this represents both our desires for new media to fool and our fantasy about not being so foolish as to be fooled ourselves. Nipper is safe because he is cute and cute because he is not threatening. Nipper's cuteness is connected to the sense of betrayal we see in his tilted head; this is why

Sianne Ngai classifies cuteness as an aesthetic of consumption.[81] We feel compelled by the cute dog (to possess and protect him, and by proxy the media on which he is emblazoned) even as we recognize his fate as our own—to be deceived by our consumerism. The new real names both that surface appeal of Nipper as representing the immediate connection with the real and the inevitable and deeper mode of media circulating in and becoming part of the world. If we want to understand media and its consumption, we can do no better than to look at and listen to the dog in front of, within, and around the new media.

If we understand the representational immediacy of Nipper being fooled by the recording of his master's voice, the representational remediation of the painting of Nipper tilting his head at the record player, and the mimicry of the global circulation and dissemination of the logo as copying itself as a meme, then, of course, the above examples provide at least another few options—hypermediation, homomediation, and somamediation. Hypermediation, as Grusin and Bolter describe, occurs when mediation itself becomes the content of mediation, when we cannot help but notice the media, when such mediation makes a significant comment or presents a theory on the mediation. To their triumvirate of terms (*immediacy, remediation,* and *hypermediation*), we should add *homomediation* to name the mode of remediation wherein the remediating medium is the same as the medium it remediates. So if *remediation* names how one medium (say, the painting of Nipper) mediates another medium (gramophones), homomediation mediates its own mediation (a recording of Nipper singing and barking about his love for recorded music). Somamediation is when the medium is reduced to the most basic and hardly external medium of the body (most typically the human body), as in the case of Jōji the gangster understanding himself as a copy of the dog. It is this final form of mimesis through somamediation that is the clearest evidence of the instantiation of representational and ontological mimesis. Therefore, every chapter of the present volume deals with the body in some way.

Welcome to the New Real

The mimicry aspect of mimesis has been considered a false form of mimesis by thinkers from Plato to Adorno and Horkheimer, on through Maruyama Masao and others. Plato holds that mimesis, as both the semblance of the real in art through the imitation of nature and the dissolution of the subject into nature, must be strictly banned from the Republic.[82] Adorno and Horkheimer identify fascism as a kind of modern-day magical mimesis of the noncreative/embodied kind (mimicry): what Horkheimer calls the "repressed form" of mimesis, or mimesis of "false projection" that seeks to remake "the environment like itself."[83] In Adorno's reading of Heidegger, the transparency of mass culture (giving over the private for the public) encompasses a "diluted form of the collective mimesis of the desire to equal everyone else by knowing everything about them."[84] This kind of sociopolitical mode of knee-jerk mimicry as mimesis has been a critique in ancient Greece and twentieth-century Europe. It has also underpinned interpretations of wartime Japan, explaining the repression of self and creativity in the context of the rise of fascism.[85] This negative view of copying assumes that, in the moment of bending to power to perform and represent as commanded, the self, creativity, and freedom are lost.

But even Maruyama Masao, who shares this generally negative assessment of mimetic behavior in wartime Japan, sees the possibility of a more creative and positive aspect in the postwar era. Mimesis, as imitation of nature and the dissolution of the subject into the fluctuating semblances, is the characteristic trait that brings about the fundamental destruction of identity; and in Maruyama's version, magical or primitive mimesis in the psychopathology of Japan's wartime leaders resulted in the absolute subsumption of self for the perceived greater good. Maruyama argues that the structure of Japanese ultranationalism lacked both formal logic and subjective ethics (*shukanteki rinri*); therefore, there was no clear separation between the self and the public.[86] This notion, that in the moment of mimicry the self is given over to the nation, is, for Maruyama, not a universal claim about mimesis but rather a historical one.[87] When discussing the postwar era, for instance, even he allows for more active modes of copying:

Of course, even imagination has its existential basis, you know. I mean, if to have imagination is just a matter of ignoring physical reality and floating about with one's head in the clouds, then the highest forms of art and culture are shuffling about in the wards of mental hospitals. . . . Even realism is a method of creativity. It's not the faithful copying of a perceptible subject. It is precisely because the reality does not appear directly, but as a "mediated reality" depending on the positive participation of the human spirit, that we can call it fiction. So the decisive factor lies in the integrating force of the spirit after all.[88]

This idea resembles Benjamin's endorsement of creative mimesis over what Susan Buck-Morss calls a "knee-jerk" reaction. So, a negative understanding of mimesis only attends to one version of how mimesis can remake the world; such a remaking can be destructive, but it can just as well imagine a world into being. Such mimesis affects the world through the ontological (what Maruyama calls existential) basis of cultural material, which is to say through mediation. This book does not attempt to take sides in a normative debate about mimesis. Rather, following in the steps of Buck-Morss's, Gertrud Koch's, and Andreas Huyssen's readings of Benjamin's mimetic faculty or Vittorio Gallese's scientific cognitive behaviorist understanding of mimesis, the book understands this ambiguity of the politics of copying to be the crux of human creativity and its relation to the world.[89]

Why does it matter that two kinds of mimesis are linked through media? This link itself reveals the power (and, therefore, politics) of mimesis in the world. The concept of media alienates us from the matters at hand in the same way that, in Marx's conception, money (as a medium of exchange in the economy) alienates us from what is really going on—the exploitation of workers. Mimesis highlights this function of media. By recognizing that the concept of media itself obscures our ability to see the base, the ground, the limit, or the real, we come to see how media participates in power inequalities in and exploitations through mediations, and in doing so tends to alienate us from the mediating human bodies (from the people) in the story of mediation. The concept of mimesis ultimately helps us return the human back into the story of mediation, because media do not copy alone, nor do they make meaning in the world in the absence of human beings.[90] Just as the body has returned recently to media studies, the posthuman fantasies that new media produce (and whose arrival we may both desire and fear) do not allay this but rather reify the importance of the human.[91]

New media are interesting because of the way they create and reflect (or are symptomatic of) a desire to reframe content, not because they fulfill such desires. Media produce the perception that the old frames of content have failed, not because the sociological or cultural dynamics of reception around the frame have fundamentally changed. But such medial shifts are themselves productive, allowing us to recognize the infinite regress of the real as if anew. When new conduits open, content is remediated to fill the new channels, not because of a perceived failure at the level of production, reception, or circulation of the old ones. It is not the case that new media arise to fulfill a specific need of signification or social cohesion. Because new media arise not out of crisis, they only seem to matter anew when the old discourse flow has stopped, hits an obstacle, seems awkward, or becomes so normalized in the everyday as to have become mundane. This is why attention to media seems salient around moments of the perceived failures of the old media to connect, as well as when media seem not to matter and content reigns. On the one hand, we might want to say that media critique is more important now than it ever has been, especially in the wake of the disconnects in popular media after states of emergencies like 3/11, the rise of neofascist leaders, Covid-19, or successive climate disasters. On the other hand, of course, even in seemingly normal times, when media seem to function effortlessly and naturally to communicate the world to us, they transform our reality.

The New Real shows how we compensate for the infinite regress of the real (always beyond reach) with a continual desire for better mediation. The new real is not a better, more immediate connection with the real but rather names both our desire for such a possibility and the inevitable failure of media to provide a lasting fulfillment of that desire. The new real is a joke, something like a not-so-sly marketing ploy that both pokes fun and somehow takes seriously the notion of the real itself being remade anew (renewed) by the latest media gadget. Here we should remind ourselves that, in the vocabulary of online purchasing, *renewed* has come to mean "lightly used, refurbished, repackaged, and resold." It names the situation in which such claims for gadgets remaking the world are made with increasing regularity. The new real describes our lives after the social absorption of a new medium into the mediascape. When the new media have become quotidian and boring, when its presence in our lives is unremarkable (to be expected), when we are perhaps ready for yet another next new thing, then the new real has finally arrived, having already transformed our lives.

2

Stereomimesis

Stereograph, Panoramic Parallax, and the
3D Printing of Nostalgia

One day toward the end of the nineteenth century, perhaps during a lull in business at his Yokohama photography studio, Enami Nobukuni donned the costume of a samurai warrior and posed in front of his own stereographic camera. The resulting stereographic photo (Figure 5) was published by C. H. Graves's Universal Photo Art under the title *Ancient Warrior Costume of the Japanese* in a series of two hundred photos of Japan and later included in several other series of stereoviews of Japan. Advertised as a means of travel to distant lands, such collections promoted a particular feeling about the medium of stereography—the sense that the objects and people being gazed upon were present in the moment and place of the viewer.[1] This feeling of presence of the person in front of the viewer is contradicted in the labeling of this photo, squarely focused on the "warrior costume." It was also possible that some viewers would feel as though they beheld an actual samurai warrior as they positioned their eyes in a stereoviewer and "resolved" the two images into a single, apparently three-dimensional one. Indeed, two-dimensional images of actual samurai had been produced and circulated widely since the introduction of photography in Japan a half century earlier. Without contextual knowledge about the social changes that had already taken place in Japan long before the photo was created (including the abolition of the samurai class), Euro-American viewers were sure to apprehend the photo as though it represented an authentic view of Japan and a Japanese national. More nuanced consumers might have understood this picture to be a simulacrum of a time past, not only through the use of words like *ancient* and *costume* in the labeling of the photograph but also through the clearly visible dark vertical line of a studio corner in the backdrop to the right of the painted tree. This tension between connection with

Figure 5. Enami as Samurai (glass negative). The photo was published in 1900 by Griffith & Griffith of Philadelphia. Another image likely from the same studio session in 1898 is listed as negative "No. 1800. Japanese Armor," the first of nearly two hundred stereoviews of Japan by "T. ENAMI" that Griffith brought to the market in 1900. This image was later included in several Keystone collections (after Keystone acquired C. H. Graves, which had acquired Griffith & Griffith). Image here reproduced from Keystone-Mast Collection, UCR/California Museum of Photography, University of California, Riverside.

the real and constructedness of the mediated image functioned without relation to the individual being photographed. For consumers, the specific identity of the person modeling the armor did not likely matter.[2]

Yet, thanks to collector and independent scholar Rob Oechsle, we now know that the subject and the cameraman of this particular stereographic image were one and the same. It is a self-portrait by Enami Nobukuni (a.k.a. T. Enami), a photographer who owned a studio on Benten Avenue in Yokohama, near where foreign visitors often first disembarked in Japan, from the 1890s through the 1920s. Here Enami poses as a samurai, a class that had been abolished in 1873, a generation before this photograph was taken. Since Enami's studio advertised in English as having "costumes" for portrait photography, and indeed there are other photos that include people of both Asian and European descent posing in his studio wearing this very armor, a probably unanswerable question arises: Why did Enami sell this self-portrait, along with hundreds of other photographs, as an authentic image of Japan?

The simplest answer seems the most likely. In addition to being a skilled photographer, a colorist with a keen eye for detail, and, at least in this instance, a model, Enami was a global businessman. As a middleman, he navigated the tension between the exoticist desires of a Western world that demanded images of a vanishing Japan and the realities of a modernizing and rapidly changing Japan, the economy of which thrived under the labor of technologically minded tinkerers, early adopters, and innovators. And by all accounts, he did it well. Visitors to his studio purchased magic lantern slides that are still sought after by collectors today. Major multinational corporations, like C. H. Graves, Griffith & Griffith, the Keystone Stereoview Company, and Sears, Roebuck and Co., bought, repackaged, and sold his series of stereographic images. His name appears as the attributed photographer of three photos in D. C. Angus's *Japan: The Eastern Wonderland* (1904), of fifteen photos in Burton Holmes's *Travelogues* (1908), of ten out of the twenty-four photos in K. Ogawa's *Fuji-san* (1912), of two photos in Joan Berenice Reynolds's *Asia* (1920), and of twenty-two photos included in Sir John Hammerton's seven-volume *Peoples of All Nations* (1922). But Enami does not announce his presence in the double photo above. His name appears in no known caption for it. The open secret of the inclusion of his face was only "discovered" over one hundred years after it was taken. So a better answer may be found by considering the photo as an instantiation of the two modes of mimesis that structure this book's understanding of media. I begin with this photo to illustrate how mimesis exceeds both representational and miming functions in a given medium.

Stephen Halliwell explains "two conceptions of mimesis": a passive one, "depicting and illuminating a world," and an active "creator of an independent artistic heterocosm, a world of its own."[3] Of course, these two concepts are linked; indeed, there are times when they resolve into one. The concepts are split and yet share some of the same space—like two sides of the same coin. These are seemingly binary definitions that together form a dynamic system that is labeled "mimesis"—the heads and tails of a fixed system or economy.[4]

Stereography is both a representational medium and a tangible instance of mimicry in our world. Cognitive science has shown that our brains flutter between a dominant image received in one eye and subordinate one received in another to create the visual sensation of the spaces we inhabit. Likewise, we must understand mimesis by toggling between at least two of its conceptualizations, never entirely letting go of either image. Stereography is spatial (involving the distance between two lenses, the area of two 2D images, and the 3D rendering), as well as temporal (conjuring a past that no longer exists, encompassing the time from the moment of taking a photograph, through processing and pasting it onto two cards, to the staging of the viewing, and the resolution of the paired images in the viewer's perceptual consciousness).[5]

Karatani Kōjin's reading of Kant's *Dreams of a Visionary* uses the parallax effect (which is at the heart of stereoscopy) to articulate the essence of radical critique. For Kant, the two views of parallax are irreconcilable antinomies from which transcendental deduction derives. Movement over time and across space between two views gives perspective, which then has the potential not only to bring understanding of such things as our distance from heavenly bodies but also to suggest that other truths lie beyond experience alone. From Kant's intuition, Karatani concludes that since neither of the two fundamentally irreconcilable parallax positions yields false views, only toggling between them allows a more complete perception of a view that is more than the sum of its parts. For Karatani, this becomes a method for finding a radical perspective, or what he calls a transcritique. Switching from one position to the next while continuing to hold the previous position in the mind's eye is a nimble positionality that rejects the Hegelian sublation of the two positions into a higher form, showing, rather, how any heightened awareness is in the parallax effect that occurs while shuttling between them.[6]

In another reading of Kant's work, Derrida shows how Kant's aesthetics are bifurcated. Derrida highlights a tension in Kant's view of art; on the one hand, there is the ability of art to document nature (how art simply is, *physis*), while on the other, art is necessarily of a constructed nature (how art is skillfully cultivated to taste, *technê*). The artist is free to create (to let nature flow through her), yet the artist is a mercenary and, therefore, a prisoner of the market economy of taste. Here again we have a seemingly fixed system of mimesis that produces not only a passive or transparent representation of nature but also an active construction of a version of the natural world (one for which there is a viable market); Derrida labels this system economimesis. Elsewhere, Derrida connects this economy between the physis and technê of art to the archival and artificial within photographs that seem, on the one hand, to have passively captured light through chemical reaction occurring in an instant and, on the other hand, to be the product of skillful use of the apparatus of the camera and the processing and viewing moments.[7]

Derrida speaks of our obligation "to reconsider the supposed referentiality or passivity in relation to the referent from the very beginning, the very first epoch, so to speak, of photography."[8] Challenging the common view of the "chrono-logic of what has taken place only once" at an instant of a photograph being taken, Derrida encourages us to think beyond the flash of the photo to see photography as occupying "a heterogenous time" or "differential duration." Once we understand the *longue durée* of exposure, we can see that: "If technics intervenes from the moment a view or shot is taken, and beginning with the time of exposure, there is no longer any pure passivity, certainly, but this does not simply mean that activity effaces passivity. It is a question of another structure, another sort of acti/passivity."[9] In other words, photography combines subjective technique or artistry with objective chemical and technological forces that seem to happen on their own. Deeply connected to the time of a photograph (the blink of the machinic shutter, the duration of exposure of the film to light, the durability of the photo as an object, the time of apprehension of the image), *acti/passivity* names the characteristic of a work that is the result of an activity that involves an automatic process, during which the actor is passive; it is a combination of automatic process and conscious activity.

Having exposed the dynamic economy between free and mercenary artists, nature and construction, active and passive, flash and duration, Derrida's innovation, of course, highlights the surplus or supplement of the emetic (vomit that spews forth or expresses itself from behind the understated economy) of the Kantian system of taste. This supplement is similar to Karatani's transcritique—the sum of the antinomies is greater than its parts.[10] In other words, Derrida's recognition of the economy or binary systems of mimesis (through art generally and photography more specifically) is a deconstruction that seems to simply lay bare how the system functions but in doing so gives a new or critical perspective. This doubled mode of the photograph that both documents and transforms nature I would like to call *stereomimesis*.

The tension within stereomimesis is key to various historical conceptions of media and their power. In addition to Derrida's identification of the dynamic with photography, the tension is also central to Erich Auerbach's analysis of background and foreground of literature, in which the play between the figure of Homer and the ground of the Bible produces varying senses of Western modern realism. Considering stereography in terms of these questions of mimesis suggests that the sense of depth created by the gap between foreground and background is equally as important as the fact of irreconcilability (unresolveability) that the gap presents.[11] Here Edgar Rubin's well-known gestalt model of the ground-figure or vase-face illusion is helpful. In the black and white painting with squiggles that can alternately be perceived as the outline of a vase or the profile of two faces approaching each other as though about to kiss, it is not that one view is more correct. Both views are equally true. Similarly, though two two-dimensional photographs create the sense of a single three-dimensional image, viewers of stereography do not suddenly forget that they are still staring at two photographs. They become active participant-observers holding an apparatus to their faces; their eyes relay images to their minds, which then interpret those images. As during any communication, viewers are always to some degree conscious of the medium. Only in instances when the medium is momentarily ignored, as when viewers are tricked into thinking their view is transparent or immediate, do they require reminders about the apparatus or a study of the media.[12]

Stereomimesis names the recognition that both modes of mimesis—representationality and mimicry—are mutually present at any given moment, even when one may become so dominant as to almost obscure the other. Stereomimesis helps us to understand perceptual media in the real world. By taking a deep look at the history of stereography in Japan through four lenses, the two or more modes of mimesis can be rendered more visible. This chapter is divided in two and then in two again. First, two modes of circulation and dissemination—the handheld stereoviewer and the vending machine stereopanorama—are shown to re-present the world even as those media transform the world. Second, the chapter considers two ways of thinking about the technology standing in the world (mimicry)—on the one hand, the literary and eventually surrealist and cubist imagination of the medium considered stereoscopy as world-creating moments of poesis, as the realism of 3D began to see it as a surreal trick that was only 2.5D at best; on the other hand, the rise of a 3D scanning and printing business for the creation of bronze sculptures in the late 1920s to 1930s shows just how transformative the world of stereoscopy could be. Stereoscopy would be cyclically rebranded as new through these alternate technologies of dissemination. The point of these four views is not to fix an image out of the gaps and incongruities defined by the distance and time between them; that is, it is not to resolve them into a singular image but rather to gain a better sense of the depth and duration afforded by thinking about a multiplicity of moments of mediation. To do so can expose the range of affordances of the stereographic medium in hopes of articulating a point of critique—namely that the media alone can never dictate or determine their specific perceptions or receptions. The mediation of media happens outside of that frame—sometimes through marketing and always through the body.

Enami in Cosplay: Left Eye, Looking In, Figure

The example of Enami's self-portrait presents stereomimesis in a nutshell by juxtaposing his mode of production (selling the "real Japan" through stereoscopy) with his impersonation of a samurai in the photograph (offering a carefully constructed artifice through his mimicry). The stereograph market involved a mix of European and American visitors, Japanese consumers, and armchair travelers around the world. After the first wave of photographic images from Japan (largely taken by Westerners or their often-uncredited Japanese assistants) from 1850 to 1890, the photograph market was renewed by the influx of stereographic images of Japan. The images produced for that market demonstrate that Western primitivism and orientalism was matched in Japan not only with Japanese versions of those aesthetic systems but also with a nostalgia for a premodern, fetishistically longed-for past, imagined as refined and pastoral.

Enami participated in a global network of trade in stereoscopic photographs of Japan. As part of a vibrant photography community in Yokohama, he trained under Ogawa Kazumasa in the 1880s and joined the Photographic Society of Japan on March 22, 1890.[13] From 1892 to 1926, he ran a studio on Benten dōri (his son would later take over, running it from 1929 to 1938).[14] This shop was named one of only seven recognized studios for tourists and collectors in Japan in 1904. Enami was awarded a silver medal at the 1905 Exposition Universelle et Internationale de Liège.[15] He embedded with Japanese forces during the Russo-Japanese War and documented battles and victory poses with both stereographs and glass lantern slides.[16] He also traveled beyond the Japanese Empire, processing photos from Manila, Singapore, Hong Kong, Shanghai, Beijing, and Tianjin. He published several stunning photos in *National Geographic* in the 1920s under his own name.[17] After his original studio burned down in the 1923 earthquake, Enami successfully litigated to receive owed payment from Raphael Eduard Liesegang, heir to the Liesegang magic lantern and photography factory in Düsseldorf, who had ordered and received 1,080 lantern slides (totaling 677 yen and 80 sen) from Enami prior to the war.[18] His talents were touted to the president of the National Geographic Society, Gilbert H. Grosvenor, by photographer Sakamoto Kiyoshi in a letter dated September 11, 1928, preparing Grosvenor for his trip to Japan: "I like Enami best especially for developing your own films. He is thoroughly trustworthy."[19] And thanks to the studious work of Rob Oechsle, Enami continues to be thought of as the "foremost producer of Japanese stereo view scenes."[20] Despite this formidable commercial and professional information and his photographic legacy, not much is known about Enami as an individual or thinker. He left behind no diaries or collections of letters. He did not write any treatise on stereoscopy, guidebook on the aesthetics of composition and color, or essay on good business practices. So from scant resources—the foreground minutiae of his photographic legacy and the broader background discourse on photography and stereography—we can only conjecture the middle ground, what he thought about stereoscopy as a medium.

Such photography studios as Enami's commonly provided photos of Japan to foreigners and tourists, as well as played a memorial and documentary role for Japanese people seeking to commemorate important life moments. Cameras were still a new enough technology that they were not yet widely circulating at the mass consumer level; they were mostly in the hands of professionals who then charged a hefty price for their products. Their studios also typically offered foreigners and locals the opportunity to have their portraits taken, sometimes in local garb or historical costumes. A 1902 English-language advertisement for Enami's studio in *Japan Directory* promotes "Views and Costumes of Japan," in addition to enlargements, portraits, stereoscopic views, and lantern slides.[21] The photographic record shows Enami's customers in kimonos, armor, and *yukata*. This market for dress-up or cosplay as masquerade celebrates the past.

Enami's eye for nostalgia extended beyond his studio to his outdoor, on-location landscape photos. His most stunning, colorful, and stereotypical magic lantern slides were single images, originally selected from a stereograph, depicting small groups of people (between two and five) in front of some impressive background. Enami was skilled at capturing the already stereotypical views of Japan, not only through stereoviews of landscapes featuring Mount Fuji, bridges, and local flora but also through figures populating those landscapes: farmers, students, artisans, geisha, tattooed laborers, wrestlers, and samurai. And, indeed, according to stereograph historian and theorist Jonathan Crary, the positioning of figures in the middle ground with a landscape in the background is typical of stereography as a medium.[22] Enami's compositional practice in nature exemplifies Crary's theorization about the medium writ large.

Enami's stereo-self-portrait captures two gazes: one, an imperialist or anthropological gaze of a Western viewer that desires connection with the world and the other (a gaze at the stereograph), and another, his gaze-back that punctures or pierces the two-dimensional plane, seeming to hit back at the viewer.[23] The trick of this photograph is that the foreign corporations to which Enami sold the stereograph probably had little idea that what they were seeing was anything less than an authentic Japan. They were not completely wrong. After all, what could be more authentic than a photographer's self-portrait? Yet, the anonymity of the model had to be maintained for the photo to be representative of Japan in the form of its "ancient warrior" rather than a specific person. A more recent photographer's costumed self-portraits present an inversion of Enami's photo. In Cindy Sherman's self-portraiture in masquerade (and doubly so for Yasumasa Morimura's self-impersonations of Sherman), the inclusion of the self in disguise is subversive.[24] The same might be said of the transcritical, acti-passivity of Enami's cosplay. But Sherman's photos of herself impersonating famous, iconic, or archetypal women of popular culture are subversive because we know they are self-portraits. Her gaze confounds ours because as photographer she is in more control of the image than is typical for a model. Conversely, Enami's self-portraiture is so gripping because it was a secret not to be opened for decades. Nevertheless, his masquerade is incomplete; rather than submitting to the structure of the gaze, he confounds us with his look, a pose of military might.[25] And yet, does any sense of presence or frisson emanating from the photo originate in the gaze depicted within it or the exterior knowledge of whose visage it captures?

At the time of its initial circulation, the Enami photo was trading on what Daniel Novak highlights as the "alienation, anonymity, fragmentation, and abstraction" of nineteenth-century photography. Novak argues that the labor of the human bodies or models framed in early photography is abstracted in the same way that capitalism more broadly abstracts labor from workers: "Using the technology of 're- alism,' these photographers produced new and fictional bodies that existed only in a photographic space. In other words, the technology of realism produced what appears to be its opposite: the nonexistent, the fictional, and the abstract."[26] Of course, this composite of documentation and artifice, fact and fiction, might be evident in all photographs, but it is particularly salient in the stereo exemplar above. That is, Enami entered the capitalist marketplace by abstracting his own labor as a model in order to make himself into the anonymous likeness of other such samurai images already circulating. Abstraction mattered, and Enami was a master of economimesis, at once a salesman and a master artist. The model being the photographer (controlling the means of production) does not necessitate or determine that the photo could transcend the structure of the gaze. But our knowledge of the doubled role adds an extra perspective to the photo. Viewing this stereograph as connected to both a desire for ancient Japan and the modern moment of the photo studio is a way of grasping the reality of Enami's predicament.

Enami was caught between at least two worlds. For instance, there was, on the one hand, the market that wanted him to vanish and provide a transparent view of Japan and, on the other, his own artistry and craft that sought beauty and affect. Baudrillard writes that "the photographer too has disappeared" in photography and that "there is indeed a symbolic murder that is part of the photographic act. But it is not simply the murder of the object. On the other side of the lens, the subject too is made to disappear."[27] Here, he is really blind to the other eye that might also see the birth of the modern split subject in that very disappearing of the unified subject. With the studio and his face, plain as day in the photographs, always awaiting discovery or recovery, Enami drew on anonymity and self-abstraction to incompletely disappear; he cannot hide, just as viewers of the stereograph never escape the fact of their own gazing.

In a way, Enami achieves through this stereomimesis the position that Donna Haraway advocates in her feminist deconstruction of what she calls the "god-trick" of "infinite vision" associated with the Cartesian male gaze in effect in so much photography. Haraway insists on the embodiment of the gaze to counter the very illusion of a "conquering gaze from nowhere," an "infinitely mobile vision," the position of "seeing everything from nowhere." She writes, "That view of infinite vision is an illusion, a god-trick." In its place she proposes "insisting metaphorically on the particularity and embodiment of all vision."[28] Rather than a disembodied technological or institutional gaze, Enami, by inserting himself into the frame, perpetrates a doubled embodiment: as the photographer, he is the gazer; as the model, he is the gazed upon. And there is even more to it than that: as the model, he redirects his own gaze; as photographer he directs ours back at himself and his viewers. So here stereoscopy is marking not only a nostalgia for a past Japan but also a longing for a unified subject (which is, of course, always already in absentia). What is captured in Enami's self-portrait is the tension between the pose of passively presenting the reality of ever-vanishing history and the present reality of actively cultivating a mythic past.

The story of Enami's self-portrait presents an alternative to the gazer/gazed upon binary set out by a common narrative of the imperial photographic encounter with the other, which imagines that native people have a binary choice "either to be the victim of imperialist reality, or to play their allotted role in the white man's fantasy."[29] Enami declines to choose, instead playing the "allotted role" of Japanese as other to "the West" while simultaneously learning to inhabit that new world through the technology of the other. He became both the victimizing holder of the gaze and its subject. As the gazed-upon subject, Enami was not simply turning the gaze back on the viewer but recasting the gaze as much for a Japanese audience as for the world. This constant shifting—for us, between eyes, and for Enami, between being the framer of the shot and the object of the shot—allows for an alternative positionality of the split subject that is fundamentally modern. Stereomodernism here lies in the constructed, virtual reality of his self-portrait, at the nexus between the real and the imaginary, between new media and old tradition, between 2D and 3D, between east and west, between left eye and right, between gazing in at the self and out at the world. The perspective provided by Enami's landscapes and figures is not so much that of the solipsistic Cartesian worlds of erasing the I/eye of the beholder but the staging of the I/eye of the subject as in the functioning of the panorama and diorama.

The Panoramic Stereoscope: Right Eye, Gazing Out, Ground

A regular advertisement that ran in the *Asahi* newspaper several times from the fall of 1902 through the following year announced a "major invention of photology that will astound!" (odoroku beki kōsenga-kujō no daihatsumei), "an even greater product than the ordinary panorama photos and panorama stereoscopes [*panorama jittai kyō*] used in typical classrooms." The advertisement for "the automatic panoramic peep-o-scope" (panorama jidō nozoki-kyō) called it "a novel curiosity [*zanshin chinki*] about to become a craze." The machine in question was akin to August Fuhrmann's massive stereoscopic Kaiserpanorama (ca. 1880) but closer to another viewing device, patented by William Reeves in 1897, that, for a few coins, would automatically flip through a series of stereoscopic images at a set pace for one viewer at a time.[30] This newspaper ad was aimed not at viewers but rather at proprietors of businesses who might allocate a space in their shops or businesses for the automated entertainment/amusement machine, promising "a reliable daily revenue of 12 yen for the collection of funds for schools to educate poor children or for orphanage charities. . . . A money maker beyond expectations." The advertisement concludes with a call for interested readers to request a detailed mail-order pamphlet, offering "regional special contracts for individual sales" of this "innovative and unusual automatic money profit machine." Here the economy of mimesis (the zero-sum game between nature and artifice that Derrida describes) is superimposed on the entertainment economy, as views automatically provided by the device (in a closed system of representation and mimicry) become a source of revenue.

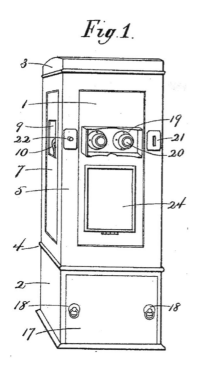

Fig.1.

Figure 6. Designs for similar coin-operated, automatic stereoscopic "panorama" viewing machines. *Clockwise from top left:* Reeves 1897, Kimura Kōseikan 1904, Shigeru shōten 1910. Images from Reeves's U.S. patent application and the *Asahi Shinbun.*

This type of viewing apparatus was neither popular nor long-lasting, but it exposes something important about that moment in the history of mass visual media in Japan: for a brief time, the private, solitary viewing of stereoscopy and the public experience of the panorama hall were linked through the public installation of this kind of vending-machine viewer. This apparatus seems to have been available in various forms from roughly 1897 to 1916, and in nearly every instance the relationship between panorama and stereoscope was part of the marketing. This link between panorama and stereoscope provides a key to understanding how such media transformed cityscapes.

By the late nineteenth century, photography had become familiar, losing some of its early allure as a spectacle. But that sense of excitement would be renewed by both the stereoscopic photography boom from the 1890s through the First World War and the new mechanized viewing machines that proliferated during the same period. Though the name of the coin-operated "panorama stereoscope" suggests a fusion of two seemingly antipodal optical affordances, what it reveals is that what seems like two forms with two different functions today were considered more closely associated then. At one level, the fusion can be seen as a brilliant marketing strategy. What seems at first blush to be inaccurate nomenclature reflects an effort not only to capture the burgeoning Japanese market for binary vision devices and viewing opportunities offering a three-dimensional perspective but also to tap into the well-known and much-discussed urban architectural destination for visual spectacle, the panorama hall. But at another level, the broader discourse around such devices reveals structural and functional similarities. In addition, the unity in the naming of these visual regimes in this kind of device reveals much about the capacious definitions around stereoscopic photography during the first decade and a half of the twentieth century. Further, the fact that "the panorama stereoscope" is linked to the rise of the vending machine in Japan shows how the machine's mediation and dissemination of realistic and fantastic images is as important as its mediation of commerce.

As stereography lost some of its sense of novelty both in Japan and abroad by the turn of the twentieth century, new efforts began to revitalize the experience of stereoscopy. In the United States, the Keystone Stereoview Company sought to charge the medium with an educational role, for instance, by printing a "Descriptive Text for

Stereographs and Lantern Slides" to accompany the series *A Scenic Tour of Japan* (1905). At the same time in Japan, the stereograph was being reinvigorated with the tinge of new spectacle through photographic reporting on the Russo-Japanese War. This push to capture newsworthy events visually has its own history. At once the result of the stereomimetic technique of documentation or recording as well as one of spectacle and spectacularization learned from the popularity of violent panoramas imported to Japan a generation after the U.S. Civil War in the 1890s, 2D war photography was also the legacy of a generation of photographers like K. Ogawa (Enami's teacher), who sold several photo collections of the previous decade's military encounter in China.[31] Such photographic mediations of the latest war afforded the next generation of photographers like Enami a new opportunity to document and, indeed, produce the visual discourse on the latest war. As part of a burgeoning military-industrial complex, Enami traveled to the front to earn money by taking war photos as an embedded photographer.

In addition to the renewal of the media through the incorporation of timely content, the technology of the medium itself was ripe for a reboot. By 1902, there was already something old and nostalgic about the stereograph as a medium (the double photos mounted on cards) and the stereoscope as a gadget (the handheld viewers). Both had been introduced in Japan by 1862 and circulated there more widely in the 1870s, but they really became a consumer form in the 1890s, when photographers like Enami first began to mass-produce and market them.[32] An advertisement for the Katsugakan photo shop in Kanda, Tokyo, carried in the July 2, 1902, issue of the *Yomiuri Shinbun* emphasizes the astounding representation of the already aging media, claiming that "the true images of figures vibrantly appear before your eyes" and "one glance is worth a thousand"; yet, the advertisement, even as it celebrates the format, seems to protest too much in the image it presents. A print rendering of a stereographic photograph of a traditional landscape subject for woodblock prints and labeled "Fuji from Suruga" adorns the top of the advertisement, which also features other print images of two different stereoscopic viewing apparatuses along with the word *Stereoscope* as an English gloss over *sōgan shashin* (literally, "binocular photographs"). Because widespread adoption of photostatic reproduction in newspapers was still a decade away, using a double image print etching of Mount Fuji to represent a stereoscopic photograph was necessary. Here, the new media is sold through the old medium, which cannot quite capture the effect, so it resorts to the textual rhetoric of realism in representation and appeal through the use of one of the most traditional landscape vistas imaginable—the national, natural symbol of Fuji, a medium for conjuring the myth of nation—as a totem pole stands in a village center for conjuring a dead family.[33] The cognitive dissonance between the advertisement's claims about the stereograph's vibrant and new representations and the means by which this can be reproduced in the remediated form of the newspaper reveals not just a gap between new and old media (stereography and newsprint) but also two basic problems of stereography: first, that it was difficult to circulate widely because it required a stereoscope, and second, that it was to be populated with remediated nostalgic images like the national icon. Or, in short, the advertisement is both a sign of troubles of a stereograph market that was ripe for a renewal and a meager attempt to renew it.

That renewal would come in both content and form. The medium of the panorama hall (a circular building for viewing an expansive painting on the walls, which gave a sense of 360-degree immersion in the landscape of the painting when viewed from the center) had circulated globally in the last quarter of the nineteenth century. It was an immediate success in Japan, with panorama halls springing up across Tokyo and over forty halls built nationwide in the twenty years after the 1890 opening of the Ueno Panorama Hall.[34] Memorialized by literati (such as Mori Ōgai, Hagiwara Sakutarō, and Edogawa Rampo, among many others) who wrote about the enchanting experience and bewildering effects of the spectacle, the panorama halls became so exceedingly popular that they, in turn, spawned spin-off gadgets.

In addition to the panorama halls, the German Kaiserpanorama also transformed and renewed the stereographic media. It is not clear whether the "panoramic stereoscope" devices bear any direct lineage from August Fuhrmann's 1883 invention (patented in 1888) for between ten and twenty-five people to view an automatically advancing series of stereographs or from a similar coin-operated device (patented by William Reeves in 1897) for one person to view a series of stereographs over a set period. But there seem to have been at least circuitous connections. The Kaiserpanorama was popular and well known throughout Germany, and penny arcades were all the rage in the United States at a time when many Japanese officials, students, and other technological appropriators visited the West specifically in order to glean the latest innovations. Most technological and visual apparatuses developed in Europe and America found their way into the Japanese technical literature of the time, though there is no mention of the Kaiserpanorama until 1902, nearly two decades after its invention.[35] And some Japanese content appeared in the German Kaiserpanorama soon after: a series of more than forty Russo-Japanese War stereographs, some colored in the Enami studio's style, were exhibited in the Wilhelmshaven Kaiserpanorama in April 1906 and remain in the Deutsches Historisches Museum's Kaiserpanorama collection.[36] Back in Japan, Kimura Kōseikan's April 1904 advertisement for a panoramic stereoscope (see Figure 6, center) touted the fact that the machine would exhibit binocular photos (*sōgan shashin*) from the Russo-Japanese War in Asakusa (near one of the famed panorama halls) for ten days in May.[37] So it would seem that the histories of war stereography, public panorama, and machinic viewing were at the least nearly simultaneous, if not mutually constitutive. Even if divergent evolution cannot explain the similarity with Fuhrmann's and Reeves's inventions, at least convergent evolution might. Perhaps confronted with the popularity of the panorama halls, Japanese marketers of these devices also adopted the term *panorama* for another form of visual spectacle just like Fuhrmann had done earlier in Berlin.[38]

Of course, today we recognize that in form and function the stereoscope and the panorama hall have very little to do with one another.[39] Scholar of human behavior Hosoma Hiromichi recognizes the confusion as experiential, stemming from a blurring of the lines between the "real world (environment)" produced by the mechanism of the panorama hall and the "feeling of presence" produced by stereographs. He notes that the two forms are distinct because the viewer is oriented outward to a landscape vista with the panorama, where the viewer is oriented inward toward the interior of the trick of the apparatus in the case of the stereoscope.[40] And yet the fact that the stereographic viewing mechanism was billed as "panoramic" in both European and Japanese contexts exhibits the durability of a powerful marketing strategy.

A more fundamental link between these two affordances can be seen in the architectural phenomenon of the twelve-story tower in Asakusa, the first skyscraper in Japan where visitors could pay a fee to enter the viewing deck on the upper floors. It is significant that, in contrast to the simple, box-like designs of Fuhrmann's Kaiserpanorama and Reeves's coin-operated apparatus, the Japanese panoramic stereographs were often decorated with ornaments resembling architectural features. The above-mentioned 1904 advertisement, for instance, features a particularly intricate design that seems to have been relatively resilient over several versions of the machine produced over the following decade in Japan. With its cresting, pinnacles, cupola, spires, and flèche, the exterior design of the machine's wooden cabinet are consonant with the look of the skyscraping, "cloud-penetrating" brick and wood tower, which had opened fourteen years earlier. The exterior of the panoramic stereo-machines would be the first impression that all purchasers and consumers would have of the machine, before deciding to approach it, insert coins, and peer inside. In this sense, the exterior of the machines placed throughout the city echoes the presence of the tower in the city and preceded the gaze at the stereographs inside it.

The stereoscope, the Kaiserpanorama, the panorama hall, and skyscraping tower offer different viewing experiences: the solitary gaze of the stereoscope is multiplied into a number of simultaneous parallel experiences by the Kaiserpanorama; the panorama hall and tower both offer spectacles to be enjoyed as part of a crowd. With the first two devices, a gaze into lenses is required. In the latter two buildings, a gaze outward from a center is the norm. But there are also some important similarities. The very presence of such devices in the world means that they begin to transform their environs even before they are "used."[41] Those who use the stereoscope must insert and switch the stereograph cards before and between looking through the lenses, thus holding and beholding the apparatus as such; the panorama hall and the Kaiserpanorama are urban destinations; the tower is a spectacle not only for those who go to the top but for all city dwellers who marvel at its dizzying height; and the automatic panoramic stereoscope stands in a room, beckoning potential customers to insert a coin and peruse the images behind the lenses. The consumers who sit around the Kaiserpanorama in chairs staring into the binocular lenses of the machine are paralleled by the potential consumers who stand lined up in anticipation of sitting down and looking inside.[42]

Unlike the tower, a unique location as the only structure of its kind in Tokyo, the panoramic stereograph was sold with the purpose of being "set up at key points around the city" (shigai no yōsho ni set-chi).[43] In other words, the private moment of a singular view through the machines must be contextualized by the fact that, like the multiple panorama halls dotting the cities, the goal was to install the panoramic stereographs throughout the country. As a network, the machines potentially widened the reach and market penetration of stereoscopic views, broadly casting images across the cityscape in a way that anticipates television. To peep, one need not have purchased a series of photos and a viewer (or know someone who did); rather, one could walk up to a public device, deposit a coin, and begin viewing.

The consumption of such viewing apparatuses does not start when one stares into the machine or enters the hall to view; it begins at the moment when the environment in which it is placed is transformed by the presence of the mechanism itself. Before the machine can serve up its stereocards, before it can become a machine that stages sights, these staging sites are themselves staged sights to behold. Acknowledging that the viewing of the device itself becomes part of the viewing experience shows that the views mediated by these various devices are already premediated or doubly mediated. The double views themselves are layered with another view—the view of the device. This view external to the device (the view of the exterior) itself guarantees that the later, secondary view into the machine will be recalled as a constructed or mediated trick. There is a stereomimetic tension between these two seemingly antipodal ways of understanding the media: even as viewers know it is a trick, they are to be fascinated by the trick.

The visual discourse on the tower in Asakusa reveals this binary structure, that the tower was both to be seen and to afford seeing. Early marketing materials emphasized not only its height and panoramic view but also its interior features. For instance, a series of four posters titled "Diagram of the Great Japanese Cloud Piercing Tower," published soon after the red-brick tower opened in 1890, advertised it with a tableau of rooftop and interior views alongside a print of the tower, their vertical arrangement emphasizing its height. This juxtaposition of the external view with internal images of the spiral staircase, the elevator cars, the elevator motor gears, and panoramic view were common, positioning the viewer both outside and within the structure.[44] Two of the four posters advertised the panoramic views of the city, reflecting the context of the panorama hall boom. But that three of the four advertise the interior marks an important aspect of the historical allure of the tower—it was not only a site to gaze out of but also a sight to see into.[45] Similarly, even though there was less emphasis on the interior mechanisms and workings of the panoramic stereoscope machines of the late Meiji, they were also promoted, instilling the desire to be both gazed upon and gazed into.

The very fact that a building could transform the landscape was part of the experience. As with the panorama halls in which the observer was "placed in the center of an expansive spectacle that extends across the walls around him,"[46] the tower in Asakusa provided an expansive view of the cityscape around it. Similarly, the panorama halls gave observers "a sense of visual power and control they could never hope to experience while being swallowed up in, distracted and consumed by the busy, noisy, confusing metropolises in which they lived."[47] Clearly, part of the thrill that these structures imbued in their consumers had much to do with the buildings themselves. This is why even decades after the debut of the panorama halls, advertisements were still featuring images of the exteriors of the halls.

The interior and exterior affordances of these architectural sites (the halls and the tower that enable the sensation of distance and perspective on the city spread out before and around them) give us further insight into thinking about stereoscopy. Brian Massumi reminds us that the panorama hall is not contrary to a Cartesian view often associated with stereoscopy and its underlying desire to penetrate the z-axis: "The panoramic image did not in fact break with traditional perspective, but multiplied it."[48] As binocular viewing glasses and monocular telescopes were often provided in the centers of the panorama pavilions, so too were they affixed atop the biggest panorama of all, the view from atop the twelve-story tower in Asakusa. Edogawa Rampo's story "The Man Traveling with the Brocade Portrait," for example, is premised on the scopophilia of a man who spies a woman through binoculars while gazing out from the tower.[49] At the very moment of getting a lifelike panorama or a presumably unadulterated unmediated glimpse of a real city vista, visitors were already being shown that looking through binocular lenses might enhance the optical experience.

In addition to the privileged position of the paid consumer from within and atop these buildings, there was the open-access position of people all around the outside of the tower and the halls who paid

Figure 7. Poster for the twelve-story tower in Asakusa, featuring views of the building from the inside and outside. Image from the Edo Tokyo Hakubutsukan.

no entrance fee. The tower's primary optical affordance was for the casual observer who had no ticket for admission, as a landmark orienting the city walker.[50] Just as the view from within may separate the viewer from the city, as Seiji M. Lippit suggests, the tower also grounds the city around it.[51] Rampo's character remarks: "All you had to do was find a slight rise anywhere in Tokyo, and you could see what everyone called the 'Red Ghost.'"[52] City dwellers gazing toward the tower gained a sense of perspective and distance. Just as the architecture itself offered a transformative view of the city from on high, the presence of the early skyscraper in the city transformed the city around it even for those on the ground. Similarly, the presence of a "stereographic panorama" (a mini tower resembling the full-sized one in Asakusa) in a room transforms the space around it, imbuing it with spectacle, wonder, and desire.

The similarities between the panoramic stereograph, panorama halls, and the twelve-story tower are not limited to this dynamic between exterior and interior. The content of the views was also in a complex relation. Responding to the claim that the French city literature of Balzac corresponded directly to the panorama, scholar Maeda Ai notes an absence of panorama in early modern Japan. Instead, he writes that peeping devices were the best visual correspondence to Hattori Bushō's literary *New Tales of Tokyo Prosperity* (1874). For devices providing three-dimensional perspectives in early modern Tokyo, vignettes of city life were more common than sweeping panoramas. Maeda emphasizes the relations of "people and things" that populate horizontal landscapes.[53] Timon Screech's descriptions of such *nozoki karakuri* (peeping boxes) significantly include both panoramic-like landscapes (of hell, heaven, China, factories in Jakarta) and portraits of elephants and green-grocer girls.[54] What happened two decades later, when the panorama halls themselves came to Japan around the same time that stereoscopy was an active consumer phenomenon, seems to be, if not a unification of forms, at least a continuous play between them.

All these media emphasized the play between landscape in the background or distant view and "people and things" in the middle or foreground. From the beginning, panoramas in Japan were part diorama. For instance, a Battle of Vicksburg panorama was displayed in Tokyo with real U.S. Civil War artifacts and weapons in front of the walls painted with vistas. And the Automatic Panorama (Jidō Panorama) in October 1894 featured automatons *(jidō ningyō)* populating the diorama in front of the panorama walls. Panorama pavilions were also related to a lens-mediated view, insofar as binoculars were available to visitors.[55] This play between figure and ground, portrait and landscape, dummies representing corpses and paintings of battle-fields was deemed to give unique perspective. And the play is doubled in the dichotomy between panorama hall and the stereoscope that finds perhaps a moment of unity in the panoramic stereoscope. Crary explains, "Pronounced stereoscopic effects depend on the presence of objects or obtrusive forms in the near or middle ground."[56] It is significant, in this regard, that Crary includes in his book *Suspensions of Perception* three copies of stereographic images from the historical Kaiserpanorama, which he claims have nothing to do with panorama. One of these images—of Niagara Falls—is all background. In contrast, the second image provides a London streetscape background and middle ground. And the third, a group of Japanese women in kimonos situated against a backdrop of a bamboo fence in a garden.[57] According to Crary's own logic, the 3D effect of the Japanese stereograph is the most pronounced of the three and also happens to share a structural characteristic of panorama halls, which often had diorama-like dummies staged in front of the walls. What began as a way to enhance the stereoscopic effect (by placing human figures in the foreground) became a trope in Japanese stereographs of Enami and others with the full-body nostalgic portraits of Japanese men in samurai ward-robe and women in kimonos.

Such images found their way into the panoramic stereograph machines. Hosoma describes the contents of the photos of people displaying various manners and customs *(fuzoku jinbutsu),* such as "beautiful women and ikebana," "peony field and beautiful woman," and "beautiful women playing go."[58] He quotes the explanatory pamphlet for one of the panoramic stereoscope machines as discussing the distance between the things (flowers) in the background and the people (beauties) in the foreground. Hosoma writes:

> Why did this writer [of the pamphlet] mistake "panoramic photo-graph" and "stereoscopic photograph"? ... There is the particular expression, "real things, real environments [*jitsubutsu jikkyō*]," to describe the feeling of being present [*rinjōkan*] in a panorama pavilion. ... This writer took his image of the panorama pavilion,

then confused the presence obtained from the panorama pavilion and the presence obtained from the stereoscopic photograph, and then mistakenly called the stereoscopic photograph a "panoramic photograph."[59]

Here, Hosoma suggests that whether the bodies in the foreground were Japanese beauties or Russian war dead, beautiful or dreadful, it was the feeling of presence that mattered over the specific content. In addition, there were photographic beauty contests hosted within the Asakusa tower. Soon after its opening in 1890, William K. Burton, the designer of the tower, hosted a beauty contest featuring photos of geisha; such exhibitions would become something of a trend there.[60] Thus, where the panorama hall tended toward morbid depictions of wars to evoke the feeling of presence and the tower featured landscapes populated by beauties to create the same effect, stereoscopic panorama machines unified such genres of content, both the allure of Japanese beauties and morbid curiosity about war.[61]

The new machines were also marketed as wonders of automation and vending. On October 22, 1903, the *Yomiuri Shinbun* ran a brief article on an "innovative inventive apparatus" (zanshin hatsumei kikai). As the article described it, a company near the Yoroi bridge was turning out "panoramic photographs and panorama stereoscopes" that, besides "being suitable for classroom use," would also be "mechanisms for naturally earning revenue" (shizen ni shūnyū o eru yō no shikumi). The writer was cryptic in describing the device but was clearly impressed by the fact that it had "automatic functions requiring no manual labor."[62] This focus on automation emphasizes the lack of a hand crank seen in earlier versions of column stereographs. Like the many and sundry hand-operated or cranked cabinet stereoviewers marketed primarily for the private home from the 1850s to the 1920s, these Japanese machines provided multiple views of a series of photos, but with the twist of automatically advancing images.[63]

Crary emphasizes the constraints on the body of the stereoscopic viewer (who had to fit their eyes into a single particular position in a viewfinder or wear ill-fitting glasses) and the subject's cognitive role in the "radical abstraction and reconstruction of optical experience" that stereoscopy occasions.[64] The fact is that we never encounter the stereoscope solely from the position of our eyes plugged into the viewing machine. We do not remain exclusively in that Cartesian and solitary space. Rather, as Crary and Mark B. N. Hansen remind us, we are necessarily also always simultaneously aware of the apparatus in our world. Indeed, the function of the apparatus depends on our "manual action."[65] In other words, as in a film, there is the ordering and composing of the viewing; but unlike a film, such ordering and composition is accomplished by the viewer. Since stereographs were most often meant to be viewed in a series, there is a fourth axis of time that needs to be considered. And yet the labor involved in manual composition with the traditional stereoscope in which the viewer had to manipulate cards by hand differs from the automatically rendered (pre)compositing of the vending machine. This temporal factor of viewing through the automatic panorama stereoscope collapses or connects differences between still photography and motion pictures.

Unlike film, the automatic stereopanorama did not animate movement but rather created montage effects. This emphasis on the automatic viewing of stereoscopic images in the advertisement and labeling of the devices mirrors what Walter Benjamin writes about the Kaiserpanorama—namely, that it resembles cinematic viewing. Whereas Benjamin's early experiences of the Kaiserpanorama predated the advent of film, the introduction of the stereopanorama in Japan was virtually simultaneous (for many Japanese citizens, motion pictures would have been the earlier medium). Benjamin was particularly interested in the montage-like way in which the Kaiserpanorama brought a sequence of images before its viewer. In the end, he contrasts the bell that rang between views with the music that seamlessly stitched together the montage of images in the cinema.[66] But the absence of music was not necessarily characteristic of Japanese panoramic stereoscopes, several of which had "organ included" (orugan iri) or "music included" (ongaku iri) printed right on the machine.[67] Benjamin emphasizes the machinic time of the imaginary travel to foreign places ordered by the Kaiserpanorama's bell, while the cinematic music of the organ in the Japanese machines could help smooth potentially jarring juxtapositions and transitions. In Benjamin's sense, then, these Japanese machines were more cinematic than the Kaiserpanorama for the viewers. But the different sounds may have had similar marketing effects. Benjamin argues that the bell punctuating the montage of images created a sort of Pavlovian response of desire for the next image. The music could do the same for people near a Japanese stereographic panorama, who could hear the music play as they watched those with their brows pressed to the machine, for whom the music might also have helped to smooth the transitions between the images flipping by.

Hosoma refers to panoramic stereoscope machines as providing "scenery as sales items" (urimono toshite no keishiki).[68] The innovative vending machines sold not just these visual amusements but also trinkets and goods.[69] In 1906, Kuroki Shingo of Osaka applied for (and received the following year) the patent for an "automatic binocular fortune vending apparatus" (jidō sōgankyō tsujiura-shutsu sōchi), which sold paper fortunes along with its views. The innovation was the vending method, so the patent gives details not about the stereograph-changing mechanism employed but rather about the coin-operated sales mechanism.[70] Advertising, too, increasingly focused on the varied earning potential of automatic vending machines. Early advertisements for the stereoscopic panoramas made vague promises about "mechanisms for earning revenue," but by 1914, the Arita company advertised machines that were able to sell fortunes (omikuji and tsujiura), cigarettes, and strong liquor (shurui).[71] A similar vending/viewing machine from 1905 (on exhibition today at the Takahara Kyōdokan in Gifu Prefecture) not only sold a series of thirteen pictures with musical organ accompaniment but also dispensed packets of the popular Jintan mint. The advertisement for this Jintan machine on exhibit with the machine details the placement of this panoramic stereoscope. The vending machine debuted at the Jintan Park tower directly next door to the taller cloud-piercing tower in Asakusa.[72]

What these machines display is photographic culture in transition between handicraft and speed—a moment after hand-painted lantern slides and before feature-length films. The automatization of scrolling machine views is doubled by the automatization of the sales. Both automatizations are labor-saving: no one is needed to crank the machine for the next stereocard or to sell the Jintan (or other widgets). The legacy of this new medium for spectacle and sales persists in the continued success of Japanese vending machines (jidōhanbaiki, lit. "automatic sales machines") today. But, as Marxist theory explains, such mechanisms do not, in fact, "save" labor but rather merely obscure or alienate the labor to another hidden level. In the example of the automatic viewing/vending machine, the labor of advancing the images and selling the mints is merely shifted to the industries that arose to stock the machines and constantly create new spectacular products with which to load them. In this sale of goods and illusions, we are presented a bifurcated vision of a Debordian society of spectacle in which some of the goods themselves are illusions.[73]

Following Maeda Ai's interpretation of the panorama of Tokyo as seen in Japanese literature in terms of Henri Lefebvre's ideas of urban organization of space, we can say that these new media as monuments in the city became symbolic spaces of spectacle (the panorama hall and the skyscraping tower were spectacular monuments worthy of visits, as were the vending machines that miniaturized sightseeing experiences). But the gap between these symbolic spectacular spaces and what Maeda and Lefebvre might call their paradigmatic spaces (what Lefebvre defines in relational and binary terms, or what we can think of as oppositional parallax spaces characterized by dichotomies of left/right, inside/outside, center/periphery, or town/country) provides some perspective. And ultimately the conduit for this perspective would be the so-called syntagmatic space (for Lefebvre and Maeda, the transportations systems of rivers or roads, but we might do better to think of these media themselves as the syntagmatic infrastructural connectors for this networking of spaces).[74] Rather than staring into the future, these spectacular panoramic parallax devices created a nostalgia, the seeming ability to stare into the vanishing and distant past. But, of course, they were simply conduits creating new televisual spectacles not meant for catching a glimpse of a past that had been frozen in time but meant for cultivating longing for the vanishing beautiful past or aestheticized violence of the recent past in the present.

Solid-State Nostalgia and 2.5D Anamorphosis: When 3D Was Surreal

Stereoscopy is said to be about viewing solid objects, and yet it so often leaves its viewers disappointed. Physician, poet, and early theorist of stereoscopy Oliver Wendell Holmes used the word *solid* intentionally in reference to the hard card format of stereographic images. Here it is useful to consider the Greek etymologies of the compounds *stereograph*—the writing of a solid—and *stereoscope*—the gazing upon a solid.[75] When talking specifically about the stereo-optics of image, Holmes seems aware that the solid could be related not in opposition to a gas or a liquid, but to an empty husk that is only a surface—a nonsubstantial empty shell, only skin deep. Holmes also talks of collecting stereographs as akin to hunters collecting "skins": "The time will come when a man who wishes to see any object, natural or artificial, will go to the Imperial, National, or City Stereographic Library and call for its skin or form, as he would for a book at any common library."[76] The word *skin* is important not only because it might conjure, for contemporary readers, racialized anthropological depictions of the world in early stereoscopy but also because it relates to what would become a common critique of stereoscopy—namely, that the three-dimensional effect looks thin, false, or somewhat attenuated. Here the common critique that the trick of stereoscopy is apparent in the way that depth looks anamorphic rather than rounded, that the edges around figures make them seem as though thin onionskins or paper cutouts popping up in children's dioramas.[77]

Consideration of the two most common Japanese language translations for the *stereo* in *stereoscope* or *stereograph* provides a different perspective on the contrasts between skin and surface and between depth and solid. *Rittai* (standing-body) and *jittai* (real-body) echo the sense of solidity and reality of a body seeming to stand before the viewer; the "body" (*-tai*) in both words captures the notion of figure and physique—that which would have to stand out against the background for the effect of presence to be produced.[78] Through these Japanese etymologies, stereoscopy discourse shares the notion of ground and figure discussed above in reference to both the stereoscopic technology (Crary) and panorama aesthetics (Maeda) and reflections on what I have called stereomimesis from Karatani, Kant, Derrida, Erich Auerbach, and Edgar Rubin, among others. But the word *rittai* is also related to a later Japanese critique of the falsity of realism and praise of the surreality of stereoscopy, in that the abstract modernist style of cubism would be translated using the same term. In the early 1920s when *rittai-shashin* meant "stereoscopic photography" and *rittai-shugi* meant "cubism," stereoscopy could no longer be thought of solely as adhering to things as they are in the world.

The supposed truth of the 3D imagination produced by the two 2D photographs lies not in the images alone but in some "mode of ideation," to use the words of Wilhelm Max Wundt.[79] Wundt's book *Lectures on Human and Animal Psychology* was translated into Japanese in 1902 and explores the ramifications of the then recent innovations in stereoscopy for psychology.[80] In Wundt's view (later supported by cognitive science), the 3D image is not, in fact, instantaneously apprehended as a single image composed equally of the two images on the card but rather results from an uneven shifting between two images, one of which is dominant, while the other performs a supplementary function.[81]

Foregrounding the viewer's role in image construction through "the operation of reconciling disparity" shows stereoscopy to be a mind–body–machine nexus. As such, it raises the very question of the use value of the apparatus. The fact that there are some people who can train not just their eyes but themselves to resolve three dimensions from the stereocards without the aid of lenses in stereoscopes reminds us that the machine is only part of the mediated experience. And even those who do not need the stereoscope must use their brains and eye muscles. This intervention of and interpretation in the brain contrasts with the notion of the immediacy of the techno-image, the seemingly immediate multiplanar parallax, a parallax of instantaneous apprehension of two positions. The brain's role suggests a movement over time (a toggling) between positions and foregrounds the spectator position, resolution, rendering, or interpretation. This tension—between the power of the image, on the one hand, lying in the image itself (immediacy) and, on the other, residing in the minds of the viewers (interpretation)—is why the supposedly realistic medium has been called false and even horrific.

Edogawa Rampo writes of the horror of viewing simple red/blue 3D films where beasts lunge at the camera or poles jut out toward the eyes of the viewer.[82] His horror is consonant with that of the future death capture in every snapshot that Roland Barthes identifies as the future-anterior capture inherent of all photography. But the duration of a photo is not simply within the snap of the shot or the flash of a bulb. As Derrida notes, the idea of an instant captured on film is not quite right in the first place. So when photographs or stereographs are the impetus for an affective nostalgic response, it helps to think of the duration of the exposure, the emulsion, and the developing process, as well as the time elapsed between these actions, all of which is typically lumped together as the instant of photo-taking and the flash of the view.[83] The feeling of presence created by such 3D images is said to feel like a "click" (namely, an instant when the images are thought to resolve, though this click too is a myth with the toggling between images continuing through a duration or period of the so-called resolve).[84] Even when mechanically automated in the panorama machine or the cinema, a singular view or peep is never an instant but instead has a duration. Superimposed onto all these durations for stereoscopy is the duration for the mind to resolve the two images also leading to an affective response or feeling of presence that itself may have an undetermined duration. Of course, quasi-realistic and nostalgic perspectives on time and history produced by the stereograph may be present in all photographs, as Susan Sontag suggests, but the effect seems somehow enhanced through the 3D perspective of the stereograph.[85]

The question here is whether the trick of 3D has any effect, whether enhancing or mitigating, on the falseness or horror already inherent in the 2D photo. Crary puts the problem down to the fact that the 3D effect of stereoscopy is spotty at best, "a disunified and aggregate field of disjunct elements," because the two two-dimensional photos mean that "the fundamental organization of the stereoscopic image is planar."[86] In other words, stereoscopy is not a 3D but a 2.5D: a view that suggests and approximates actual embodied stereovision without quite reproducing it. For Crary, this fact about stereoscopy ends up foregrounding precisely that which photography seeks to erase—the falseness of Adorno's and Benjamin's phantasmagoria of media—and is the reason for its obsolescence. And yet, the openness or opacity of its own trickery and fakery is the reason for it being taken up by surrealists.[87] That is to say, artists looking to transcend the limitations of scientific fidelity to representation of nature turned to stereoscopy precisely because it was so clearly a trick. And this sense of trickery would not be dissolved by the innovation of incorporating ocular convergence into the apparatus for taking or viewing stereographs (in 1953) and stereoscopic films (in 1973).[88] Indeed, the brief rebirth and quicker death of stereoscopy around the convergence technology of RealD 3D (color 3D video-drawing on convergence techniques and polarized or flicker lenses) beginning in 2009 seemed to many observers' eyes to be an improvement on the planarity of two side-by-side images because it took into account the way our eyes cross and converge on objects to see them. But the adoption of RealD 3D for the motion picture *Avatar* and by major Japanese television and cinema production companies would wane with inevitable tiring of the trick and the development of other tricky media like VR technologies.[89]

All media work necessarily as filters or lenses distorting our spatially and temporally finite experiences of the infinite world, reducing such experiences to an even more limited scope. Of course, some media will be considered even more exciting than our experience for a time, but ultimately our experience of reality proves to be more fully stimulating or at least unparalleled by our media. This does not stop the dream of better, clearer, more fully rendered representation. This cyclical nature of realist desire was recognized by surrealists.

Writing in 1939, when stereoscopy itself had long been a throwback to a bygone age,[90] the surrealist poet Hagiwara Sakutarō reflected on his deep, lingering fascination with stereoscopic photography as a hobby. In an essay titled "My Camera," Hagiwara too finds the stereoscope compelling not as an embodiment of the real and not because it is kitsch but precisely as a solid medium of gloom and nostalgia.

> This stereoscope alone is my one and only companion. And I myself have an essential reason for this. The reason I have a camera is neither for taking so-called art pictures nor for documentary photographs that preserve memory. In a word, through the optical effects of the machine, I want to reflect or project [*utsushitai*]

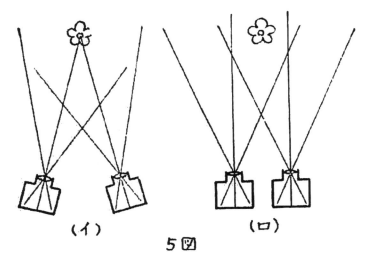

Figure 8. The Minimal Difference and Maximal Effect: Planar stereographic setup versus biplanar convergence stereographic setup, from Otagi Michifusa, "Sutereo ni kansuru moro mondai," *Shashin kōgyō*, August 1953.

the nostalgia [*kyōshū*] of my own heart as it is reflected in natural scenery. From a long time ago, there has been a spot in my heart for that kind of nostalgia, like the so-called loneliness of *haiku,* the lullaby heard in those days of innocence, some limitless romantic yearning, or even some extremely miserable and pathetic song. So in order to project or reflect the nostalgia within me, the "stereo" standing-form [cubist] photos [*sutereo no rittai shashin*] cannot be beat. And that is because those stereographs (a kind of miniature original panorama [*honrai panorama no ko mokei*]) themselves have their essence in their particular gloom of the panorama; the panorama is something that gives the feeling of a mysterious nostalgic desolation. . . . I want to say here it is "like the real view [*jikkei*]," but the reason I will not say it is that the panorama of stereographs are different than the real view, because they are mysterious and illusory. Here, like the paintings and the objects in the panorama hall, the distance between the background and the foreground gives the illusion of spatial representation [*kūkan hyōzō*]. . . . I don't have any interest in regular photos, because only stereograms reflect or project this. Regular photos are planar [*heimen*], merely copying two dimensions of the world. So, to the extent that photorealism exists, it is all the more far from the poems and dreams of my heart. That is because the nostalgia of my heart is dreamily composed only in three-dimensional space.[91]

In Hagiwara's view, the stereoscope fails in its promise of presenting some better, clearer vision of a reality for a passive viewer and gives only a version of nostalgia for a solid state of things, albeit one that never actually existed but is distilled through a gloomy, lonely heart.[92] The fact that he openly compares the panorama hall with the "miniature" panorama of the stereoscope comes from his sense that the panorama hall also provided a three-dimensional perspective. And his configuration "*sutereo no rittai shashin*" (translated above as "'stereo' standing-form [cubist] photos") is odd because Hagiwara, an otherwise careful wordsmith, essentially doubles the term. Here he is either just being redundant or in his mind *stereo* and *rittai* are not equal.

In an earlier essay recalling his childhood visits to the Ueno Panorama Pavilion where he saw exhibits on the U.S. Civil War and the Battle of Waterloo, Hagiwara also mentions this sense of depth in the play between the "real objects and the picture" (jitsubutsu to e) in the hall, recounting a game he used to play after hearing about the structure of the hall (i.e., that there were both paintings and real objects): "with the curiosity of a child, I would passionately try to discover the borders between the real objects and the painting."[93] And the composition of his actual photos adheres to his recollection of the panorama. Over 40 percent of the extant photos taken by Hagiwara are stereoscopic, and 33 percent of those capture people.[94] Some critics remark that the soft, almost hazy focus of Hagiwara's photos has the effect of emphasizing the gap between close-up and background.[95] His theorization of panorama hall and practice of stereographic photos are not some sideline hobbyist comments but would become core principle understandings for his poetics.[96] In the end, Hagiwara, whether through photographs or poetry, was more interested in the play between the objects and paintings or panorama and city that produced the effect than in the effect itself. Similarly, the stereoscopic images he took conveyed not the solid objects that Holmes envisioned but poetry, dreams, and fantasies (no longer a connection to the world but a retreat from it). In this view, the cognitive space between the images of the hollow skins (between two planar images) in stereographs requires a filling in, and this requirement inspires the surrealist poet.[97] In Hagiwara's stereograph as poetry or poetry as stereograph, the medium's reality lies beyond the medium, elsewhere, in nostalgia, a dream of a time in which something (some solid object in reality) could be recorded and documented in time and space.

This powerful understanding of the nostalgia of the stereoscope seems to have rubbed off on Hagiwara's daughter, but for her, the medium connects through its very loneliness. In an article commemorating her father, titled "By My Father's Bed," Hagiwara Yōko (a novelist and prize-winning essayist) writes:

> Of all the things around my father's bedside the ones that left the biggest impression were the stereographs. Beginning in his twenties he became absorbed in photos—taking and developing them himself, but by the time of my childhood memories he was already taking stereographs.[98]

She writes of disturbing her solitary father alone in the gloom of his room to bring him tea and taking some time to examine his stereographs with avid curiosity. "For a father who could not clean up after himself at all, he sure took care of those stereographs arranging them neatly in the glass cabinet." The first time she tried to see the photos it was too dark and gloomy. And when she tried a second time:

> I thought that they would be boring photos [*tsumaranai shashin*], but it was exactly as though living things were coming out of the picture. I became enthralled and tried swapping in various photos.
>
> However, just as I was looking, as only a world of frustrating illusion came to appear, I began to feel inexpressibly lonely for a long time while sitting on my father's cold hard mattress.[99]

The passage is short but contains the entire history of stereoscopy, compressed—the fascination, doubt, mystery, and allure for the strange object, the desire to behold it, suspicion, the first use, the impressiveness of the representation, the feeling of presence, and then estrangement from it. And, finally, the essay as a whole connotes a sort of nostalgia with which the genre was always already imbued. At last, she connects across time to the memory of her father not as a primitive other from the past but as a surreal ghostly image and memory of loneliness. The medium is at once connecting and alienating; it is the primary means by which she connects to her father's alienation.

Bernard Stiegler describes photography as "two technical systems [of lens and shutter and chemical and paper] and two separate viewings: those of the photographer and of the spectator."[100] I want to emphasize that stereography does all of this in a similar manner, only more intensely, and that the binocular image presents the odd temporality of the photo in its most solid state. Stereoscopy also puts the subject in a relationship with the object that stages a missed connection up front, as a figure popping out of a flat landscape or background. In other words, with its play between figure and ground over time, stereography makes salient nothing less than the multiple long durations of the photograph always already hidden or hiding behind the apparent flash of the moment of taking and glimpsing.

The sense of sullen nostalgia in the stereograph for both Hagiwaras lies in its temporal gap between the taking and the viewing that Stiegler identifies and the spatial parallax gap that is the exploited technê of the stereo apparatus. This gloom is not the dark space of the horror of getting one's eye poked out, as it is for Rampo's idea of

3D cinema, but rather the gloom of the temporal and spatial abyss of modernity as the gap between the dream of being present and experiencing a sense of reality always belatedly through mediation, a gap between the image chemically recording the light bouncing off the object and the darkness of the solitary mind that must make sense of the double images alone in the machine. It is the solitary failure to concretize a connection with the object, the failure to ever truly realize or resolve presence. In this view, stereoscopic images are less about representing solid bodies in perspective, as in the grotesque (horrific or beautiful) appropriations of the technology, than they are about a kind of nostalgia for a long-absent way of life (for presence).

Panorama Islands, Additive Manufacturing for Posterity, and the Return of the Real

In *The Strange Tale of Panorama Island,* Rampo creates a world in which a madman transforms an island wilderness into the semblance of a panorama hall by erecting a viewing tower at the center of the titular island and creating various scenes that trick visitors' perceptions. The story of the murderous, single-minded antihero Hitomi Hirosuke serves as an allegory for the moral consequences of cycloptic spectacles that suggest a Cartesian mind–body divide. In one of the climactic scenes, Hitomi (lit. "one-view") explains to his wife his theory of creation behind his construction of the island and describes a key function of the panorama hall. The fascinating thing about the panorama halls of his youth, he says, was their spatial doubling:

> Outside the panorama hall, the streets that one was accustomed to seeing everyday exist. And inside the panorama hall, no matter the direction in which you look, there's no sign of that world, and the Manchurian plains extend to the horizon line far away. In other words, the double worlds of the streets and the plains exist in the same spot. At least, it gives rise to such an illusion . . . displayed in such a way that you cannot distinguish the boundary between the real things and the painting.[101]

The doubling of the spaces makes the entire panorama hall into a medium for conjuring another world that is contiguous but also at a remove. The story of Panorama Island stages what might happen if the walls of the panorama hall were to evaporate, so that the world itself became a panorama. In the fantasy novel, the answer is that deceitful things—murder, impersonation, crimes of passion, etc.—happen. Rampo's story suggests that there is something fundamentally perverse about the nature of virtual worlds, simulacra, and representation. Ultimately, it shows that mimesis has the potential not only to create transformative fictive worlds but also to transform space and behavior in the real world. This story then presents something like a budding haunted media critique *avant la théorie* that explores the darkest repercussions of both aspects of mimesis.

The story's depiction of a completely human-designed island environment evokes an almost magical transformation or manifestation of spaces through technology that is nothing particularly new. Indeed, one of the oldest forms of human artifice is gardening. Though vision was always important for such transformations, in modernity the mediation of such sites through lenses and film have made the stakes of such artifice more tangible. For instance, Enami's stereographs (ca. 1898) of the great bronze Buddha statue at Kamakura illuminate one aspect of the media as totem pole. Though once gilded, the statue today exhibits a green patina with only faint remnants of its golden past visible near the ears of the great figure that towers over ten meters in height. The statue is hollow, so visitors have been able to appreciate both the inside and outside of the monument for hundreds of years, and ancient graffiti still mark the inside of its walls. Today, the Kotoku-in shrine garden that houses the Buddha forbids specific kinds of new photographic gadgets—selfie sticks and drones.[102] But along with Mount Fuji, the statue was one of the major subjects for early photographers of Japan, including Enami.

One of Enami's stereographs of the Kamakura Buddha differs from the vast number of photos of it from the time, which tend to immortalize the monument from a frontal angle. Enami's stereograph views the statue instead from a three-quarter angle, which has the effect of enhancing the feeling of depth, not only because trees in the foreground frame the statue and a man stands in front of it but also because the angle highlights the statue's profile.[103] The paper diorama-like setup of Enami's photo reminds viewers that, like so many ancient monuments, the statue is hollow or thin in its monumentality; indeed, there is no direct connection with the original statue that stood on this spot: the current verdigris-covered statue is a rebuilding of a wooden original, and yet it is still prized as ancient in its own right, having withstood the tests of time since its thirteenth-century reconstruction.[104] One rare photo from circa 1890, included in the New York Public Library Photography Collection, shows the statue from behind with doors open in the back airing it out.[105] Enami's photo, without similarly showing the statue's interior, has a similar effect of revealing a depth through perspective while emphasizing the thinness of the diorama-like layers of fore-, mid-, and background.

In these thin skins of the stereography, the medium of hollow yet solid bronze statue would be reborn. A rebirth of stereoscopic photography in the late 1920s was founded on the use of the technology to create monuments occupying space in our world. The 3D scanning and printing developed by Morioka Isao, inspired by François Willème's breakthrough stereoscopic photosculptures of the mid-nineteenth century, present a stunning case of the transformational possibilities of stereomimesis. In a series of articles in 1927 and 1928, published in prominent photography journals and mainstream general interest magazines and newspapers, Morioka wrote and was interviewed about his experiments using photography to quickly create accurate and precise sculptures. He claimed to have had a deep interest in the faces of the literati, such as Akutagawa Ryūnosuke and Kikuchi Kan, whom he had befriended when he worked for the journal *Shinshōsetsu* (*New Novels*) upon graduation from university. In articles and patent applications, Morioka described his system of portrait photography from multiple angles that could act as templates for the precise building of 3D busts and eventually full-body sculptures. Long after Morioka's "stereophoto-sculptures" (*rittaishashin-zō*) would be rebranded as 3D scanning and additive manufacturing, his method would be described thus:

> In some of the earliest work in Japan, Morioka developed a hybrid process between photosculpture and topography. This method uses structured light (black and white bands of light) to photographically create contour lines of an object. These lines could then be developed into sheets and then cut and stacked or projected onto stock material for carving.[106]

Though today we would recognize the process as "scanning" and "printing," many of the contemporary articles from when the technology was debuted did not know what to make of the images of the process that depicted multiple thin white lines of light being shone longitudinally down the face of a model, so they compared the squiggly lines along the stark silhouettes to snakes. The amalgamation of the cutout "snakes" printed on hard stock would then be arranged to form the basis for the mold of the statue.[107]

Morioka soon put his technique into practice, founding his Stereographic Sculptures Corporation, which over several decades produced statues and sculptures of prominent military leaders, businessmen, scientists, celebrities, and politicians, such as the Marquis Tōgō Heihachirō, Prime Ministers Kishi Nobusuke and Fukuda Takeo, architect Itō Chūta, statesman and postmaster Maejima Hisoka, mechanical engineer Kamo Masao, epidemiologist Ōshima Fukuzō, international film star Douglas Fairbanks, author Helen Keller, and world-famous aviator Charles Lindbergh (as well as Presidents Johnson, Ford, Carter, and Reagan).[108]

Morioka's stereographic sculptures of bronze share a lot with the much larger premodern Kamakura Buddha, but the two modes of memorialization are not identical. Where the Daibutsu, with its much-larger-than-life stature and stylized beauty, does not attempt mimetic fidelity to a once-living human, it still remains representative of a figure (in this case, a deity), as well as signifying first and foremost that it is a substitute for the actual real thing.[109] If the old medium allowed for a larger-than-life stand-in for and mystification of the human form, the new one is a move toward measurable reality. Though Morioka's technique could certainly be used to scale up or down the model's size, commentary on his method consistently emphasizes fidelity and realism. Evoking problematic notions about the potential of reverse mimesis, the U.S. patent for which Morioka filed is fittingly titled "Photographic Method of Reproducing Original Objects."[110] Rather than discussion of how the technique itself cultivates and conjures a particular kind of reproduction, the patent simply claims to reproduce the "original."

And more than that, it is the Fordist model of reproduction—speed, efficiency, and the trading of artistic craftsmanship for scientific technical precision (it has been called "mechanical sculpture" in other contexts)—that is emphasized in the discourse around Morioka's

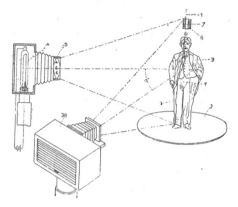

Figure 9. Photos of Morioka Isao's
process using Morioka as the model,
displaying his patented technique of
photographing slices of hundreds of
silhouettes using a powerful strobe
with a slit of light. The images would
be printed onto zinc plates, cut to
form a last or mold on which bronze sculptures would be cast. *Top left*:
Morioka is the model in the photo illustrating the process (akin to scanning
today). He sits with thin beams of light illuminating the contours of his
body and is photographed from hundreds of angles. *Top right*: Next, the
accumulated photographs of the squiggles ("snakes") are printed at scale
and meticulously cut by hand. *Bottom left*: Then the cut images are stitched
together to form the mold for the sculpture. *Bottom right*: The copyright
application depicts the camera setup. Photos taken from Morioka Isao, "Rittai
shashin-zō," *Supekutoru shashin: Shashin-yō kenchiku, Kōjō shashin-jutsu
(saishin shashin kagaku taikei),* vol. 9, ed. Nakamura Michitarō, 1–19 (Tokyo:
Seibundō shinkōsha, 1936), and Morioka's U.S. patent application.

process. Here it is unclear whether we have an instantiation of Kant's mercenary artist who produces for the market or the artist who has been freed by technology of one kind of labor even as the technology requires another. Morioka's technique does not seem like a passive or natural mechanism for recording objective reality as a sculpted object, but the discourse consistently refers to the representation itself as being realistic. This active mechanism that requires labor (shifted from trained artist to the less skilled handicraft of factory workers) shares much in common with additive manufacturing today. The reduction of labor of the singular artist and its multiplication outward (outsourcing) to a number of people is captured in the articles about the method in the fascination with the speed of production—from the model sitting for the photos, which takes "only five seconds" to modeling a "bronze sculpture within a week."[111] As an early version of what would come to be labeled "rapid prototyping" and "3D printing," writers compared this short sitting time and rapid build (from photos to sculpture in a matter of days) with the weeks and months a lone artist might take to produce a similar sculpture. Although the process is spoken of as though it is entirely machinic in the historical articles, detailed descriptions of the process reveal the role of the human hand in the process of cutting the forms from the photographic outlines, in using sewing machine technology to stitch the forms together, and in molding the casts for the bronze.[112]

The process involved in getting several hundred beams of light to be cast onto the surface of an object/subject of the photograph in less than a minute was seen to be at once quite fast—giving an "eerie" (*bukimi*) feel (like a "death mask") to many of the statues—as well as too slow: for example, in some cases capturing a distorted facial look produced during the few seconds required to take the series of photos when enough time had passed for a model's expression to change; the result could be a statue memorializing a face half with a smile and half with a stern expression. Noting the resemblance to detective fiction rather than real life, one writer conjectures uses for the stereographic sculpture technology that extend beyond the 3D printing of statues: psychological diagnosis (presuming an association between facial structure and behavior) and the apprehension of criminals (through something like facial recognition).[113]

The discourse around the technology suggests that the skill of the artist has been outsourced to the immediacy of the machine. So that now a team of unskilled, presumably low-cost workers can do in a short time what an expensive, skilled artist would have taken more time to do. And the other imagined uses for catching psychopathology in physical form and criminal recognition, too, are about the labor-saving efficiencies of the sculpture. It is no coincidence that today a 1935 sculpture by Morioka of Paul Harris, the founder of the Rotary International organization promoting goodwill among international professionals, stands at the world headquarters in Evanston, Illinois. Morioka was an international businessman, deeply invested in the economies of scale to be reaped from technologies of mechanical reproduction and his connection with the Rotary Club was simply a product of these efforts. Here, the economy of stereomimetic production clearly renders a medium into our physical spaces, transforming how we might understand not only whose visage it captures but also the environment in which the sculpture stands, as well as the modes of production and labor required to produce it. Notable here are the close ties with the consumer markets Morioka cultivated displaying his wares in Daimaru and setting up a "Solid Photograph Statue" studio in Shiseido on the Ginza. In the historical wonderment around the technology, we can read an economimetic spectacle of the medium as commodity fetish akin to Guy Debord's society of spectacle that pushes consumerism.

Debord marked the beginning of the society of spectacle as the 1920s, when Morioka was first patenting his inventions, likely because of another parallel invention—television.[114] Around the same time Morioka was scanning the surfaces of human bodies using stereography, Takayanagi Kenjirō was first scanning the world with an electron gun using a Nipkow disc that effectively sliced the light bouncing off objects in the world into segments that could then be converted to electric signals for transmission. We need not be crassly historicist to see that the technical parallels and near-historical coincidence of these two modes of capturing and reproducing repeat a well-known and more or less long-standing structure of the commodification of everyday life that Debord was attempting to describe as a new or modern phenomenon that seemed to sever us from the past to create an infinite present.

Debord's description of the society of spectacle may mistake present nostalgia for presentism. What panoramic stereograph, photosculptures, and television display is a present that is nostalgic for an always already vanishing past, an objective reality that can never be completely given presence. These technologies did not so much sever us from the past as show us how the past was always irrecoverable, gone even as it was happening, slipping by through the snap of the shutter. It is not that the advent of these technologies marks the moment in history beyond which everything is simulacra (as Jean Baudrillard claims) but rather that their surveilling and spectacular reproduction of the world is always behind the times, necessarily belated (even when "live").[115] They simply mark a clear moment in the history of human mediation of the world in which we can see manifest the structure of our cultural mediations laid bare. The machinic reproduction makes the totalization (depth and breadth) of the society of spectacle seem present or new, but of course language had already been working this kind of mimetic magic—with its labeling of the world (representation) and thus conjuring into existence (mimicry) that which had never been conceived as such prior to its naming through its ontological trick.

What these Japanese media histories display is an intermediate or blended (what Debord would later call "integrated") mode between Debord's two poles of the society of spectacle—the concentrated (fascistic or imperial) and the diffuse (capitalistic) in which consumers are interpellated by a surveilling authority of the system and the advertising regime. We could narrate this media regime transition from panorama stereograph to printed bronze monumental statues as a slow descent from consumer spectacle to fascistic, as the spell of the production efficiencies of Morioka's new means of statue production turned to serve the memorial interests of the state.[116] But I think we do well to think of both concentrated and diffuse modes as present even when one is more salient than the other. The early *gaitō terebi* (public televisions) of Japan's 1950s were set up not as great interpellators of the public to serve the national interest by, for instance, pumping up a cult of personality around the emperor or a prime minister (as they were planned for Nazi Germany and Stalinist Russia) but rather as opportunities to sell the public on the use value of the new appliances for the home primarily through the broadcasting of sports. But the nascent television industry was not solely driven by a consumerist purchase for the private consumption of the spectacle of sports; the wedding of the emperor in April 1959 also gave a notable boost in home sales of the units.[117] And this integrated form of spectacle continues today.

None of Morioka's bronze sculptures of the 1930s came close to realizing the use to which the body artist Rokudenashiko (a.k.a. Igarashi Megumi) would put to a derivative technology eight decades later. Much to the chagrin of Japanese authorities, in 2014 Rokudenashiko 3D scanned and printed images of her "pussy" (the colloquial *manko* is the term she insists on over more clinical terms like *chitsu*, "vagina"). She was arrested for offering 3D modeling files as gifts to sponsors of her crowdsourcing efforts to 3D print a blown-up version to make into a pussy-shaped kayak. With the files, she offered ideas for fun uses to which sponsors could put her pussy molds, such as coffee cup lids and smartphone covers. In a sense, her work remediates the awkward embodiment of the apparatus during the viewing of stereoscopic images into the realm of 3D printing.

At a broad and abstract level, we might begin a conclusion to this chapter by suggesting that stereoscopy is to representation what 3D printing is to mimicry. In other words, the two sides of the mimetic coin are captured by the two forms of stereographic media. And yet it should have been clear already from the discussion of Enami's photos and the panorama stereoscope that even then the position of the media in the world mattered as much as what content they bore. For 3D printing simply makes manifest what we already knew—that representation and mimicry are indeed two sides of the same coin. In this way, stereomimesis clarifies the seeming contradiction that the media contain: on the one hand, media may contain or capture a truth of objective reality, and on the other hand, media clearly construct such representations as they exist as objects in the world. The new real names this media spectacle produced around the state of this seeming contradiction in which neither natural, passive representation nor active, artistic construct wholly eclipses the other. The point of recognizing and discussing the two modes is to try to move beyond what Hal Foster, in his *The Return of the Real,* calls the "reductive either/or" constraints on reading as either representation or autoreferential.[118] Such acknowledgment of the modalities of mimesis could render a more complete picture of media that is aware of the pitfalls in thinking both that we have finally captured a historical, objective real with media and that what is captured is a construct of the artist or beholder.

Rokudenashiko's work differs from that of Morioka Isao in content, form, and mediation (here, files circulated for free on the internet). Ultimately, the Japanese courts deemed the potential to seemingly conjure a pussy out of thin air to be obscene. Though the artist herself connects this offense-taking to a general cultural unease about female genitalia, which contributes to body image problems the world over (a content issue), it seems clear that more is at work for those who take offense.[119] In Japan, no comparable legal actions are taken against the commodification of genitalia when their reproductions are sold as "adult toys" (*otona no omocha*) in the forms of dildos and functional artificial vaginas (such as the "onanism cup" [*onakappu*] series marketed by the TENGA company for the express purpose of masturbation). So it seems the mode of distribution as 3D scan files provided for free with the potential ease of proliferation and reproduction was at least a branch of the root of the perceived offense. Where Morioka's bronzes were public, monumental, expensive, and primarily of men, Rokudenashiko's radical edge lies in the female private (parts) made public, pervasive (widely available), and not monumental or maternal, so much as what she terms as "cute and cuddly." To some degree Rokudenashiko's work threatens the economy and marketplace not because it competes with sex toys but because it uses technology to provide free or seemingly free copies. It produces pussies outside of both the commerce economy and the sexual economy. This is its threat. Indeed, this problem of spectacle around representation as reproduction is not solely a problem of style or aesthetics. And this is why it is possible to declare, as Crary does, that "the problem of mimesis, then, is not one of aesthetics but one of social power."[120] Ultimately, stereomimesis is a problem of aesthetic and social power.

Rokudenashiko's work is but one of the many cyclical returns of stereoscopy since its dawn in the mid-nineteenth century. To some degree, its continual return attests to its longevity and our interest, but to some extent it also marks our continual disappointment with it. In the recent market failures of RealD 3D movies and televisions, such as Sony's BRAVIA 3D (in addition to the ongoing slow market failure of VR headsets), there is an echo of the earlier successive fading of interest in stereography over the late nineteenth and early twentieth centuries. So in a way stereoscopy continually dies and lives on in some zombie forms.

Whether this is due to what film critic Ogi Masahiro calls (after the advent of 3D TV in the first decade of the twenty-first century) a shutting down of the viewer's imagination or something else, there is likely a bigger frame in which to consider the passing of 3D—its multi-planarity.[121] All of the cyclical marketing hype over 3D technologies makes similar claims about the immediacy of the 3D techno-image, but, in fact, the products continue to be multiplanar and, therefore, share much with the discourse on the so-called superflat aesthetics and the attendant multiplanar apparatus of Japanese animation. Thomas Lamarre's explanations of the multiplanarity of anime understand recent innovations in computer graphics animation, video gaming, and film to be part of a multiplanar series of media. In other words, there is a visual media convergence toward the multiplanar. If, as Lamarre quotes Oshii Mamoru, with the advent of CG films, "all film is becoming animation," then all film is also becoming multi-planar.[122] The fundamental difference between multiplanar animation, video games, and films and multiplanar stereoscopy is not insignificant. Where in the former cases the multiple planes are layered atop one another (for instance, as the thin, indeed transparent, cels of early film animation), in stereoscopy, of course, the planes are presented side by side or respectively to each eye. The multiplanarity of the convergence media that Lamarre discusses at length lies within the form of the media themselves, yet with stereoscopy a body or brain is required to complete the ontological multiplanarity, to stitch the images together.

Statuary is erected to monumentalize and memorialize that which no longer exists or will soon fade. Statuary's promise is that the essence of the thing can last in an iterative form beyond the thing itself. And 3D printing pushes beyond traditional statuary, suggesting we can do away with the thing itself or that the printout can be the thing, not simply its simulacrum. With 3D printing, we might dispose of the thing itself here and rebuild it elsewhere. It marks the obsolescence of the real. This might have been the ultimate threat of Rokudena-shiko's file circulation. If we can conjure pussy from "thin air" (for free, free from financial or sexual economies), is not the power of the pussy reduced? And yet this offense-taking marks the utopian dream of creation that defies the laws of physics—to produce something from nothing. Indeed, as physics and economics agree, no thing is free. Rokudenashiko paid for vaginal rejuvenation surgery, fans donated to her crowdfunded kayak project and in doing so purchased the rights to the files, fans paid for 3D printers and the 3D printer filament through which to print "her" pussies.

All such projects hinge on a hype of better production and distribution (ones without externalities of labor and resource exploitation). But even the Open Meal design project that calls for the digitalization and 3D printing of food toward a "food singularity" will not defeat the laws of physics and economics. Sushi Singularity, Open Meals' concept restaurant, was launched on the idea that the *Star Trek* vision of a replicator providing the food we need and desire out of thin air is ready to hand. While the 1960s-era TV show version materializes food at the atomic level through some fantastical as-yet-unfathomable science, the coming Sushi Singularity—engineered by Yamagata University, Yawaraka 3D, Cykinso, and Hydroid, among others—relies on extruding processed and edible food into various shapes from "digital oden" and daikon to cube-shaped hamburgers and "cyber wagashi." The product of Dentsu (one of Japan's leading advertising agencies), the slickly marketed imagery of the various projects advertised on the Open Meals website tends to focus on the issues of circulation (we can "teleport" sushi into space) and consumption (the singular sushi will contain precisely the nutrients your body needs because it will be "hyper-personalized" after health analysis data has been provided to the restaurant).[123] But clearly all of this fascination with the concepts behind Open Meals is overturned by the fact that resources found the realization of the dream. The tell in the lie that is the Open Meals website is the very fact that to enjoy the teleported sushi one will first have to go to the Sushi Singularity restaurant or eventually own one of the printing machines. Like the marketing of armchair stereoscopic travel in the nineteenth century, such teleportation comes at a cost and operation of the mechanism despite any or all coming automation.

In a sense, the projection of stereoscopy onto the real world that 3D printing produces, whether as statues, pussies, or sushi, seeks to augment reality through mimicry. As futuristic as the Sushi Singularity website wants to seem, there is something deeply nostalgic about its dream, a dream that is not dissimilar to the infantile fantasy of imagining what if our favorite fictional characters or monsters were real. Such dreams of truly augmenting reality explain the runaway success of *Pokemon Go!* After all, what is such augmentation of reality if not yet another dream that the sum could equal more than the whole of its parts? This kind of mathematical impossibility that enables the dream reveals what the dream really is—a willful ignorance to the whole of its parts. When we say that something is more than the whole of its parts, it is because, unbeknownst to us, another part, a provisionally ignorable part, a part that we did not count, contributed to the sum. Our ignorance of the net parts, whether labor, material, or conceptual, produces our ability to believe in utopic ideas.

The projecting onto the world of 3D photography in the form of 3D printing is what we might call the old media stage or, if we oppose that teleological model, a resting stage in the cyclical narrative of media when a recently developed medium has become so ingrained that it has transformed our everyday reality, sometimes in mundane ways like the positioning of a new vending machine or bronze statue in the city and sometimes in fantastic ways like the teleported sushi. We could state the flow of this chapter as a history: early in its circulation (Enami as samurai), the medium is prized for its connection to reality and authenticity (however false and cultivated and nostalgic that created reality might be); in a later phase (automatic panoramic stereoscope), the media needs remarketing and finds new angles in war and sex content, machinic delivery, and media convergence; in later stages (stereoscope as fantastic fetish and surreal wonder), a critique of the originally perceived affordances (as more realistic perspective on the world and deeper connection to the world) of the medium nearly reverses its claims. And finally (with stereographic sculptures), the medium projects itself into our world in some unexpected way, becoming part of the lived and built environment. These shifts have much to do with binarism at the core of parallax vision and, indeed, philosophical thinking about mimesis. But rather than thinking of these shifts and changes over time as in a teleological history, such shifts might be considered as different modes of mediality that are more or less salient at different moments, that rise and fall in undulating and unpredictable cycles.

If there is any of Karatani's parallax radicality to this stereomimetic critique, it lies in the surplus value when toggling or flashing between binaries such as nature and composition or art, machine and individual, objective and subjective, anonymous and personal, disembodied and embodied, abstract and named, or stereo and panorama. But while we recognize both modes of mimesis (representation and mimicry), we might also recall that any sense of such radicality itself is ungrounded utopic thinking that is necessarily and even willfully ignoring what really constitutes its perspective. It emanates not from a revealing or uncovering, nor from having transitioned to a new moment of seeing one image to another moment in seeing a different image, but from dwelling in the gap or incongruity between both views. This means viewing Enami's labor as both anonymous complicity with a capitalist system that is beyond the capability of any single individual to transform and a radical secret that resists by remaining open to eventual discovery and recovery in the future. For the stereoscopic panorama vending machine, it means understanding the automatic views and the physical machine both as a televisually cinematic phantasmagoria and as a totemic, talismanic fetish. These convergences and remediations of media are perhaps best realized in the stereophotographic sculpture. With the technologically produced bronze sculptures, the flash of media as duration of labor saved as well as value squandered (a fading of Benjamin's aura or Barthes's punctum in the mechanical ease of reproduction wherein skilled labor seems traded for the technê of the machine itself) becomes easily apparent on the surface. Or rather, the new medium itself records or documents that loss; therefore, enabling punctum or aura to return in the statue not as a marker of the human but as a marker of loss of labor or labor saved. In a way, the media stand in then not as substitutes for but as markers of lack of presence or lack of body. The media in a backward way insist on the body in the machine by impressing upon us the lack of presence as we dream of disembodied media or immaterial sustenance. They insist on the figure against the ground, not a figure over ground or ground over figure as the unconcealment of ground, but rather figure and ground—the system or economy of antinomy itself that necessitates an apparent surplus that gives more than the sum of its parts.

3

Schizoasthenic Media

Record, Reappropriation, and Copyright

From the ether, a disembodied voice beckons. A mysterious distress signal emanates from a space station that is empty of human life, but where robots continue to function, repair, and rebuild. Kon Satoshi's short anime *Magnetic Rose* (*Kanojo no omoide,* lit. "her memories," 1995) echoes the outer-space eeriness of Stanley Kubrick's *2001: A Space Odyssey,* Andrei Tarkovsky's *Solaris,* and Ridley Scott's *Alien,* among others. Ōtomo Katsuhiro's 1990 manga on which the anime is based displayed many fantastical elements: the shape of the space station resembles a rose; the welcoming killer robots serve high tea and talk about their mistress; a seventeenth-century baroque style decorates the interior of the otherwise futuristic facility. But what differs in the anime version is the nature of the distress signal. The manga's peculiar rescue call emanating from the station—Glenn Miller's "Moonlight Serenade"—is transformed in the anime to a disembodied aria from *Madame Butterfly.*[1]

It is not clear why Kon made this specific substitution in translating the story from one medium to another, but there are clues to be found in both the story line and the limitations and affordances of such remediations. In the plot of both versions, the original owner of the space station was a distraught prima donna whose husband had been tragically murdered. Long after the demise of "the madame" (*okusama*), her robots continue performing their daily tasks, while dream images recalling moments of the prima donna's life haunt the virtual reality rooms of the station and the minds of her would-be rescuers. By meshing the virtual reality dreams of the long-dead opera singer with the dreamy desires of the space-salvage team, the anime blends dreams and reality through both media and mental states. The salvage team can survive only by escaping from the simulacrum on the space station. The music of Giacomo Puccini's opera, especially the aria, enhances this blurring of the lines and raises the question of mediation. After all, multiple media depicted in the short film hold important positions in the plot: beyond the communications systems and holographic rooms, the space station as a whole is a medium for channeling the madame; the ghost and her long-past love that are conjured by the station are also traditional tropes evoking opera.

The aria as a signal then directly connects opera with anime in a way Glenn Miller's song could not have. Miller's jazzy tune about a June evening's rendezvous would have set a tone very different from that of the operatic voice. Michel Chion's notion of phonogeny posits that the absence of a body enabled by sound technologies leads to a presence or overabundance of particular kinds of voices. The ghostly presence of the madame of the space station operates according to the logic of Chion's notion of the acousmatic disembodied voice; because she is no longer there, we find multiple versions of her via virtual simulacra projected in the holographic rooms of the space station.[2] Following Chion's logic, perhaps it is because the space station is really just a medium for recording, storing, and replaying the life of the madame that a pathos similar to that of Puccini's opera permeates the anime. In this sense, the operatic voice is particularly well-suited to the eerie animation. The aria, evoking the themes of suicide and love lost, sets a more appropriate tone for the story to come and is, thus, an improvement. But the shift from jazz to opera may also have had to do with budget and copyright—*Madama Butterfly* had gone out of copyright and could, therefore, be used without permission and at no cost, whereas Glenn Miller's tune would still have been protected under Japanese law.

Copyright seeks to resist the disembodying effects of recording media by reconnecting song to real bodies (traditionally, living creators or their heirs and, more recently, the less corporeal but nevertheless legally embodied entities of multinational corporations). Copyright performs in the sphere of law what at the narrative level Chion calls "de-acousmatization" or what we might think of as a re-embodiment. Copies linger long after the body is gone. Recordings and broadcasting provide acousmatic sound—a disembodied voice and dislocated site available for sampling, remixing, and redeploying to create what Steven Feld calls "schizophonic mimesis." Picking up on R. Murray Schafer's idea of schizophonia that occurs when a body is separated from voice in a sound recording, Feld describes the new way that recording media enable the "use, circulation, and absorption of sound recordings . . . split from their source through the chain of audio production, circulation, and consumption."[3] This schizophonic mimesis, the audible pastiche and sound sampling made possible by recording technology, is also what copyright tries to secure against. Though it inevitably fails to do so completely, copyright seeks to restore original links between the real world and the mediated world through legal and financial means.

Viewers of the animation hear Renata Tebaldi's rendition of the aria as the initial signal, and its somber tone persists throughout Kanno Yōko's soundtrack for this short anime, echoing the mood of Puccini's opera. The fact that Tebaldi's rendition is accredited (and presumably paid for) is itself an example of the legal reconnection of a disembodied voice on-screen and a particular performer. In this way, copyright itself mediates, connecting creators with their creations: composers with the compositions, singers with the songs, bodies with the recorded voices. Yet some bodies are more easily reconnected than others.

This chapter considers another animated film, one in which the aria from *Madama Butterfly* was replaced with yet another song created to echo it. After the Rome Convention of 1928 expanded concepts of cultural property to cover the new media of records and radio, German lawyer Wilhelm Plage used the ensuing legal protections to put the brakes on Japanese use of European music. In response, Japanese media moguls united to resist what they saw as a scourge from the West. In 1940, Miura Tamaki, the world-renowned opera singer who for all intents and purposes *was* Madame Butterfly for over a decade, wrote the score to a short cut-paper silhouette animated film that hearkened back to Puccini but avoided the wrath of Plage, a move that ultimately coincided with the alteration of Japanese copyright law. This chapter—a tale of music and law, a copyright hound and a prima donna, medium and mimesis—suggests the stakes of cultural property and reappropriation, mediation and remediation, representation and mimicry.

The aim of this chapter is to recast the notion of schizophonic mimesis back onto a previous era of globalization. Luce Irigaray's feminist version of Plato's cave shows how her call for mimesis to undo gender stereotypes and male desire might be successfully employed to skirt the law or transform it. The last section of the chapter reflects on the role of the Japanese "screen" or "window" in the various media ecologies of *Madama Butterfly* to show how the space articulated for Japan generally and Madame Butterfly specifically is a mediated space of desire not dissimilar to Plato's cave as read by Irigaray. Butterfly's space is walled and therefore always already confined to the phallogo-centric universe of Western male will. Within this space, Madame can assert forms of will and agency, though they are curtailed and she is ultimately doomed to suicide.[4] As a medium conjuring *Madama Butterfly,* Miura manages to work like Irigaray within and against this doomed cultural scenario to achieve a modicum of success at transcending it.

Roger Caillois's theory of mimesis as a form of mimicry that allows the individual member of a species to sink into their environment is useful in rethinking questions of gestalt that arose in chapter 1's discussion of stereomimesis. If the last chapter focused our attention on how media can help to show perspective in a toggling between figure and ground, Caillois's ideas of mimicry, Joan Riviere's ideas of masquerade, and Irigaray's notions of mimesis are instructive when distinguishing between the environment and the individual becomes impossible, when the camouflage of a butterfly is so good that the difference between the original and the simulacrum are almost imperceptible, and, thus, when the possibilities of the perspective of stereomimesis (standing out from background) have been squashed or flattened. Miura's skill at becoming Madame Butterfly is not Caillois's simple "psychasthenia" (a weakening of the self or soul to blend in with an environment) but rather a schizoasthenic agency, a strengthening and garnering of power through acquiescence to the system, a camouflage that allows both survival and domination of the mediascape. Ultimately, this chapter shows how the figure (of Madame Miura) and ground (of the screen or window) can merge through mimicry and mediation, if not to rise above environment (here, the culture industry) then at least to be transformative of it.

Infinite Regress from the Real: The Butterfly Boom and Schizophonic Mimesis

In 1940, long after cut-paper animation had ceased to be a mainstay of Japanese cinema, professional dentist and amateur animator Arai Wagorō produced an intricate, twelve-minute masterpiece of the genre. Two facts about the single 332-meter-reel film make it a case study of the peculiar relationship between media and law that continues to shape the Japanese cultural industry today.[5] First, Arai's *Madame Butterfly's Fantasy* (*Ochōfujin no gensō*) features the singing and compositions of the preeminent twentieth-century prima donna of Puccini's opera, Miura Tamaki. Second, the film depicts the denouement of the famous opera in black-and-white silhouette with a round window (*marumado*) at its center. It is my contention that these two aesthetic choices (one aural, the other visual) are the result of long cultural and legal histories of media and mimesis, representation and mimicry. Together, they demonstrate what happens when cultural products are copied and remediated in other forms: occasionally a new version copies so well that, despite the new media contexts, it fades into the cultural background of other, older versions; in other cases, occasionally a new version stands out because of its difference. How can a given musical performance or recording harmonize with the historical cultural context and how can it stand out? Are there times when a copied song can do both? When does faithful mimicry seem powerful and even original? What inspired Miura Tamaki, already a global star, to help with the production of the short film? Why did she compose her own abridged Japanese version of the opera rather than simply sing the aria she had sung over two thousand times in at least fifty countries?

The simple answer carried in newspapers at the time is that Miura took pity on the amateur animator Arai, whose film comprising over eighteen thousand meticulously composed frames had incurred fees from the German copyright lawyer Wilhelm Plage, who claimed to be representing the estate of Puccini.[6] The proposed fees were so high that the film could never have been screened were it to include music from what Arai called "the real thing" (*honmono*); so Miura stepped in. But this simple story does not provide the context, with which newspaper readers at the time would have been familiar, that explains why Miura would be predisposed to help out anyone against Plage. The explanation of Miura's motivation cuts to the heart of the Japanese broadcast and recording industry in the late 1920s and 1930s, when the law and industry were beginning to come to terms with the new disembodying aural media of records and broadcast radio. The determining aspects of the new media and copyright contexts of Miura's work include the 1920s to 1930s boom in music inspired

Figure 10. Madame Butterfly and Trouble stand before the round window or screen in Arai Wagorō's masterpiece. Screengrab from *Madame Butterfly's Fantasy* (*Ochōfujin no gensō*), dir. Arai Wagorō (1940; Nihon ātoanimēshon eiga senshū, Kinokuniya, 2004), DVD.

by *Madama Butterfly,* the rise of a global recording industry, and the impact on Japanese copyright law of the Rome Convention of 1928, which updated the Berne Copyright Convention laws to account for new media.

Prior to the phonograph record, the first true medium for the circulation of music was the globalization of Western sheet music notation in the nineteenth century. Published in Osaka and Leipzig in 1891 and 1894 respectively, two scores of Japanese folk music compiled by musicologists Y. Nagai, K. Kobatake, and Rudolph Dittrich would become sources for Puccini's operatic copies.[7] Scholars Hara Kunio and Arthur Groos, among others, document how the opera musically transposes several melodies without attribution directly from *Japanese Popular Music: A Collection of the Popular Music of Japan Rendered in to the Staff Notation* (1891) and *Six Japanese Popular Songs* (1894).[8] The Berne Convention of 1886 covered sheet music in the form of such written notation, so it would have been possible for such recorders of music to bring suit against Puccini. However, there were relatively few cases in Japan that dealt exclusively with scores prior to mechanical methods for recording music, and there was doubt about the ability to copyright folk songs, long considered to be in the public domain.[9] The new medium of the record also provides a direct connection between Puccini and Japanese music. And further, because of the capital investments involved and the perceived lack of special knowledge involved in spotting copies (the idea that anyone could hear and recognize a musical copy, whereas only those who had studied music could understand a copied score), records were more likely grounds for copyright suits.

Puccini's own record collection indicates a direct connection to the nascent Japanese record industry. Reminiscing many years later about her visit to Puccini's house, prima donna Miura Tamaki recalled this connection:

> Puccini pointed to the piano, "Madame Miura, fifteen years ago I composed *Madama Butterfly* at that piano. Back then I heard Japanese music from Ōyama Hisako, the wife of the counsel to the ambassador from Japan in Italy. She gave me records of Japanese music. With those as a foundation, I aesthetically wove in the melodies of 'Takai yama kara,' 'Genroku hanami odori,' 'Kimigayo,' 'Miyasan miyasan,' and 'Echigojishi,' as I composed *Madama Butterfly*."[10]

Miura's account of the diplomat's wife, who not only played records but also performed on the koto for Puccini, is bolstered by evidence from Puccini's extant record collection and his record orders.[11] Puccini's admission that he employed themes without changing them significantly should not be shocking. At the time, such borrowing from what were perceived as vernacular sources would not be considered worthy of a lawsuit or even something to hide.

After recounting these cases and remembering the fact that Puccini copied from multiple sources, it is not the place here to trace Puccini's sources or to label him a plagiarist, copyright infringer, or derivative artist but rather to recognize the fact that, in Japan's first major record copyright suit, even the same person performing the same song was not deemed to violate copyright.[12] In addition, we need to remember that all art takes place within conditions of small changes, sampling, repetition with differences—in other words, through being mimetic not only of reality but also to other arts. As one of the most studied, commodified, global cultural productions of the twentieth century, *Madama Butterfly* exemplifies this dynamic. The fact that music can be smoothly adapted and adopted is characteristic of the schizophonic mimesis prevalent in the age of recorded music, but such smoothness is in the ear of the beholder. If we know nothing about the putative original sonic culture of a series of sounds, such appropriations might seem smooth. If we know enough, such appropriations are never imperceptible or smooth. In other words, our distance from the source of music stands in direct relation to the ability to consider an adaptation or adoption legitimate.

Developed to name the appropriation by major music industry figures like Herbie Hancock and Madonna of ethnographic and musicological recordings of Indigenous peoples to their own monetary and cultural gain, schizophonic mimesis occurs precisely at the intersection between cultural production and copyright law. But Feld's lament about the practice sidesteps what is often taken to be the latent critique in his development of the notion. It is claimed that the negative concept of schizophonic mimesis (pathologized as it is) overlooks what is ubiquitous in cultural appropriation and creativity. Indeed, as problematic as they may be, Herbie Hancock's controversial claim to Feld that his unacknowledged borrowing from anthropologist Colin Turnbull's recordings of *hindewhu* music is a "brother thing" and copyright law's inability to assign jurisdiction over folk music both acknowledge that community and individual ownership of culture differ. Arguments centered on identity suggest property is communal or folk and thus cannot be stolen.

Much of the "schizo" quality of some forms of phonic mimesis has to do with how jarring or smooth the fit is between musical types. The examples Feld provides are quite jarring. But Roger Caillois's notion of a tendency toward evolutionary and legendary "psychasthenic" camouflage as mimetic mimicry would seem to indicate that our ability to distinguish between Italian operatic music and Japanese folk song in *Madama Butterfly* might be equivalent to the degree to which the opera can be called mimetic: for some, it might seem like an operatic mode representing the truth about Japan; for others, it might seem like schizophonic mimesis through its pastiche that mimes several genres of music. When Schafer coined the term *schizophonic* in

1969, he did so to name the unease of encountering sounds split from their origin.[13] But this unease indicates that the person feeling it already held beliefs about the correct assignment of origins. Such beliefs connote their own logics of authority to seek and recover origins. As vibrations moving through a medium outside of the putative sound-makers, however, sounds are always already removed from their origin. Voices splitting from bodies happens even prior to the advent of recording media and is natural because voices travel through the medium of air. In other words, schizophonia suffers from its presumption of a unified subject—here presented as a mythic moment when a voice and body were one. A schizoasthenic approach, however, takes the split (or schizo) as given and shows how one can overtly perform in multiple registers to fit in with a variegated background.

When we think of the orientalism of the Western male creators of *Madama Butterfly*—including Pierre Loti, John Long, David Belasco, and Puccini—we must recognize that these are but individual names in a longer chain of signification through which the repetition of mimetic representation and mimicry plays the high stakes game of identity, identification, difference, and differentiation. If none of their orientalist representations are proper or appropriate to the infinite reality of the real Japan, we should not be surprised—no mirrors (as finite distillations) can ever perfectly reflect that which they purport to represent. But that such imperfect reflections would affect Japan itself is a function of power inequalities. Further, that both records and legal conceptions of copyright would also have iterations in Japan is only natural. The foreign and new in Japan would be mediated through the known and close at hand, just as the Japanese music had been filtered through the operatic form by Puccini.[14] This is the situation in which Miura was enabled to create through reappropriation.

By 1940, when Miura recorded her own composition for the short animated film, she had already made at least nine recordings of music from the opera between 1917 and 1937 for the Columbia, Victor, and Nipponophone record labels in Japan.[15] These best-selling records (sales were in the hundreds of thousands) and more than a dozen performances of songs from the opera on the national radio network JOAK between 1932 and 1939 made Miura Tamaki a household name in Japan by the 1930s. Along with covers by other Japanese divas, they also made Puccini's *Madama Butterfly* familiar to the Japanese public.

As a result, *Madama Butterfly* became something of a musical sub-culture in and of itself in Japan, birthing a spate of spin-off records. Between 1933 and 1939, at least ten different popular songs with lyrics or motifs derived from the opera were recorded in Japan. With titles like "Mourning Butterfly" ("Nageki no chō"), "Ms. Butterfly of Nagasaki" ("Nagasaki no Ochōsan"), and "Cio Cio's Love" ("Koi no Chōchō"), song lyrics evoked the opera, transposing its situations into modern contemporary life with jazzy and even boogie-woogie popular melodies rather than those of the more foreign-sounding opera and situations deemed too last century. "Ms. Butterfly of Nagasaki" (1939), sung by Watanabe Hamako, even picked up on the melody of Puccini's "Un Bel di, Vedremo" transposing a riff from the aria into the middle of the otherwise popular-style song.[16] It is important to note in this context that Puccini's aria itself lifts a piece of the traditional Japanese folk song "Jizuki-Uta," most likely from Dittrich's score.[17] On the one hand, we can distinguish the riffs; on the other hand, the context is so new and different it seems not to matter legally. Identifying origins in this dizzying array of sampling is almost beside the point of such schizoasthenic mimesis. The more important and more historically accurate point is that the mediation, the circulation of records themselves, fundamentally transformed the music on them so much so as to be thought outside the realm of legal adjudication.

In May 1929, after a long tour of European and American stages playing Madame Butterfly in Puccini's opera, Miura returned to Japan to much fanfare. Though she had recorded tunes from Puccini's opera in Italian with Japanese record labels on previous returns home from her world tours, this time Miura recorded in Japanese.[18] Although print translations of the opera had been circulating for at least a decade, it was the combination of translation and recorded music that led to the viral spread of derivative recordings in the late 1920s through the mid-1930s. The lyrics for the Victor release had been translated into Japanese by Senō Kōyō.[19] This was an attempt to repeat the commercial success that Miura enjoyed in July 1922 when, in a banner month for the record industry, her Italian-language recordings of Puccini's opera with Nipponophone sold over eighty thousand records.[20] And yet the translation and domestication of *Madama Butterfly* was a new beginning. It was after the success of this opera in translation record that the sales of *Madama Butterfly*–derivative works flourished.

Senō's Japanese translation of the aria is remarkably accurate in its rough match of the meter of the original, such that Miura's performative talent for subtly stretching a few syllables here and there to fit the tune is hardly perceptible. The inevitable iterative differences are more noticeable between the translation and the translated. For instance, Madame Butterfly's American paramour Pinkerton climbs the hill not like "a little speck" (*un picciol punto*) because he is distant, as in the original Italian, but like "a doll" (*ningyō*) in Senō's translation. As a result, the Western male is more than trivialized, almost castrated here. And Butterfly's teasing by staying hidden so as "to not die" a little (Un po' per non morire) becomes teasing "so as not to draw attention" (ki no nukenu yō ni). So the association of Japanese culture with the exoticized death of prideful suicide foreshadowed in the Italian disappears in Senō's translation. The "little dear wife, blossom of orange" (Piccina mogliettina Olezzo di verbena) becomes simply the more generic "my pretty wife, beautiful flower" (Kawaii watashi no tsuma yo utsukushii hana yo).[21] Here, the specific floral reference in the original Italian is flattened in the Japanese version, perhaps to downplay the specific aesthetic connotations of white verbena in Japanese poetics, which would point toward death.

Differing from Senō's work, Miura's own translations, which contributed to something of a rebirth for her celebrity in the mid-1930s, add a tinge of nationalism. Her translation retains the "my pretty wife, beautiful flower" but adds to it a flavor of the tradition of ancient works using such poetic archaisms as *unaji*, which appears in both the *Nihon shoki* (*Chronicles of Japan*) and the *Manyōshū* (*Poetry Collection of Ten Thousand Leaves*) to mean "sea way," in referring to Pinkerton's return from overseas.[22] In her 1935 Japanese translation of "To Die with Honor" ("Con Onor Muore"), Miura replaces the specificity of the lily and rose flower references ("Fior di giglio e di rosa") in favor of the more generic "Oh my Boy, more beautiful than flowers" (hana yori mo kirei na utsukushii bōya yo).[23] That the local Japanese translations of the original soften some of the exoticism and fetishization of the "foreign" Japaneseness should not be surprising. These Japanese versions shift the emphasis from an infatuation with the exotic other to the tragedy of an impossible love, bringing the story more into tune with the trope of tension between social duties (*giri*) and individual passions (*ninjō*) popular on stage since at least the days of dramaturgist Chikamatsu Monzaemon (1653–1725).

All of this copying of *Madama Butterfly* offered ripe ground for a copyright lawyer to go fishing for lawsuits, and Plage brought the music industry to a near standstill with what was dubbed in the papers at the time the "Plage Whirlwind" (Purage senpū). His pursuit of copyright might be seen as legally correct and just were it not for these facts about the musical origins of *Madama Butterfly* and the unequal role of Japan in the global order. In terms of geopolitical considerations, the case of *Madama Butterfly* on Japanese records exemplifies an openness to globalization and international relations as well as a reaction against unequal terms. When confronted with an obstacle, culture production can be ramped up by the enforcement of copyright law rather than simply restricted. For a time when foreign songs were not allowed on records or radio, derivative works were produced that echoed their sounds, content, and aura.

Two Mediums: The Prima Donna and the Copyright Hound

New media produce a demand for material content. To no small degree, much of the "new" content begins as a remediation of material available on older media, so it is no surprise that when the Japanese record industry and radio broadcasting corporations were hungry for material in the 1920s and 1930s, they turned to print media and musical scores. In Japan, print infringements of copyright were rarely adjudicated in the courts or even by capitalist middlemen, not because the law had no such protections (it did) but because particular factors impeded enforcement of the law. These factors included the linguistic inabilities of would-be enforcers, the limited purview of potential litigants, and the crafty hidden work of publishers and translators. However, with the new media of records, broadcasting, and film, culture did not have to be translated to be transmitted and understood as a copy, and corporate producers could hear and see infringements and so sent copyright lawyers around the world in search of new revenue (particularly after the Rome Convention, which solidified music rights in new media). The case of *Madama Butterfly* in Japan flitted around the problems of who could stand for whom and who could possess what culture, revealing the crises of new media to be a problem of the original medium—of people. This section examines both Plage and Miura as media that transmitted or conjured two realms for a Japanese audience—those of the law and those of opera.

Medium One: The Plage Storm

Almost immediately following the 1931 Japanese ratification of the Rome Convention of 1928, Plage established the Plage Organization (Purage kikan) to represent the Bureau Internationale de l'Edition Musique Méchanique and the Cartel des Sociétés d'Auteurs de Perception non-Théâtrale, the rights holders and representative to several thousand Europe-based artists, including Puccini, Franz Lehár, and Gustav Mahler.[24] He then began to lodge requests for usage fees from broadcasting stations, orchestra performances, theater owners, record companies, and other music businesses. Plage made hundreds of requests for fees and engaged in several lawsuits, putting a damper on the vibrant Japanese culture industry for nearly a decade.[25] Finally, in 1940, various government ministers, music industry leaders, and creators (including Miura Tamaki) developed legal and extralegal means to remedy the situation, by adhering to international copyright law and expelling the foreign invader.

The story of Plage and *Madama Butterfly* is significant for understanding the metamorphosis of Japanese copyright law in the wake of new media of recorded and broadcast music. The story begins not with records or radio but with film. As early as April 1932, the shooting on location in Kyoto of the Paramount film *Madame Butterfly*, starring Sylvia Sidney and Cary Grant, had been hyped by the Japanese press.[26] On the debut screening of the film at the Shōchiku Theater in Asakusa in 1933, the *Yomiuri* saw through the film's claims to authenticity calling it, either an "American-esque Japanese film or a Japanese-esque American film" (Amerika-teki Nihon eiga, mata Nihon-teki Amerika eiga).[27] The *Asahi* review of the film similarly criticized the exoticist and orientalist elements of the film—"Viewed by Japanese eyes, there are many foolish elements in the film"—and asserted that it must have "used as advisors people who clearly knew nothing about Japan" (kanari Nihon o shiranu jinbutsu o jōgensha to shite tsukatta).[28] The review was surprisingly favorable toward Sylvia Sidney in yellowface, and most interest in the film seemed to be focused on the strange (*bukimi*) elements of the film and recognizing how those facets contrasted with the seriousness of its content.

The Shōchiku entertainment company, which screened the film in its famed theater, capitalized on the interest the celluloid version garnered. As a related attraction, announced in a five-column spread in the *Asahi Shinbun,* the all-female Shōchiku Musical Theatre Company (Shōchiku Rakugeki-bu) performed a live broadcast of *Fantasy of Madame Butterfly: A Radio Revue (Rajio rebyū: Ochōfujin no genso)* from the Asakusa Shōchiku theater.[29] The Paramount film was based on David Belasco's play adaptation of the story by John Luther Long and lacked the singing of Puccini's opera, but much of the underscore evoked musical themes from the opera.[30] The Shōchiku broadcast would place the music back on center stage. Described as a musical revue of *Madama Butterfly (Rebyūka sareta kageki "Ochōfujin"),* the event was billed as an abridged version of the longer work by Puccini, compressing the opera into two acts. Performances continued a month later, when the show was advertised in the *Yomiuri* as an "operetta" in "four scenes" by the "Shōchiku Women's Musical Performance" (Shōchiku shōjo kageki kōen).[31] Though a shortened version of the opera, the revue also extended its possibilities not only with the gender-bending necessitated to tell the story with an all-female company but also by stretching the material to include spoken dialogue and scenes not present in the original.[32] *Madama Butterfly's* strongest reverse mimetic impact in Japan is to be found not in the audience or mass media reception of this revue but in the legal response it provoked.

That legal impact is evident in the suits brought against Shōchiku for this stage production and radio broadcast. In October 1933, the Ricordi company of Milan brought a suit against Shōchiku's director, Kido Shirō, for infringement of the Rome update of the Berne Convention because of the performance at the Shōchiku theater in Asakusa in March.[33] In spite of this suit, in May 1934 Shōchiku staged around thirty performances of *The Fantasy of Madame Butterfly* at the Osaka kabuki-za without obtaining the rights, sparking a more lasting case. It began on June 12, when Kido Yoshihiko (no relation to Shirō), a lawyer in Plage's office acting as representative for the Ricordi company, brought a suit against Shōchiku for copyright infringement, freely changing the title, using the opera without permission, and presenting a simulacrum (*gisaku,* counterfeit version) of the original. On October 3, at the Tokyo Public Prosecutor's Office, Judge Yuta Tamon deemed the charges appropriate and handed down a fine of fifty yen.[34]

But the Plage Whirlwind raged on. The legal cases around the performance and radio broadcast of *The Fantasy of Madame Butterfly* provided impetus for pushing back and fundamentally transforming Japanese copyright law. Likely given confidence by the precedent that another all-female troupe had performed a similarly curtailed one-hour version of the opera only a couple of years before, Kido Shirō of Shōchiku resisted the ruling. He objected to the fine and made a motion for a formal trial, sarcastically offering Ricordi, in lieu of a performance fee, a meal at an expensive restaurant, a colored print (*nishi-kie*), or a fancy Kyoto doll.[35] The ensuing trial was finally dismissed two and a half years later. The Tokyo *Asahi* labeled the dismissal "a windproofed forest disposing of the Plage Whirlwind" (Purāge senpū ni kikyaku no bōfūrin).[36] Because of the force of the suit's rejection, the case provided the grounds for the conceptualization and adoption of a 1939 revision to the copyright laws in Japan that continue to hold today. It is, therefore, necessary to understand the gist of the 1936 decision to dismiss Plage's efforts to understand that revision and, indeed, the continued presence of the Japanese intermediating body for copyright, the Japanese Society for Rights of Authors, Composers, and Publishers (JASRAC).

The decision in the Shōchiku *Butterfly* case hinged on the question of who could legally stand for whom in questions of copyright. This question of legal representation or, as it was called in the parlance of the day, "copyright intermediation" stemmed from article 28 of Japanese copyright law, which stated the circumstances in which foreign copyright law applied. The court ruled that, since the Rome Convention's reworking of the Berne Convention did not adequately account for the question of the ability to transfer copyright to "countervailing powers" (*taikōryoku*), Japanese law still applied. According to article 15 of the Japanese law, a third party could only sue on behalf of the rights of others if the transfer of copyright had been registered (*toroku*, lit. "recorded"). In other words, those who do not register copyright transfer cannot be referred to as victims under article 44 of the Copyright Act, so such complaints would not be deemed legitimate under Japanese law. In this case, Plage's office could not represent Puccini because the transfer of copyright had not been registered.[37]

Having lost the penal case, Plage filed a complaint in March 1937 for damages by the Shōchiku company in a civil case, which he won on June 14, 1940, but by that point the culture industry and the government had already united to resist the threats from the German copyright hound and other would-be representatives of foreign copyright by further changing the law.[38] This resistance first manifested in the formation of a league of luminaries of cultural production, industry bigwigs, and government officials. This association orchestrated the 1939 revision of Japanese copyright law specifically on the basis of the question of transfer of copyright authority or the ability of one person to stand legally for another—for one person to legally act as a medium for another.

This legal transformation is rooted in the tensions around Plage between the first *Butterfly* case in 1933 and the new law of 1939. In 1933, when Plage had managed to all but prevent NHK from playing foreign music, the broadcaster tried to work around him by using some Japanese associations such as the Greater Japan Composers Association (Dai Nippon sakkyokka kyōkai) and the Japanese Song Writers Association (Nihon sakka-sha kyōkai), but to no avail. Plage himself was involved in trying to set up an alternative intermediary copyright association, in the hopes that by convincing Japanese artists to sign up to earn fees for selling their international rights for their work, he might also increase his foothold in the Japanese culture industry and, thereby, his ability to collect fees for his European clients.

In December 1937, having nearly shut down his own source of revenue by making it prohibitively expensive for NHK to play foreign music, Plage's office established the Greater Japan Musician and Publishers Association (Dai Nippon Ongaku Sakka Shuppansha Kyōkai) to act as an intermediary between industry and artists and recoup losses.[39] Perhaps a reflection of the atmosphere of rising nationalism in 1930s Japan, famed music critic Masuzawa Takemi wrote anti-Plage essays arguing that it would be better to have a Japanese organization than one run by a foreigner. Also opposing Plage's attempt to set up an intermediary organization, Kunishio Kōichirō, a Home Ministry and police bureaucrat, established the Japan Music Copyright Association (Nippon ongaku chosakuken kyōkai) in 1935.[40] Kunishio's Japanese association brought together various parties with interests in copyright, including famous writers (Shimazaki Tōson, Kikuchi Kan, Yamamoto Yūzō, and Tokuda Shūsei), painters (Yokoyama Taikan), ceramicists (Ono Kenichirō), music conductors, composers, and directors (Konoe Hidemaro, Norisugi Yoshihisa, and Yamada Kōsaku), as well as print publishers (Masuda Gi'ichi, Meguro Jinshichi), culture industry businessmen (Kobayashi Ichizō, the head of Tōhō and its Takarazuka company; Ono Kenichiro, the head of NHK; and Kido

Shirō, the aforementioned head of Shōchiku), and government bureaucrats (Kuriyama Shigeru, Foreign Office; Karasawa Toshiji, Peace Preservation Bureau; Omori Kota, minister of justice; and Gotō Fumio, home minister).[41] With the establishment of this organization including such powerful government leaders, the culture industry was finally in a position to make headway, not simply lobbying for change but contributing to the process of making new law.

Such actions were consistently tinged with a kind of racialist and nationalist bias against Plage. Proletarian writer and strike activist Kishi Yamaji, in the second of a series of three articles in *Yomiuri Shinbun,* advocated for a withdrawal from the Berne Convention, arguing: "Obtaining the benefits of the cultural advancement of the entire people of a single nation transcends the individual rights that are the subject of copyright. Under this rallying cry, Japanese writers must resist the second 'Plage Whirlwind' emanating from Nazi Berlin."[42] Here, anticapitalist and antifascist tendencies aligned to advocate for national culture. In such moves, radical left and right were in alignment. In order to defend the Japanese culture industry, as well as maintain Japan's adherence to the Berne Convention, head of the Metropolitan Police office Kunishio Kōichirō, who had also been integral in the 1934 copyright revisions, established the Music Police Squad (Keishichō ongakutai) in August of 1935. Continuing to explore ways to resist Plage, Kunishio conceived of another legal method around July of 1937—that the Japanese should develop their own version of the German Law Regarding the Intermediation of Musical Performance Copyrights (Reichsgesetz über die Vermittlung von Musikaufführungsrechten, 1933).[43] Kunishio was deeply interested in the adjudication of copyright law in terms of the still-new medium of records. In a detailed article titled "The Playing of Phonograph Records and Copyright," he argued that records complicated the role of musical copyright into at least two sets of issues—those to do with the records, the copyright of creators and performers, as well as those dealing with makers/recorders (*seisakusha/shachōsha*) and sellers; and those to do with the problem of copyright consent (*kyodaku*) pitted people holding discretionary or voluntary consent (*nin'i kyodaku*) against those holding legally designated or required consent (*hōtei kyodaku*).[44] Ten years after the Rome Convention was supposed to have settled questions of copyright and the new media, this policer of the law was still at pains to elaborate its full ramifications.

At the heart of the question was not what qualified as intellectual property but rather who could lay claim to it—fundamentally, a question of mediation.[45]

On April 5, 1939, due to the dealings of Kunishio and other power-players in the Japan Music Copyright Association, the Law Concerning Intermediary Work Relating to Copyright (Chosakken ni kansuru chūkai gyōmu ni kansuru hōritsu) was enacted. The law gave rise to the Great Japanese Literary Copyright Protection League (Dai Nihon bungei chosakukenhogo dōmei) in 1940, which would later become today's JASRAC. The so-called intermediary industry law (chūkaigyō hō) of 1939 established Kunishio's association as the legal copyright mediator for both domestic and foreign interests by formally licensing it "as an administrator of musical copyrights and a collector of royalties on behalf of the composers and authors."[46] And like the German ordinance on which it was based, it also included the function of "expelling undesired lobbyists and agents from abroad."[47] Masuzawa Takemi, an outspoken music critic who had been vehement in his public opposition to Plage, was made chief director of the new association.[48] These events combined to make it difficult for Plage to continue to participate in the Japanese media industry.

If the result of the law was not clear enough to the public, Plage himself referred to it in opinion pieces as "Lex Kunishio" or "Lex Anti-Plage."[49] On March 29, 1940, Plage was hauled into the police metropolitan office for illegally practicing copyright law. Interrogated for more than five hours, he claimed his Mukden office that opened on March 8 was unrelated to copyright issues.[50] After these police interrogations, after the license for Plage's society was refused, and after some very public pleading in the press, Plage left the country.[51] Upon his exit, his colleague Kido Yoshihiko stated that "even if Plage is prohibited to remain on the job in Japan, Japanese translators and performers will have to ask the owners of copyright for permission directly. This will require a long and arduous procedure, whereas Dr. Plage's presence as an *intermediary* could have simplified it to only a matter of one telephone call."[52] In the Japanese press, Plage was almost always depicted in a negative light in newspapers and magazines. So his role in the Japanese legal world and culture industry raises several questions. Was he a powerful European bringing the law of Europe to the fringes of its reach? Or was he a middleman, who, as a foreigner in Japan, was only able to eke out a living until his nationality and insensitivity to the local business culture left his bold moves open to reprisal in the Japanese media system? These two possibilities are not as antipodal as it may seem at first glance.

This juridical history of Plage's work with copyright in Japan gives a sense of how the new laws affected Japanese culture. The account of Plage's interactions with *Butterfly* reveals how integral to the transformations of the copyright/media nexus they were. In many ways, the precipitating issue that allowed figures like Kunishio Kōichirō and Masuzawa Takemi to advocate for changing the law in 1939 was the series of cases around *Madama Butterfly*. One reason for its significance is that *Butterfly* was one cluster of a handful of cases that Plage (who largely was able to achieve his goals with only the threat of lawsuit) actually took to court. Because of that and because of the stature of the players involved, the press covered the *Butterfly* copyright story extensively, giving it an outsized impact on views of Plage and the need for domestic control of international copyright.

Medium Two: Plage's Last Storm — All about Miura

Philosopher Luce Irigaray might have been talking about Pinkerton and his witless friend Sharpless, Loti and Long, or Puccini and Plage when she wrote that the "process of mimesis" in Plato's story of the cave takes at minimum two men, one to project the image and another to respond to it. This male spectacle produced for men on the walls of a womblike cave suggests for Irigaray that the distinctions between the inner and outer cave vanish in the production of such images.[53] And her version of the cave narrative, then, invites the question of what happens when Irigaray or Miura Tamaki insert themselves into such images, assuming predefined roles, and beginning to play with and alter these images. Can they be successful at shifting discourse? Are the poses or roleplays of the male philosopher or the demure Japanese woman doomed from the start to remain in the economy of the cave? Miura's successful mimicry, playing the role of Madame Butterfly, gave her power to lead an outsized life and indeed become part of the pushback against Plage.

Variously a singer, philanthropist, wife, divorcée, widow, proletarian, bourgeoisie, and ultranationalist sympathizer, Miura lived a colorful and adventurous life of the globetrotting prima donna that would become the stuff of novels and films. For more than a decade, her ability to become the fictional character of Madame Butterfly made her the most globally recognizable person of Japanese descent.[54] Born in Kyōbashi Tokyo in 1884, Miura (née Shibata) Tamaki enrolled to study piano, violin, and singing at the Tokyo Music Institute (now the Music Department of Tokyo University of the Arts) in 1900. As a student, she cut an outlandish figure, commuting to school on her bicycle; at that time when cycling was thought of as a men's sport, she became known as the "bicycle beauty" (*jitensha no bijin*) as she donned purple or red *hakama* to cycle from Ueno to Sakuradamon.[55] Singing in her first opera (a performance of *Orpheus*) in 1903 at the Imperial Theatre in Tokyo, Miura would be typecast in the role of Butterfly, playing Cio-Cio in London, Boston, New York, Chicago, San Francisco, Monte Carlo, Barcelona, Florence, Rome, Milan, Naples, Buenos Aires, and many other places in over forty countries and two thousand performances over the ensuing decades.[56] Miura became the embodiment of fiction becoming reality or reverse mimesis; and this transformation of the diva by the role was embraced by Miura herself, who in many ways became synonymous with the fictional character she played.

In his study of the diva's last performances, music historian Kunio Hara identifies what he calls "repeated identification of Miura with the fictional character of Cio-Cio-San."[57] This identification is clear from Miura's earliest performances through the final ones. Miura always remained the Madame in the opera. Just as historians have sought to identify historical personages upon whom the fictional stories of Madame Butterfly (and her counterpart in Loti's story, Madame Chrysanthemum) "must have" been based, there are many inverse representations of the character in our real world, moments when the fictional Butterfly has been said to have been made manifest in a historical personage.[58] Miura Tamaki is simply the most striking case. For all intents and purposes, for a period from around 1920 through 1946, Miura Tamaki *was* Madame Butterfly.

On her debut performance in 1915, the *Times* of London wrote of the cultural gap between Italian opera as an art form and the Japanese artist as an individual but hailed the perfect unity of the person of Miura with her role:

A real Japanese "Butterfly" was advertised as the principal attraction in the performance of Puccini's *Madama Butterfly* at the London Opera House last night, and unlike many advertised attractions based upon an appeal to realism, Mme. Tamaki Miura proved to be a real attraction as well as a real Japanese, because she is a real artist. . . . A clear, birdlike voice and a way of indicating changes of expression by subtle changes of timbre, like this sudden little movements of hands and figure which are her chief methods of acting, are wonderfully engaging.[59]

The article fixates on the spectacle of Miura in terms of "attractions." The piece attributes the performer's realism to the embodiment of putatively Japanese qualities: the "birdlike voice" and the diminutive subtleties of her gestures. In the constant referral to Miura as "Mme. Miura," we can begin to note a slippage between the character and her impersonator, culminating in the final line of the review: "Madama Butterfly made all her companions look irredeemably Western." But what is meant is that Miura did so.

The reviews hailing Miura's national origin as the key to the opera's "reality" rest on an implicit, if false, syllogism: Butterfly is Japanese; Miura is Japanese; therefore, Miura is Butterfly. The repeated conclusion that Miura essentially *is* Butterfly was underlined in the April 1920 meeting between the maestro and the madame, when Miura traveled to Puccini's estate in Torre del Lago, Italy. The two posed together for a widely circulated photograph, and the meeting was viewed in the Japanese press as giving an imprimatur to Miura's performances.[60] That version of the meeting is reproduced in Miura's memoir, which quotes Puccini as saying:

"Your Madame Butterfly is, of all the Madame Butterflies that I have seen, the most ideal Cio Cio. Many prima donnas in Italy (and, of course, places like America and Spain, too) will walk about on stage carrying the parasol as if they do it every night; then they'll sing, but none of them have been my ideal Madame Butterfly. . . . But Madame Miura, your Cio Cio exemplified in the first act the fantastic childish Cio Cio-san of a fifteen-year-old. And in the first scene of the second act, you completely expressed the love of a mother and the love of a young wife who waits for her husband to return home.

"When I saw your Madame Butterfly, I thought Madame Miura is not singing. I thought that what appeared on stage was the illusive

Madame Butterfly which I had described in my heart. Truly Madame Miura, you have realized my dream with your Madame Butterfly. For you, having none of the faults of other prima donnas like forgetting to express the personality of Cio Cio-san for the purpose of their own self-confidence and esteem; you, because you are a Japanese prima donna, exude Japanese affect and the virtues of a Japanese wife. There is only one of you in the world, truly my ideal Cio Cio-san!"

. . .

In addition, Puccini was not simply the famous composer, but the true father of Cio Cio-san; so, I felt affection for him as if he was my father. I cherish the photo taken of us at that time as my most important treasure.[61]

In this complex play of representations, Puccini (as voiced by Miura) confirms her authenticity as the medium for Madame Butterfly in a speech studded with contradictions. There is only one of her; a copy is impossible; she is Butterfly. She is the manifestation of the idea he had, one that he fathered. She is somehow both his copy and his original, his representation and mimic. Puccini here exemplifies the male orientalist who gives birth to his own image of difference and otherness only to then find it borne out in reality. Miura takes on the mantle of this "stupefying" and "irritating" situation of the binary between orientalism and reverse orientalism.[62] Her willful masquerade echoes myriad comments that Miura was constantly performing the role of Butterfly and Japanese person for audiences beyond the opera house, whether those of Japanese or non-Japanese descent, fans or journalists.[63]

Miura, then, was not only a synecdoche for Japan and Japaneseness but also a metonym for the fictional character of Madame Butterfly.[64] But Miura did not simply have the title thrust upon her; she eagerly claimed it. Often referred to as "Madamu Miura" in Japanese or "Madame Miura" in European languages, she was the medium through which the character was realized. In her biographical memoir called a "record of a life" (*ningen no kiroku*) titled *Madame Butterfly* (*Ochōfujin*), in the biography of Miura titled *The Madame Butterfly for All Time* (*Eien no chōchōfujin*), and in the fictionalization of Miura's life by novelist Setouchi Harumi that is also titled *Ochōfujin* (*Madame Butterfly*), the legend of Miura is intertwined with the role she so often played. Remarks about her May 1930 performance noted that, listening to the recording, it was impossible to tell whether it was "Miura Tamaki's *Madama Butterfly* or *Madama Butterfly*'s Miura Tamaki."[65] And this continued through the announcement of her 2,008th performance in the role to be sung in Japanese in Osaka in 1937 and broadcast on radio, which was greeted by a tongue-in-cheek question whether audiences would hear Miura Tamaki or Madame Butterfly (Miura Tamaki ka . . . Ochōfujin ka?).[66] In these versions of the life of Miura as Madame Butterfly, we find the manifestation of a desire among critics, interpreters, fans, and Miura herself to find not the fact behind the fiction or upon which it was based but the fact in front of or after the fiction. This desire for the realism of reverse mimesis, for the person who can best comport herself to fit the fictional ideal, is clearly related to Miura's ability to achieve such popularity and longevity on the global stage.

The close association between the character and the person continued through her final 1946 radio performance and recording sessions for which, despite the absence of an audience that could see her, Miura dressed in Butterfly costume and recounted her meeting with Puccini over twenty years prior.[67] In other words, from her debut performances to her final acts for Japanese and international audiences, Miura drew on her close association with the role. The Glover Garden in Nagasaki, called the "Butterfly House," commemorates a historical person who purportedly inspired the story behind the opera and also houses a bronze statue, installed in 1963, of Miura Tamaki as Butterfly. The statue stands as one more way in which Miura remains the medium for the Madame, successfully fitting herself into the image of the character projected by others.

If Miura mediated Butterfly, she did so not as a passive agent but by actively translating and transforming the role. At various points she not only transformed herself but also manipulated the press and her audiences to consolidate her agency. Being an active medium in Japan and on the global stage in the early twentieth century meant that she had to be at times openly political, but her politics over the course of her career are not easily parsed.[68] Much has been made of her final performance under the occupation.[69] But her career was full of the political signs and pivots of a public life. Her individual public actions alone trace an anomalous and variegated political portrait. At times, she was a philanthropist, traveling to a prison in Lima or the Tokyo Municipal Asylum to sing for the inmates.[70] At times, she was an internationalist, playing a benefit concert to raise funds to help send athletes to the 1936 Berlin Olympics, or a nationalist, organizing an All Japan Chorus for the 1940 Tokyo Olympics (which would soon be canceled).[71] At times, she was a feminist, performing benefits to support women's health and education and publicly criticizing the position of women in Japanese society.[72] In addition to her many comments about divorce being easier in the United States than in Japan, on her tour with Alberto Franchetti after she had separated from her husband, she was the victim of many threats to her life because of her negative comments about a woman's place in Japan. One letter calling her a "traitor to Japan" was "undoubtedly inspired by an interview with Madame Miura published recently in which she referred to woman's status in Japan as one of serfdom and predicted that someday Japanese women would rise up against tyrannical domination of the men and demand equal rights."[73] From a leftist perspective, she was a member of the bourgeoisie. Her life was threatened after a concert in Okayama for "holding bourgeois concerts."[74] But she could have been a proletarian, traveling to Moscow as a guest of honor with Kikuchi Kan, Yamada Kōsaku, and other luminaries from the Association of Proletarian Artists.[75] She might have been a fascist who performed under the flags of fascist Italy and Nazi Germany and sought to curry favor with Mussolini, presenting him with gifts of a tea set, her portrait, and her own Japanese-language translation of *Madama Butterfly*.[76] In some ways, she was complicit with the war effort, visiting wounded soldiers at military hospitals in Tokyo and traveling to China on a concert tour to entertain the troops.[77] These various public appearances do not lend themselves to easy political categorization.

Miura's celebrity may have been so monumental that typical labels for political action fail to hold. It might make more sense to see her political actions in terms of the benefits she sought from them. Perhaps her complicity with the fascists and the war effort could be read as methods to secure funding for establishing her singing school. Perhaps her philanthropy was a means to pump up her celebrity and upcoming performances. But these justifications too seem a bit too black and white to encompass the complexities of an entire life. So maybe it is best not to put such narrow labels on her myriad efforts in the public sphere, but neither is it very useful to simply see them all as pragmatic or strategic means to specific ends. In her struggle to overcome Plage in copyright battles—using her status in the culture industry and pursuing desired ends through alternative means—we can see her hacktivist approach as something of a guiding principle in her life. So when Plage managed to shut her performances down in the legal realm of suits and fines, she found ways of pushing back elsewhere in the forms of translating the book to the opera or writing the soundtrack to the cut-paper animated film.

Plage and Miura

By the 1930s, Miura's decades-long ties to the Japanese culture industry enabled her continued success. She was able to leverage galas and dinners to her ends. For instance, when Miho Kantarō, the president of Columbia Gramophone Company of Japan, gave a party for people in the press, motion pictures, and music industries at the Tokyo Kaikan in early December 1935, Miura used the occasion to begin the planning stages of a concert titled "A Night of Madame Butterfly" (Ochōfujin no yūbe) to be sponsored by Columbia at the Hibiya Hall in June 1937.[78] On June 19, 1937, the lawyer Yamashita Hiroaki on behalf of Plage filed an injunction with the Tokyo district civil court against Miura Tamaki enjoining the Columbia Record Company president Miho from the singing and performance (engeki oyobi kashō kinshi) of Madama Butterfly.[79] But the suit did not completely stop Miura who managed to regroup her troupe and play a concert with this title a few years later.[80]

This encounter left Miura with a negative image of Plage. After playing the role so many times around the world, to be halted by someone claiming to represent the Puccini estate in Japan seemed an affront to what had become a way of life for her. In a March 1940 interview about her participation in Arai Wagorō's short animated film, Miura cited Plage's excessively high fees as a motivation for the work, saying, "It was out of antipathy for Dr. Plage . . . and because I was touched by the beautiful film that I composed music for Mr. Arai's film, though composing is not in my line."[81] Another hint that the struggles with Plage were in the minds of the cut-paper film's creators is that they chose to give the film the same title as the 1933 Shōchiku production over which Plage had launched one of his early complaints: Ochōfujin no gensō (The Fantasy/Illusion of Madame Butterfly). That title can be seen as a mocking reference to Plage's earlier legal skirmish with Shōchiku, which he ultimately lost.

Taking advantage of what seemed to be new protection under the recent adoption of the intermediary copyright law, Miura used the film as publicity to promote her planned concert series, which would include a performance of *Butterfly* at Tokyo's Nichigeki Theater in May 1940.[82] But prompting fears of a return of the Plage storm, the German lawyer tried a new tactic. In an effort to extract fees and a ban against her upcoming performance of *Madama Butterfly,* Plage's EastAsian Copyright Company (Tōa Kopiiraito), representing Puccini's son, Antonio, filed a civil suit accusing Miura of "violating personal rights" (jinkakuken jingai). Under the threat of a large fine, the concert was canceled. Plage's new angle of interference from abroad managed to secure a postponement of the concert on the grounds that the excerpts to be played were a "partial performance" and, therefore, violated the integrity of the original that was protected under the copyright law.

The theater manager, Hata Tokichi, expressed doubt about the purported grounds of "desecrating" (*bōtoku*) the original by shortening it, because he had proposed running the opera in its entirety, to which the lawyer for the Plage/Puccini side responded that the same fee of two thousand yen would be required to perform the whole opera. In Hata's view, "the true purpose of the action undertaken by the other side" became "highly questionable. . . . Therefore, we decided to postpone the performance."[83] The notion that one only needed to wait these things out was a common point of view that year, as most involved perceived that Plage was in his last throes as a copyright hound in Japan. Writing in the July 1940 issue of the film industry trade magazine *Eiga Asahi,* Takebayashi Kenshichi predicted that the strength of the native-run Copyright Association of Japan would only grow stronger, that Plage would be pushed out, and that this was the reason for postponing the show rather than paying the fee.[84]

How could mimesis (a necessary and natural part of cultural production) become a legal problem? In Japan, the answer was specifically related to Plage's entrance onto the cultural industry scene as an intermediary for rights holders. Though the cases of Plage and *Madama Butterfly* are not unique, they are exemplary in the way they encompass many of the problems of copyright dealing with new media at the time and since. Laws must define what is being copied; to prove violations have occurred, litigants must prove copying has happened; they have to prove a violation has occurred (sometimes a violation of the integrity of the whole); cases often revolve around questions of mediation (*chūkai,* in this case who gets to represent for whom); they often represent fears of noncommodified circulation or of circulation that does not remunerate the creator. The *Butterfly* cases contain all these issues, so it is no coincidence that upon the eve of his expulsion from Japan in April of 1940, having been barred from doing business in Tokyo and Mukden, Plage himself referenced the various *Butterfly* cases when he wrote an open letter:

> I am firmly convinced that if only once e.g. Ichiszo Kobayashi of Takurazuka or Shiro Kido of Shōchiku had been summoned by the Metropolitan police and been grilled for two days as has been the case with me, the copyright problem would have been solved long ago.[85]

In a sense, Plage is telling it like it is. From his perspective, there was a double standard. On one hand, major culture industry corporations were getting away with taking content for free and making money on it, while, on the other hand, he who had been on the side of the law and justice was interrogated by police. Though most copyright officials today accept Plage's legal justification and credit him with shifting the Japanese culture industry to start taking copyright law more seriously, that his actions seemed motivated by cultural misalignment (and perhaps racism) made him the object of ridicule, scorn, and legal jeopardy.[86]

At the same time, Miura too seems to have become the victim of a double standard; after playing Madame Butterfly around the world and to have been told she was Madame Butterfly by no less than Puccini himself, it was unimaginable to her that the opera was not hers to sing. The postponement of Miura's *Madama Butterfly* would only last until Plage and his office were finally shuttered in the summer of 1940, but the events left a lasting impression on Miura, who recalled them in her postwar memoir:

> Lastly, I have one unforgettable memory about Puccini's son Antonio who came all the way to my hotel by car when I had

been invited to go to their country home in Torre del Lago. Around that time Antonio was always loafing about, cruising around in his car; but after his father died, it seems he's gone into the auto business. Then when I had returned to Japan and . . . when I sang *Madam Butterfly,* this guy named Plage came by without fail to take money for copyright. At first there was no way of telling whose rights he was levying fees for and the seizure was terrifying. So after I told him to bring evidence, the next time he returned carrying a copy of the documents. When I read Plage's power of attorney, I was surprised because they were signed by Antoni.[87]

Her association of her close connection with Puccini and his son and the surprising incursion of copyright fees suggests a disbelief. The fact that she had, over the course of her career, continued to play Butterfly from as early as 1914 through the late 1930s in Japan surely contributed to her sense of surprise and terror about the fees. In her personal connection to both Puccini and the role of Butterfly, we might hear echoes of the motivating example for the theorization of Feld's notion of "schizophonic mimesis." Feld cites Herbie Hancock's problematic sense of being in a simpatico relationship with the Indigenous people who created the music he lifted for "Watermelon Man." The difference between Miura's and Hancock's copying lies in the mediation of the relationship. Where Herbie Hancock supposes a world syndicate of brothers presumably based on historical inequalities, heritage, and skin tone, Miura's claim might be more about authority coming from the seemingly unmediated face-to-face relations between people, or what today in Japanese is called "skinship." In placing human relationships over identity (affiliation over filiation), Miura implies that more or less direct exchange between bodies matters more as mediation than does identity or external media in terms of who should have rights to copy. If Miura was successful in her pursuits on the global opera circuit because of her ability to take on the role melding with the background environment of the opera world, she was also able to make her perfect inhabiting of the exoticist image of Butterfly into a method for garnering her own agency. This story of fitting in to stand out, then, requires not only a figure or body but an environment, background, or architecture from which to stand out.

Of Screens and Windows: Open Locks, Paper Walls, and Silhouettes

If Miura's soundtrack for Arai's film stands out as a copy that is different enough to have skirted copyright, the visual aspects of the film are in some sense more consonant with a history of visualizations of Madame Butterfly. In its stunning silhouettes, Arai's short cut-paper animation from 1940 echoes images of the Madame present onstage and in print almost since her inception. Two important elements of the animation's context are present in John Luther Long's 1898 short story "Madame Butterfly": popular Western misperceptions of Japanese marriage and the typical architecture of Japanese homes in the late nineteenth century, which included paper windows. For Long, the illogic of locking a house with paper walls is something of a joke and metaphor:

> Some clever Japanese artisans then made the paper walls of the pretty house eye-proof, and, with their own adaptations of American hardware, the openings cunningly lockable. The rest was Japanese.
> Madame Butterfly laughed, and asked him why he had gone to all that trouble—in Japan!
> "To keep out those who are out, and in those who are in," he replied, with an amorous threat in her direction.[88]

Many of the orientalist stereotypes of the era are raised and some subverted in the story. Even though Madame Butterfly is clearly duped by Pinkerton, the American sailor, the tragedy for the reader remains that Butterfly, Pinkerton, and their son Trouble are all unwitting victims: Butterfly of Pinkerton's carefree privilege and her misunderstanding of his feelings for her, Pinkerton of his carefree privilege and misunderstandings of Japanese culture, and Trouble of his mother's tragic love. Butterfly's Japaneseness is conveyed by rendering the dialogue in her voice in a drawl resembling Black minstrelsy. On such gestures of verisimilitude by Long, Arthur Groos writes, "This attempt to confirm verbally the Japanese local colour is anything but realistic."[89] Long's story is mimetic not to reality so much as to preexisting stereotypical representations of otherness and Japan. Mimesis, to be effective, must seem like that which we already know from other mediated experiences. To seem realistic, or as Groos puts it, to construct "a convincing oriental ambience," the representation must copy enough to make its consumers swallow any differences between their expectations and the version presented.[90] In that sense, the Black minstrelsy evident in the depictions of Japan represented as the other to the white male American in this construct of Japan at the turn of the century.

Japanese houses, and by proxy Japanese loves, Pinkerton assumes, are free, open, and flimsy. There are sinister overtones in the controlling American husband's attempts to establish ownership and property rights to a woman who can, perhaps, give herself but who cannot be contained. If the tension in this scene is between American and Japanese culture, property rights and human agency, the attempt to control and the inability to do so, this dynamic repeats wider problems of cultural control happening outside the realms of fiction between privileged Western cultural logics and Japanese modernization. The space where this tension exerts itself is particularly located within or behind the Japanese fusuma (movable partitions, variously doors or walls) made of *shōji* (opaque paper glued to a wooden lattice), the opacity of which makes it a screen to vision but also a screen upon which shadows may be cast (thus giving not an eyeful but at least an alluring sense of what is going on within). The tissue paper walls transform or render the three-dimensional space of the room into a two-dimensional image. In that sense, tissue paper walls are a Japanese medium. Though this screen as shadow-bearer is part of a long visual tradition in Japanese art, in *Madama Butterfly* it is a Japanese medium constructed through the eyes of the Western male gaze.

Butterfly's room is, therefore, a female space limned by the opaque walls of male desire that act as a medium similar to Irigaray's version of the Platonic cave. The missing piece in Plato's story of the cave, according to Irigaray, is one of origins: Do the cave walls reflect a projection from outside, or is the outside a reflection of what goes on in the cave? This veiled question is the question of the feminine: Is the feminine the origin for the masculine, or is it its shadow? The Japanese home itself is thus doubly feminized by the male gaze as a womb, the movable and removable, opaque and pierceable walls that are the screen upon which images are cast or upon which dreams have always already been cast. Madame Butterfly's media are those of Irigaray's theorizations of womb and speculum.[91]

There is something more specific to this Japanese medium that grows through successive iterations of Madame Butterfly through the novel, drama, and opera: this medium particularly associated with the Madame as the meme became an international phenomenon. Among the hundreds of architectural points and home furnishing details included in art critic Moriguchi Tari's 1922 book *Bunka-teki jūtaku no kenkyū* (*Research in Cultural Homes,* written with Hayashi Itoko) is the following curious entry:

> Figure 158 looks as though it is a Japanese style room because it contains a window made by westerners imitating the Japanese taste [*Nihon shumi o manete*]. This sort of thing is made expressly for facing the garden from the dining room. They call it the "Madame Butterfly window" [*ochōfujin no mado,* glossed as *madamu batafurai uindō*]. It seems they think of the well-known Madame Butterfly as a representation of Japanese taste. It combines the *tokonoma* [display alcove] and *shōji* [paper and wooden partition commonly used as a door or window cover]. Euro-Americans say the meeting of the vertical and horizontal lines of the *shōji* gives the sense of a very simple harmony [*hijō ni kansona kaichō o kanji saseru*]. However, the sliding door is not paper, but glass.[92]

A Japanese-reading audience is introduced to the "Madame Butterfly window" as an architectural feature of a Western house. It is something both of a boon to the nation and a curiosity to have a thing so obviously related to one's own culture adopted elsewhere; mimicry is, as the old adage goes, the sincerest form of flattery. But there is a strange sense of loss and displacement accompanying such mimicry. The other thing is not the same. The Madame Butterfly window connotes Japanese style or "taste," while transforming it into something different. Such cultural appropriation requires translation and explanation for a Japanese audience. Within that definition is an implied critique—Madame Butterfly is not a representative of Japanese taste and the proof of that lies in the window that is not Japanese but perhaps could be labeled "Japanesey." The Madame Butterfly window may have the shape of paper shōji, but it is glass, making it fundamentally different from anything in the Japanese home.

Reimagined with glass in place of paper, the Butterfly partition is revealed as a medium par excellence. Glass is so closely related with

Figure 11. Glass medium: the Madame Butterfly window associates the domestic space with the woman even as it conjures something of the modern fetish for the exotic in New Jersey. Image from *House and Garden*, June 1915.

The "Madame Butterfly" window looking out from the dining-room over the garden has the characteristic Japanese sliding windows and low platform

the term *media* that windows are a standard metaphor for the concept of media.[93] A window is a border or threshold that simultaneously separates and connects two environments. Glass allows light to pass through, even as it filters, distorts, and bends its rays. Different styles of glass render different mediating affordances.

One possible source for Moriguchi's description of the Madame Butterfly window is a June 1915 *House and Garden* article about the Frank A. Pattison House in Colonia, New Jersey.[94]

The small telephone room has a high-backed settle with double casements above it, while the garden window of the dining-room is a very interesting "Madame Butterfly" window with sliding sashes

and a low platform. Here is a window, suggested by Puccini's
opera, full of Japanese tradition, charmingly picturesque, and yet
in harmony with the simplicity and the decorative interrelation-
ships of vertical and horizontal lines that make up the panel-like
treatment of the walls.[95]

The window has little to do with the content of the famed opera; the
nomenclature seems meant only to capture an idea of Japanese style.
Though labeled as part of "Japanese tradition" in the magazine, the
fact that this style window must be introduced suggests it is new (not
part of the American tradition yet) for the *House and Garden* reader-
ship. Further, the proximity of its mention with that of a small telephone room suggests something of the modern technical and design
innovation of the window style for the U.S. home.

That this window should have been remade to be Japanesey, and
rebranded with a cliché name for Japanese taste, is of interest here
because it suggests a kind of reverse mimesis—one iteration of a new
real. Madame Butterfly, the fictional character (who was by the 1920s
more typically heard on record and radio rather than the supposedly
unmediated realm of the opera house), has come to mean something
in our tangible world. Rather than the representation of, say, the realities of Japan mattering through the medium of Madame Butterfly, what matters or comes to the fore in the example of the Madame
Butterfly window is that the medium itself takes up space, becomes
part of the built environment, part of our material reality. *Madama
Butterfly* may not represent Japanese taste, but the Madame Butterfly
window is a version of the Western taste for Japan made manifest for
a suburban New Jersey home.

How does the association of Madame Butterfly with a window
work? Melissa Eriko Poulsen argues in her study of the mixed-race
identity of Butterfly and Pinkerton's son, Trouble, that there was a
clear association among nineteenth-century orientalists between objects and people:

> The desirable Japanese aesthetic—as demonstrated by *Madame
> Butterfly*—just as often included Japanese *people* as it did decora-
> tive objects. As Lafcadio Hearn wrote about purchasing Japanese
> objects, "although you may not, perhaps, confess the fact to your-
> self, what you really want to buy is not the contents of a shop; you

want the shop and the shopkeeper, and streets of shops with their draperies and their habitants, the whole city and the bay and the mountains begirdling it. . . . all Japan, in very truth."[96]

As with Hearn's summation of the desire to possess the Japanese merchandise, the Japanese merchant, and all of Japan, so too, perhaps, the inclusion of the Japanese-style window in an American house displaces desire for the Japanese (displayed by Pinkerton's "amorous threat") with the Japanesey. In addition to this logic of association of object with fictional person and displacement of desire for people to desire for objects, such taste for the new Japanese medium likely also came to be named after the ill-fated title character because of a series of associations that became magnified over several iterations or remediations of the story.

The global popularity of the opera alone (besides the short story, play, and various and sundry offshoots and modernizations) has created the myth that from the first performance of Puccini's work at Teatro alla Scala in Milan in 1904, it has been staged every night since somewhere in the world. There have been numerous versions of the opera, many of which pick up on the association of the character with the window and screen. Gradually, the Japanese window/screen as introduced in successive versions of *Madama Butterfly* had a profound-enough effect on non-Japanese audiences such that an association grew, imprinting that particular style window with the name.

Though the window and screen play small roles in textual versions of *Madama Butterfly,* something significant happened with the visual representations of the story. It seems unlikely that *Madame Chrysanthème* by Pierre Loti in 1887, the short story by John Luther Long titled "Madame Butterfly" published in 1898, or Belasco's play from 1900, for that matter, alone or in combination had made the window so potently associated with the fictional character to have crept into mainstream architectural consciousness. Although windows appear in Loti's story, of the five mentioned, only two have people staring through them, and none depicts Chrysanthème herself using the medium.[97] Though a window has a minor role in the text of Long's story (the consul looks out of one), shōji paper walls appear several times (including the scene of configuring locks on them). In one important scene, Long depicts Madame Butterfly poking three holes in the shōji in order to espy Pinkerton. The function of the translucent tissue-paper partition as an opaque demarcation of space is violated to transform it into a makeshift transparent window.[98] Belasco's play *Madame Butterfly* repeats this scene and also uses the shōji as a screen that the characters hide behind: Pinkerton to hide his presence from Butterfly, and her later to hide her suicide from her son. Shōji is used in the plot as that which one can hide behind as well as see through.

The constraints and possibilities of theatrical staging may have contributed to the association of the screen with Madame Butterfly. Screens were a relatively cheap and easy way to evoke Japan visually, and their presence is more significant in Belasco's play than in Long's short story. What does it mean to hide when the hiding is done potentially in plain sight onstage for the audience? It would be a striking visual effect that would have less impact on readers of a print story. Puccini's opera retains the scene of making holes in the shōji and, confirming their use as a window, adds the maid Suzuki looking through what the script calls the "shosi" at the garden. While these various scenes are important plot points, none of them closely associates the character of Madame Butterfly with the window.

Rather, it seems that the woman and the window became one through successive staged and visual depictions of Madame Butterfly. When Long's short story, which originally appeared in the *Century Illustrated Magazine* in January 1898, was expanded as a book published by Grosset & Dunlap in 1903, the volume included several photo illustrations. These visual additions made Butterfly's architectural environment tangible for the reading audience. Consider that all but one of the sixteen "photo illustrations" include wood and paper partitions as convenient studio backdrops behind the white models posing as characters in the story; in seven of those, Butterfly herself is depicted in kimono in front of the screen. This preponderance of images depicting Butterfly and her portals for an audience with scant experience of Japan associated the character with the Japanese-style shōji window.

From stills of the New York production of Belasco's play in 1900 and 1906, it is clear that shōji partitions (along with kimonos and flowers) played a major visual role in the staging of those productions.[99] Puccini, who saw Belasco's play in its London staging, drew not only on the plot but also on some of its visual motifs for his opera. These were amplified in the marketing materials for it. Although the original poster by Italian graphic designer Adolfo Hohenstein for the debut performance simply depicts Madame reaching from within a darkened interior for Trouble, who sits blindfolded and basked in light with a door (possibly a fusuma but no window or shōji) between them, the enduring images of the opera came from Hohenstein's disciple. Soon after, Leopoldo Metlicovitz, who had worked under Hohenstein for G. Ricordi (the rights holders to Puccini's opera), designed what would become the iconic poster and series of postcards, which prominently feature several windows and screens. Metlicovitz's classic poster shows Butterfly waiting for Pinkerton in three-quarter view from behind (the position from which the ornate hairstyle of Japanese entertainers was often displayed in Edo-period woodblock prints) gazing out of a balcony window with a lattice similar to shōji. And in Metlicovitz's series of twelve postcards depicting key scenes from the opera, nine depict the title character and shōji or windows. One striking image shows Pinkerton and Butterfly in amorous embrace silhouetted on a shōji in a *marumado* (or *yoshinomado,* a circular window that often looks out onto a garden in Japanese architecture).[100]

 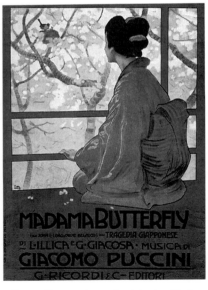

Figure 12. Figure and ground: Madame Butterfly was long depicted with the windows and screens behind her, as these two images attest. Images of Leopoldo Metlicovitz's poster and postcards from author's collection.

The power of these two images is attested to by the imprint they left behind, having been copied in many visual renderings of Madame Butterfly over the ensuing four decades.

These myriad depictions of a woman waiting by or in front of her lattice-covered window more and more transition to shadow images of the woman behind her screen in later versions. The marumado and silhouette from Metlicovitz's postcard contributed to the association of Butterfly with a screen. The Mary Pickford film has two marumado. One, shown early in the film, is a small, round window covered with shōji in Butterfly's dressing room. The second appears as an architectural feature in the garden and has simple bamboo latticework in place of paper. A brief kiss scene depicts Pinkerton and Butterfly embracing in silhouette not behind a shōji screen but in front of a bright, moonlit garden pond not far from the round window.

The 1932 Sylvia Sidney and Cary Grant film version solidified the linking of the images. When Pinkerton and his friend Lieutenant Barton (played by Charlie Ruggles) first arrive at the teahouse, geisha dance with stark shadows projected behind them on shōji. In the following scene prior to the one in which Pinkerton and Butterfly meet face-to-face, Pinkerton is "introduced" to her as she dances behind a shōji and he espies her shadow. As the scene begins, we see Butterfly nonchalantly dancing for herself (rather than for an audience). The film then cuts to her shadows dancing on the screen, then to Pinkerton as he examines a shamisen with the dancing shadow behind him. As he puts down the shamisen, he notices the movement and becomes enthralled with the shadow dance. After a big Cary Grant smile, we get a silver screen full of the shōji shadow dancing. Pinkerton then stands to go open the partitions and meet the real Butterfly for the first time. Later, as she watches Pinkerton's boat leave the harbor through binoculars, she gazes out of a marumado partially covered by a round shōji screen, and she is in the same spot again months later, now with Trouble, waiting through the night for his return. Finally, in the climactic scene, Madame Butterfly kneels in front of the shōji screen holding her father's knife, handed to her in the previous scene by her son. When she unsheathes the knife to reveal the blade, etched with the following inscription in Sinitic prosody "為名譽不生 為名譽之死," the characters dissolve before our eyes through the wonders of animation and become English: "To die with honor when one can no longer live with honor."[101] Visually, Butterfly and the window or screen become one over the decades-long series of depictions.

The visual trope of Butterfly beside or in front of the window/ screen suggests that together they act as mirrors of Western male desire, as well as provide the possibility of the tain of the mirror to invigorate and turn that image to other uses. The 1940 cut-paper animated short film is part of this network of visual representations and associations that we might label "the Madame Butterfly window nexus." The film pays homage to and innovates on these representations, picking up on the marumado used in Metlicovitz's postcard and the 1915 Pickford film, as well as drawing on the silhouette dance of the 1932 film. Indeed, the decision to use cut-paper techniques to create a silhouette film (*kage'e eiga*) in the first place seems as much an homage to Lotte Reiniger (the German cut-paper animation master whose orientalist films circulated widely in Japan) as reference to the 1932 scene of Sylvia Sidney dancing behind shōji to Cary Grant's delight.[102] The film does so at a time of highly strained U.S.–Japan relations and growing Japanese nationalism. As such, the short animation turns the story of a product of Western imperialism into an undoing of it.

The story of Pinkerton locking away his butterfly bride is a story of possession—albeit temporary. The Japanese marriage depicted in the story is a mockery of the Western institution precisely because it gestures toward longevity even as it is clear that it cannot last. The story of Pinkerton attempting to lock Butterfly away behind tissue paper walls when he wants her only temporarily seems like a parable for cultural appropriation. It seems perverse to think about Long's appropriation of Japanese culture on par with Pinkerton's roguery toward Butterfly only if we fail to understand Marxist expropriation, Lott's "cultural robbery," or Walter Benn Michaels's notion of "cultural genocide" as enabling the privileged "to treat something that didn't belong to them as if it did."[103] However perverse and misplaced questions of the propriety of culture or cultural ownership are, when culture is appropriated because of the identities attached to it, rather than solely on aesthetic grounds (and the possibility of any appropriation solely on aesthetic grounds too must be suspect), there is a sense of loss from the pilfered culture even as the spread of the culture itself may be a source of pride and even as there is a sense of expansion and inclusiveness within the culture of the pilferer/plunderer. Appreciation and copying of the art of the other is inevitable. It is what human communication does. But not all appropriation is equal. It may also be done well or done poorly. It may be done out of reverence and homage as well as out of mockery and ignorance.

Such cultural appropriation, mixing, and marriage done without respect sets the moral groundwork that enables violence. There should be no easy moral equivalence between injustice to cultural products and the human products of human reproduction. Appropriation of culture and its products play defining roles in how we understand such injustice, in how we come to know it. And, thus, culture needs to be thought together with injustice to human beings. And yet, to borrow or even appear to steal that which was never possible to be owned in the first place can be as liberating an act as a confounding one. Just as Pinkerton was wrong to think the Japanese were too free with their possessions and their morals, and therefore required foreign locks, we might also see the notion that the Japanese lacked a sense of copyright until Meiji modernization and the Berne Convention to be a modernizationist myth. In fact, the Japanese had locks to protect tangible property and laws to protect intellectual property long before Meiji.[104] Of course, to assume either such complete difference of Japanese history or a universalism that repeats familiar structures is to play at a kind of orientalism long since critiqued. Between the particularism that legal copyright in Japan has an entirely unique history and the universalism that all creation is copying with a change lies the truth of the complex genesis of a Japanese Madame Butterfly.

Cultural appropriation is, of course, a logical or even natural outcome of the mimetic faculty. If in theory copying and appropriation are natural, it is not practiced on an even playing field. In practice, some cultures (such as the Japanese one in the late nineteenth and early twentieth centuries) are easier for some people (such as white European men) to appropriate than others. Though copyright may attempt to check what is natural about the production and circulation of cultures in the world or the play between media and content (that things are copied in the process), it does not in practice check all copiers equally. We see this borne out, for instance, in the ease with which Puccini copies Japanese folk songs and the problems some of Miura's performances of Puccini incur. We can see the conflict between mimetic faculty and modern law design in the context of new media playing out in all its guises in this discussion of what might now be called media ecologies around the trope of Madame Butterfly.

The Madame Butterfly window is, thus, both a window and a screen. It is a more or less clear object that affords a view of something else on the other side, that connects two sides while demarcating their separation, that transmits light through degrees of transparency and opacity. But it is also a gridded divider that allows shadows to be cast upon it, bearing a copy, a silhouette of something standing somewhere else behind or in front of the division; it divides even as it connects. The window divides the private room of a Japanese woman from the public space of the harbor it overlooks, Pinkerton from Butterfly, East from West. What it connects, then, are body and background or figure and ground. The body is a medium, as is the environment behind it. In the Japanese architectural book, the Madame Butterfly window is both a false representation of a real Japanese architectural feature and a real Western thing to be described in the world. This tension between two modes of mimesis, one representational—having to do with a degree of fidelity and the question of accuracy of the copy—and the other ontological—marking the unavoidable, ongoing material presence of the medium—is the focus of this book. The Madame Butterfly window is but one example of how the Western desire for a traditional other occupies and transforms reality, creating a sense of a new real.

The space described by the paper walls imprisons Butterfly, and to some degree this architecture (and the infrastructures of racism and orientalism) produces her defining act—suicide. The control of the flimsy marriage and its insubstantial opaque walls can be likened to the control of copyright: it is legally binding but also bendable. Paradoxically, the right created to protect the widows of authors is both a bar to blatant copying and generative of new derivative material. In the story of *Madama Butterfly,* a mother "widows" her husband and the father of her child; in death, she becomes the posthumous author of a future for the child as yet untold.[105] In this sense, Butterfly's and Trouble's identities are linked to what Michael Taussig might call the "selfing space" of the Japanese house.[106] In contrast to Caillois's notion of mimetic psychasthenia, where an individual mimes a background to fade into it, Taussig proposes that playful agency can grow in precisely this willful choosing of identity formation. Where Taussig proposes that identity is freeing (when a culture incorporates the cultural products of the other so smoothly that they are hardly recognizable as linked to the "original"), in the opera we have the inverse case where identity is a trap. Butterfly gives up herself to free Trouble of his Japanese association so he can go and live with his father as an American. In this sense, Trouble is freed (within the rhetoric of the story), but does it make sense to talk about Butterfly as free through death? As such, the space seems more in tune with Irigaray's notion of Plato's cave as a pure projection of masculinist thought that allows little room for play but out of which play can still make meaningful critique. Indeed, Irigaray's work on mimesis is close to that of Caillois, who argues that the individual may be "tempted" by their surrounding spaces and eventually dissolve into the background. For Irigaray and Caillois, the temptation by space may be the threat of the dissolution of the individual subject. Butterfly dissolves into the space in order to individuate Trouble from it; in this sense, her room is a selfless-ing space. Fundamentally, this is the reason why, despite all statements of equivalency to the contrary, Miura Tamaki differs from the character of Madame Butterfly: where the fictional projection of Western male desire ends by relinquishing her life, Miura finds her own voice in the animated film because of the power accrued through performing the role over a lifetime.

Disembodied Ownership: Cultural Appropriation Redux

In many senses, this chapter has been simply a work of mimesis, more or less creatively copying and sampling from the work of scholars who came before. Just as many Japanese divas would take up the role of Madame Butterfly after Miura, so too for scholarly innovation. The chapter has directly engaged with issues of (inter)mediation, ownership, and cultural reappropriation that not only permeate the circulation of Madame Butterfly but constitute the very grounds for that circulation and globalization. This media history of *Madama Butterfly* in Japan provides an iteration of the kind of male-dominated and privileged situation and image of female and femininity that Irigaray critiques from within. At the center of *Butterfly* is a character who is at least triply othered by gender, race, and class (as an indentured Japanese woman) from the powerful white, male American Pinkerton, and yet Butterfly's difference as such is a construct. In the early twentieth century, Japanese popular culture appropriated the *Madama Butterfly* story and domesticated Butterfly through the promotion and circulation of versions and spin-offs. Miura Tamaki, the prima donna at the center of this cultural boom, took on the role, inhabiting the overdetermined space constructed by the desires of the Western male ego and making the image of Asian femininity her own, echoing Irigaray's problematic (yet powerful) position within philosophy. Within this framework, Miura's work of performance, translation, and composition shows just how transformative and how limited such work of mimicry and masquerade can be. There is nothing unique about the way this media history around *Madama Butterfly* in Japan reflects, recasts, and refracts issues of mimesis back at us, but rather because of its particular moment in history, its particular set of orientalist gender dynamics, and its role in the metamorphosis of copyright, the case of *Madama Butterfly* in Japan helps us to understand what is at stake in media studies.

The vast number of studies of media ecology attest to an unchangeability of aspects of the object of study (that which stays the same, such as the title and characters) even as they purport to show how media have fundamentally transformed the object. The arguments of this chapter may mime media ecologies, perhaps to simply provide one more history of myriad cultural forms in a global story. This chapter repeats Caillois's notion of mimicry, whereby the individual melds with its surroundings. And, thus, it becomes simply one more iterative study in a vast array of faulty media studies of mediation and remediation, but with a difference: it shows how mimicry and subsumption of identity itself can be a form of active being in the world. But if the practices of Irigaray and Miura truly garner agency through mimesis of dominant and even oppressive forms (and I think they do), then this chapter's repetition of other scholarly efforts to track the wider media ecology of Butterfly should have worked to perform difference through similarity, explicating how the stories of the madame and the copyright hound, the window and the screen, are not simply another media ecology but perhaps a more narrow media entomology.

Madama Butterfly in Japan proves through its infinite mimicries once again (as if we needed it) that the ideas of an origin and essence to a cultural phenomenon are mythical at best. At the same time, the booming interest in the opera after Miura's return to Japan and the subsequent recording and filmic multiplicity of versions show us how the mimetic faculty (as a compulsion and as innate mechanism) is itself tied to our fetish for and fear of new media. We can see this through navigating the odd relations of recording and broadcasting music, copyright laws, and the identities of human media like those of Plage and Miura; though this story is mainly about the mediation of music in the early twentieth century through translation, performance, recording, broadcast, filming, copyright law, and human beings, it is applicable to our contemporary concerns for digital rights management software and ownership of cultural heritage today.

Cultivated and culturally constructed in Western Europe, copyright law forced the definition not only of what constituted legal artistic borrowing and illegal copying but also of melody, media, and music itself. Indeed, the legal battles to define music through media in the wake of records and radio relegated performance to but one instantiation of "music." Radio broadcast, musical scores, and records the law would define as on a continuum with, but somehow separate from, original performance.[107] Though amended in 1971, 1999, and 2000, copyright law in Japan continues to position JASRAC as the primary intermediary between rights holders and users of cultural material. The 1971 revision of the law to account for magnetic audiotapes and record rental shops recognized "duplication rights," a change that occasioned the development of karaoke and, later, of minidisc technologies.[108] Yet were it not for the underlying centralized intermediary system, the trading of rights that enabled karaoke would not have had the content for duplication in the first place. In 1999 and 2000, copyright law in Japan was revised to reduce the power of JASRAC in the wake of the new media issues that the internet seemed to bring. Even though formally replacing intermediary rights with the Act on Management Business of Copyright and Neighboring Rights, the new law still allows a powerful place for JASRAC to continue; for instance, the rights-holding organization was integral in 2007 in working to get thirty thousand YouTube videos taken down for copyright violations.[109] So the legacy of Plage and Miura continues in the Japanese mediascape today.

The continued importance of intermediation in Japan reveals that the rise of digital media and their inevitably ensuing remediation give rise to anxiety not only over a potential loss of capital accrual but also over the very thing/message/information/music being remediated. And this ontological anxiety over what constitutes content (that was a major part of early music copyright law) continues today with music for which an originally recorded performance putatively does not exist. Virtual music that is first and foremost mediated by computational machine (without a recording of a performance as such) seems at first blush to raise an unprecedented specter of music produced without human labor. But recent controversies over copyright of the simulated and synthesized human voices sold by Yamaha as their VOCALOID software continue to place old questions of proxy ownership, media, and person at the forefront of Japanese copyright disputes. Just because the voice seems truly disembodied, it does not mean that race and body are not issues in VOCALOID circulation. We find their return in VOCALOID singer profiles and, indeed, in the way copyright seeks to maintain a space for the software production company to reembody or reincorporate the virtual voice in a corporate legal financial space. In VOCALOID, we can see the legacy of a content–media nexus (one already long evident in the Butterfly media histories discussed here).

For profit in the capitalist cultural marketplace, this means that entropy reigns and copyright continually must play catch-up to order the fact that cultural products spin away from their putative producers but that production ultimately lies beyond the limited powers and agency of a particular producer. This means that cultural production runs ahead of capitalism at every turn because of the flight patterns of mimesis.[110] Copyright is an interesting case of trying to reconnect what has been alienated and hidden—the labor of the artist or cultural producer. And yet, it runs counter to the nature of cultural production, which is necessarily to copy. The problem really is not that copyright generally seeks to remunerate the labor done but that it seeks to accrue capital over the long run of time for the labor done once long ago that was generally already remunerated.

4

Copycat Rivalries
Teleplay, Mask, and Violence

On March 30, 1959, major Japanese news media reported the tragic event of a child jumping to his death the previous day from the roof of his apartment in Nagano while imitating the first Japanese television superhero. The series *Moonlight Mask* (*Gekkō Kamen*), which ran for five seasons and inspired six spin-off films, garnered between 48 and 68 percent of the national viewership. Despite such popularity, this incident, and several others like it, led to the cancellation of the series.[1] The practice of "Moonlight Mask make-believe" (Gekkō Kamen gokko) had been the subject of much news in the weeks before the incident and seemed to speak directly to the wildest dreams and scariest nightmares of budding new media theorists, who were calling attention to the potential power of television to be a transformative agent in the world. Indeed, young and old fans found a lot to copy about the pistol-packing, motorcycle-riding mystery man who meted out justice clad in a white outfit with a cape, a turban, and, iconically, a mask. The simplest form of such real-world play was probably singing along with the show's popular theme song (which became a blockbuster record in 1958 with over one hundred thousand copies sold). In more provocative and eye-catching reports of mimetic behaviors around the new medium, photos of children dressing up as the hero for make-believe play around town or even for their more traditionally formal *shichi-go-san* (seven-five-three-year-old) Shinto coming-of-age celebrations abounded in the press.[2] Parents and pundits alike expressed concern about children sparring with toy guns in imitation of the hero, creating a nascent moral panic around television. But it is the imitation of the superhero's primary power—the ability to jump from high places—that led to tragic injuries and death.

Even the origins of *Gekkō Kamen* were deeply connected to and reliant on imitation. The show was a deliberate copy of both historical and existing fictional characters. The hero was based on wartime anti-imperial figure Tani Yutaka, a Japanese national who wore a turban while fighting against British aggression in Malaya (and whose legend was later reinvented or resuscitated in the wake of *Gekkō Kamen*'s cancellation as television's *Harimao* series). The show itself was inspired by popular American TV shows of the day, like *The Lone Ranger* and *Adventures of Superman,* both of which had been broadcast on Japanese networks.[3] Copycat behavior through this television show is emblematic of the story of the medium writ large. The medium, as conceived early in its history, depended on the belief that such transfer might reflect and create mimetic behavior: be they through viewers acting out their heroes' superpowers, becoming educated citizens of the world who will vote rationally, or purchasing irrationally what the commercials encourage them to desire. To be sure, the story of Japan's rapid economic growth is linked to the rise of television with its attendant models of commercialization and consumerism.[4] Hype around new media, whether in the form of advertising or punditry, creates a cultural and social discourse that both praises and scapegoats media. What unifies these polemics is the notion that the medium can change the world through mimicry, not merely present copies of it.

This chapter considers the role of copying from imitative gestures and mimicry to copycat crime and violence in the context of early television with particular focus on the marketing and reception of *Gekkō Kamen.* If the previous chapters examine a distinction between two kinds of a doubled mimesis, showing how the dichotomy of representation and mimicry produces conditions in which a figure can stand out in stereoscopic photography (chapter 2) or creates an environment for fitting in (mimetic camouflage through mottled behavior, chapter 3), this chapter examines how the desire for a given represented world can be the source for a violent and tragic mimetic rivalry, how the figure and event of the copycat might intervene in the real to better reveal the media-mimesis nexus.

Like other new media, television has long been held to have both positive and negative real-world effects. The promise of education—a conduit of information fed directly into the home—is balanced by the curse of mindless entertainment creating "a nation of a hundred million idiots."[5] But, of course, the real-world effects of any media, including television, are not black and white. The case study of *Gekkō*

Kamen can give us a sense of the complex role that mimicry had been ascribed. Ultimately though, television has only been correlated with mimetic behaviors; so claims about causation are dubious at best. Therefore, rather than arguing about causation, it is better to focus on the discourse, to track how the logics and illogics of causation around mimesis themselves set the basic parameters for understanding the media. In other words, the point of this chapter is not to take a side in the debate over whether television affects behavior but rather to understand how such taking of sides is itself a mimetic effect of television working in the world.

A derivation of both photographic and broadcast communications technologies, television is a kind of copying machine that reproduces and distributes images and sounds to other times and places. But not merely composed by the copying technicity of the machine or network as a mode of representational immediacy, television is thought to also provoke copying in its audience. Dreamed of as a tool of national education, the realization of television brought with it Luddite fears that have long accompanied new media—most starkly about their ludic effects on children and young adults. As such, this is a good case through which to test René Girard's theories of mimetic rivalry, which presume that human desire is ordered around miming that which others have or do and which, in turn, creates violent competition in situations of scarce resources.

Mediating Universal Mimetic Desire and Japanese *Monomane* at the Dawn of Television

Girard's notions of mimetic desire and rivalry, as well as those of mediation, violence, and scapegoating, can be helpful for thinking about copycat behavior. For Girard, *mimesis* has a negative connotation—referring to mimicry of a dark variety, that in which imitation of another's desires results in violence because of a presumed scarcity of the desired object.[6] In his zero-sum schema, it is said that we learn to desire that which another desires or possesses by means of two modes—"internal mediation" and "external mediation."[7] An "internal mediation" of desires occurs when individuals admire or desire that which others (mediators) from within their community in their same social status have or desire. In this type, accrued rivalry leads to violence in the competition for the desired object. "External mediation" of mimetic desire is between individuals on differing social planes from different communities—for instance, when a fan desires what a celebrity enjoys. It is easy to see from this latter form how this theory becomes more powerful in the televisual age.[8] This chapter focuses on a blended form of Girard's mimetic desires involving both internal and external modes. Children imitate their external mediator (a superhero) who is himself mediated by a mask and by television; but they also imitate each other (internal mediators) imitating the superhero in a game of one-upmanship that can lead to "reciprocal violence."[9] Television encourages this mimicry, marketing hero-themed goods, such as toys, masks, and vitamins.

In Girard's concept, "metaphysical desire" is the desire to become another person. In metaphysical desire, the mediator becomes despised, since the mediator's existence means that emulation can never result in complete transformation or replacement. In other words, the continued existence of the mediator threatens the imitator so that the imitator feels animosity toward the mediator. To ensure that this system of desire continues, Girard posits that in the mimetic rivalry for the desired, some level of violence will be displaced onto a scapegoat, so that others refrain from mutual annihilation. The scapegoat provides a steam valve to ameliorate the intensity of the violence. Girard writes that the scapegoat eventually becomes sacred through its function as a peacemaker between the parties in the mimetic rivalry. It is, therefore, key to his understanding of Judeo-Christian religion and the societies deemed to be influenced by those ideologies.

Girard's discussion of violence and scapegoating is further limited because he forgets the primary question of mediation beyond the mediation of the human body within the tribalism of his focus. Though he studies the human body as media(tor) in his work on mimetic possession in ancient rituals and on close body mimetic surrogates such as masks, he neglects examination of the ways such bodies themselves are mediated by other media (an odd oversight considering so many of his examples are mythical and fictional bodies).[10] In doing so, he forgets to study the way media and mediation (rather than human mediators or their fictional/mythical representations) transform desires. The study of history of the mediation of culture on such desires would deflect his transhistorical universal humanism or at least qualify it. Just as he limits himself to the Western Judeo-Christian tradition and, thereby, gives up on the potential of his universalism, he ignores the historicity of mediation and how such mimetic rivalries must necessarily be transformed over time and place and, therefore, loses out on elaborating any nuanced specificity to his argument. Girardian thinking is a symptom. It articulates a world of human behaviors that could but does not necessarily exist. So rather than thinking of the theory as a brilliant, all-encompassing lens through which to understand the universal reality of social relations, we need to read it as a mode of thinking itself produced by the trauma of realizing or suppressing the realization that all desire is always already mediated and mimetic. Ultimately, such symptoms reveal the necessity for historicization, as well as broader, more abstract thinking. For instance, we should recognize Girard's thought not just as postwar and post-Holocaust thinking but as television-age philosophy.

Copycat behaviors have been connected to the question of creativity and originality, representation and mediation. Too often over the course of Japan's modern history, the nation has been seen as an egregious copycat, violating Western copyright and patents to produce a belated and imitative modernity.[11] And yet this narrative presumes that there was ever a particular original modernity that sprang sui generis onto the world stage. It presumes that innovation and creativity (whether aesthetic, technical, or progressive) can ever be original, a notion at base contrary to an understanding of development as always achieved through response to the past. What this chapter hopes to expose is that copycatism is a question of framing, context, or media. The degree to which a person, a message, a work of art, or a nation is considered a copycat has to do with the level of attention to other such frames.

In modernity, originality was valued and imitation disparaged, even in Japan. For example, poet Hagiwara Sakutarō, who celebrated the surrealism of stereoscopy (as we have seen in chapter 2), was vehemently opposed to copycat artists. In the 1922 prose poem "Annoyed by Copiers/Mimes" ("Mohōsha ni yotte haradatashiku sareru"), he writes: "Oh, how my imitators make my thoughts, art, and special turns of phrases into boring everyday commonplaces."[12] Hagiwara takes a standard view of copying as an inferior version of an original, but this sort of rage against the human copying machine can be seen as an empty pose if cultural production is considered at base to be necessarily copied and modified—when culture is seen as an unceasing echo chamber with no original scream. In this light, it is global, singular modernity in all its varied possible forms that, with its myriad possibilities of machinic reproduction, produces the priority of the singular creative artist. When we recognize that there can be no production or creation without copying, we recognize (as did Walter Benjamin) the mimetic faculty as an innate tendency. In circumstances of scarcity, then, mimetic rivalry will necessarily arise. In fact, to copycat is not necessarily to degrade, but it must involve some change or difference from the putative original or model. Indeed, Hagiwara's own creative poetry is a pastiche of others' work. All of this suggests that Hagiwara's complaint against copying at the level of content is balanced at the level of form by appropriation of modernist norms. He must be conscious of this, and, therefore, his work should be read as ironic. Just as Hagiwara's rage emerged from a vibrant publishing world of print media innovations, which made reproduction cheaper, this issue of the moral value of copying becomes particularly clear through the lens of media and mediation and around crises of new media, especially television.

Hagiwara's views arose from a combination of modern and native traditions of copying—theories of copying that prize creativity as well as mimicry.[13] For instance, the aesthetics of the iterative arts in Japan extend through the salon tradition of storytelling that produced the retold *Tales of Ise* and *Tale of Genji* and the oral storytelling traditions of *The Tale of the Heike,*[14] through the tutorial tradition of calligraphy, in which students learn by copying the works of their masters,[15] and through the Noh theater tradition of *monomane* (the imitation/impersonation of things) where players are said to take on the characteristics of that which they imitate, distilling and refining the thing (object, plant, insect, animal, or person) in order to become it. The historical person Ariwara no Narihira was understood through tales on scrolls about previous legendary lovers even as he himself would become the inspiration for *Tales of Ise* and later *Tale of Genji*. The copybook method of calligraphic education is not just part of the tradition, it is the primary means for its transmission. And the Noh mask makes plain (or performs the opacity of) the face of mediation. And, therefore, such copying, whether in the various derivations of tales about the playboy and poet, the numbering of masters in calligraphy, or the mask of Noh was always already mediated. Indeed, at base, copies are mediations. And thinkers of the televisual age looked back to these traditions, and particularly to Noh, for insight about the new gadget increasingly penetrating Japanese homes.

According to Noh scholar Steven T. Brown, the practice of mono-mane "includes mimicry, miming, impersonation, and simulation as well as nonrepresentational forms of becoming-other."[16] The fourteenth-to-fifteenth-century Noh practitioner, playwright, and theorist Zeami Motokiyo saw the uses of monomane as a mode not simply of realism but of clarification.[17] The Noh mask meant such "becoming other" through role-playing was never transparent but always layered with an opaque sense of the constructedness of any impersonation. Therefore, it should have been no surprise that, when televisions first were appearing in Japanese homes, a significant discourse theorizing copying and imitation returned to the fore in Japan. This theoretical discourse concerned with dramaturgy and media found an echo in more mainstream and direct concerns with how the new medium of television would affect society, particularly the children within it. Not only does twentieth-century monomane discourse begin to resolve a tension in the notion of applying a theory from the West (mimesis) to the cultural materials of the rest (not Western), it also served to domesticate, translate, and remediate the new medium of Japanese within more familiar terms.

During the broad context of the birth of television, three prominent public intellectuals—Abe Kōbō, Ōoka Shōhei, and Takahashi Yoshitaka—all wrote important essays struggling with monomane, touching on questions of the social importance of culture in a time of televisual mediation. The essays do not engage directly with television per se (indeed, if mentioned at all in these essays, television is but a side or passing point), but they formulate a state of the discourse in thinking about how actors copying onstage or otherwise in the public arena might, in turn, affect how audiences act in their daily lives. The thought of these three luminaries on the role of copying and monomane in the context of rising television ownership provides a nascent theory of the value and risks of such copycat behavior.

In a December 1957 essay titled "About Imitation" ("Monomane ni tsuite"), published in the magazine *Film Arts* (*Eiga Geijutsu*), world-renowned avant-garde novelist, absurdist playwright, and abstract multimedia artist Abe Kōbō laments the lack of quality role-playing monomane in Japanese film. In his short article, written just before the widespread proliferation of television, Abe surveys Japanese and Western aesthetic traditions of impersonation and concludes with a call for the return of monomane to the public arena. Citing Bertolt Brecht on the notion that it is a mistake to insist that the popular arts awaken by naturalizing feelings, Abe makes the case that performance is rooted in actions that simply and imitatively reproduce (*subokuna mohō saigen*) rather than through the objectification of self. After acknowledging many types of mimesis in Plato, Abe then quotes Aristotle, from chapter 4 of the *Poetics,* on the cathartic function of mimesis, discussed both in terms of *mimos* (*mimosu*) and mimesis (*mimēshisu*):

> Tragedy . . . is an imitation through action rather than narration, of a serious, complete, and ample action, by means of language rendered pleasant . . . in which imitation there is also effected through pity and fear its catharsis of these and similar emotions.[18]

Abe places this Aristotelian notion into dialogue with Zeami's idea about acting, that "the vernacular is what makes people laugh; what makes a fine actor is their possession of an innate sorrow or pathos."[19] Here Abe (in a contradiction to the contemporary "realist" film acting practice of becoming the role through method acting or the Stanislavski system) goes on to argue that the best kind of imitation (*mohō*) is not simple imitation but rather theatrical imitation, one that foregrounds something like the performativity of the mask in Noh. He connects this to the common belief that imitation is boring and opposed to creation and creativity: Abe mentions that the word *to ape* (*sarumane,* monkey see, monkey do) generally signifies that imitation is unfortunately treated as a boring or less than human activity. If simple copying is animalistic, Abe leans toward something higher. He then calls for a thorough reevaluation of imitation "no matter how big the scale of imitation, how fragmentary, impressionistic, or detailed imitation, which is to say that which is included in the domain of *monomane.*"[20] In other words, he wants to foreground the constructedness of mediation; the frame or the mask must be exposed for imitation as monomane to be successful.

After quoting Marx on the role of reality's mastery over mythology, Abe intimates how in the age when reality trumps myth, new imitations must be found.[21] He then goes on to cite the biography of

Charlie Chaplin by Peter Cotes and Thelma Niklaus on the relation of mimicry to humor. There, Chaplin's satiric mimicry is admired for its ability to create empathy for the tragic downtrodden.[22] Chaplin's skills on film effect response in the audience; that is to say, representational mimesis through mimicry effect a mimicked response of the cinematic public. Ultimately, Abe argues that successful imitation is that which not only copies the external "physical" (*butsuriteki*) form of the object but also captures and performs something of its internal "physiological" (*seiriteki*) composition. This recognition—that acting that moves an audience (mimicry) is skillful in capturing not only an outward realism (representation) but also a metaphysical essence—is what Abe understands to be the goal of monomane. In other words, copying of acting is not a passive or transparent becoming of the role but rather a subjective activity that makes its own artifice opaque.

Abe ends the essay by tying his view of the meaninglessness of recent film musicals directly to this question of imitation. For him, musicals are superior to melodramas (and recent comedy) in which actors imitate imitation to achieve this opacity. The best vaudevillians, slapstick comedians, and musical players, he argues, have a way of creative imitation that can reinvigorate imitation globally in the way of filmmakers like Shinkichi Okada and Jules Dassin. Perhaps in reaction to the radio show genre called monomane in which comedians and singers impersonate the work of others, this essay anticipates that genre's remediation on television. It should be no surprise that this short essay—which succinctly reviews a thousand years of mimetic thinking and deals with various media from film to radio drama, from parades and circuses to opera, and from song recordings to stage performances—never deals directly with the new medium of television because it would not become a widespread mainstream media until the following year. This praise for mimos or mime and monomane as a higher form of copying just prior to the advent of mass consumption of television in Japan simply sets the late 1950s mediascape as hungry for new approaches to questions of copying and impersonation.

About a year and a half later, novelist Ōoka Shōhei wrote an article titled "Enough Already with Imitative Arts," which in some ways echoes Abe's view but defines *monomane* in opposing terms not as opaque copying but rather as transparent aping.[23] Ōoka rails against the globalized, derivative copycat culture already visible on early television and draws attention more directly to television by mentioning several media, from the supposedly unmediated performance arts of drama, ballet and opera to more obviously mediated ones of print literature, film, LP records, and television. Even as he recognizes the recent successes of an always already mediated Japan on the world stage (such as through the success of the film *Rashomon* in winning international attention and prizes), he critiques a perceived lack of Japanese cultural ingenuity in the face of what is now called globalization.

Simple copying of Western form and content, Ōoka argues, gives contemporary Japanese art an attenuated feel. On the one hand, his argument about the oddity of Western-style drama in Japan is similar to Abe's. On the other hand, he says that the attempt to globalize Japanese traditions through Western stereotypes also falls short. On Western-style drama in Japan, Ōoka writes that Japanese actors who "wake up on tatami mats and, at most, move around the wooden flooring of a bungalow with slippers on" probably cannot imitate the movements of foreign actors "who usually walk into rooms with their shoes on, typically sit on chairs, and open doors to exit and enter."[24] In other words, the unnaturalness of daily life depicted in Western drama makes Japanese actors imitating the daily life of non-Japanese onstage appear strange or fake, such that the characters seem like "incomplete foreigners" (hanpa-na gaikokujin).

Unlike Abe, who might have seen thin fakeness as precisely what was needed, Ōoka praises the Stanislavski method and condemns that which misses the realism mark. Calling the recent Osaka Festival a miscalculation in terms of its potential appeal to a global audience, Ōoka makes the case for more contemporary mediated representations. At the same time, however, he critiques the recent television show *Spectacular Japan,* which was made for American television but also aired in Japan and starred the internationally famous Japanese actress Kyō Machiko. Despite the participation of the foremost global female star of the Japanese silver screen, Ōoka derides the show's orientalism (without using the word).

> They [Americans] are impressed with Kyō Machiko's western
> dramatic performance as Japanese kabuki style. The questionable
> Japanese dance on *Japan Spectacular* as a kind of geisha waltz in
> a single layer kimono made many people indignant at the "na-
> tional disgrace" [kokujoku], but there is nothing that can be done

if the American observer thinks that geisha dances are that sort of thing.[25]

Even as he critiques the mishmash of Japanese stereotypes and the wrong and even scandalous choice of costume for a dance that itself was neither traditional nor Western, he recognizes the bind inherent in presenting Japan to spectators with particular stereotypical expectations already in place. In the end, Ōoka (whose novels are themselves often considered derivative copies of Stendhal's) advocates not for a return to some pure premodern Japanese tradition but for a more thorough engagement between Japanese tradition and (Western) modernity. For models of such conscientious mixing, he cites the aesthetic rage in prewar Japanese modernism for mélange work by artists such as Masamune Hakuchō, Tanizaki Jun'ichirō, and Mushanokōji Saneatsu, all of whom melded the contemporary with deep concerns about vanishing traditions to create thoughtful intermixings. Thus, advocating not a return to native Japanese arts but a turn away from the crass postwar globalization and back to the smarter cosmopolitanism of Taishō—when creativity and creative translation, adaptation, adoption, and originality coalesced—Ōoka rails against the simple copycat culture he saw at the time. For him, the monomane (imitation) he opposes names simple copying or animal-like aping rather than the careful digestion and reinterpretation of a previous generation's work.

Literary critic Takahashi Yoshitaka is more squarely focused than either Abe or Ōoka on a comparison of the Japanese monomane and European mimesis traditions. After showing how Aristotle's and Zeami's views of impersonation are quite close in many respects, Takahashi argues that most stage acting differs from other forms of art as representation. He notes that with most forms of art, something other than the thing itself conveys the imitation (i.e., a medium): in literature, letters create a literary world; in painting, colors do so; in sculpture and architecture, it is wood and stone that provide the medium for world-building. But in dramatic performance, generally a human actor is the "same single human subject" (onaji hitotsu no ningen shutai) as the object of imitation.[26] Of course, Takahashi slips in a false equivalence between the generally represented (fictional) human and the performing actual human. So in articulating a difference for drama, he then ignores how pivotal and foundational particularly insular works have been for understanding literature and the arts: the literary worlds created by words alone (such as the anomalous *Finnegans Wake*), paintings of paint (think Jackson Pollock), sculptures of trees made out of wood (such as John Grade's work or bonsai). And yet Takahashi wants to preserve a particular place for drama because he conceives of a human actor playing a human character to be an unmediated form of art.

Here, Takahashi says Zeami fundamentally differs from Aristotle in his view on drama: for Zeami, actors do not need to deny or abandon personality—rather, he considers "personality as essential to imitation."[27] He then cites Zeami's preference for a mixed form of representation and mimicry wherein an actor should both become the object to be imitated as well as let something of the actor's own style and personality show through. For Zeami, this effect can best be achieved by older performers (over the age of fifty). Takahashi fixates on another mediated aspect of Noh theater—that there are traditionally no female actors so that male actors must become female characters—to get at the notion that one can never truly leave the self behind in acts of imitation. Ultimately, this for Takahashi suggests that all attempts at realism carry within them the notion that the thing represented is not the thing itself. Isomorphism is a contradiction in terms. Takahashi writes: "Even when a 'young vivacious man' takes a woman's role, Europeans should not care. This is because Japanese mimesis is oriented towards something fundamentally different from European mimesis."[28] Here, Takahashi perhaps mistakes the variegated forms of mimesis in the Western tradition for the one literary form (representational) canonized by literary scholars of the twentieth century. But what he inadvertently identifies is a similarity between both traditions—namely, the tension between becoming other and remaining the same. He names this as a desire. What Takahashi ultimately sees as the Japanese difference in mimetic thinking—the desire to become things rather than humans and animism or an abandonment of anthropocentricism (*ningenchūshinshugi*)—is, in fact, rooted in a base similarity to the desire to become other than the self—the use of the nonpresent (demons, women, stones, heroes) in the becoming present of worlding—that the multifarious Western mimetic tradition of mimicry shares.[29]

This question of realism is an important point to raise again in the context of television. If Takahashi wants to foreground something like an opacity to mimicry of a native Japanese mimicry that reveals itself as artifice (that never calls for a complete suspension of disbelief) whether in age or gender of actors versus characters, then he also implicitly suggests that such opacity (a critique of transparency) could potentially inure television audiences from the threat of the media. Indeed, the potency or threat of all dramatic cultures from Noh through Kabuki to modern plays, films, and television to arouse audiences to action should be lessened by such violations of realism. And yet debate around who could not resist media and who would give themselves up entirely to that which they were mimicking would rage around television.

Abe, Ōoka, and Takahashi present a variegated yet coherent discourse on copying that coincided and spanned television mainstreaming. Abe is interested in monomane as more than simple copying that which gestures toward the artifice of copying itself. Though confusingly he calls aping "monomane" perhaps not so much after the Noh theater practice but after the radio (and later television) show genre in which contestants compete to imitate animals and impersonate famous people (wherein the more transparent the mimicry, the better), Ōoka also opposes aping. He calls for more opaque creativity (i.e., mimicry that can be read qua mimicry) in the inevitable adoption of Western culture concomitant with modernity. Takahashi sees the problem of mimesis—Western realist representation—as displaced by Zeami's theorization of monomane as more than simple copying. It is precisely in the supposedly unmediated human form of drama with an obvious mediated mask that we can view Takahashi's internal contradictions. Regardless of whether the opacity and transparency are both equally part of the Western tradition, all three thinkers prize some opacity of mediation as a mode of not only aesthetic but ethically responsible copying. And television becomes the media for this new mode of theatrically foregrounded copying.

Masking Justice from Elsewhere

Such opacity would be found in the mask of the television superhero Gekkō Kamen. In the mask we can find an instantiation of Girard's concept of the "monstrous double," wherein the subject recognizes their own mimicry as well as the behavior of their mimetic rival as monstrous, interpreting their own copying as coming from else-where (externally outside of themselves as though possessed). The monstrous reminder of our mimetic tendencies resembles concepts of haunted media and media possession. In the Girardian schema, masks, monstrous doubles, and media are effectively the same. In other words, we scapegoat masks, others, and media because we do not like how we ourselves copy the represented realities and positions brought to us by them.[30]

In addition to being media that bridge or communicate from one fictional or impossible world to another possible one, masks also cover the individuality of the face to create an iconic face behind which nearly any humanoid figure might lurk. In the case of Gekkō Kamen make-believe, Girard's mimetic rivalry seems particularly apropos because the mystery behind the mask allows and encourages viewers to imagine themselves as the secret identity behind the hero. This question of who Gekkō Kamen is permeated the show, from the opening theme song to multiple plots, images, and promotional events.

Even those Japanese who were not among the show's viewers during its late 1950s run would at least have heard the theme song, which sold over one hundred thousand copies and was frequently played in public spaces such as shopping streets. Its lyrics were among the most frequently quoted pieces of popular culture in 1958 and 1959.

"Who Is Moonlight Mask?"
No one knows who he is or where he came from
Yet everyone knows him
That guy, Moonlight Mask
Is an ally of justice, a good guy
Appearing and disappearing
Like a gale force wind.
Who is Moonlight Mask?
Who is Moonlight Mask?[31]

Since the theme song introduced the hero at the start of every episode and played again during key scenes within the episodes, it can tell us much about his character and the reasons for his popularity in the late 1950s. First, the existence of the superhero is self-contradictory. Gekkō Kamen is known but not known, as his origins and true self are hidden. Second, the mysterious hero appears and disappears with

Figure 13. Mask as medium: Promotional still of the iconically masked superhero mounted on his Honda Dream C70. Courtesy of Senkōsha Productions, 1959.

a flash to mete out justice. These two points together suggest a sense that, like the hero, justice comes suddenly and sporadically ("like a gale force wind") and that it is not something with a definite origin or associated with a particular nameable individual. It appears that justice is an outside, coming to Japan from somewhere else.[32]

The key to this mysterious (unspecifiable) identity is clearly the hero's mask, which covers his face enough to keep secret the identity of the individual behind it. Echoes of the famed *Lone Ranger* tagline "Who was that masked man?" reverberate through the *Gekkō Kamen* theme song, but there are also important dissonances. Unlike *The Lone Ranger* series and many later masked heroes, whose alter egos are known to the audience and to a few close characters within the narrative, the *Gekkō Kamen* series does not openly reveal the true self behind the mask or depict scenes of transformation (*henshin*). Sasaki Mamoru suggests that the difference between early postwar Japanese heroes lies in their transformations: Ultraman is a human evolved or metamorphosed into an alien (a symbiote), and Kamen Rider also transforms his body, but Gekkō Kamen is only disguised, not physically transformed, and therefore, potentially, one of us, the viewers.[33] The audience never knows Gekkō Kamen's name or motivation. Typically American, British, and Japanese superhero stories (from the Lone Ranger and Batman, through Judge Dredd, Kamen Rider, and Sailor Moon) feature a dichotomy between private life as regular citizen and public life as hero as part of the narrative.[34] Yet, reflecting postwar ambiguities about justice and the domestic capacity to mete it out, the identity and aims of both criminal and hero were masked in the *Gekkō Kamen* series, even to the viewing audience. Whereas the recent spate of Hollywood hero films seeks to provide origins in order "to provide a psychological rationale . . . so we see that the early lives of superheroes are marked by tragedy, which gives rise to a righteous thirst for justice and even revenge," *Gekkō Kamen* gives no clear backstory to explain his past and justify his present actions.[35] Instead, we are told anyone could be Gekkō Kamen; so, in a sense, the Japanese people are all potentially Gekkō Kamen. It is implied that the backstory is the national backstory; a recent war that ended with the imposition of a victor's justice from which Japanese had felt alienated. In this context, donning the mask of justice could restore that from which any one of us in the viewing public might have been alienated.

Examining the creators of the series, Sasaki Mamoru states:

In the Japanese postwar way of life in the context of our experience of the end of the war as a defeat, this [sense of how to find justice] is the core challenge. What exactly was the war? What does the Japanese race mean? And the Emperor? What did the occupation mean? Was the democracy taught to us by the US a form of justice? Does gender equality and majority vote equal justice? . . . Here justice is always an uncertain thing.[36]

The uncertainty about justice was, according to Sasaki, never resolved in the real political struggles of postwar Japan. Rather, he implies that the series' creators believed justice could only be resolved by the imagination and creativity of televisual production.

The producers of the series included elements within the narrative that encourage an allegorical reading. Critic Tzvetan Todorov defines *allegory* as follows: "First of all, allegory implies the existence of at least two meanings. . . . Secondly, this double meaning is indicated in the work *in an explicit fashion*: it does not proceed from the reader's interpretation (whether arbitrary or not)."[37] In order for the allegorical reading to be justified, there must be explicit references to the doubled allegorical meaning. According to Todorov, allegory arises when direct speech about a situation becomes impossible (for any reason from political or epistemological), but nevertheless there must be a flash of direct speaking to actualize the allegorical reading.

There are several points of direct speaking that would justify reading the series allegorically in Todorov's terms. Takahashi Yasuo finds the "Ghost Party Strikes Back" ("Yūrei-tō no gyakushū") episode to be a direct allegory of the Sunagawa Struggle of 1955 (a precursor to the 1960 demonstrations against the revision of the U.S.–Japan Security Treaty), in which the expansion of the Tachikawa Airfield in Tokyo was opposed by the local residents who were to be displaced by the construction.[38] But it is probably the words of Kawauchi Kōhan (the series creator and writer) that best justify this mode of allegorical reading. In the opening introduction and closing afterword to the first volume of the initial novelization of the series, he writes:

Boys and girls!
The things written about in this book do not actually exist in the Japan of today. But incidents that fairly resemble them really do. In addition, there is the future possibility that some of them

will come to fruition. So please believe that someone like Gekkō Kamen, who has the heart of a god and does good deeds without anyone knowing, fights to make the world a better place!

And:

> As I wrote this novel a number of events have taken place all over the world.
> In the area of the Middle East (battles in places like Lebanon, Iran, Jordan) are but one instance. But whatever the circumstances, military altercations are not laudable. However, from now on peace in this world will be more and more dependent on today's young boys and girls.[39]

Recognizing that today's youth inherit the problems created by the adults, Kawauchi implies that children today should believe in the possibility of justice even in world affairs. He states elsewhere that the particular justice of Gekkō Kamen resides in his slogan "Don't hate, don't kill, forgive!," which we can read as a direct address to the televisual audience rather than solely to the characters within the narrative world.[40]

Perhaps the best articulation of the explicit doubling in *Gekkō Kamen* occurs in the final scene of the series, in which the superhero himself says, "If the peace of love and justice filled this world, a person like me would no longer be necessary."[41] This simple statement clarifies the allegory by making the fiction's relation to reality explicit from within the story itself. This final scene makes the claim that only in a warring, unjust, and unloving world (that is to say, in our real world) do we desire the existence of a superhero. Within the world of the narrative, it means simply that, since the world is broken, we need a superhero to save it. But in the real world where peace, love, and justice are also considered lacking, where millions of viewers enjoy the story of a masked ally of justice on television, it means that we long for justice, even if only in the form of fantastical and fictional superheroes who mete out justice along with compassion, aiming for peace.

As we shall see, what was always an implicit allegorical message within the series itself (that the series with its fantastic and phantasmagoric depiction of justice represented or symbolized something displaced from the real) would itself become a root form for understanding justice in the world. The character Gekkō Kamen would become a primary metaphor or synecdoche for describing the need for justice in the real world. That is, his name would be invoked to name the lamentable state of justice in the real world while also maintaining a fantastic hope for future justice. This real-world function of Gekkō Kamen could be thought to be simply a figure of speech, but it in fact reflects a mode of thinking about justice itself. The mask is Todorov's link between the allegoric and the actual or Lacan's stitching point *(point de capiton)* that binds together the symbolic and the real and that brings together two layers of meaning, one diegetic and the other extradiegetic, one representative and the other mimicking. Gekkō Kamen's mask is the medium that binds the world on television with the world affected by television.

Of Masks and Media: A True X-Man

Fans of the show are in general agreement that the masked avenger, a turbaned tornado, a motorcycling man of mystery must be the private eye Iwai Jūrō, who is somehow involved in all of Gekkō Kamen's adventures and never appears in a scene with the superhero. However, there is a significant difference between this kind of latent understanding implied by circumstantial evidence and the kind of overt, diegetic on-screen connection revealed to audiences, for instance, when Clark Kent goes into a telephone booth and reappears as Superman. There are no equivalent phone booth transformation (*henshin*) scenes in the *Gekkō Kamen* series, so the audience's hunch is never confirmed or disproved.

That this uncertainty was a deliberate part of the series is clear from the opening title sequence of the first episode in season two, when an overt mistake was made. As the opening credits role, while the theme song repeatedly asks, "Who is Moonlight Mask?," the parts of both Iwai Jūrō and Moonlight Mask are listed together as being played by the single actor Ōse Kōichi. This fleeting slip in the titles listing the same actor as both the private investigator and the superhero reveals perhaps some truth of the extradiegetic world (a truth already presumed about the diegetic one by most viewers), but the evidence would be erased from the credits in the very next and all subsequent episodes, where the actor's name in the dramatis personae for the character of Moonlight Mask is replaced simply with question marks.

Within the story itself, since Iwai's investigations overlap with Gekkō Kamen's just causes, it is never clear whether Iwai is simply working on the same case as Gekkō Kamen, is in cahoots with him, or, in fact, is the hero himself.[42]

Given the narratological premium placed on the mystery of the superhero's true private identity, it comes as no surprise that in the third season, the villains who Gekkō Kamen battles are inversions of himself—literal X-men (goons with huge *X*s painted across their shirts) whose true identities are unnecessary to the functioning of the plot. And though these X-men are clear carryovers from the wartime *kamishibai* (paper theater) hero series *Golden Bat* (*Ōgon batto*), their resurrection in the new medium corroborates two distinct postwar ideas. First, it reinforces the notion that television is a kind of "*denki kamishibai*" (electronic paper theater). Second, it underlines postwar confusion between injustice and justice, criminals and law enforcers, and threats to social stability and their resolution.[43]

The hero's mask connects the postwar situation with the wartime one. This is apparent in the final episode of season two, called "Justice Does Not Die," in which a "Meton bomb" seems to kill Gekkō Kamen. The scene depicting his death is intense. We see the hero on his motorcycle chasing a carful of bad guys who throw the bomb at him. The explosion leaves behind nothing but a cloud of dust. The scene cuts to Detective Iwai's house where the news has just been reported, and a crowd of friends gathers to mourn the loss of their hero. Then slowly the masked face of Gekkō Kamen is superimposed one by one on each member of the entire Iwai household, friends, and staff still sobbing from news of their hero's demise.[44] The otherworldly quality of Gekkō Kamen is grounded in the domestic space of a Japanese family. This grounding renders his superiority, superpower, and aura in this moment not lost but diffused out into the national family. Gekkō Kamen becomes part of the Japanese household, as his enemies are decidedly foreign. Finally, Gekkō Kamen appears, demonstrating that he is alive; but the audience now knows that it would not matter if the hero had died, because he tells us that justice will not die. As the ally of justice, Gekkō Kamen resides inside every one of us—hence the superimpositions; we each have the potential to inhabit the super position of the ally or protector of justice. The scene signifies both the perceived absence of justice and a deep desire for local jurors.

How can we describe this particular form of postwar Japanese justice? Rather than a blind justice that treats all who come before it equally, the show blinds its audience as to the origin of its justice. There is clarity of purpose to this justice. The criminals are known and obvious. But it takes a hero to hold them accountable. This raises questions that surround superhero tales from many cultures: Does superhero justice advocate vigilantism? Is justice or revenge in the name of the nation being pursued? Without a jury, vigilante justice relies on those with rare superpowers rather than on the public.

Of course, the series attempts to relieve anxiety about this tension by leaving open the possibility that we can all become Gekkō Kamen. This possibility of potentially becoming the superhero is what inspires mimetic rivalry. And the mimetic rivalry is itself at least doubled: first, we the audience members are supposed to desire justice so much that we might want to occupy the position of the superhero/judge here in the real world; second, the series itself represents that justice is foreign—they have justice over there (in the United States, in the West) and we Japanese do not; we need justice, they have it; we want what they have. What guarantees the mystery and the possibility that we can occupy the position of the hero through mimetic rivalry is the mask. Because the mask covers identity, it enables substitution and identification even as it reveals anxiety about absence. Frantz Fanon's idea that "black people" need to wear a white mask in the world articulates the larger structure of a world of racial hierarchies at the global level of empire.[45] And the *Gekkō Kamen* series reveals a particular postwar Japanese tinge to this desire for a literally white mask. The Japanese people who crave justice because they have seen it arrive "like a gale force wind" from elsewhere must have a white-masked justice. But the cosplay (dress-up) of the mask ends by revealing that the only possibility of justice is one that is forestalled, deferred, and removed from the here and now. Anyone can take the place of the ally of justice, but in practice it may be that no one will.

Moral Panic, Play, and the Media of Revealing Disguises

If mimicry, imitation, or impersonation (monomane) was a mode of thinking abstractly about media and the question of mimicry at the advent of television for Abe, Ōoka, and Takahashi, *copycatism* (*mohō*) became the term of anxiety that early theorists of the mass medium used in considering the sociological issues around television by the time a child dressed up in a Gekkō Kamen mask and jumped to his death. It was not the first time that media were made the scapegoats for the damage that resulted from mimetic rivalry.

In the early twentieth century, as the new science of psychology was gaining ground, there was already an understanding of the dangers of the then new media of newspapers and film in terms of copycat behaviors. For instance, Terada Seiichi's landmark 1918 book on criminal psychology spends forty of its six-hundred-odd pages on the topic of imitation with section titles like "Imitation and Crime" and "The Essence of Imitation."[46] Terada sees imitation in terms of two roles: the subject or imitator (*mohōsha*) and the object or model. In considering the imitator, he argues that the essence or content and context differ for everyone. In predictably problematic ageist and sexist assertions of his time, he claims that children are more suggestible and open to influence than adults and that women are more susceptible to influence than men. He then categorizes the object of imitation into two subtypes: experiential (*keikenteki*) and external (*gaiteki,* where the object of mimicry lies outside of experience). After citing the mass media of the day (newspapers and magazines) as problematic, Terada suggests that boys are particularly susceptible to adventure novels, crime stories, and their attendant photographs in newspapers.[47]

Such concern for youth and copycat behavior in play or make-believe (*gokko*) have returned cyclically. To be sure, make-believe and new media had a long history going back to the late nineteenth and early twentieth centuries with war make-believe (*sensō gokko*), sword play (*chanbara gokko*), sumo play (*sumo gokko*), and *Zigomar* make-believe *(Jigomaru gokko),* in which children imitated the mediated images they saw in photographs of war and filmic stories of premodern samurai, as well as French films like *Zigomar*.[48] Gekkō Kamen play is but one moment within this long connection between media and copycat make-believe, but it is emblematic of the specific ways in which television could intervene in that history. In the wake of the *Gekkō Kamen* incidents, concerns about imitation and impersonation would become crystalized in a discourse about the relationship between media and make-believe.

With the postwar advent of television, old fears and concerns surrounding new media took on renewed urgency with the growing presence of televisions in Japanese homes. Children leaping into harm's way in their imaginative Gekkō Kamen play not only led to a stigma against the show but also gave credence to the notion that the media and mediated had changed our world. Skepticism toward the new medium resulted in new measures for self-regulation by television stations to proscribe violent content even prior to the cancellation of the show.[49]

The coincidence of violent, copycat, imaginative play and inadvertent or accidental violence prompted the search for scapegoats. Initially, pundits blamed the television, but blaming the new medium became increasingly untenable. This was because television was fast becoming a familiar and fundamental part of life for a growing portion of the Japanese population. Infrastructures, once built, quickly seem self-evident and inevitable parts of the world and unchangeable. So, in the search for a new scapegoat, the content (especially the hero at its center) was next to take the blame, ultimately resulting in the cancellation of the *Gekkō Kamen* series. We scapegoat media then the mediated to displace the rivalry we (critics, psychologists, criminologists, politicians, scholars, and parents) have with one another. It is a rivalry over influence (particularly around children and also over citizens).

The story of scapegoating the form and content of a new medium to atone for the tragic consequences of the mimetic rivalry between youth and the hero also suggests another rivalry—among those who seek to exert ideological influence. In placing blame on the medium (television) and the mediated (the show), educators, public officials, and cultural producers (of older media) reveal their desire to influence the nation's youth and their fear of losing power to the new media. In their rivalry with television, they tried to scapegoat it, but ultimately the medium was spared and only the content sacrificed. It was not so much a displacement of ire toward media onto content (which would suggest that the original target was legitimate) as it was a fetishistic substitution, which led to a repetition of the content to be sacrificed. This substitution that overvalues the power of the content explains why so many masked riders continue the legacy on Japanese television in the wake of *Gekkō Kamen*.

Beyond the cancellation of the *Gekkō Kamen* series, fears of the pernicious influence of television had a lasting impact on how the networks functioned and the kinds of content they were willing to broadcast. In June and July of 1960, new controls on radio and television were announced, including a requirement to delete scenes of violence (*bōryoku bamen*) and flag any such alteration of content.[50] But even after these measures were in place, a televised event once again crystalized fears around the new medium as a scapegoat: the inadvertent live broadcast of the assassination of socialist political leader Asanuma Inejirō on October 12.[51]

In the aftermath of the assassination, in which a seventeen-year-old right-wing terrorist rushed onto the stage during a televised political debate and lethally stabbed Asanuma, the *Asahi* hosted a discussion between prominent social theorist and women's rights activist Ohama Hideko and playwright Uchimura Naoya on the subject of violence on television. Beginning the discussion with the recent instance of televised terrorism, Uchimura comments that the Asanuma incident was shocking and overstimulating (*shigeki-sugimasu*): "If children saw it, they probably thought it was heroic." Then Uchimura expands out beyond the frame of the particular incident to the kind of realism being broadcast into the home, including the recent demonstrations against the renewal of the U.S.–Japan Security Treaty. In response, Ohama laments that there had not been better explanations of the news images for children, claiming that kids were becoming numb (*mahi*) to televisual violence. At this point, she conflates the news images with the sword and pistol play modeled on violent fictional shows (*bōryoku bangumi*), even mentioning the recent incidents of children getting hurt by jumping from rooftops in imitation of Gekkō Kamen. On the one hand, Ohama laments the flattening of the real and fictional images of violence, asking for better context and explanation; on the other hand, this lament about the conflation of the real and fictive acknowledges the means by which the medium acts as a transformative agent.

In thinking about television and its impact on the world, Ohama and Uchimura engage with a theory of the medium proposed as recently as November 1957 when Shimizu Ikutarō published one of the earliest media critiques of television in the journal *Thought* (*Shisō*). In "The Televisual Age," Shimizu famously contrasts print and television. He argues that print actively engages the critical thinking skills of its readers to construct not only the real worlds of fiction in their imagination but indeed their own relation to fiction and, thereby, their identity and subjectivity. By contrast, passive watchers of television simply experience the preconstructed or given televisual world without the possibility of a critically aware self or subject to intervene:

> The anguish, reflection, and study that can only be done in leisure time has become impossible due to television, and human beings are absorbed by reality in the daytime and knocked out by reality in the night, and the given human tendency to transcend reality has no chance to be born.[52]

This notion of the medium spoon-feeding a reality rather than determining what constitutes reality puts all viewers in the naive position of the mesmerized child. Indeed, Shimizu's notion of reality here seems split, like the Lacanian notion of reality and the real, between the mediated reality and a larger objective reality wherein the infant becomes uncritically fascinated by the mirrors of mediation. That a mediating frontal lobe might be short-circuited by the medium itself makes television, for Shimizu, ultimately a reactionary medium that supports the status quo. Though such early ideas that posited television as basically conservative yet implicitly transformative of the world through the subtle ways in which the televisual gaze constructs subjects' views of reality abounded at the level of theory, when Shimizu was publishing they had yet to be given concrete evidence.[53]

By 1960, this notion of the medium as transformative became the subject of a major series of surveys by the Ministry of Education (Monbushō). Using the survey results, children's literature scholar Namekawa Michio wrote a popular sociological book titled *Television and Children* (*Terebi to kodomo*). Published in 1961, just two years after the *Gekkō Kamen* incident, the book focuses on the various ways in which the new medium might transform daily life, paying significant attention to the copycat phenomenon.[54] In addition to raising perennial worries about the consequences of sitting too close to the screen and the impact of lengthy viewing on eyesight, school preparation, concentration, and sleep patterns, the book is most concerned with delinquent and violent behavior correlated to television viewing. From murders and robberies to mundane family arguments over channel selection, the book chronicles undesirable behavior associated with television. Concluding not that television itself is bad but that "watching too much" (*misugiru koto*) might be, Namekawa recognizes television as one medium among many that may have problematic impacts on the lives of young viewers. He writes, "I agree with the survey's conclusion that 'television alone cannot be considered the cause of delinquency,' but I have to admit that, of all the many causes, 'TV is one of them.'"[55] Namekawa calls for a holistic view of the medium to understand the cause of its social impact, insisting that "it is necessary to consider clearly whether it is the 'machine' called the television, the functions that make it work, or the contents of the television shows, or all of these together."[56] In the end, he argues that it is not just the producers but also the receivers who share the blame for the social transformations around television. For Namekawa, the medium's proximity to such acts means that it must at least be a factor. But, of course, defining what kind of factor and determining the degree of ethical culpability for the medium and for acts of violence to which it seems related remain unsolved problems.

Namekawa's concern for the social impact of the new media at the center of many households is most evident in a chapter titled "Imitative Behaviors" ("Kōi no mohō"). Acknowledging that problems similarly accrue around learning from movies, plays, and even family members, Namekawa goes on to make the case that juvenile imitation of the dynamism and excitement on television is only natural. Agreeing with Ministry of Education reports that conclude that "television alone is not the sole cause," Namekawa writes, "although not the sole cause, as a cultural material around the child, it forms part of a very influential 'environment' and thus affects the child's developing mentality."[57] As proof of this impact, Namekawa focuses on behavior. He considers not only the proliferation of children imitating the ubiquitous kisses on television (kissu gokko) but also Gekkō Kamen's popularity and the accompanying craze for "Gekkō Kamen make-believe." He is, of course, particularly concerned with criminal acts and what he terms the "see it, copy it" (miyō mimane) mode of juvenile interaction with television. Even as he repeatedly acknowledges that copycatism may be for good or ill, Namekawa emphasizes the impressionable minds of youth, contrasting "the strength of children's mimicry" with the "weakness" of their "mental capacity for resistance."[58] In this view, television is transformative of society, and especially so for children.

Noting that those juveniles already predisposed to delinquency are most likely to imitate criminal behavior seen on television, the book suggests that the majority of children will not simply carry out actions of the fantastic worlds depicted on television. Far more prevalent than copycat crime, copying television via make-believe is both prevalent and unpredictable. Tellingly, Namekawa mentions that in *Gekkō Kamen* pistol play, homemade pistols are preferred to the uncool (*kakkō yokunai*) mass-produced plastic toy pistols and other goods associated with the show.[59] This sort of opting out of the consumerism overtly promoted by television advertising exemplifies both the inevitability of copycatism (everyone wants to play Gekkō Kamen) and its unpredictability (kids prefer their own homemade costumes to the advertised ones). Recognizing that "the old dream of television as the best media to educate and inform democratic people has never materialized," Namekawa finds a new situation (or new real) in place of that old dream, wherein the effects of television on everyday activities are undeniable but have also become mundane.[60]

Soon after the Gekkō Kamen–play incidents, the *Yomiuri* ran an article titled "Children's Play: Little 'Gekkō Kamens' Take Leaps Unwittingly." Recounting a different incident, the article ponders "dangerous forms of play" in relation to television. Citing the series *Superman,* it suggests that children's longing for heroes is the reason "why they imitate Gekkō Kamen and Akado Suzunosuke and leap off of things." To correct this behavior, it continues, "simply scolding without taking the opportunity for explanation will have no effect." Instead, it explains, the goal of parents and society at large should be to guide "children through bad environments and to bring them up to be obedient." On the one hand, the article notes that it is natural and appropriate for the little Gekkō Kamens "with their *furoshiki* hanging from their shoulders [like capes] while holding pistols in their hands (of course, just toys), to pose with serious faces and say 'I'm an ally of justice'"; after all, the reasoning went, Gekkō Kamen's winning record over one bad guy after another makes him an admirable object of emulation. On the other hand, it cites the many examples of boys injured by tumbling from high places and recalls the story of a young body covered in a furoshiki cape being pulled out of an irrigation canal in the Adachi district and warns that such danger must not be overlooked. The article narrates childish mentality: "In the course of play, they get caught up in the dream and forget . . . , getting caught up in the illusion [*sakkaku*] that they themselves have become the real Gekkō Kamen [*honmono no Gekkō Kamen*] they go for it." Widening the frame of analysis beyond just children, the article recognizes that even adults watch films and identify with the characters, crying or feeling happy, but "this tendency is stronger in immature children."[61] Explaining how the prevalence of this form of play cannot be stopped, it suggests mitigating the dangerous effects and bad influences of the medium by reminding children that the stunts of a fictional story cannot be performed in reality.[62] Whether this was good and realistic advice or simply the human interest grist of a paper looking to address a common middle-class concern, what is clear from the piece is the ubiquity and intractability of such play.

Even though television viewers were unreliable consumers (who occasionally prefer homemade costumes of bath-towel turbans, improvised guns, and furoshiki capes to store-bought ones), the sale of series-related goods and advertising show that copycatism was at the heart of the capitalist media complex. The documentary photographer Hamaya Hiroshi's striking photo of three skiing little Gekkō Kamens gives a sense of this.[63]

What is striking about the photograph is the fact that the three children are all playing at being Gekkō Kamen at the same time. With printed capes of the hero aflutter, they trudge up a hill, skis and poles in hand, to engage in sport while maintaining their make-believe world and realizing not only the wildest dreams of commodifiers of the Gekkō Kamen image but also the in-show message that, in some sense, we can all be Gekkō Kamen. And that message itself was good for sales: instead of one Gekkō Kamen at a time, meaning one mask for three kids, marketers could sell three.

For the ultimate realization of this surplus success of marketing, one need only look to in-character television commercial spots by the stars of *Gekkō Kamen*. For instance, Takeda Pharmaceutical, the sponsor of KRTV's "Takeda Hour," which featured *Gekkō Kamen* and other programs, sought not to merely sell the generic toy masks like those in Hamaya's photo but to relate the hero to products that had little to do with the series by having the actors promote the company's vitamin supplements. An instructive example is the television advertisement for Arinamin, a vitamin B1 supplement. In the advertisement, the actors Ōse Kōichi (in the guise of his character Iwai Jūrō on the show) and Tani Ken'ichi (in the guise of Iwai's sidekick Fukuro Gorohachi) look directly into the camera and implore viewers to take Arinamin to grow strong like Gekkō Kamen, an obvious

Figure 14. Three Moonlight Mask skiers in Hokkaidō. Original caption reads in part: "When it snows, kids in Hokkaidō want Old Man Gekkō Kamen to take them skiing." Hamaya Hiroshi, *Kodomo fudoki: Shashinshū* (Tokyo: Chūō Kōronsha, 1959), 25. Photograph by Hiroshi Hamaya. Copyright Keisuke Katano.

televised gesture encouraging copycatism.[64] The fact that this vitamin supplement was initially developed for the Imperial army to combat beriberi in the colonial pursuits of an earlier era reflects the repurposing of wartime experiences toward marketing copycat behavior—that is, getting viewers to take action in the real world by going out and purchasing the supplement.[65]

In some related marketing gimmicks, the direct play to the mimetic desire through the televisual can be easily sensed. Another Takeda Pharmaceutical *Gekkō Kamen* tie-in advertised the multivitamin Pan-Vitan Pere not only on television but also via a giveaway of *Gekkō Kamen* cardboard masks, complete with turban and blue-tinted cellophane sunglasses for children to wear while playing make-believe.[66] The company was taking advantage of the fact that young fans were already engaged in dressing up as their hero. Obviously, having an army of striking-looking young kids running around with the masks on and "PanVitan" written in big red letters across the mask over their mouths would be useful advertising.

A print newspaper advertisement for PanVitan that appeared in

Figure 15. A Takeda Pharmaceutical advertisement giveaway mask marketing the PanVitan multivitamin. Image from author's collection.

the *Yomiuri* five days before the first death associated with the show cuts to the heart of this marketing of mimetic desires. The ad depicts a young boy staring wistfully into the sky with the tagline "Children dream of jumping like Gekkō Kamen" and a floating image of the hero jumping just above and to the right of the child's head. That drives

Figure 16. Takeda's PanVitan Pere advertisement markets vitamins to realize the desires of children who dream of jumping like their hero. Image reprinted from *Yomiuri Shinbun,* March 24, 1959.

home the point: television had already transformed the dreams of children. The text of this ad promoting Takeda Pharmaceutical's sponsorship would go on to implore parents to capitalize on those desires by purchasing PanVitan Pere to help their kids grow up strong and realize their dreams.[67]

This advertisement is no smoking gun proving a causal relationship between the marketing, the medium, and the tragedy just a few days later, but rather it should remind us of René Girard's studies of mimetic desires. If we desire to be like our heroes, it may be that the ensuing rivalry destroys the trace of the hero or of our individuality. The quest to leap like the hero might have the result of injury. And injury has the result of scapegoating the marketing and media, rather than pointing a finger at individual responsibility.

The role of the mask in postwar Japan was of paramount importance in relation to not only television heroes but also larger issues of psychosocial identity. Critic and philosopher Hanada Kiyoteru writes of the clarity in identity that a mask can provide in this world where nothing is as it seems. Arguing that a mask might better reveal true expressions from its seeming to cover direct access to the face, the essay has been read as the philosophical counterpart to Hanada's interpretation of Mishima Yukio's *Confessions of a Mask*.[68] But its thesis is applicable to the case of a pop cultural product that both depicts mask wearing and behaves like a mask in its stark caricatures and exaggerations. Even though Hanada makes explicit reference to the high culture of Noh theater in the essay, he attempts to show how a particular mode of masking in reaction to the influx of "Western things" (*seiyōteki na mono*) could lead to wartime attitudes.

What Hanada terms the "prototypical schizophrenia" of Japanese nationalism is characterized, he argues, by the attempt to grasp a true face that lies behind a mask. But as he acknowledges this split psychology that maintains a mask as well as a belief in a true face beneath it, Hanada maintains that the face itself is a mask beyond which one cannot penetrate. In other words, even as a face is discovered beneath a mask, the true face moves to a deeper level in a sort of infinite regress of the truth hiding beneath surfaces.[69] Hanada decidedly emphasizes the surface appearance of the mask; the mask is a key medium that illuminates the connection not only between an allegorical fictional world and reality but also between "Japanese things" and "Western things." Although to a certain degree Hanada's choice of the traditional Noh mask fulfills this function, the masks of pop cultural superheroes make his case even starker. For the *Gekkō Kamen* series, the mask does not hide an inner face or truth of postwar justice but rather is itself the truth. The mask (re)presents the contemporary perception of justice—a masked justice that cannot be easily located, identified, or named.

Hanada's thinking about masks as bridges between this surface and another hidden one and as powerful surfaces in and of themselves parallels the thinking of other important philosophers of masks, including Girard, as well as anthropologist Tanigawa Ken'ichi and media guru Matsumoto Toshio. For all of these later thinkers, masks bring god(s) and man together: they are connections between our world and the magical or spiritual one. So wearing a mask becomes a kind of evasion of responsibility—wearing it, the wearer is neither human nor god but somewhere in between. In miming possession from beyond our world, questions of responsibility fade. In rituals, masks inhabit the reclaiming of trauma or performance of a horror, the mimetic desire or copying that needs to be accomplished. In this sense, masks are similar to Girard's monstrous double.[70] For Tanigawa, the medium of the mask between the world of the dead and that of the living is precisely the space where free flow between the two worlds is established; through a kind of mask play, the bridge is maintained.[71] Matsumoto sees the mask in these terms as the medium through which the other world can be performed but also as the means through which the wearer can be transformed.[72] If these thinkers cast masks in terms of the magical and spiritual, it is not hard to see that justice itself was placed in this mystical and mythical position in postwar Japan by the *Gekkō Kamen* series.

The aspirational quality of the series—that it encouraged viewers to strive to be an ally of justice—can similarly exemplify Matsumoto's vision of the transformational power of masks. Matsumoto writes:

> When wearing a scary form of mask, a person unwittingly draws a scary expression inside of the mask. . . . In general, assimilation into a mask is manifested as a desire for transformation into others with great spiritual power, beyond the limits of oneself.[73]

Matsumoto was fascinated by Jean-Louis Bédouin's notion that masks were "attached to supernatural spirits" and, therefore, were in some cultures thought to confer superhuman (*chōningenteki*) powers on their wearers. This understanding of the mask doubles the religiosity or transcendentalism of the media concept, insofar as it parallels the way the tangible (the mask, as a known or visible marker of the unknown, unknowable, or invisible) is connected to the intangible. Here, the notion is that the mask orders, renders, or makes the man and is parallel to the idea of media making content. This is ultimately why, for Matsumoto, masks are but another medium. In his thinking about masks, Matsumoto writes: "The mask [*kamen*] is not a veil [*fukumen*] but a medium of transformation [*henbō no media*]. It not only hides the real face [or bare face, *sugao*], but at the same time actively shows another face. . . . It is the face that you want to be projected into the eyes of others."[74] Matsumoto argues that the mask can ultimately transform its wearer, as well as those around it: "Masks, in that sense, are also media that transform the relationship between us and the world."[75] Here, Matsumoto's idea that a mask is a medium for conveying the inner desires of the wearer and takes into account the gaze of those who witness the performer is similar to Gilbert Simondon's idea of media as enabling a "transindividual"—namely, one who is able to embody more than one identity because of such mediation. This understanding of a mask as a medium of transformation that presents the desires of the masked rather than obscuring them is key to seeing the superhero mask, television series, and medium for what they are—technology or, rather, cultural material that both represents and constitutes reality.[76] More than an allegorical interpretation, it allows us to read the mask for what it is (rather than for what lies beneath it or what it stands for). The mask is a blank screen upon which imagination from both sides (within the mask and outside it) has run amok. The mask, then, is of course but another television screen for broadcasting and receiving.

Unpredictability and the Mask

Writing about more recent television history, Thomas Lamarre brings to light the embodiment and unpredictability of mimetic actions around the medium. Lamarre argues that televisual anime mediation particularly lays bare the dispositif or mechanism of control at the center of television as a network medium. Though his book does not claim that what it describes begins with anime, it argues that with anime, and especially its attendant epileptiform seizure discourse around the Pokémon Shock of 1997, what is true of television writ large rises to the surface—namely, that it has the power to control society in direct and indirect ways that are nevertheless unpredictable. If the epileptic seizures purportedly induced by the flashing lights of *Pokémon,* the sensational reporting around the Pokémon Shock incident reflects a fear of media contagion around television, even though the root mechanism is a transmedial effect more cinematic (flicker and dark room related) than televisual. What creates the shocking sense of viral contagion or pandemic around "haunted media" is the combination of both forms, the cinematic transmitted across the national television network (a cinema all at once: if not one with a liveness, at least one with a togetherness).[77]

For Lamarre, television anime shows like *Pokémon, Detective Conan,* and *Crayon Shin-chan* reveal more clearly than nonanime the transformative and unpredictable role of television in our lives. For example, he discusses the young impish manga and anime character Crayon Shin-chan, who dances wildly in front of the television while watching his hero, Action Mask (Akushon Kamen), a masked rider in the Gekkō Kamen and Kamen Rider lineage. The *Crayon Shin-chan* series rehearses some of Plato's and Aristotle's greatest fears about the iniquities around mimesis. Lamarre writes:

> The charged field in front of the TV becomes a zone for a particular kind of play—the kind Walter Benjamin evokes in his accounts of semblance and the mimetic faculty: the child mimicking the windmill or imitating the passage of clouds. So do the movements on the television screen course through Shin-chan's body. He does not internalize its messages. He may not even hear them, and if he did, Shin-chan would not grant them any more authority than he grants any other figures of authority—parents, teachers, shop clerks, which is to say adults in general. Consequently, as a result of his general rejection of authority and hierarchy, Shin-chan introduces a tentative split within the one-to-many tendency of broadcast television, a split between a hierarchical tendency (centralized authority) and a unidirectional tendency. The result is a very different way of understanding (and performing) the effects of television.[78]

We see a copying or miming occurs, but whether the message or ideology behind the hero is internalized (whether the miming of movements corresponds to a faith in the hero's principles or presents ironic critique of them) remains up for grabs. Here, Lamarre uncovers the inevitability, indeterminacy, and unpredictability of mimicry at the heart of the medium. The fact that this theorization of the mimetic tendencies of the Shin-chan/television nexus happens in manga is of significance for Lamarre because it reveals anime's transmedial mix. It is not that anime alone does this but that anime's remediation as manga presents a critique of anime and television. This notion can return us to Matsumoto Toshio's notions of mediation through mask. Matsumoto ends with the notion that the mask bridges the visible and the invisible: the interior and exterior dichotomy is doubled by the mask and, therefore, exposed or put on display by the mask. This is a mediation of mediation already present in something like the body's mediation of the mind. But that too presumes a mind–body split. What is clear in Lamarre's understanding of the television as media is that there is no split. The mind is body. The body mind. Shin-chan, like the Pokémon-shocked children, just goes into his thing; without any frontal lobe thinking, television is simply embodied.

To understand this role of mimesis and mimicry, our return to the dawn of television heroes is useful. In 1958—the same year in which Lamarre makes a point of telling us that Usui Yoshito, the creator of Shin-chan, was born—the new technology of television created the need to produce content for broadcast. In Japan, at least in the short term, much of that content initially came from outside the country, where it was already being produced—specifically from Hollywood. Indeed, *Gekkō Kamen* was created using a transmedial method that emulated American shows like *Laramie, Adventures of Superman,* and *The Lone Ranger.* The new mixed media format was developed for the sole purpose of capturing American-style action stories, the "television film" (*terebi eiga*)—shot on film stock, edited in a film studio, and then broadcast on television. This brought filmic special effects and stunts into the medium of television, which was still largely dominated by live broadcasts. This transfer of 16-millimeter films to television (like anime taking on filmic and manga-like characteristics in Lamarre's view) works against the idea that the essence of the televisual medium was its liveness; rather, this kind of remediation shows how one medium can amplify another.[79] Indeed, the remediation of older forms is part of what makes new media seem new, because they can package and deliver the familiar in a different way. And because of the success of the *Gekkō Kamen* television series, six films featuring the hero were shot in 1958 and 1959 on one of the newest film formats: the wide-aspect-ratio proprietary medium TōeiScope, which like other "scopes" of the late 1950s used an anamorphic lens to give a panoramic experience during projection. The scope experience remade cinema in relation to television. Cinema became a distinct spectacular experience from the boxier 4:3 aspect ratio (formerly of film) seen as mundane and everyday with the entrance of the television into the home. Even in its early moments, television was, therefore, already justifying and affecting the film production world.

The unconscious, embodied, and unpredictable reverse mimesis characterizing the response to television that Lamarre exposes can be found even in this early moment of the media. The unconscious and unintended impact of the media on our world (such as those of the Pokémon Shock) can be found, for instance, in the media reports of fires caused by new electronics in the home. Long before the Pokémon Shock, not flashes but sparks caused a particular kind of anxiety about the new media. In those early years, the press conflated fears of new media as a gadget in the home with fears of the mediated. A case in point, in 1962 a newspaper reported that a fire in Tokyo's Shiinamachi was caused by the new electric gadget overheating; the excitement around the cathode-ray tube was not only what it projected onto a screen but also the heat it generated behind it. To be sure, some of the "'dangers' of television" were not mimetic in the representational sense, but they did threaten households in real ways. The fact that the article puts quotation marks around "dangers," as if to draw attention to this unexpected danger, suggests that readers had been aware of other dangers around the new medium. Indeed, the article presents itself as a public relations message to raise awareness because, while the dangers of propane gas and washing machines were well understood, "the average housewife cannot be expected to have a wariness of such things as television fires."[80] Beyond the overheating appliance fires that were the source of one kind of panic, the molding of how children and adults alike saw the world was the cause of a moral panic that scapegoated the media itself.

Gekkō Kamen represented mediation and its intervention in the world via in-story newscasts about crimes to the ever-present radio and telephone mediation linking characters with crimes and criminals. This was conspicuously clear in the television backdrop that included a structure actually being erected in Tokyo and captured in episode nine of the "Treasures of Baradai Kingdom" season and in episodes two and three of the "Dokuro Mask" season. The now-iconic Tokyo Tower was completed in 1958 to boost transmission of television signals across the Kantō region. Though television had been broadcast to mass audiences in Japan since 1953, it was not until the production of mass market units and payment schemes were developed that Nippon Denpatō NHK invested more to build a larger broadcasting hub in the megalopolis.[81] The construction of the tower coincided with the shooting of these two seasons of *Gekkō Kamen,* and it was used as a backdrop in both. The appearance of the broadcasting tower within a television show itself is not so much a reflection or representation of the changed landscape that television brought to the city and nation as an instantiation of that change. By including the tower under construction, the show documented the arrival and captured the future of television, even as that future was being realized in the transitional remediated form of television film (*terebi eiga*).

In the above fire report and the depiction of the rise of the TV broadcast network tower caught in the backgrounds of *Gekkō Kamen,* the presence of television in daily life can be glimpsed. But the mimicry that happens in front of the screen or in the daily presence of television in the home with unexpected results dominated the early discourse on the new medium. The expectation was that people would mimic what they saw on television, but the discourse reflects a disappointment about the unpredictable results of such mimetic behaviors. Acts resembling Shin-chan's unruly mimicry abound in the media reports around *Gekkō Kamen.* One variety was a kind of internal entertainment industry mimicry, including mundane attempts to capitalize on the success of the series through the spin-off show *Harimao* or Ōsei's subsequent career on the Takeda Hour action shows. There are also less directly related examples, such as the 1959 Tōei thriller *The Squirrel and the American* (*Risu to Amerika-jin*), which tried to capitalize on the image of a man in a turban and white mask depicting a character in a white mask and head covering on all of the posters and promotional materials, leading a *Yomiuri* review to call it an "imitation [*magai*] *Gekko kamen.*"[82] This discourse presents a slow rewiring of the understanding of the world through the series such that questions of justice eventually become synonymous with the hero, as well as evidence of a new real.

The debates around the role of television in transforming the home, society, and nation were certainly not limited to *Gekkō Kamen,* but the series brings into focus how the medium changed the environment. There were both negative and positive stories about mimetic behaviors that grew beyond simple make-believe. Though not exactly a copycat case, one reference to the *Gekkō Kamen* series appeared in nonentertainment news just days before the story associating the series with the death of a child, in an odd crime story of a gang robbing public telephones caught in a restaurant in Nagoya. One of the nineteen-year-old members of the gang was an actor who had played a policeman and been a stuntman in the *Gekkō Kamen* series. The news stories covering the story all headlined with this fact versus fiction reversal, the *Yomiuri* leading with "*Gekkō Kamen* Actor Arrested," and the *Japan Times* echoing with "Young TV 'Cop' Turns Out to Be Crook in Real Life."[83] This surprise or thrill at the inversion between representation and reality was countered several months later with a story of an eighteen-year-old night watchman for a bank in Ikebukuro whom the papers would label Gekkō Kamen after he jumped down from a six-foot concrete wall to apprehend a knife-wielding bank robber.[84] This night watchman and everyday hero in our real world stands in relation to the fictional superhero, whether he was inspired to take action by the television or was simply understood after the fact through the televisual metaphor. Both of these true crime stories are forms of a reverse mimesis, which mimes the mediated image or uses it to make sense of the real occurrence.

This was not a one-off event but can be seen in many real-life events that occurred during the run of the series. An example can be found in a July 1960 news reel that compared the striking Miike miners to Gekkō Kamen not only for wearing masks (to avoid the tear gas of police) but also for behaving like allies of justice by avoiding bloodshed in their strike.[85] This sort of cultural embedding of the popularly mediated image can be seen again a few years later in a February 20, 1963, *Asahi* article titled "We Should Be Scared of Young Teens: What Creates Them?" The article answers its titular question with the simple assertion that the root cause of increasing adolescent violence is copycat behavior mimed from television and film. Mentioning a recent incident of delinquency in which middle schoolers stole money from their teacher in imitation of the *Baby Gang* series of films that debuted in 1961, the article cites psychology scholar Yamashita Toshio imploring producers of television and film content to consider this phenomenon of juvenile imitation in the creation of their work. The article also notes work being done by a research group within the National Police Agency (Keisatsuchō kagaku kenkyūjo kankyō kenkyūshitsu) that found that direct imitation (*chokusetsu mohōsei*) was prevalent among elementary to middle schoolers and indirect or mediated imitation (*kansetsu mohōsei*) was more common among middle school and older students. This meant that "early teens" partake in "adventure" play, mixing reality and fantasy such that excessive violence can easily transform "whatever-whatever make-believe" into "whatever-whatever crime" (*OO-gokko ga OO-hanzai ni kawari yasui*). The article concludes by referencing critic Ohama Hideko's claim that children doing poorly at school fell into these types of crimes due to the high-pressured game of school advancement and a lack of guidance.[86] This rewiring of our outlook on the world through the medium is what Heidegger means when he writes that it has become impossible to hear the raw sound of an engine—for such mediated technological material mediates our experience of the world.[87]

Second Wave: The Politics of Moonlight Mask

Seeing the world through the lens of the series would have profound effects on those who had grown up with it. The impact of the series can be seen everywhere. What is sacrificed in the belief in the hero is a sense that justice is here in normal, daily life. The superhero series shows how justice is not anything but mediated, fantastical, magical, or mythical. Conversely, when the dream of a superhero-style justice is relinquished, it is not just that youth dies but that maturity itself is sacrificed. Those who grow up believing that someone else (not from around here) will provide justice may never grow up to become responsible citizens to take over the real mantle of enforcement of justice.

After a nearly two-decade lull, *Gekkō Kamen* experienced a resurgence in its influence on popular culture in the late 1970s. But there was something different about the show's renewed popularity. In the late 1950s, cultural references to the series cashed in by connecting to a new fad, but by the 1970s, it was the show's retro cult status that made it useful for explaining nonmainstream culture. Decades after its airing, the show continued to have a lingering cultural cachet for those who had grown up with it, giving it an air of the avant-garde even as a new anime version would revive the character for a younger audience.[88] In this transformation, we can see nostalgia for a time when pure justice seemed like a worthwhile fantasy.

In the 1950s, the series was evoked in mainstream culture often to justify nonstandard behaviors as just. Its pervasiveness can be seen in a brief flash in Ozu Yasujirō's *Ohayō* (*Good Morning*, 1959), a film that depicts a story in which children pester their parents for a television set to watch sumo. This depiction of children's culture would not be complete without at least a quick reference to the pop-culture television superhero: in a game of *shiritori* (a word-chain game), the schoolteacher calls for a word that begins with a final sound in the word *kiku, ku*. A young boy eagerly raises his hand to give the answer and he is called on. He stands, blurting out, "Gekkō Kamen!," only to be told he has made a mistake by giving a word that begins with *ge*. This sort of passing reference evokes the buzz around the series without directly referencing its content. And it also shows how something like the actual *Gekkō Kamen*–themed iroha card games had helped to rewire young brains by illustrating the sounds of the Japanese syllabary with phrases connected to the show. In a version of the syllabary game marketed to coincide with one of the six Tōei *Gekkō Kamen* films, the card for the hiragana character *mi,* for instance, gives the phrase "Mina terebi de *Gekkō Kamen*" (Everyone watches *Gekkō Kamen* on television). Here, the goods sold to promote the spin-off movie of the remediated TV movie series announce the truth that television had superseded the older medium.[89]

New wave director Ōshima Nagisa's film *Street of Love and Hope* (*Ai to kibō no machi,* 1959) referenced the show's content to suggest the political naivete of a young woman. When the middle-class, Pollyanna-type character Kuhara Yoko is challenged by her brother to justify her behavior toward the working-class student Masao, who resells pigeons to make money, she claims that she is simply "an ally of justice, Gekkō Kamen." The statement suggests her childlike view of the real world. This scene about the role of the superhero in the real world was then used by critic and philosopher Hanada Kiyoteru (who had a decade before connected masks to wartime schizophrenia) to explain the false sense of justice held by the still relatively obscure but up-and-coming director Ōshima himself in an article titled "An Ally of Justice: Theorizing Ōshima Nagisa."[90] Ōshima's entire political project of pursuing justice in the real world through art that exposes inequalities, abuse, and corruption cuts against the childishness of the faceless justice meted out in the *Gekkō Kamen* series.

But for Hanada, even Ōshima's staunch idealism seems childish and removed from reality precisely because it remains naive and impractical. He writes that a mask allows "A to be both A and not-A," thus enabling a truth-telling about identity through erasure: we are all both ourselves and not ourselves alone.[91] Ōshima's critical film successes stemmed from his ability to mask critique with a sly appeal to the masses through sensual youth drama. But what Hanada's critique of Ōshima's and, implicitly, of our superhero's mask reveals is that our own true selves are simply masks. To unmask Ōshima or Gekkō Kamen is to render them no longer who they are. Rather than revealing a buried identity, unmasking them would remove their identities altogether.

Ozu and Ōshima were not the only serious filmmakers who reflected interest in the pop phenomenon. Terayama Shūji's cult classic *Emperor Tomato Ketchup* (1971) features an army of children dressed in shirts marked with an X as both a mark of negativity and as a satire of fascism through the Anpo demonstrations as well as paying homage to the *kamishibai* and *Gekkō Kamen* villains of decades before.[92] Soon after, Terayama made direct reference to the early television series in a detailed explication titled "Tiny Colossus: Gekkō Kamen." As precisely as Umberto Eco's allegorical reading of *The Amazing Adventures of Superman* series homes in on the problems of identification and repetition in the protection of private property, Terayama focuses particularly on the issue of justice and vigilantism in the *Gekkō Kamen* series. The article is perhaps the most interpretive piece on the series from that later time period and is, therefore, worth quoting at length:

> Beginning with World War II (when the true face of justice became perverted towards the true face of evil, and justice was lost), ethics had to hide its face. So we placed our hopes and despairs on a champion of justice who "appears like a whirlwind, and disappears like a whirlwind." It wasn't the champion of justice, but justice itself that we had begun to doubt. We came to think that the very criterion for determining justice did not exist. . . .
>
> That is to say, Gekkō Kamen and young detectives cannot be mobilized during an international incident like the Vietnam War. There, things like justice and evil become confused and intermeshed; and both sides claim the mantle of just cause, so participants are forced to choose their justice. That guy Gekkō Kamen

and the young detectives, who cannot hold views of justice that account for such things, work for an already pre-defined justice. . . .

The Japanese Red Army had their own laws and justice, their own executions and people's trials for comrades. . . . If Gekkō Kamen were to suddenly appear, as a champion of justice, I wonder what actions he would take.

"The Law is the killy-loo bird of the sciences," wrote Fred Rodel (*Woe Unto You, Lawyers!* 1939). A killy-loo is a bird that flies backwards. Law too is based on the principle of the past and adherence to precedent making "a vice of innovation and a virtue of hoariness." . . . When Gekkō Kamen retreats behind his cape, I often wonder if he is flying progressively into the future or flying backwards.[93]

Part of the generation that grew up watching *Gekkō Kamen*, Terayama links the contemporary (tele)vision of justice directly to larger social ills, deftly weaving connections between seemingly disparate phenomena—the sense of justice lost after World War II and the contemporary issues of the Vietnam War and the Japanese Red Army—through the guise of the mysterious protector of an ambiguous justice. Terayama's justice is either progressively flying toward some future place when its essence will always be clear and present or wildly flitting away like some backward-flying killy-loo (presumably a regression into aggressive and oppressive wartime imperial justice). When it is masked, Terayama seems to intimate, the possibilities for justice are open and ambivalent. What is ultimately hidden under Gekkō Kamen's mask, then, is the fact that there is no universal justice. But the fact that Terayama uses Gekkō Kamen to explain what at the time seemed to the mass media as unexplainable (the televisual spectacles of the Vietnam War and the Red Army) should tell us that *Gekkō Kamen* had become a useful tool for understanding the mediated world. Terayama transformed a signifier of the childishness of unquestioned universal justice to a symbol that could explain the ambiguities and ambivalences of any justice.

The tendency to see the problems of postwar Japan in stark relief through the guise of *Gekkō Kamen* continues into the twenty-first century. For instance, economist Kaneko Masaru reads former prime minister Koizumi Junichirō's deflationary-era policies of bailing out banks as an attempt to become a "Gekkō Kamen" who saves the economy by enabling those responsible for the bubble economy to get off the hook, but implicit in his Marxist critique is that only fundamental structural reform of the economy could rescue Japan.[94] More recently, one of Terashima Jitsurō's series of articles in the general interest magazine *The World* (*Sekai*) sees the latent passivity of postwar Japanese society prefigured in children's television programming of the late 1950s; in his view, the long-running young swordsman series *Akado Suzunosuke*, whose hero magically waves his hands in the air, and Gekkō Kamen, who appeared out of thin air on a Honda motorcycle (an engine of the postwar economy) to mete out justice, contributed to the recent drift toward remilitarization and belligerent mindsets among those fifty- and sixty-year-olds who grew up in the late 1950s and early 1960s and who run the country today.[95] This sort of oneiric reading of the real world through the series is best seen in its use by a recent politician. By the 1980s, forty-year-old right-wing activist Tsujiyama Kiyoshi (a child at the time of the original television series) famously began dressing up as Gekkō Kamen to protest a number of things from scandals involving Aum Shinrikyō to the Kobe child murders (*Kōbe renzoku jidō sasshō jiken*) and what he felt had been poor treatment by the press.[96] As his web profile stated, he saw himself as "Moonlight Mask, admirer of justice" (seigi wo ai suru Gekkō Kamen).[97] He donned the cape and white turban, complete with crescent moon, to portray himself on the side of an imaginary justice that no longer seemed to him to exist in the real world, perhaps as the only way he saw as possible to bring that kind of justice into the real world. There is also a significant difference between the case of a child jumping to his own harm in the late 1950s and the cosplay of an aging activist through the 1980s and 1990s; if the child in the early postwar years was jumping out of respect and admiration for the hero's sense of justice, the avant-garde activist in the 1990s wore the garb to grab attention and highlight frustration, hypocrisy, and a general lack of justice in the real world.

Regarding the dynamic that implicates violent representations and the cultures that accrue around them, it helps to consider our presentist notions of the content of the media (anime or video game sex and violence) and its supposed connection to such real-world behaviors. By rerouting such present interests today through a *détournement* into a similar historical concern around an early postwar version of a similar problem of supposed copycat accidents, crimes, and misdemeanors, this chapter has shown that the *Gekkō Kamen* series was neither the first nor the last in a long line of pop cultural icons that seemingly produced reprehensible actions. Our distance from it in time and space may make it seem less incendiary than consideration of the same issues around the real-world effects of cultural material from porn to horror, from video gaming to web 2.0 social media interactivity, and from online bullying to radicalization. The effects of mimetic rivalry can be seen not only in the viewer's relation to the media's creation of fictional worlds but also through the role of mediated information transforming our world.

In a February 1979 special issue of *The Tide* (*Ushio*) magazine dedicated to the issue of "Television and the Japanese people," critic Akatsuka Yukio argues that television is transforming our desires in an article titled "The Topicalization of 'Copycat Crime.'" For instance, Akatsuka cites how television advertising created the perceived necessity for an electric futon drier where there had previously been no such perception. This sort of creation of desire was all well and good, he claims, when it came to selling goods, but, in the wake of televised coverage of a high school prostitution scandal, he cautions that television was too powerful a factor on the impressionable minds of youth. Introducing the recently coined neologism *copycat crime* (*mohō hanzai*) as German in origin (presumably from *Nachahmungstäter,* which appears in 1978), Akatsuka discusses the rise of these kinds of crimes across Europe and the United States, finally pointing to the Japanese television coverage of the Klaxon Incident, in which a driver who excessively used his horn was killed in an act of road rage, as the cause for multiple subsequent road crimes. The article finally concludes with a sentiment that still resonates in the era of fake news transforming reality: more than reality or facts being recorded as information on the new media, Akatsuka claims that nowadays "there are many times when information creates reality."[98] While this view would gain force during the successive televised terrorist events, as well as the lone wolf otaku incidents of the 1970s to 2000s, at its base is the way reality and imagination or fiction could intertwine through the television.[99] The slippage between the mediated reality of televisual coverage of the news and the creation of events

designed for livestreamed news coverage overlaps and cyclically repeats to the point where distinguishing between origin and copy no
longer makes sense, like some oneiric ouroboros.

Miyabe Miyuki's crime novel *Copycat Crime* (*Mohōhan*, 1995), the
film based on it (directed by Morita Yoshimitsu, 2002), and the recent
TV Tokyo television miniseries (2016) based on the novel together
portray copycat crime and true crime discourse in Japan over the
past fifty years through the televisual lens. The multivolume novel
foregrounds the media and features technologies of reproduction,
capture, replication, and distortion from copying handwriting, to
scanners and voice distorters, video recorders, photography, and
faxes. And the episodic tale repeats itself, retelling or copying the
story out in each successive volume of the paperback edition with
increasing detail from various perspectives: from the point of view
of the policeman, then the journalist, and later a suspect, dwelling at
length on the perspective of the victims' families, and finally taking
the perpetrators' vantage points.

Author Miyabe's doppelgänger in the character of journalist Maehata Shigeko stages the infinite regress of copying. Maehata is trying
to solve the murders, but at the same time, she is caught up in the ethics of collecting, copying, and circulating the grisly details of personal
and private horrors and violence committed upon a group of young
women and two men. Maehata's character gives Miyabe the chance
to comment on and theorize the primary social function of true crime
stories as well as crime fiction. The journalist justifies her own prying
into the private lives of the victims' families knowing that her work
of publishing (copying out and repeating) the details of the crimes
in public can have a feminist cause—exposing the deep moral trans-
gressions of the crimes, short-circuiting the twisted logic of the individuals perpetrating them, and hopefully causing a social shift that
will begin from the recognition that something is deeply amiss with
a society that produces violence against women on such a mass scale
(of which the string of murders is but the tip of the iceberg). Here,
Maehata believes strongly that her writing (just words) can have an
impact if it exposes the facts. But her ultimate direct action in the
world consists of a fiction (words of a different sort).

In her final confrontation on national television with the perpetrator, Maehata does her best to expose the truth by creating a fiction.
With the goal of provoking a confession from the criminal master-

mind inaptly named Peace, Maehata takes everything she knows about the truth of the case to create a fiction or lie. The perpetrator desires to be a mastermind, desires to control and manipulate, desires to be creative, desires in short to be the bohemian artiste born sui generis—that is, one who produces totally unique art, unlike anything before. Maehata asks a friend who is a crime fiction buff to borrow a very old and obscure American paperback that has not been translated: "I wonder if you could lend me one? The older the better. I don't mind what it's about—just as long as it's a book that hardly anyone's ever heard about."[100] She then holds the book up before Peace (the would-be mastermind) on television and says that everything we know about the serial crime spree was copied from this book. This lie, the fiction, or fake news has its desired effect and Peace is provoked to confess. This kind of mimesis, a mimetological view of mimesis, a metamimesis, or a reverse mimesis becomes obvious when our attention shifts from the contents or image being mimed to the form or media of its miming. This is the "perpetual allusion" elaborated by Derrida on Stéphane Mallarmé and Plato: mimesis without a mimed original. It is the problem noted by Erich Auerbach to have been of a Western concern, a desire for a reality and a fictional veneer over it.

In the 2002 film version, the perpetrator recognizes the journalist's bluff and encourages television viewers to check the internet about the facts; and then, as though to add another piece of evidence to prove that the crimes were original, nevertheless confesses. The 2016 television miniseries version of the scene is more closely faithful to the novel. The confrontation is depicted amid intensifying music and frenetic cutting between the televised show and the televisual audience such that it becomes clear that what motivates the confession from the murderer is the thought that his audience might consider him to have copied. Here, the artist/murderer is insulted that his audience might think of him as a plagiarist criminal. And, indeed, since Maehata is lying to trap the egomaniac, we the audience of the television miniseries understand what the audience of the reality television show within it do not—namely, that the murderer is telling the truth when he claims to be an original and the journalist is lying. This is to say the titular copying of *Copycat Crime* is not a copy of a specific mediated crime per se. But we also know that Maehata's lie in the story about a book representing a crime (like Miyabe's real-world novel) itself is a fictional truth. That is, though Maehata's story about the

American book is false, as Miyabe's story about it is a fiction, both are based on truth.

We know there are, of course, other mediated copycat crimes in reality, and even if this one is not a direct copy, it is iterative of others. Indeed, Miyabe's book, which was originally serialized in the *Weekly Post* (*Shūkan posuto*) from November 1995 to October 1999, is to some degree a light fictionalization of the real-world crimes of otaku Miyazaki Tsutomu's killing spree known as the Saitama-Tokyo kidnapping and murder incidents (1988–89) and the Kobe child serial murders (which played out during the serialization of Miyabe's book in 1997). That Miyabe chooses these incidents and ones like it to replay in her fiction is a way for her to stage the media's role in the spectacle and sensationalization of crime. In this way, the book and subsequent versions of *Copycat Crime* show in stark relief the kind of moral panic and real-world repercussions of mimetic rivalry that are ever present but somehow more salient in our hyper-media-saturated world today. Miyabe seems to recognize that copycat crime is both a "moral panic" and a possible reality that routes through media. That is, she shows us the power of journalistic narrative and fantastical stories for reality, as well as the power they cannot possess—namely, the power to be perfect predictors of future crime. This is because of both a mimetic fallacy (Brewer's idea that a mediation can ever accurately portray reality) and the mimetic faculty (Benjamin's notion that humans are inherently mimetic machines). We all copy, but we necessarily copy imperfectly.

Since worries about the corrupting effects of cultural material on the supple minds of youth have returned cyclically in recent years, promoted by pop psychologists, politicians, and television pundits, lamenting a seeming increase of violence in manga and video games and the seeming parallel increase in real violence among children, then it may be time once again to return to the question of the real-world repercussions of fictional representations. If individual responsibility must be assigned for such crimes, whether the 2008 Akihabara stabbing incident (*Tōrima Jiken*) or the 2019 Kyoto animation arson attack (*Kyōto Animēshon hōka satsujin jiken*), the cultural material environments in which these incidents appeared to be saturated must also be examined to assess the question of culpability. The following chapter examines this aspect of representation and mimicry in terms of environment through the concept of ecomimesis.

5

Interpassive Ecomimesis
Gaming the Real

Since their debut in mainstream consumer culture in the mid-1970s, computers and their consumer-entertainment interfaces have been connected to a futurist imagination of new and cutting-edge technologies within their marketing rhetoric, remediations in other media, and the worlds depicted in the games. Central to these utopian dreams have been presumptions about virtual interaction, education, social connection, and world-building. Along with these promises of new media came moral panics around games that featured role-playing murder, mayhem, and visions of the end of our world (and of hitherto unknown worlds). So, as in the earlier case of television, video games have been imbued with the hopes of a society seeking new tools for education and family bonding and the fears of a society that needs a scapegoat to blame for its dissolution.

This chapter examines the tendency of video games to posit player avatars who control the fate of a world. In terms of the effects they may have on the world through reverse mimesis, such games are not necessarily good or bad; these games could just as easily be argued to convince people to act together to do incremental things in which participation constructs and affects the world as we know it (like recycling and voting) as they might overplay the role of the individual, appealing to the powerless who fantasize about megalomaniacal control. The first tendency is actually disregarded in many video games, especially ones that depict a dystopian (realist?) world in which social institutions of government, school, family, media, etc., have failed, such that all that is left to transform the world is the individual. The genre that names this type of narrative is the "world type" (or *sekai-kei*). Though not identified as a genre until the early 2000s, its roots can be traced to science fiction novels in the 1980s. Over the ensuing decades, sekai-kei became a mainstay in manga, anime, light novels, and video games. This chapter argues that because of its claims on control, video games in particular became one natural home for the genre. In reinscribing the game/metagame division, these sekai-kei games speak to the problem of the perceived failure of social institutions in the real world; at the same time, they are realized as another mechanism for building the social.

Early video-gaming culture produced few great theories of gaming but rather staged theory in the form of thought experiments played out in other media (because as yet, games were thought to simply suggest what they could later become). Again and again throughout the 1980s, the cultural material around games such as advertisements, novels, television shows, and films depicted games in their glory as educational media that might reunite the family, as well as in their most problematic form as artifacts of moral panics around both the future of schools and family and the fate of the world. So prior to examining a specific sekai-kei game to show how it intervenes in this history, it will help to look at three key early moments through other media: at the time when video game consoles were becoming dominant in the home, the 1983 film *The Family Game* by Morita Yoshimitsu subtly centers on an almost absent video game, a 1985 novel by Murakami Haruki depicts games as one of several media demarcating and connecting bifurcated worlds, and a 1986 essay by Betsuyaku Minoru about sports television became the foundation for sekai-kei theory. If the notion that life is a game is a way of bracketing or softening the harsh realities of postwar economic struggles, then in essence *The Family Game* rehearses an early version of Robert Pfaller's interpassivity through the outsourcing of education to a tutor.[1] The consideration of everyday life as a game gives over to the notion that the geostrategic fate of the world is a kind of game in *Hard-Boiled Wonderland and the End of the World,* a novel in which the protagonist will ultimately have to choose one of two worlds in which to dwell. By positing that an individual has control over their own harmonization with their environment, the novel marks a kind of romantic ecomimesis that intends to construct a safe space for its protagonist, built entirely for him. And yet in doing so, it instantiates the lack of harmony it seeks to shore up. It is only in the later sekai-kei video games where these tensions are brought to the fore and made overt.

Drawing on and extending theories of interpassivity (the notion that technology allows us to outsource our activities in order that we achieve some homeostasis) and ecomimesis (the notion that media record our incessant desire to harmonize with our environment), this chapter then traces two major intersecting strains of gaming discourse in Japan—family disconnect and the end of the world. The 2009 visual novel game *Steins;Gate* attempts to resolve the inherent conflicts arising out of long-standing early gaming concepts (the myth of interactivity, the loss of family and the atomization of the individual, the megalomaniacal individual desire to control or save the world), though it fails to do so because of the rigidity of the medium. Yet, the contemporary practice of *jikkyō purei* (playthrough videos with running commentary, or literally "real, on-the-spot play") mimetically affects social interaction from the vantage point of social media and advertising. If interpassivity is part of the labor precarity of the stagnation of postindustrial economies, then such play—as preparation for underemployment—is most visible when outsourced to the game itself.[2] If ecomimesis reveals the fiction of a clear demarcation between environment (metagame or real world) and subjective world (game world), its natural genre must be sekai-kei (world-lineage) and its natural medium video games. This look into the game and beyond it illustrates how the complex medium of the video game plays at representing the real and how such play itself transforms the world.

W(h)ither the Family and the World? Interpassive Play and Ecomimesis

Robert Pfaller marks an increase in "interpassivity" writ large as part of the contemporary search for play, suggesting that play itself is a parallel to interpassivity.[3] *Interpassivity* refers to the dynamic whereby the normal actions and activities of everyday life move to media: recording a television show replaces watching, as the consumer merely plays at watching by collecting videotapes or DVR files.[4] The outsourcing of parenting to a tutor upon which the 1983 film *The Family Game* is premised establishes the interpassive mechanics of play and gaming as its undergirding theme.

Gaming is important to the film not only because trailers featured the 8-bit sounds of gaming but also because *The Family Game* forces its viewers into the position of a player of a video game, there simply to enjoy the characters and play rather than find a deeper underlying meaning. Game critic Yoshioka Hiroshi compares it to the world of the 1987 film *Hatchaki Sensei's Tokyo Game,* where game and reality can be distinguished:

> The film *Family Game* (1983) by Morita Yoshimitsu eerily predicts the form of our current situation, in which reality and game are fused. In short, the message of this film is that that even family life is no more than a kind of role-playing. As game logic has penetrated even into the most intimate of living spaces, the boundary between the game and reality has disappeared. In other words, it has become difficult to see the programming for this world that generates "games as reality."[5]

The notion that our postmodern global reality is simply a game in which humanity has drifted so far from engagement with the brutal realities of the world has become a commonplace. That daily struggles are trivialized through their gamification is the drivel and grist of a particular contemporary pose of critical theory that sleekly seeks to align postwar performances of apolitical stances, abstractions from the reality of game theory, and risk-bundling strategies with the growth and bursting of bubble economies and the postmodern disavowal of meaning. But what has allowed critics to even argue that everything is a game, that life is a game, is not simply the advent and proliferation of game theory, computer modeling, and derivative markets but the prevalence of video games themselves in daily life. This notion that all the world is a game has become such a commonplace saying in our postmodern global reality that it is hard to imagine that it once seemed a critical revelation. The film's ambiguity does not encourage viewers to take an active role in playing the film, in order to interpret a moral to the story. Rather, the ambiguity itself can be seen as video-game-like insofar as the plot matters less than the play and gags along the journey; in short, we are being told to interpassively outsource or simply give up our interpreting of the film and enjoy. And yet this interpretation misses an actual game at the center of the film.

The obvious specific connection between game and family for Japanese viewers at the time of *The Family Game*'s release would have been the video game console. In 1983, the year that the film was released, Nintendo first marketed its historic NES (Nintendo Entertainment System) console in Japan as the Famicom (a portmanteau abbreviation of "family computer") gaming system. From this perspective, the name *Famicom* attempts to hide the medium's supposed role in the further atomization of family, begun perhaps with radio and television. Japanese viewers would have been aware that advertising connected family and education with video gaming. And, though no critics of the film discuss the actual video game in it, gaming was touted in the television ads for the film and centered (albeit briefly) within the film itself.[6]

Critics and audiences of *The Family Game* frequently note the unusual and visually striking placement of the chairs at the family's dining table, all in a row on one side.[7] This placement gives the dining scenes an unrealistic, staged look, a stark visualization of a disconnected family that never meets eye to eye. But there is also at least one practical, diegetic reason for this, beyond the simple extradiegetic one that it allows for one nearly consistent camera setup during family meals: the family television (shown briefly in the corner of the room, when the camera, for a flash, crosses the dining-table line) is on the camera's-eye side of the line. That is, the family may be lining up like this at the table to watch TV; and the camera that stands in the place of the TV (the eye that prevents them from seeing each other eye to eye) is watching them. Notably, the Famicom video game system was named in part for its imagined resting place atop the family television set, so that "parents and grandparents could enjoy watching the children play."[8]

But more than this, there is a flash of a video game within the film, sandwiched between a scene of Shigeyuki Numata getting beat up by a group of boys in a field on his way home from school and another at home, in which a neighbor discusses intimate details of a family crisis. The six-second scene occurs almost exactly in the middle of the film (fifty-three minutes into the film with about fifty-two minutes remaining). It is also a pivot-shot for the entire film that is bifurcated at that moment between the setup in the first half of the film and the denouement in the second. Though it would be too simplistic to suggest that this scene (which itself contains a division between analog and digital games) provides a template for reading the film as a split between real and virtual family games, the scene's presence stitches together the first half of the film that sets up the climax and dissolution of the film, suggesting that traditional social interactions may have been replaced by gamic ones, and that both have led to atomization.

Figure 17. A flash of games: the 2D and 3D ice hockey games at the center of *The Family Game* are played in the absence of family. Screengrab from *The Family Game* (*Kazoku Gēmu*), dir. Morita Yoshimitsu (1983; Long Beach, Calif.: Geneon, 2006), DVD.

In the foreground, three of the boys crowd around a tabletop hockey action game (the Champion Hockey Pola 400 game made in Finland by Bock-Plast), and in the background two boys are playing what appears to be Bandai's release of the Mattel Intellivision's *NHL Hockey* console game.[9] Though the boys laugh, there is no clear dialogue; the beeps from the video game saturate the soundscape. Through the juxtaposition of these two forms of hockey, this scene sharply places into comparison two kinds of gaming: tabletop games and video games. In the analog foreground, the boys stare intently at the 3D board where plastic figures swat around a miniature puck. The figures, of course, move because they are connected below the board to metal rods that are manipulated by players. In contrast, the boys in the background stare at a 2D virtual world on the television set that achieves a minimal sense of depth through perspective by angling the ice rink to be smaller at the top of the screen than at the bottom, though a lack of shadows makes this effect fall flat. As such, the scene raises the question of whether, beyond these details of difference, there is a categorical difference between the old and new regimes of gaming.

This hockey scene, then, anticipates what will become explicit, for instance, in the 1987 Japanese television advertisement for an ice hockey game on Famicom's new "disk system"—a fleeting mise en abyme that suggests a real in which our media remake our world. In the advertisement, a family gathered around the console is surprised when a hockey player, presumably from the digital game they play, crawls out of the television screen and into the living room saying, "Sorry for barging in." The hockey player then joins the family in playing the game on the console from whence he came. The commercial ends with the hockey player declaring, "It's more fun than the real thing!," to which the father responds, "That's because it's Nintendo" (Honmono yori omoshiroi desu ne! Nintendo desu kara). This sort of hokey reverse mimesis is clearly intended to suggest that the new system has vastly improved the resolution and realism of Famicom games.[10] In other words, it suggests a kind of surface improvement of representation and immediacy, in terms of colors, sounds, action, and resolution. It is essentially a celebration of the increasing amount and variety of information that it was possible to convey in a short time, the media becoming "hotter" to use Marshall McLuhan's term.[11] And yet, the fact the virtual-turned-real hockey player wants to play the digital version of the game rather than the real one suggests that the priorities of our world have been either completely reorganized by games or simply brought to the point of enabling us to joke about the possibility of such desire. Of course, the real reverse mimesis that the ad intends for viewers to complete is the purchasing of Nintendo products, the conversion of passive viewers into active consumers. The ad (like all such ads) interpellates the viewer, in fact, to disconnect from the television and go to the store to buy new media to reconnect to the television in a new way.

This separation of the world of human constructs and the real world is precisely the distinction that the theory of ecomimesis seeks to negotiate. In the course of the development of the concept, ecomimesis has had at least two competing—at times overlapping and at times contradictory—meanings in recent discussions in the fields of, on the one hand, architecture and design and, on the other hand, cultural critique and ecocriticism. Coined by systems ecologist and business strategist Gil Friend in 1996, the term initially referred to Sisyphean efforts to mime the environment in architecture and design, but it gradually evolved into a label for more or less successful attempts to harmonize built construction with the environment.[12] Later, for instance, Timothy Morton ecologically repurposes the term to address and critique the ecological writing language of immediacy (characterized by tropes like "even as I write . . ." used since the Romantics) to convey a writer's harmony with nature.[13] According to Morton's critique, in rhetorically positioning oneself in the midst of nature, such (romantic) writing reveals or instantiates the very gap that it intends to close—the gap between the writing moment that is necessarily out of nature and the ecological/ecocritical one of action that must occur in the world. As such, *ecomimesis* names a tendency of human creative construction in the world (whether in building and fabrication or in discourse and fabulation) to represent a human fitting-in (immersing in the environment) even as such representations inevitably display the impossibility of the task because concepts of nature have been constructed in contradistinction to those of the human. In short, it is a transcendental tendency toward the impossible goal of completely accounting for ecosystems affected by the tension between world-awareness and world-building.

Alenda Y. Chang makes the persuasive argument that such tension is repeated in video games. She writes:

> The concept of ecomimesis can easily extend to encompass photography, film, music, and games. . . . Game texts, unlike conventional texts, demand action—games are "richly designed problem spaces" or "possibility spaces" in which we come face to face with our knowledge of and impact on the environment.[14]

Though I agree that video games stage the problem of ecomimesis well, I am skeptical of the notion that (inter)action within games allows them to overcome the old romantic problems of reification that Morton outlines. In its efforts to harmonize or eradicate the borders between human individual and nature, of course, ecomimetic writing and gaming end up often muddying, reifying, and demarcating.[15]

In the idiosyncratic and insular worlds of Murakami Haruki's early fiction, social and community organizations and ideological state apparatuses such as family, school, police, military, and religious organizations are all but absent, at most relegated to minor roles in the plot. In their place, readers of his *Hard-Boiled Wonderland and the End of the World* (1985), for instance, are presented with meditations of lone selves on the spaces in which they dwell, such as the following scene of video game play.

The book is bifurcated between two sections representing two apparently separate worlds. One is a near-future world familiar to sci-fi enthusiasts, in which a technologist is pursued by a mysterious cabal. The other is a psychological world within the protagonist's head, from which he is unlikely to escape; this is a surreal and dystopic world more familiar perhaps to readers of Kafka than to detective, speculative, or science fiction. But in the end, of course, the worlds are connected. We soon realize the one world is simply the world within the protagonist of the other world's head. But when we consider the nature of the diegetic links between the two worlds, the primary role of media in the novel becomes clear. What is interesting about the two worlds of the novel's "double helix structure" is the fact that such media are the rungs of the ladder that connect them.[16] A recording of "Danny Boy" by Bing Crosby floats up in both worlds and a unicorn skull that sits atop the television set (in place of a video game console) in the "Hard-Boiled Wonderland" is paralleled by the skulls the reader examines in the library in the "End of the World" world.

The medium of games provides another such point of connection between the two worlds. With games as one of its mise en abymes, the novel depicts game centers of the late 1970s (as well as a variant of chess) to correspond to the plot structure noted for placing the importance of personal relations and decisions on a level with decision-making about the fate of the world.

> It was five-twenty-five when I stopped at *the library*. Since I had more than enough time, I got out of the car and took a stroll down the streets still wet with rain. In that sort of coffee shop which has a service counter, I watched a *golf match on television* while drinking coffee, then I went to a *game center and played a video game*. It was a game where you destroy tanks with antitank guns as they cross a river. I was dominating at first, but as the game went on, the number of enemy tanks increased like lemmings, destroying my base. When my position was destroyed, the screen went

completely white *like the incandescent glow of a nuclear explosion.* Then the words "game over—insert coin" appeared. As instructed, I put another hundred-yen coin into the slot. As music rang out, my base reappeared, completely unscathed. *It was precisely a battle to be lost. If I didn't lose, the game would go on forever. And a game without end somehow has no meaning. That's trouble for a game center and trouble for me.* In time, my position was destroyed again and the glowing light reappeared on the screen. Then the words "game over—insert coin" floated to the surface.[17]

In this passage on video gaming, the connections between the personal and the global are represented insofar as the private individual plays alone in the arcade (game center). Characteristically, the narrator plays alone while waiting to meet his date. The intimate relationship of dating is directly connected to the narrator's decision to kill time in public and semipublic spaces for cultural consumption (the library, the coffee shop, and the game center), as well as to the game's featured denouement at the geostrategic level of nuclear annihilation. Indeed, the game center locates gaming in a middle ground perhaps between the private domestic sphere of the home and the public space of the library, but one largely devoid of human contact. In the arcade, the player is out in the world, but only nominally. But rather than having the game itself affect the "real" of the diegetic world, Murakami limits the global damage of nuclear war to the world of the game, leaving readers to make any allegoric connections to the novel as a whole.

Alone in public, staring at a screen, and deciding the fate of the world in the machine, the narrator contemplates the meaning of all games. The necessary and inevitable failure of the protagonist to have his game avatar survive is at once both tantamount to ending the world in which his avatar dwells and to ending what is putatively only a game in his world (the novel world).[18] The narrator will invert this kind of game ending in his final choice of the novel to stay in the psychic space of the "End of the World" rather than going back to the "Hard-Boiled Wonderland." This final decision is effectively opting to continue forever playing the game of the rule-bound, fantasy world that is both personal and private (because in his head) and to give up the messier but social hard-boiled world. If the novel's ending is unsatisfying for some readers, it is because of the observation that the narrator makes here. An eternal game has no meaning; or, conversely, there must be an end for the game to exist as a game. Rather than allowing the world to die at the end of the gamelike novel, the narrator chooses the gamelike world of the narrator's unconscious (the static end of the world), remaining perpetually in what seems to be an endless game.[19]

Recent theories about the sekai-kei genre help clarify this broad abstract issue about the gamification of the world even as some of them point to Murakami as an early example while relying on an obscure essay by Betsuyaku (a.k.a. Betchaku) Minoru to explain the structure of the genre. In his 1986 essay collection *Tange Sazen Riding a Horse,* Betsuyaku considers several media and their corresponding sociostructural forms. Beyond the 1920s serial fiction and samurai films featuring the famous one-eyed character of the title, the media discussed in the book range from stage through newspapers, novels, and photographs, to word processors and television. But it is particularly the collection's first essay, titled "The Loss of a Middle Ground," that became an important basis for later theorizers of sekai-kei. The essay uses the aesthetics of sports television as its primary example. Focusing on the framing of shots in a live televised baseball game, Betsuyaku muses about a perceived overuse of the close-up and lack of mid-shots. He writes that if watching a baseball game in the ballpark or stadium is like reading a detective novel, the "near view" or close-up presented on broadcast television makes the game more similar to the psychological portrayals of an I-novel. This essay introduces an idea that he goes on to elaborate in subsequent rethinkings of the idea of close-up, mid-shot, and long shot. Ignoring the sociality of, say, watching a baseball game in an *izayakaya* restaurant, he argues that the middle ground of social interpersonal connections through community is losing ground to a myopic view that raises and distorts the importance of the individual directly against the background (which he connects to belief in mystical divination) with no mediation in between.[20]

According to critic Kasai Kiyoshi, the sekai-kei form has a layered structure (like Murakami's book) with inner and outer worlds. As Kasai presents it, path-blazing sekai-kei in the mid- to late 1990s depicted bifurcated worlds—both a real, everyday, individual interior and an extraordinary, fantastic exterior with a global reach. Kasai writes, "Creative work that continues to describe the pure love of the powerless boy and fighting girl is the world's real reflection of the simple fact that the everyday is Armageddon and the Armageddon is everyday."[21] This view presents a three-venue understanding of the sekai-kei form; first, a personal everyday (micro level); second, the intermediating social arena (mid-level); and last, the world Armageddon (macro level). Drawing on Betsuyaku's schema, critics Azuma Hiroki, Maejima Satoshi, and Saitō Tamaki reconceive this subcultural form to discuss a middle or intermediary layer lacking in the structure of the genre.[22] The three areas (personal, social, and global) in the genre of sekai-kei correspond to Betsuyaku's terminology of foreground (close-up), middle ground (medium shot, middle view), and background (backdrop, landscape) or Jacques Lacan's schema of the Imaginary, the Symbolic, and the Real.

The importance of the meta level of sekai-kei cultural products as the middle-level mediators (symbolic) is clear even without this psychoanalytic close reading. The works themselves continually provide their own intrastory critique on media and its meta levels by using media not just as background elements setting the scene but as integral drivers of the plot. This turn toward addressing mediation within the stories themselves enacts a return of the social middle ground supposedly lost within the genre. Though school, family, police, government, and press have weakened or vanished in the stories, they are replaced by intervening technological connections between individuals and their environment through gadgets. The fantasy of sekai-kei is the fantasy of ecomimesis—the notion that one could live without a middle level of society or media directly in the world. This fantasy is always revealed as such by the fact that characters live in hypermediated worlds. In other words, disconnect from traditional mid-level social organizations spurs creation of a bypass or is enabled through mediated connections. This supplementary function of media within the genre replicates a function that the genre itself serves for its consumers and in a sense reifies the purportedly vanished middle ground. The market success of the sekai-kei genre in so many media (novels, light novels, manga, anime, films, and video games) attests to the return of the social at both the mediated and meta levels. If sekai-kei is the genre for a lost generation of people who feel disconnected from government, work, school, and family, it is precisely through this mass genre that they are able to socially reconnect with an entire community or society of fans. In short, the massively popular genre itself has replaced absent social relations represented in the works with mediation, information, communication, and infrastructure.

In recent years, a number of media theorists have begun to question the sociological politics of this divorce from the immediate social situation around the fantasy of direct connection to the global. Critic Uno Tsunehiro calls the entire sekai-kei genre "decisionist," after Carl Schmitt's notion that decisions by a citizenry tend to be left to the authorities during states of exception like 3.11, insinuating that Miyadai Shinji's "laying back" itself assumes a sort of reactionary complicity with the status quo and that the status quo cannot be changed during a state of exception.[23] This decisionism names the interpassivity of generations of game players who, feeling disenfranchised from the activities of world politics, seem to have retreated to the seemingly hermetic virtual digital realms of games, thus in effect allowing traditional mid-level actors to continue on as though nothing has changed.

Gaming the Frames of Human Relations: Giving Up on Media, Forgetting the World

The remainder of this chapter considers family life and the end of the world from the vantage point of a single, simple, visual novel game from more recent sekai-kei genre history. The game *Steins;Gate,* which debuted in 2009, foregrounds family without direct representation of a putatively traditional nuclear family. Like most Japanese visual novel games, *Steins;Gate* is a kind of choose-your-own-adventure story that involves remarkably little "play" and a lot of reading (about ten times as many words as Sōseki Natsume's famed novel *Kokoro*). In the game's multiple narratives, preventing the untimely end of the world is within the control of a small group of friends who become a kind of surrogate new family. The gameplay (such as it is) also revolves around the depiction of a newer medium than video games—the smartphone.

Developed as an "imaginable science" (*sōtei kagaku*) adventure game, *Steins;Gate* was promoted as "ninety-nine percent science and one percent fantasy."[24] The game's developers took extra care at the level of setting to ground the game world in reality through an obsessive focus on detail. For instance, the setting of the game in Tokyo's "Electric Town" Akihabara is by no means unique, but the level of detail to which real locations and addresses are explicitly and meticulously reproduced within the game world was of special importance to both game producers and fans alike. More important, because it self-consciously remediates devices and engages in gaming theory, *Steins;Gate* is particularly useful for understanding how video games function to create a new real. This particular game represents just a snapshot in gaming history, but, as a node in that timeline, it helps us understand what came before and what might come later. There is nothing particularly new or unique about the game, but it exemplifies the evolution of sekai-kei and the dating sim game form as they transformed over the first decade of the 2000s.

The marketing of the game as being close to reality is not entirely a ploy designed to intrigue customers; it became an important part of the ways in which people engaged with it, even beyond the level of play. This is evident not simply from the details of representationally mimetic mise-en-scène within the game but also from the metagame materials that facilitated connections between fantasy and reality. For instance, in the "Akihabara Guide" section of the *Steins;Gate Official Resources Collection* book, game producers included a map of the real-world locations of game-world events. Fans of the game made so-called pilgrimages to sacred sites (*seichi junrei*) from the game. Some discovered other real sites thinly veiled by the fictional world of the game and posted their findings and evidence on various fan blogs and social media platforms across the web.[25]

The marketing of the game for a time transformed the world directly through a kind of reverse mimesis. The Radio Assembly Hall (Rajio kaikan, or Rajikan), where the game starts and, in some senses, ends, has been a home to Tokyo's electronics industry and gadget hobbyists since it opened in 1950. It also became an important site for the real-world advertising of the game. The game world was hyped in the fall of 2011 (a few months after the anime version of it debuted) when marketers built a physical, life-size mock-up of the futuristic satellite-cum-time-machine, seemingly having crashed into the top floor of the Rajikan building, as it does in the game and anime. The building instantly became a site for both otaku game fans and passersby to consider anew.[26]

In addition, key images and plot points that seem far-fetched are actually echoes of factual elements of the real world. For instance, the international cabal SERN behind time travel research in the game is based on the real-life CERN (Conseil Européen pour la Recherche

Figure 18. Images of the crash from within the game world and a fan photo of the marketing ploy in real life. Diptych composed from screengrab and image from Wikimedia Commons. Photo credit 禁樹なずな, "Time Machine Representation on the Radio Kaikan.jpg," Wikimedia Commons, October 29, 2011, https://commons.wikimedia.org/w/index.php?curid=17254384.

Nucléaire), which has been deeply engaged in dark matter research. The use of basic household technologies, such as a modified microwave oven, in the creation of the "future gadgets" (*mirai gajetto*) that the lab produces makes the inventions seem almost realizable. The Divergence Meter (a device that measures the divergence of a particular alternative timeline from the events of the original timeline) is built from Nixie tubes, a popular pre-digital-era device for the display of numbers that had recently been revived by electronics enthusiasts with a penchant for retro style. In one subplot, the protagonist Okabe Rintarō (hereafter Rintarō) searches for an old computer, the IBN 5100. This fictional computer is loosely modeled on the real-world IBM 5100, which was also featured in a real-world net-based time travel hoax referenced in the *Steins;Gate* narrative. The computer is depicted in both the game and the hoax as a combination of a Rosetta stone and a time machine because, as a computer with both APL and BASIC languages, the IBM 5100 served as a threshold medium allowing contemporary computers to access older ones through translation or code transcription. Whether or not such meshing of game world and real world amounts to the advertised "ninety-nine percent," the grounding of the game's look and tone in reality, even as many of the ideas, images, and scenarios stray far beyond it, is a fundamental characteristic of the game.

Beyond the setting, the game uses visual and textual frames that integrate contemporary reality within the world of the game to present multiple and varied mise en abymes. In fact, as we shall see, the only significant interaction or gaming comes in how players choose to interact with Rintarō's cell phone, which serves both as a medium for emails and bulletin boards within the game world and as a frame that encompasses the entire game world itself. Cell phone icons indicating battery strength and connectivity (see Figure 20) give a sense of this layered visualization of the game world. For a visual novel game that was originally intended to be played on a cell phone, the use of the most ubiquitous portable gadget of contemporary life as the primary mise-en-scène is significant not only for the narrative play and functionality within the diegesis but also for its impact on the user in the real world.[27] These frames provide windows into different aspects of and information about the game, but at another level, they produce a kind of coordinated cognitive dissonance, one purposefully tuned to promote neither confusion between game and reality nor an immersion in a game reality but rather continual comparison between the two, a toggling back and forth. This stereomimesis (see chapter 2) cultivates an aesthetic akin to what Richard Grusin and Jay David Bolter label hypermediacy—namely, the overt inclusion of gaps of mediated, overlapping realms so as to render the mediation opaque.[28]

The narrative of *Steins;Gate* features a bizarre series of events and murders that occur within a group of friendly tinkerers and gadgeteers in the electronics shopping district of Tokyo as they discover a way to send email messages to the past via "d-mail" (short for "De-Lorean mail") and later to "time slip" between alternative timelines. The time machine is not the sleek 1980s stainless steel DeLorean sports car used as a time travel machine in the film *Back to the Future* but rather a modified regular smartphone. The point of view is almost entirely from the vantage of Okabe Rintarō, the over-the-top persona who envisions himself as a mad scientist but is actually neither mad nor much of a scientist. An eighteen-year-old student at Tokyo Denki University, Rintarō surrounds himself with a cohort of friends in his invention laboratory. Shiina Mayuri (sometimes called Mayushii) is a cute, performatively childish junior member of the lab who seems to be more of a mascot than a participant. Hashida Itaru (a.k.a. Daru) is an overweight computer otaku who enjoys hacking, hanging out at maid cafés, and eating fast food.

Each of the game's various story lines closely relates to one of the main characters with whom Rintarō is in some way in love. Each of the potential love interests represents a specific plotline and a given playthrough and contains an ending corresponding to the character. This information can be drawn from both various playthroughs and discussion boards and the structure of the data of the game. These potential couplings are part of the core structure of the game, even encoded in the game files: at the end of each chapter, there is a text file that is stored within the chapter folder but that is normally invisible to players (unless they hack into the code). These files mark the end of the chapter, but in so doing, they also highlight the game producer's view of the chapter's primary goal. For instance, at the end of the Suzuha story, the file reads in abbreviated English "END_SUZ"; likewise, the file ending the Feirisu story reads "END_FEI"; the Ruka chapter ends with "END_RUK"; Mayuri ends "END_MAY"; the first and fake Kurisu ending reads "END_CRS. . . . END_FAKE"; and the true ending tells readers of the code with "END_TRUE." So this seemingly surface organization of the plot is also deeply embedded into the very DNA of the game itself. And the deep structure tells us that, despite the title's runaway success in the media mix, it is at base a dating sim game, a popular and long-standing genre with questionable ethical values.

When Mother Disintegrates: Harem as Queer Family

Steins;Gate takes the narrative structure of Japanese dating sim games and *otome* (maiden) games, in which a player has the task of developing a relationship with one of several characters. However, instead of the successful or "true" ending being rewarded with sex or love, as in most dating sim games, the success of the "true end" in *Steins;Gate* is achieved simply by the preservation of the lives of all the lab members. Unsuccessful endings are marked not by the failure to consummate a relationship but by the death of one or more of Rintarō's friends/lab members. Though sharing its structure with *eroge* (sex games), *Steins;Gate* might be called an Eros game, if we follow Freud to take Eros as the "life instinct" or a will to life, in opposition to Thanatos or death.

To the extent that it makes sense to consider *Steins;Gate* within the context of the sekai-kei genre rubric at all, it is because there are, indeed, several existential threats to the planet pitted against the personal desires of Rintarō and the survival of the other lab members. As with more typical sekai-kei, *Steins;Gate* is marked by an almost complete absence of traditional social structures in a middle ground between the protagonists and the world. Though many of the characters are university students, game players never get a glimpse of their school lives. Religious, police, and government authorities seem to have no power against SERN and, thus, are not considered as adequate to the task of addressing the moral conundrums of the story or even investigating murders in a just manner.

When parents play key roles, as they do in two of the story lines, it is mainly as a negative force. The father is a prime motivator of Feirisu's backstory, but it is her father's death that enables her to become a maid café proprietress. Makise Kurisu's mother is far away in the United States, while her father is directly linked to the story as the mad scientist who would steal secrets from his child to give to enemy nations and organizations. His actions in some timelines have a direct impact on the end of the world, but in terms of his treachery and betrayal, his actions are equal to the degree of his estrangement from his daughter, so in this sense, in those timelines, he is no father at all. It also is significant that we know nothing of Rintarō's own family. In short, nuclear families hardly exist in the game.

This thematic point is also statistically borne out. For instance, of the sixty-three uses of the Japanese character for *mother* (母) in the entire textual corpus, including every possible playthrough of *Steins;Gate*, none refer to mothers who are present and active in their children's lives.[29] This reflects the notable absence of active mothers who play a major part in the plot or in the consciousness of their children. This lack, disappearance, or disintegration of the mother is often cited as a marker of Japanese gender politics and family dynamics in the postwar information society. Perhaps best exemplified by Ueno Chizuko's 1993 reflection on Etō Jun's *Maturity and Loss* (1967), the basic notion that the postwar Japanese mother is both a victim of and an enabler of her husband's abuse, while becoming a victimizer of her children and eventually their victims, too, is widespread in cultural theory.[30] The absence of the father (who is away from home working) precariously positions the mother, in this understanding, as simultaneously the all-powerful ruler of the home finances and the completely powerless double prisoner to the education system that places undue burden on her and to a capitalist system built on stark gender disparities.[31] Whether or not they are true of actual families in Japan, the fact that such theories continue to circulate and prop up such beliefs means that they hold interpretive power. *Steins;Gate* depicts just such a world in which these myths about social institutions such as family hold. And in this it contributes to and cultivates nostalgia for a strong nuclear family that probably never really existed. This does not mean that *Steins;Gate* is in tune with the social reality of postwar Japan, but rather that *Steins;Gate* is in tune with or part of this discourse on social reality that helps to give this particularly skewed sense of the real.[32]

This is to say, whether or not we agree with Tomiko Yoda and Uno Tsunehiro that mothers are becoming stronger or with Etō, Ueno, and Ōtsuka Eiji that they are vanishing (and perhaps becoming stronger in their absence), the fact that *Steins;Gate* presents nearly familyless and motherless children is significant in and of itself, insofar as it forces us to consider what might be left after the putative disintegration of the family and disappearance of the mother. This perception of a loss of family in the real world precedes and parallels the absence of family in fictional sekai-kei worlds. So to some extent the discourses are linked and overlapping, becoming mutually productive over time.

This desire for a family of affiliation is not only part of the post-modern culture of pop literature but also a significant part of the mass culture of the video game world since at least the video game *Mother* (*Mazā*, introduced in 1989). The origin of the meaning behind the title *Mother* (marketed in English under the title *Earthbound*) is the stuff of legends: it is *mother* as in *mother computer* (like in the movie *Alien*) or *mother* as in a game so large as to be the mother of all games or *mother* as in the opening cry at the beginning of John Lennon's song "Mother" (1970). In a 2003 interview, the game's creator, Itoi Shigesato, listed all of these possibilities in response to a question about the title of the game but then referenced his own marketing background and how he chose the word *mother* because he thought that "it would be best to use a word that was not at all game-like" (gemu-rashikunai yatta hō ga ii).[33] This answer acknowledges the absent presence of mothers haunting not only the worlds of video games but also contemporary culture, showing how such a perceived absence can return to make the presence all the more desired and central to cultural products.

Although the family as a reality or concept is not evoked very often in *Steins;Gate,* the structure of relationships between friends is very much familial. In the entire *Steins;Gate* corpus, the word *family* (*kazoku*) is only used thirteen times and in reference to primarily Ruka's and secondarily Makise's families, never to the group of lab members. This would seem to suggest that family is not overtly thematized in the game. Yet, its unspoken existence on the periphery of the characters' lives centers its importance for consideration of the relationships within the game. If families are tight-knit groups of people dwelling together and caring for one another, then the lab members are, indeed, a family, whether or not the word is used to name them as such.

Online discussions and character groupings suggest that players themselves in many cases view the lab members as a family of affiliation. For instance, one blogger conjectures that the absences of mothers and the relationships between Rintarō and the group of young women makes this a game about fathers and daughters.[34] Some fans have gone so far as to literalize the metaphor and create family trees that attempt to explain complex relationships through time loops. For instance, a frequent point of interest for fans is the genealogy of Amane Suzuha—so much so that one fan constructed a family tree for

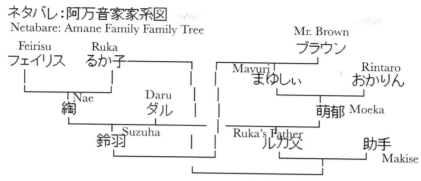

Figure 19. Spoiler alert: Amane family tree. "Netabare: Amane-ka kakei-zu (Shutainzu gēto)" posted August 28, 2012, on the "Shutainzu gēto TwitAA 2012-06-23 06:20:37" discussion board at http://zugtierlaster56.rssing.com/chan-26939252/latest.php.

the Amane family that weaves almost all the main characters into one extended family (Figure 19).[35]

Perhaps the most apt example is an archive of tweets by fans explicitly and directly addressing the notion that the members of the lab were a kind of family. Three fans tweeting in January 2010 proposed different scenarios in considering family in the game. For instance, one placed Ruka as the younger brother, Daru as the older brother, Ferris as the younger sister, Suzuha as the middle daughter, Makise and/or Mayu as the wives or wife, with Okarin or Mr. Braun as the father.[36] The founding of a gadget lab in the middle of Akihabara is an effective mechanism for constructing a new family of affiliation. With the members of the lab in *Steins;Gate,* we have a group of otherwise atomized individuals coming together around a common interest and purpose. The stable nuclear family of nostalgia (presented in Etō's critique as one of the undergirding desires of Japanese mass culture) is, of course, all but absent in *Steins;Gate,* but this constructed family of affiliation orders the plot in all playthroughs and timelines.

Paying attention to family in *Steins;Gate* is important because, in a story in which actual families are tangential or broken, saving the family of lab members constitutes a partially successful effort to undo the gender politics thought to be intractable and inherent both in the sekai-kei genre and in the basic structure of dating, otome, and erotic games. In a scathing gender critique of sekai-kei narratives and dating games, Uno Tsunehiro argues that they are thinly masked "rape fan-tasies" in which supposedly helpless, powerless men are able to give powerful yet broken women the healing they need through forced sex acts. Uno's first articulation of his theory of sexual violence focuses mainly on anime, specifically the works of famed animator Yoshi-kazu Yasuhiko. Uno writes, "These rapes are not depicted positively. However, there is no doubt about the development of the desire that should be called an implicit complicity between the author and the reader. . . . This structure corresponds to the structure of the created world."[37] In other words, the structure of desire in the sekai-kei world itself places the consumer of the cultural material in our real world in a position that is supposed to desire possession and, indeed, control. But rather than putting consumers in the active rapist position, such exercise of power itself is outsourced or becomes interpassive in games like *Steins;Gate.*

Uno later develops the idea of self-reflexivity as part of his argu-ment on rape fantasy, claiming, "So that male consumers, who have the anti-feminist desire to possess, can enjoy beautiful girl (porno-graphic) gamelike rape fantasies without guilt, self-reflexive elements towards those desires are built into the works."[38] In *Steins;Gate,* we are often given Rintarō's interior monologues, which express all sorts of desires played for laughs. His self-reflexive sexual longings therein are primarily directed toward Makise and Ruka. Rintarō agonizes the most over his desires for Ruka, which are not easily classifiable as heterosexual or homosexual (or as bisexual, polysexual, or flex-ual for that matter). Embarrassed about his own attraction to the cross-dressing boy, Rintarō continually reminds himself, whenever he compliments or feels attracted to Ruka, ". . . but, he is a boy," in a refrain that echoes his deep anxieties. Such anxieties get played up over various timelines to the point where the question of gender becomes something of a Schrödinger's cat, and Rintarō will be the brute who has to tear open the box to peer inside for genital confir-mation. Rintarō's anxiety is both a heuristic and a joke for players who presumably can also be safely attracted to the two-dimensional character and at the same time laugh at Rintarō's anxiety about such attraction. We need to understand this self-reflexivity as one of the ways the form can at once maintain a problematic politics and appear to transgress it. And this feeling of transgression is doubled for the consumer/player who may feel that they are engaging in transgressive acts through their purchase and gameplay when in fact little of the kind is happening, because play itself is bracketed in these games that are read more than played.

A large number of works in the sekai-kei genre, upon which Uno builds his understanding of decisionism and rape fantasy, are, indeed, video games. In his study of sekai-kei, Okawada Akira categorizes sekai-kei games into five types: reemergence of "World Civil War," gardening space and "freedom," originality of closed space, mobile games and communication, and transformations of user community.[39] Although we may dispute Okawada's categorization of specific games under these rubrics in any sort of rigid classification of genres, as his list does, the categories do articulate many of the elements found in sekai-kei games. It may be more useful to think of them as properties that are more or less salient in particular games than as mutually exclusive subgenres. In *Steins;Gate* we have a kind of "World Civil War" being fought between SERN and Russia. We have the nested, relatively closed spaces of Rintarō's mind, his phone, his laboratory, his immediate environs (Akihabara), Japan, the world of *Steins;Gate,* and, finally, the real world (that of the player). The staging of the transformation of communications through portable gadgets is internalized not only by the presence of the cell phone but by the fact that the phone within the game is the primary means of accessing d-mail and, therefore, for slipping between timelines; the phone becomes the time machine. The depiction of a user community in the game's BBS bulletin board postings give the backstory of John Titor and SERN that players are free to read or ignore. This leaves only what Okawada describes as a "gardening space" as not really present. And yet, the game suggests the question of freedom everywhere—for instance, in its extreme limitations on freedom (part of the visual novel game forking narrative genre) and in its content that focuses on the freedom to slip from one timestream to another with memory of the previous alternative timeline. Though it is clear that *Steins;Gate* is no sandbox game, *Steins;Gate* stages the issues of freedom versus fate and player action versus system control at every turn.

Although *Steins;Gate* ought to fit Uno's paradigm, his critique that sekai-kei generic conventions render hope for radical change impossible (decisionism) and that the structure of dating games thinly disguises rape fantasy as popular culture does not hold for the game.[40] There are multiple reasons for this. First, the form of sekai-kei developed in dialogue with theorizations of the genre.[41] A second reason lies within the game itself. Despite the fact that the structure of the timelines parallels the structure of dating, otome, and eroge games (in that there is a separate story line for each character from which the main character can choose but one), ultimately *Steins;Gate* actively violates the norm by depicting Rintarō's desire to have it all and save everyone. Furthermore, this outcome desired by the character is equivalent to the player's "true end"—not a choice between the friends (family) but the saving (not dating, copulating, raping, or killing) everyone. In this sense, the game might seem more like *harem mono* (eroge in which a protagonist is surrounded by a plethora of possible mates). But by replacing the sex of eroge with saving the lives of characters, *Steins;Gate* presents a very different model, one that militates against the troubling ethics Uno ascribes to sekai-kei and eroge writ large. Indeed, *Steins;Gate* might be considered as the exact opposite of the world-type (sekai-kei) narrative: what we might call a home- or family-type (*uchi-kei*) story, or perhaps the return of middle-ground (*chūkei*) narrative.

Players are supposed to learn from their play of this moralistic game that this type of saving of society/family comes at the cost of media. But rather than through following Rintarō's successive failures and final success at saving his friends, another perhaps unintended lesson can also be gleaned from playing the game. And it comes not through a kind of copycat play in which players like Rintarō give up on technology but through play itself. It is neither structure nor resolution, however, but the interpassive play style that determines the ultimate politics of a narrative. *Steins;Gate* manages within this fraught structure to produce a problematic narrative that nevertheless actively seeks to overcome the rape fantasy (or harem mono) structure through a play with play, a remediation of mediation. Its success, however, depends not on how well it violates the genre but on how well it masks the underlying structure as something other than that of a dating game with the veneer of a sekai-kei employing the old science fiction trope of time travel played through a seemingly new interface. Ultimately, Rintarō throws out technology (the phone) to dwell in an ecomimetic fantasy of unmediated living in the world, so that we (players) do not have to. This is the final interpassivity of the game to the extent that we are mimetically transformed gaining some homeostasis (by watching another achieve his goal by getting rid of technology). In other words, by indulging interpassively through our media in this ecomimetic fantasy, we can move beyond the dangerous romanticism that posits that we could ever exist unmediated in an environment.

Save the Family, Save the World: Reconnect, Reframe, and Console

Steins;Gate is not unique or cutting-edge in its use of the latest technologies. Since their debut in the mid-1980s, the genre of visual novel games like it has remained remarkably resistant to technical innovations in computer processing speed, gaming console design, and graphics and audio rendering. Of course, there are more images shown with higher resolution and longer stories with more text and audio in the visual novels of recent years, as compared to those appearing early in gaming history. But the basic structure of the games and the limited level of player control (or interactivity) remains largely unchanged from its earliest inception.[42] This relative continuity of the form over time is evident in a *Steins;Gate*'s spin-off called *Steins;Gate: Variant Space Octet* (*Hen'i kūkan no octet*), which is rendered in a retro 8-bit format but does not substantially reduce the level of gaming compared to other *Steins;Gate* titles. What continues to pique consumer interest over time and constantly changes with cultural trends are the themes, motifs, aesthetic style, and content of the stories. These games can change with culture because visual games are closely linked to the trendy anime and manga media mix industry.

As a game that can hardly be considered a game, *Steins;Gate* illuminates the gray areas between concepts such as narrative, play, and reality even more than games that rely on the latest technologies such as *Metal Gear Solid, Final Fantasy,* or *Death Stranding*. In contrast, the minimal play involved in visual novel games prompts questions as to whether the genre can really be considered a video game at all. How can a game that does not play much like a game still feel like a game? How can it perform gameness? *Steins;Gate* manages these tricks through innovative techniques of structuring both play and narrative. The way one nominally plays *Steins;Gate* (besides simply reading successive screens of text) is by choosing at various points to read or send emails on the mobile phone, and these decisions in the game's cyberspace have a direct effect on the player experience. At the level of narrative, the game also incorporates and represents play in innovative ways. By incorporating fiddling with the phone as the significant, narrative-altering part of play, the game remediates the contemporary medium and thereby theorizes how freedoms are offered and impinged by the smartphone as a medium.

But within the narrative itself, the experience of gameplay is represented in the form of "reading steiner," the ability for a character to recall various timelines. Where in many time travel stories, narrators lose their ability to recall and therefore learn from the alternative timelines, "reading steiner" provides a metagamelike experience of each timeline for Rintarō, who can learn from his mistakes. In this way, *Steins;Gate* seems to be responding to Azuma Hiroki's notion of a gamelike realism: "reading steiner" introduces the gaming experience of the player outside the game into the experience of the game itself.[43] Through allowing characters to relive various decision points, the game incorporates a metagame experience within the game. That is, it remediates the metagame experience of learning how to play the game, thereby cultivating what Bolter and Grusin refer to as "hypermediation." In doing so, *Steins;Gate* allegorically and interpassively theorizes and critiques gaming itself. And so ultimately, it is in this play with the phone and the representation or remediation of play itself that the effects of play and, indeed, of reverse mimesis can be most directly experienced.

The Interpassivity of World Lines and Time Loops: Reading Steiner as Metagame Remediation

At first, the timelines of *Steins;Gate* seem to be multilinear narratives—that is, separate and contradictory plotlines. And to be sure, what is true in one plotline (for instance, in which Mayuri lives) cannot be true for another (in which she dies). But it is only in experience and comparison of the net sum of all narrative paths that players can apprehend the pat message of *Steins;Gate*: that technology matters less than human relations.

Rintarō (through his reading steiner) and, indeed, the makers of *Steins;Gate* construct a single repetitively defamiliarizing organization of the story lines from the multilinear possibilities to create a single "true ending."[44] The player realizes by the end of the game that all other narrative lines, which they should have experienced en route, are subordinate to the true end. What drives and motivates the desire for the so-called true ending are the two endings of Mayuri and Makise. Their almost certain (99.99 percent chance) demise drives the player's desire for the "improbable." And so, players may not be blamed for feeling that the "true end" is actually a false one, a tacked-on and hackneyed Hollywood or Confucian ending in which all the hard work seems to pay off. Indeed, the true ending resolves the problems of all the other possible endings, thus rewarding virtue and punishing vice; however, it also defers endings.

The endings in *Steins;Gate* only seem mutually exclusive. As players eventually learn, in order to get to the true ending, they must explore (fail) all the other possible endings. In other words, Makise's and Mayuri's deaths (the denouement of two false endings) have been necessary to even comprehend the "truth" of the supposed "true ending" in which they are alive.[45] Far from mutually exclusive, the endings are actually mutually dependent! In fact, they are not really endings at all: rather, the endings are the completion of stages or levels in the game in which players must retain trans-timeline memory (the real-life version of the game world's reading steiner). Game theorist Jesper Juul writes that when a character in the game dies, the player outside of the game obtains "a kind of bonus: additional knowledge on death," but here in *Steins;Gate* the bonus is conferred both to the player and to Rintarō. Through play of the game, both players and Rintarō learn how not to have other characters (or, from Rintarō's perspective, people) die, so as to arrive at the true end.[46]

The narrative depends on trans-world-line memory for meaning. The lines are relative—only insofar as we can imagine other possible world lines can one given world line be understood. In this way, to flirt with other possible world lines is to imagine the contingencies of the current line rather than to give in to a status quo situation and decisionism. In this regard, Lubomír Doležel's ideas about heterocosmic spaces or possible worlds of literary fiction are perhaps even more relevant for games: "Having reconstructed the fictional world as a mental image, the reader can ponder it and make it a part of her experience, just as she experientially appropriates the actual world. The appropriation, which ranges from enjoyment through knowledge acquisition to following it as a script, integrates fictional worlds into the reader's reality."[47] By incorporating this reading process, which typically happens outside of the game, within the story as "reading steiner," *Steins;Gate* players play interpassively.

In *Steins;Gate,* no textual responses are allowed. The game openly mocks the interactive fiction (IF) and AI mode of interaction by including within it some visuals and descriptions of a seemingly silly "interactive game called 'Alpacaman 2' that will reply when you speak with the included microphone."[48] But when Rintarō plays the game, there is no response and the cute alpaca with a man's head just stares back at him from the screen. Even though *Steins;Gate* is set up in opposition to console gamelike interaction, some claims about IF are useful for understanding this visual novel game. For instance, Nick Montfort explains that the core of IF play is a riddle "presenting a metaphorical system that the listener or reader must inhabit and figure out in order to fully experience."[49] The same is true of *Steins;Gate.* Indeed, the riddle structure, which posits a solution, is what makes sense of the idea of a "true end" in visual novel games. In *Steins;Gate,* the player inhabits the role of Rintarō. And yet to play, to become Rintarō, is to become a virtual zombie, bot, or nonplaying character with extremely limited autonomy, whose only freedom is to gaze at the cell phone and choose whether to reply to an email.

This remediation of new media (smartphone) by the old media (game) itself offers a comment on gaming and smartphone use. In so doing, *Steins;Gate* becomes but part of the discourse constructing a living reality of the new media in our society (the theory and discourse in which it lives). N. Katherine Hayles's *Electronic Literature* examines this widespread phenomenon through Moulthrop's *Reagan Library*: "'This is not a game' and 'This is not not a game.'"[50] Hayles points out that the action of the avatar that performs functions unlocking other narrative lines behaves as a kind of "embodied metaphor." Rather than commonality between two disparate things being routed through memory, in IF they are routed through player action. The accomplishment of a specific task, such as reading or sending email in *Steins;Gate,* then, is doubled with arriving at a specific end of the story. What is embodied or cyberbodied in gamic characters of IF becomes remediated or cybermediated through the phone interface in *Steins;Gate.* This visual novel game tries not so much to capture but rather to become one with the new media—the smartphone. This is how the game plays with the notion of blurring the lines between our world and the game world more than encouraging literal confusion. It stages the staging of the abyss, not the abyss as such.

To the extent that game avatars are generally not like a first-generation Tamagotchi pet, which once dead remained dead, or an early arcade game with high stakes of a quarter for entry, gamic interaction tends to be measured by the level of control over the lives of the game characters. To the extent that our interaction with games can be found in the fact that we can activate, reactivate, reanimate, or reset several lives in a game, this interactivity is itself reencoded back into the story of the game through reading steiner. Rintarō's ability to read steiner—to recall his own various experiences of alternative timelines—is equivalent to the traditional player's metagame experience of multiple playthroughs. In this way, the game production company 5bp has largely given up on interactivity between the game world and the real world of the player outside the game by remediating the experience of game-playing.

When play itself is interpassively bracketed off into play by proxy, when even our play is at a level of remove from our activity, we play by watching another play. This does not deplete the metagame. The metagame world of goods, marketing stunts, cosplay, hosted playthroughs, and online discussions does not disappear into the game through such incorporation of gamic aspects within the game. Rather, in *Steins;Gate* the game itself has found a way to represent these reverse mimetic experiences of the fan world, rebracketing them within the game, even as they continue to flourish outside of it.

That is, when interactivity happens between the avatar and his own world (via, for example, both delusions in the game *Chaos;Head* and time travel in *Steins;Gate*), it is no longer structurally speaking required that players learn from their own mistakes outside of the game space, because the avatar (here through reading steiner) does that for them. Of course, interpassivity does not render unnecessary user communities posting timelines of events or flow charts for navigating through the game world, but it makes gameplay itself less relevant to its consumers than the mediated social interactions that share such tips and pointers. The ultimate sign of this interpassivity is the ability to run an "autoplay" mode in these games, which advances the pages automatically for the "player" so the player does not even have to press any buttons—the traditional sign of video game interaction.

"Autoplay" makes the game appear more like a movie or video of a "speedrunning" playthrough than playing the game, and yet it is itself still one way to play the game. Players on autoplay watch as the protagonist essentially plays for them or even as the game plays them.[51]

In his theorization of the term, Pfaller contrasts interpassivity with the marketing of interactivity, which itself conflates positive connotations of activism with the utopianism of new media phantasmagoria:

> The discourse of interactivity, facilitated mainly by new media, was a revival of very old wishes and utopias, which had become unquestioned facts—consequently, this discourse was more of an ideology than a theory. Contrary to this, the thinking of interpassivity consisted of a series of disturbing observations, questions and considerations, regarding which initially no one—not even those who advanced them—knew where they would lead. It is precisely this uncertainty and openness that distinguishes a theory from an ideology.[52]

In other words, according to Pfaller, the politics of this interpassivity are not as clearly decisionist as they may seem, or decisionism as a passive mode of existence in a state of emergency may open a road hitherto unexplored in philosophy and written off by political activism.[53] This interpassivity is precisely what the game not only enables in its minimal play but also explicitly calls for in its narrative message. As we shall see, through the aesthetics of remediation and the moral of the game (to relinquish gadgets), this supposedly unideological "openness" is precisely the mode of dealing with gaming and media for which *Steins;Gate* will advocate and that overdetermines its politics.

The Aesthetics of Remediation: Of Frame and Phone

Originally planned as a cell phone game, *Steins;Gate* stages the new media of the smartphone, or internet-connected phone. A clue to the importance of the phone for the story world can be found in the fact that all versions of the game use a smartphone as the key component for time travel.[54] So not merely confined to the status of an object, the handheld phone in the worlds and timelines of *Steins;Gate* holds a key role for the progression of plot and, therefore, for understanding the game's interpassivity and ecomimesis.

Most important, the smartphone is the primary interface within the game. Although there is an out-of-phone narrative layer, in which the point of view of the player largely mirrors that of Rintarō, players move passively through it. They cannot speak for Rintarō when other characters interact with him, nor can they decide where he looks or what he says or does. Since a player's only decision is whether and when Rintarō looks at his smartphone, access to that device is the only means by which we control him.

Steins;Gate exhibits a conflation of the first and second person that is common in visual novel games. If the I and You are left out of the grammar of typical IF games in order to suspend the confusion of first and second person, this is an odd feature only in languages that require the naming of the subject. In Japanese, where the subject (if contextually known) is typically dropped, IF games become more natural.[55] Yet visual novel games rarely capitalize on this potential aspect of gaming, labeling the speaking parts of characters rather like a script, while leaving the POV visuals to give a similar sense of embodied confusion. While IF makes confusion or immersion a significant portion of the affect, visual novel games remind players that immersion is a pose and that they are always playing a role. But more than the typical visual novel convention of POV visuals, the foregrounding

Figure 20. Multifarious forms of media overlay the view of the fourth floor of the Rajikan building, while receiving an email from an unknown sender. Screengrab from *Steins;Gate,* iOS edition (MAGES. Inc., 2009).

of the pose of confusion can best be seen in *Steins;Gate*'s innovative addition of the "phone trigger" to the game.

The smartphone is also important as the occasional interface by which the player perceives the entire world of the game (see Figure 20). For instance, early in the first chapter, on the fourth floor of the Rajikan building, the orange phone is "triggered" from Rintarō's pocket and appears in our view with the background environment visible behind it. But at the same time, something odd happens. Immediately, our view of the stairwell in the hall has layered over it in the upper left of our screen the date of the game world, "7/28 (Wed)," a "battery full" icon, and connection signal icon, repeating information given within the orange frame of the phone, as though the screen of the device on which the game is being played (Xbox, PlayStation 3, PSVita, desktop computer, or more recently a real-world smartphone) has become another framing phone. On the one hand, this seems to suggest that when the player has Rintarō remove the phone from his pocket, that adds a layer of distraction or interface to the world of the game, augmenting the gaming reality. Rintarō's access to his real world in the moment he stares at his phone is somehow transformed. On the other hand, the clear layer over the game world appears as though a gesture to the game itself as a game in the real world that can be framed, a gesture toward the game as a phone, interface, or platform that augments the player's reality. In this way, *Steins;Gate* literalizes what is already true virtually in our world—that smartphones perpetrate a kind of overlay on the world. We see the world as though mediated through the new medium (rather than seeing a world recast in the medium, we see the medium in the world). And yet use of this interface is not consistent within the game.

This layering becomes confusing later in the game when the player viewing the lab is directly addressed by Rintarō, who in his paranoia (or is it?) stares into a monitor in his laboratory and asks whether someone is watching them. The same date, battery, and connection icons are layered over the interface as when the player has Rintarō check his cell phone. But in this case, the cell phone remains in his pocket. What this means is unclear. How can the player at once be inside the head of Rintarō and outside it enough to see him? Is the player still in Rintarō's head, seeing his own avatar's reflection in the monitor? It would seem so, because the fish-eye of the monitor's glass is suggested in the image's bending of space around the edges of

Figure 21. " 'Hey, you over there! Are you watching us?' —Rintarō." Screengrab from *Steins;Gate,* iOS edition (MAGES. Inc., 2009).

the frame. We see ourselves through both the monitor and the lens of the cell phone augmenting our reality now. Or we are on the other side, as it were, as though in the TV monitor cabinet in the lab, as if the monitor has become a surveillance camera. He addresses the player directly, and his friends can hear him, thinking this is just another of his performances of being a paranoiac mad scientist. But his apparent paranoia points to something real, both within and outside of the game. He is being watched by Alpacaman (the character within the game running on this very monitor) and by us, the player. This scene is precisely the same sort of staging of a border between an inner world and an outer one that Timothy Morton, in their explanation of ecomimesis, considers to be a failed attempt at immediacy. In foregrounding the mediatedness of the moment, the border between game world and real world seems to vanish, even though this is the very moment in which that border is thoroughly reinscribed.

Through the means of the smartphone interface, *Steins;Gate* tries to break the fourth wall and dissolve the distinction between reality and the game. Though players generally see only what Rintarō sees,

未来のことは、誰にも分からない。

AUTO ▷

Figure 22. "No one knows what the future will bring." Screengrab from *Steins;Gate,* iOS edition (MAGES. Inc., 2009).

there is an occasional image of Rintarō himself, such as in the final scene. These glimpses work to dissociate the player from immersion in the game to perhaps a higher degree than simply seeing the text of his name below all his lines or asides. In such moments, the first-/second-person slip becomes a first-/second-/third-person slip.

The tension between the player and the avatar is resolved in the third-person viewpoint of the true end, in which Rintarō and Makise Kurisu at last meet again as if for the first time (in the game, a scene of ships passing in the night). In this scene, the player sees Rintarō as though through an out-of-body experience. He has just returned everything back to the way he wants it in the true end. Everyone he cares for is still alive. Time travel has yet to be discovered. Rintarō gives up the technology of time travel through his smartphone at precisely the same moment that the player, too, finishes playing with Rintarō's phone. In doing so, players and Rintarō effectively give up the game (of shifting between timelines to find the best ending). Instead, Rintarō learns to be content with everyone living in the present and not knowing the future. The fate of the world is left unknown and precarious, but, for now, earth abides. In this moment, there is a face-to-face encounter that is relatively unmediated: there is no smartphone battery, signal, or date information here, though there is still a voice-over and script on the screen, as well as a spinning CD-ROM icon, an anachronism left over from when such games would be read entirely from disk rather than an internal drive. The depiction of faces in hard profile gives up on the frontality of the POV shot so normalized in visual novel games. Rather than our line of sight being incorporated within the frame as consonant with Rintarō's, here the players are remediated outside of the frame. They are no longer even putatively Rintarō; their screens become their own medium once again.

The game's ultimate message is that forgoing technology is the only way to win, but the play of the game contradicts this message. The unmediated person-to-person final scene of the "true" ending (a meeting of faces or virtual kiss scene) presents nothing that feels true but rather a kind of patently false and unattainable fantasy. For the entire thirty-odd hour game up until that moment, technology was shown to control the fate of the world and the destiny of individuals. Then only in the flash of this true ending is it revealed that technology was itself part of the problem. The only way for everyone to live (at least for a time) is for them to remain in the precarious and unlikely final timeline, the outcome of which is itself undecidable because the game truly ends, and because Rintarō has learned not to try to figure out how it will go beyond the game's end. But the full experience of the game up to that point pushes its players the other way; rather than a catharsis, the end will provide game fans with frustration. The game suggests everywhere that this "true end" is just the idealistic hope for happiness, which feels quite tenuous after the long hours spent learning that such happiness is fleeting, that death will end all families, and that the end of the world is coming. Here, the lesson for the players diverges from the lesson for the character Rintarō. Whereas he sees this as the best possible ending, players may not be willing to swallow the Luddite moral of the story. Indeed, the sentimentality of the true end is possible because it represents not a realistic hope for human interaction today but nostalgia for unmediated moments that never could have existed, such as those for a perfect family now lost.

Steins;Gate thematizes electronics fetishism as well as the moral panic around such obsessive behaviors; if there is a message (albeit a self-contradictory one) to the game, it is that we are better off opting out of technological mediation of personal relationships, exemplified within the game by d-mail. In short, the game seems to support Brian Ruh's critique of the visual novel series *Higurashi no naku koro ni* that it is its "refusal to accept history and adapt, and a subsequent preference for continual states of play and the consumption of counterfactual worlds, that is the real horror."[56] But the failure of this game, at least at the level of conforming to a genre, is the degree to which it gives up on radical possibilities of change, taking ethical action, and historical contingency. In the end, the notion that Rintarō can actually do anything to save the girls feels false. As sekai-kei, the game fails because the narrative calls into question the possibility that individuals have any control over the world. But it also seems to fulfill Uno's assertion that sekai-kei writ large is decisionist, supporting status quo complicity and complacency. In *Steins;Gate,* decisionism manifests as a particularly Panglossian (cultivate one's own garden or family) variety of giving up; act locally to save one's own family (or in-group) and leave the global problems to the world-level actors.

The point of the game is to snap players, viewers, and readers out of their (inter)passivity and into a mode of relinquishing both technology and crazy conspiracy theories—in short, growing up. But this, too, entails a possibly frustrating acceptance of the status quo. Players are left in the true end in a timeline that is indeterminate but in a position of having reset and without the promise of continued play. With all other timelines having been exhausted and determined to end in death, the final timeline ends in stasis. The game must end for it to be a game; but must it end in this way? Is not replayability part of games too? Of course, one could replay *Steins;Gate,* but in practice one would not. With the true end, the future is unknown, but at least for the time being, everyone is alive, echoing the temporality of family: everyone in a family will die someday. A nuclear family necessarily becomes less nuclear over time. But the game's embrace of the ephemerality of family coincides with its fantastic denial of the technology that enabled such an understanding in the first place. Only through engaging in the gadget lab's experiments with time travel is the ephemerality of family to be appreciated. But, of course, opting out of technology today is a fantasy that denies the state of the world. In a sense, Rintarō throws out technology so we do not have to.

On the escapism of using technology to avoid using technology, Pfaller suggests that the problem of allowing our things to define us is what drives interpassive behaviors.[57] So the giving up of technology encouraged by *Steins;Gate* can be thought of as providing the means by which we escape from the need to play that might identify us or subject us to the otaku or nerd identity, for instance. But by having Rintarō do it for us, we can continue to play other games and simply appreciate Rintarō's effort as a fiction. The game then suggests an ecomimetic escape from technological/digital media is possible, but this possibility lies only within the game world. It appeals to gamers who no more want to be imprisoned by their games than by their smartphones, but the game enables the gadget addiction from which it depicts a break. In our contemporary moment, the ultimate escapist fantasy is the ability to go off-grid and give up technological connections.

The Never-Ending (Meta)game

On the difference between traditional literature and metagame, Azuma Hiroki writes:

> In modern naturalist literature, it was imagined that the reader emotionally transferred themselves into the character, the character totally lived in the story, and the story reflects reality. On the contrary, in postmodern literature, at least in some of its works, it is impossible to secure the relationship between the story and reality, so the character's life diverges to a meta/artificial environment or database. Correspondingly, the place of empathy of the reader also moves from the character to the player, in other words from the subject of the story to the subject of the meta story.[58]

Steins;Gate attempts to remediate this postmodern shift by including the character of the player within the story. Such efforts make the game more interesting at the metalevel as well. For instance, fans continually post new timeline maps and trees that explain or complicate the story. But it is the practice of *jikkyō purei* (video playthroughs with commentary) that shows the impact of the game's interpassivity—namely, shifting interactivity almost entirely to the realm outside of the game. In a sense, *Steins;Gate* represents the ultimate instance of remediation and media convergence because it internalizes both the structure of gaming (something many games such as *Chaos;Head* and *Magical Girl Madoka Magica* did before it) and the intended platform (the smartphone).[59] So, *Steins;Gate* remediates its own gamelike mediation. But such attempts will always fail to be complete because there is always another frame outside of the frames of the object of inquiry. Today we can find that frame in online fan interaction.

Bolter and Grusin propose "hypermediacy" (as opposed to transparent media) as that which multiplies frames of mediation revealing mediation itself. For them, hypermediacy foregrounds mediation, making it visible or opaque. In contrast to traditional computer programming, which "employs erasure or effacement," hypermediacy might reveal the code that constructs the user interface within the interface.[60] The traditional mode of transparent programming, such that the program can remain hidden below the surface, is the computing form of representational mimesis, which traditionally (whether in realist novels or painting) seeks to make the subjectivity or hand of the artist into a clear window that is hardly noticed. In Bolter and Grusin's analysis of games employing the aesthetics of hypermedia, cinematic virtual reality games like *Doom* and *Myst* in their multiple remediations of other media turn "out to be an allegory about the remediation of the book [and film] in an age of digital graphics."[61] Similarly, *Steins;Gate* turns out to be an allegory about the remediation of video games and anime in the age of internet connectivity (BBS and social media) and smartphone gaming. Hypermedia games that gesture to the code or interface like *Steins;Gate* (and *Doki Doki Literature Club!*) achieve a degree of hyperrealism when all such reality is revealed to be always already mediated. Whether or not code is revealed in the game itself, the place where the programmers recede from view and cede control over the game is the metagame, where new creators or fans take over where the program, as well as programmers and marketers, necessarily leaves off.

The play with the frame of the media that both marketers and fans enact in the real world is precisely what constitutes the play such as it is in this minimal-decision, forking narrative. Beyond the embodied reverse mimesis of the carpal tunnel syndrome or "thumb twitching" that comes from excessive typical game-playing, the drama of *Steins;Gate* on the surface tries to intervene in our mediascapes to inspire us to put down the tech gadget in our hands, to step away from our computers and phones.[62] But as it does so, the game depends on our fetish and the fact that the only way to access the message is to first give over to media, dwelling in the game environment for thirty hours. In video gaming, mimesis might be found in the marketing of new technology to better represent gaming worlds, in legalistic concerns over copying of the games, or in the moral panics around copycat behaviors in real life. But there is also another path—that of reverse mimesis most obviously present in playthroughs.

Real-world copying behaviors take on a number of local guises. Piracy was but one avenue of copying that became a problem in the vibrant gaming culture of the 1990s and early 2000s, yet legal copying of games by corporations and fans had been an integral part of the early history of gaming in Japan. In the pre-Famicom world of 1970s gaming, Japanese corporations bought rights from American companies to clone games and market them in Japan. And since the advent of home computing, fans have been trying to modify, personalize, and extract pieces from the most popular games.[63] But rather than the digital duplication of games themselves, it is the marketing extension enabled by broadband video sharing over social media that reveals the most obvious copying issues that help to elaborate how games exist in the world today.

Marketing and advertising are keys to understanding mimicry in tandem with the discourses of moral panic around how gaming affects players. While cultural products like *Family Game* and *Steins;Gate* depict media as harmful, advertisements of video games are created for the very purpose of giving the products a positive image.[64] Taking seriously the proposition that advertising plays a decisive role in the consumption and understanding of new media by early adopters, we should recognize alternative realities of the game world not only through modeling consumer behavior depicted in the 1980s and early 1990s Japanese video game advertisements but also through the affective adulation around gaming on social media in the first decade of the 2000s.

Demonstrating a pronounced attention to the creation of new worlds and to capturing a realistic, live-action sports gaming experience in a home gaming environment, television commercials for early gaming consoles focused on the ways in which the games could change people, families, homes, and, ultimately, their realities outside of the games they play.[65] Almost invariably, Japanese commercials for new video game systems in the 1980s and early 1990s depicted not the latest graphics on the game screens, not merely the console box holding the game cartridge, but also the place in the home where the console would live, sometimes connected to the television in a living room or, for computer games, on top of a desk in a lucky teenager's bedroom. Typically, the scene also includes the players (as in the hockey commercial previously mentioned), usually more than one person in the case of console games and one person watching another play in the case of computer games. Often an entire family is shown gathered closely around the machine. For example, a 1979 television advertisement for the early Nintendo console *Color TV-Game Block Breaker* (*Karā Terebi-Gēmu Burokku Kuzushi*, a *Breakout* copy) has a silent but smiling family of four (father, mother, older daughter, and younger son) crowded around a television set as the young boy plays *Block Fighter* (*Burokku Faitā*). Sometimes two boys play the games, or occasionally a boy and a girl. If a parent participates, it is inevitably the father. Mothers, when they are represented at all, tend to be passive observers, lingering in the background with expressions of satisfaction and awe.

Family Game presents video games as a symptom of social decay, the only interaction left that is not potentially violent in the real world. Advertisements, in contrast, present them as an undeteriorated middle ground, a tool for reuniting the family. Even as they oversell the games in terms of representationality, print ads are especially savvy about the metagame world. A 1990 advertisement for Super Famicom made its appeal not only on the basis of representation but with the claim that it provided important access to two alternative fantastic worlds. It did this by toggling between two characters, Link and Mario.[66]

With the title "For Your Review" ("Osarai"), the advertisement has a defensively postured Link with shield in hand and sword drawn, floating on a plain, flat, yellow background beside a happy Mario flashing the peace sign. The text next to a small image of a Super NES console begins by emphasizing such higher resolution factors as the 16-bit upgrade, the 32,768 color possibilities, and the eight-channel sound system but ends with the hard sell in red lettering: "But actually what we think is the most important thing is the fact that it can do 'Zelda' and 'Mario,' an often neglected truth. This, at base, is the Super Famicom's biggest specialty!" Resolution, speed, and fidelity may be all well and good, but the reality is that this was the only box that played games with both Mario and Link. By 1994, this had become a standard method of advertising. For instance, a television commercial for *Wario's Woods* (*Wario no mori*) features all the Nintendo characters animated and living within the plastic console.

Figure 23. Parallax advertisement featuring the biggest selling points of the new 16-bit console, Link and Mario. Advertisement from the back cover of *Weekly Famikon tsūshin,* no. 180 7(2), May 29, 1992.

Representational reality was thus replaced by meta-gamelike realism or fidelity to the character-led market, which is, of course, now manifest within the gaming world in games such as the *Super Smash Bros.* series that allow characters from different games to be played against one another.

As important as such TV, print, and web advertisements may be, in recent years, a major form of new media marketing has developed in the form of online metagame cultures of fan-created videos. Several subgenres of this category of unauthorized or quasi-authorized advertising have proliferated for all varieties of new media products in recent years. Straight-up reviews, featuring a reviewer talking directly into the camera about a product and occasionally showing off its functions, are aimed primarily at giving information and criticism providing context and detailed comparisons with other games. Unboxing videos, sharing the exciting moment of taking a new product out of its package, elevate the status of the latest gadget or software to a fetishistic ritual and enmesh the packaging of the product into the new media worship. But in the Japanese gaming world (and, indeed, the international one as well) nothing quite equals the power to ignite desire for video game goods like playthrough videos.

Despite its affective performance, the phenomenon of *jikkyō purei* (on-the-spot playthroughs with fan narration, hereafter "real play") is widespread and often commented on but seldom made an object of inquiry into the world of gaming. Significantly, the term *jikkyō* ("real situation" or "on-the-spot") here evokes another form of vicarious play, one routed through journalists in the world of broadcast television sports in which live commentary is known as *jikkyō hōsō* (on-the-spot broadcasting) or *jikkyō chūkei* (on-the-spot relay). The player-cum-MC is removed from the game through their running commentary on the feel of the action, the visuals of the game, the affective impression it makes, and their comparison to other games. Like the romantic nature writers of Timothy Morton's critique, who purport to be in nature at the moment they must be writing, the real-play hosts perform for the audience instead of immersing themselves in the game. Real play on YouTube or Niko Niko dōga is not about how real the game world is; it is about connecting to the experience of play in the way a sports commentator connects the audience at home to audiences in the stands. The quality of the playthrough is assessed based on how "real" the video of the play is to an actual experience of playing through the game. This is why comments submitted by viewers of a particular video often mention they feel as though they have played the game themselves. In fact, stated reasons for buying the game appear, then, to come from commenters who sense a gap in the system, a failure of the reality of the playthrough, and the necessity of having to experience it for themselves. If real play is the display of ownership and experience, it is also a marketing of the pride of ownership and experience, a show of what viewers may not possess physically or have yet to experience or have experienced thus far only alone.

Here interpassivity is at play, but not wholly. Viewers of the video watch another person play, but they interact and communicate with the poster of the video and with other viewers through comments. If it were completely and satisfactorily interpassive, no one would buy the game after watching because the experience of the video would be enough. And, therefore, corporations would be stricter about enforcing copyright control over the violations of posting playthroughs. But this is not the case. Real play is allowed precisely because marketers implicitly understand Morton's ecomimetical critique. In the end, "real play" is ultimately frustrating, marking a failure of interpassivity and ecomimesis.

Indeed, as the legal status of playthroughs suggests, the marketing success of a game depends on real play. On the one hand, as legal scholar and lawyer Fujita Akiko affirms, real play is an infringement on copyright via the stipulations protecting the "film production" (*eiga no chosakubutsu*) provision (Statute 21) of the Japanese Copyright Law. On the other hand, game corporations for the most part seem happy to have free advertising building the depth (passion) and breadth (size) of their fan base.[67] The promotion and marketing of games apparently outweighs the cost to the corporation of images from the game (and sometimes video of the entire game) circulating freely; therefore, the game producers tend not to pursue copyright infringement. Clearly, the problem surrounding how the medium alters the real is not wholly contained within this legal discourse.

Of course, most real playthroughs are fun fan interactions that add metagame depth to games that may already incorporate metagame depth within themselves. For instance, one playthrough of *Steins;Gate* features interesting fan commentary on a side point of the game. When the entry for "1.21 jigowatts" is displayed in the playthrough video of the "tips list," one commenter calls it "a translation error." The text on the bulletin board within the game features a "tips list" page that mentions that the original script for the Japanese subtitles for the film *Back to the Future* misspelled *gigawatt* as *jigowatt* and this error was transcribed uncorrected into the game world. Then another commenter responds, citing a 2008 *New York Times* blog on the mistake as a mispronunciation within the film of *Back to the Future*.[68] Such layering of the player experience with additional fan commentary is natural to the Niko Niko dōga website where the clip was posted (a video platform that allows users to comment directly on a particular moment in the video's playback). Occasionally, such commentary is more substantive, rising to the level of a budding game criticism. On the previously mentioned scene in which Rintarō seems to stare into the *Alpacaman 2* monitor and, hence, at the player, one commenter recognizes the gesture to the metagame, commenting, "This is a gamelike game" (gēmu mitai X gēmu desu).[69] This sort of interaction helps viewers understand the game and confirm their experience of a game already played.

Of course, there are more direct and clear ways in which such videos affect viewers—for instance, those relating to consumption. Another video playthrough of *Steins;Gate* suggests the marketing value of the genre. After a nearly five-hour playthrough of the demo version video, there are several comments from different viewers about purchasing the game:

14:56 I've decided to buy it. [Ore wa kau koto ni shita.]
15:16 I've watched the entire thing from the start [Saisho kara mita ze]
15:38 I bought the computer version
15:42 This makes me think I am glad to have been born in Japan
15:46 The voices are great!
16:05 Hey, the PC version is coming out July 30!!![70]

This brief excerpt from over 250 responses to the video gives a sense of the variety and joy that watchers of such videos display. It is as much a joy about the content of the game as about the ability to purchase and play the game themselves. This brief dialogue displays something like the contentless communication described by Azuma, wherein isolated participants can feel community, but, rather than formed around an empty topic, it is formed around consumption and accumulation of frivolous goods.[71]

Not all real play in this marketing vein is fan-produced. A ten-minute video features both the star Imai Asami (the voice actress who plays the role of Makise Kurisu in the game and anime) in cosplay as Makise and the script director Matsubara Tatsuya. The minor celebrities play *Steins;Gate* on Xbox. This playthrough video garnered over 16,000 views and 208 comments on Niko Niko dōga. While most comments deal with the appeal of Imai (commenting on her voice and appearance), some are simply about the game. Such anonymous participation in the viewing of the video on Niko Niko dōga visualizes the sociality transformed not only by *Steins;Gate* but by the world into which the game has been released, a world/community that, for instance, included the (then still new) website with the branded name "Niconico douga."[72] Such playthrough videos by both players and producers have the effect of socially reorganizing human interactions around the media even when, at base, their undisguised purpose is only to sell and buy games. To limit the discussion of marketing solely to the obvious capitalist concerns ignores the willing participation and the amount of time and effort spent by players/consumers in not playing or consuming but dwelling in these mediascapes.

Reverse mimesis is not simply about purchasing goods or making SG001 orange phones, as the 5bp corporation did for a promotional event for *Steins;Gate: Linear Bounded Phenogram,* but about us behaving differently. If the message of the game of *Steins;Gate* fails to get us to leave our devices, it is because it overestimates the kind of behavioral change it might evoke in players and the degree to which such change is controllable or predictable at the level of content. But we might best see player/consumer metagame community formation as reverse mimesis: games are not only gamed or tricked out to make us addicted to gaming (and this serves the profit motive of makers) but also set up to require and anticipate this real-world interaction of fans.

This metagame real-play experience around *Steins;Gate* reveals that the sekai-kei genre itself replaces the loss of mediation between individual and world that makes up its content. Today the near and distant seem suddenly reconnected through the network of distant and near views; but the internet is precisely the mid-level medium that can both connect us to the global world reality and alienate us from our local mid-level cultural realities. Similarly, the sekai-kei genre (that depicts a world without effective mid-level actors) itself becomes the cultural mediation between nerdy otaku selves and the world, a way of connecting and creating a community otherwise deemed lacking. Sekai-kei is a medium in this sense documenting a culture in which traditional connections of family, school, and religion have been deemed inadequate for connecting people and drawing together community. But even as it marks this symptom, sekai-kei becomes a genre that remakes such community into a mass of fans consuming similar materials. Real play proves this. In other words, we should not be surprised to find that the genre and the media in which such play is consumed often coalesce.[73]

Not all online interaction is productive at forming communities or families of chosen affiliation and not all communities thus formed are productive. Bullying, trolling, and other online mob behaviors have solidified the rising nationalism in Japan since before the disasters of 2011. And to some degree, shared gaming sociality has been as much a part of rebuilding as it has contributed to complicity with ongoing inequalities.

Nintendo's *Jishin DS 72 jikan* (2009), a disaster-education game designed to emphasize survival in the first seventy-two hours after an earthquake, tries to educate on the surface, but its overt function to educate, like the ending of *Steins;Gate,* rings false. Indeed, its sales have not been impressive, and the final product was not much different from the nongame smartphone apps like Tokyo Disaster Preparedness (localized in Japanese, English, Korean, and Chinese), which was promoted by the Tokyo metropolitan government in the aftermath of Fukushima.[74] Though this app may have raised communal awareness, it did not reshape social bonds.

But the Fukushima Game Jam that sought to game the building of games by competing teams of game designers and programmers in the wake of the disaster suggests a different possibility for community building. Hosted in various venues from Minamisōma, Kōriyama, Nagoya, and Fukuoka to Taiwan, Colombia, and Chile annually from 2011, the event promotes video games in order to support, "restore, and revive" the 3.11-affected region. The labor of the game-building is itself gamified: multiple teams each composed of seven people for the thirty-hour competition give each prototype game produced the equivalent of one man-month of work invested in it. The initial goal of bringing game-building to the devasted region where there had been no game developers worked at the local, national, regional, and global levels. Starting with a session that brought students together with Tokyo game producers and designers, the initial idea was to help build careers in game production as well as continued awareness of the suffering region. But with the excitement around the profession-ally produced livestreaming of the events, the Fukushima Game Jam has grown over the years. This sort of gaming the construction not only of games but also of community and economy in the wake of adversity marks the degree to which gaming now structures reality.[75]

And such gamic reality is more widespread and totalizing than the Fukushima Game Jam alone might suggest. With broad digitaliza-tion, game theory and related probabilistic thinking began to occupy a growing and significant role in military strategy, financial specula-tion, and infrastructure development under the theory that regres-sion analysis of complex problems would lead to unprecedented new efficiencies. And, indeed, to some it seemed that Japan's rapid eco-nomic growth in the 1960s and 1970s was due in part to investments made using the new math of risk analysis.[76] By the 1990s, a reversal of understanding began to place partial responsibility on the algorithms for everything from the bursting of the real-estate-speculation bubble to the decisions based on risk-assessment models to build nuclear fa-cilities in the historic paths of tsunamis. More recent and more global financial bubble bursts have brought the ends of the binary thinking that computerized algorithmic thinking would either save or destroy economies. The notion that computers are simply mere tools in our daily lives cannot cover the myriad ways in which computers and computational programs inescapably have gamed daily life.[77]

This gamification of real life raises a number of questions: What if we considered the idea that games are realms or worlds shut off from the real world to be a damaging lie from the beginning? In other words, what if we take seriously the game world as part of our world from the outset? What if we (following Morton's identification of the nature versus human romantic myth) ultimately refuse such facile distinction between media and its environment? The wager would be that (through overt recognition that there is no difference between in-game and out-of-game) such a refusal of distinctions could allow us to act more ethically. Perhaps we will never be able to fully recog-nize that the identity shifting that the games allow us through role-playing is no different from other forms of identity transformation we play between work, family, and friends, that no individual has an indi-vidual role to play in society, that our roles are always played in layers, not multiple personalities but intersectional ones. The fantasy of so many games is that the roles played there do not matter because they are fantasy, but the reality is that they matter precisely because they are actual (real) fantasies manifest in presumably harmless forms. But there is no such thing as a harm-free or ineffectual fantasy.

If this seems far blown and beyond the realm of the video game, it will help to remember that a player must be able to quit a game for it to be a game. Indeed, game historian Yoshioka Hiroshi writes:

> You can always quit a game. That is the difference between a game and reality. However, precisely because you can always quit, you somehow really cannot quit. Lately, it seems that the dynamic relationship that captured such tension between the game and the reality has become a thing of the past. This is because, I think, the relationship between the game and reality is gradually taking another form. To put it simply, reality itself is gameified. Even without playing games, gaming logic [gēmu teki na ronri] is present in our social life today. Everything from corporate activities to university research and education, every activity such as quantification of capabilities and performance, mission evaluation of the level of configurations and achievement, to visualization of ranking and so on has been spoken about through gaming metaphors [gēmu teki na hiyu]. We cannot escape from the game.[78]

The idea that gaming has become the real is a remarkably Lacanian statement about gaming. For Lacan, the real is seen as the infinite ever-present environment or world in which we dwell, distinguished from finite realities. The real may encompass all finite realities, including everything as vast as the sum of the experiences of all individuals. But the infinitude of the real seemingly renders all realities of equal significance or triviality. If games make up part of the real, gaming is now also a characteristic of the real: the real, of course, is that which we cannot wake from, turn off, or hit a reset button on. In this regard, Uno writes that games are the basis of postmodern life and cannot be avoided.[79] The game of the real never ends, and all other finite realities must dwell within this gaming. Players cannot lose because the end is always deferred, or, rather, we continually lose because the game world from which we cannot escape is rigged against us.

For example, the finance speculation that bubbled real estate economies based on models of bundled risk probabilities abstracted not just from labor and material conditions but from the data about those factors. Such algorithmic decision-making assumes away the complexities of the real by carving it into computable realities, transforming the real into a mediated reality or game not because it creates and sets rules for a game but because the algorithms it puts into practice ignore the enigma of the human. So we realize (always one crisis too late) how the minimal risk assessed was either higher than expected or simply one we were not ever willing to wager at any cost.

This is why the experimental video game *Credit Game* was developed by Kuwakubo Ryōta—in order to stage playing the market without risk in a Japan still reeling from the credit, housing, and land bubble economy of the 1980s. The 2001 exhibition of the game was touted as a virtual delight at its core, putting into direct relation this big world gaming and the metagame of the discourse of virtuality around video games:

> Day trading can even be considered the most exciting and action-packed network-based game around. Real-life day trading is, of course, full of risks. This game allows players to explore the exciting and fun aspects of day trading—a world virtually unknown in Japan—without incurring any of the risks involved in the "real game."[80]

On the one hand, the game might be read representationally as a smaller, twisted, virtual version of the bigger reality, but on the other hand, the game gives a real-world instance to learn about risk, potentially teaching would-be investors to keep from engaging in frivolous unsafe market behavior. *Credit Game* does not prove that games have become real or that the real has been gamified; rather, the gamelike real is now—after successive gaming miscalculations and the birth of the situation in which a game such as *Credit Game* is even possible—more visible.

.

6

Mediated Expressions
Emoji's E-mimesis

The modes of mimesis are necessarily most visible in overtly embodied mediations. Representation and mimicry can be seen clearly, for instance, in the popular phenomenon of cosplayers copying the dances of anime characters and posting their performances on video-sharing platforms like YouTube and Niko Niko dōga.[1] These dances echo the dynamic of real play *(jikkyō purei)* clips posted by video gamers of their game playthrough (discussed in chapter 5) but with a twist. If in reality gameplay, gamers simply try to post a true-to-life game with the value added of their affective comments about the immediate experience of gaming, with these dances we get something different, innovation on the worlds of anime and game characters. Media theorist Hamano Satoshi argues that such dancing suggests new "meanings brought about by Japanese cyberspace":

Since the advent of the internet, there has been a lot of discourse critiquing its lack of corporeality [*shintaisei,* embodiedness or somato-psychic links]. For instance, the notions that there are no face-to-face relations, that the space is anonymous, and that "the appearance" (Arendt) of flesh and blood bodies does not exist, all lead to the fact that this cannot establish "the public sphere" (Habermas), in which subjects resolve to take responsibility and have exchange and discussion. This is what has long been said. But our internet society has found a completely different path for this sort of modern subject; that is to say, a form of imitation or mimicry [*mohō*] of the fictional character-like [*kyarakuta-teki*] "Haruhi" body gives way to the "appearance" of countless flesh and blood living bodies on the web. The addenda I want to add here is that this unmistakeable reality [*jijitsu*] is probably the limit of the possibility of a Japanese networked society.[2]

Hamano's comments here resemble those of Ueno Toshiya, who was among the early wave of thinkers who found techno-orientalism to be a useful concept. Whereas Ueno contrasts the techno-orientalism of Japanimation with the "media-tribalism" of rave culture, Hamano presents an example that exhibits both.[3] It is significant that Hamano's "Japanese cyberspace" (*Nihon no netto kūkan*) provides a moment of mimicry (that Hamano himself glosses as "mimesis," *mimeshīsu*) in which netizens copy the dance in the anime adaptation of the breakout, highly self-reflexive sci-fi light novel *The Melancholy of Haruhi Suzumiya*. Far from either Silicon Valley's utopian visions around media connectivity or notions that Sony's high-definition screens and crystal-clear headphones will realize our wildest dreams of democracy manifesting virtual reality through immediacy, Hamano suggests that the most sustainable connection to the real that we can hope for through our new media is people dressing up and line dancing together and posting for others to see, copy, and repeat. He fundamentally contradicts what Azuma Hiroki describes as a "game-like realism" *(gēmu-teki rīarizumu),* in which cultural products gain reality through their verisimilitude to other products rather than to objective reality (which might seem apropos of cosplayers imitating their favorite game or anime) and the cyber-mediated participatory cultures that he elsewhere labels the instantiation of Rousseau's ideals.[4] By contrast, what Hamano calls the base, incontrovertible truth (*magirenai jijitsu*) is precisely the new real. And the sheer popularity of the *Dance Dance Revolution* (1998–2022) and *Just Dance* (2009–2021) video game series confirm the prevalence of this new real. The new real is the humdrum everyday of living with, in, and through our media that may seem so commonplace and boring as to hardly warrant notice or mention. However, it is precisely through focus on the new real that we can assess the integrative as well as sinister impacts of media on our economic, political, social, sexual, and other realities.

Body: The Medium of Identity

The reason that the body has become a center of media studies is because it seems to be the first, last, and ultimate medium.[5] Broadening the concept of media to include the body clarifies the relation of the mediated and the mediators, revealing the intertwining or entangle-

ment of two otherwise seemingly antipodal strands of mimesis (representation and mimicry). If we move beyond a static concept of media
in which external objects (print, screen, canvas) are the only viable
media to a relational one that includes the flesh-and-blood bodies
working with such objects, within them, and themselves as objects—a
continuum of mediation rather than discrete media per se—we begin
to understand that repetition and copying of mediation cannot be ac-
counted for solely by the conditions or affordances of lifeless frames.
Considering the human body as yet another medium to represent
reality and to mime such representations shows how representation
and mimicry can both be captured by the concept of mimesis as a remediation of content with attention to fidelity. Furthermore, the concept of body as a threshold brings into question the binary notions of
an inside and an outside, human and nature, and recasts notions not
only of media as between but also of mimesis as a simple question of
transparent copying. In the two-sides-in-one or Möbius strip concept
of body that contains an inside as it touches an outside, we find an
exemplary instantiation of the paradox of a medium that is both part
of a message and the means for that message's transference.[6]

Drawing deeply on Walter Benjamin's understandings of mimesis, theorist of mediation and embodiment Mark B. N. Hansen develops the notion (similar to Jacques Lacan's distinctions between
realities and the real) that all reality is mixed reality (composed of the
virtual and the real) in order to argue that our bodies are the means
through which the real world and, indeed, all media eventually must
pass. Hansen's view (like Marshall McLuhan's idea of the "extensions
of man") is that all media and mediation are subordinate to the concerns of the body. Rather than understanding the body as an ontology constructed through experience, memory, and culture, Hansen
argues for "the de jure primacy of embodiment over cultural construction."[7] He persuasively argues that since all media are received
through the body, it is, therefore, the ultimate medium. But his fundamentally ahistorical and presentist argument that the experience
of the body takes primacy over culture is a logical leap and, indeed,
contradictory of the point that the body is the ultimate medium.

The very fact that all mediation comes through the body also
means that mediation of the body comes through the body. This
leaves us with an undecidable moment or a binary: either the body

takes precedence in experience of the world (including the mediation of the body) or the mediation of the body as a medium does. It is the chicken-or-the-egg of constructivism (or the nature–nurture tension; or, as Benjamin puts it, the mimetic faculty is both phylogenetic and ontogenetic) that is not really an either/or but a dialectic tension.[8] Something like a body *is* (exists) even before we may name it as such; yet the body as we know it only comes (begins to exist) with the naming (its concept). Ultimately, the priority of the body or its concept does not matter, because for all intents and purposes, we live after any such moment when one might have preceded the other. Rather, we dwell in a world that must deal with a situation in which both a body in the world (even in utero) exists and its emergent concept continues to be developed.

This tension or gradation itself comprises how we know anything about not only the body but also anything in the world. It is not that the body simply is, but that it is and that its "is-ness" (ontology) is mediated over time just as existence of mind, thought, and memory are mediated by the body. Mind, thought, and memory may be contents that are mediated by a body, and this body (media) exists as a concept, thought, or memory mediated in turn by that same body. Just as there can be no a priori existence of a body without its concept, there can be no concept without its concept-forming body. More than Kantian, it may be Hegelian (in the same way the master needs slave and slave needs the master, according to his system) or more akin to what Karen Barad refers to as "entanglement."[9] Media needs the content and content needs the media, or body needs culture and culture needs body; media needs mimesis and mimesis needs media. They exist as systems in tension, so to posit an a priori is itself to mistake what the (ecology or economy of the) system is.

But for Hansen, our Being-with technological media is never to be reduced to the level of simply a mind and cultural construct or discourse.[10] Citing Benjamin's understanding of *Erlebnis,* he argues for direct engagement (or the lived experience of technology) rather than knowledge through memory (*Erfahrung*). However, Hansen goes too far in arguing for the potential of the direct sensuous touching between body and media. Experience, memory, language, and discourse have roles in marking how we exist alongside and with our tech even prior to some moment of a Merleau-Ponty-like touch. Yet for Hansen, the emphasis is always on the ways in which such embodiment is directly experienced by the body: "the ways in which technology's power over our bodies (domination) actually gets experienced."[11] He claims such body experience is unmediated (by, for instance, memories of other experiences, our linguistic thought processes, our cultures, our media); for him, it is directly encountered and experienced knowledge.[12] But this is magical thinking that ignores the body as but one more medium through which such immediacy can be apprehended.

The argument of this book runs parallel to Hansen's important idea that we need to recognize the power of technology in our everyday lived experience, but the idea that such dwelling with our media happens as though through a short circuit around culture, memory, ideology, and other forms of mediation and is sensed directly through our bodies must continually be called into question. Hansen is right in pointing out that for Benjamin mimesis is part of nature, part of the way the world and the human machines living in it work. But this is precisely why he is wrong in thinking that Benjamin is writing against a kind of cognitivized (linguistic/discursive) experience and thinking anyone at any time can dwell in pure experience. Rather, Benjamin's argument (clearer in his "The Storyteller" essay than in his essay "On the Mimetic Faculty") is that there is nothing unnatural about discourse, as it is but one of several manifestations of our natural mimetic faculties—in this, emoji discourse does not substantively differ from that written in other scripts.

The crass, false, or mythical history of mimesis (the nostalgia for a prehistorical moment of premodern external [to body] media) is nothing if not useful. It articulates the range of mimesis as a story of human progress over time. Benjamin and McLuhan share the notion that writing and inscription marked a difference in how human beings related to the world. Whereas, for McLuhan, writing alienated us from our visual worlds, for Benjamin writing was but the most recent stage in the growth of nonsensuous mimesis, which may not have alienated us from the world so much as provided another natural moment of being human within it. This sort of nostalgia for the preprint era also holds in Saitō Tamaki's media theory:

> In cultures since the advent of the use of character writing [*moji shiyō*] mimesis itself is dominant. . . . Mimesis is recognition of the object and the whole, pointing to the experience of the

divide between subject and object disappearing. In oral cultures, the mimetic faculty was helpful for the memory of poetry and such. However, the appearance of the alphabet brought about the distance between subject and object through vision. Here "objectivity" was born. However, at the same time, the good [*kōfuku*] unity or integrity of mimesis was lost.[13]

This notion of a time when there was a unity of subject and object is a fiction we tell ourselves to continue to dwell in the world as split subjects in the here and now. Saitō's notion of mimesis as being embodied in a pre-media-laden world and tangibly changed in a mediated one ignores the notion of the body itself as media for mimesis.[14] So, what I want to argue through attention to the body here is that the body is both semiotic and sensuous. This dual tension runs the course of the history of mimetic thinking through Benjamin and continuing today—and is quite evident in emoji. This is not to say that the tension is ahistorical or constant but rather to say that, because it is a modal tension configured differently at different moments, it needs to be historicized. The point here should not be to take a side (to assign to one mode a modern, unnatural derivative position and to the other an original, essential, natural, and timeless one) but to recognize the state of being as such is torn between both modes. So, for example, it is not whether emoji are a new language or a return to pictures on cave walls but to recognize that the script is actualized by the tension between the two. The task of this book has been to identify how such tension is manifest at various times in various media histories and mediations.

Benjamin senses that human mimesis (as opposed to naturally occurring resemblances between things) requires and draws on human ingenuity and creativity. To read the stars, dances, and entrails, he argues, was not a kind of unthinking mimicry or copying but required some "nonsensuous" (not directly embodied) interventions or innervations—which is to say, it required what we would now call some frontal-lobe thinking even as it deeply engaged the body. As Susan Buck-Morss puts it, it is not that the kind of mimesis that needs to be recuperated from primitive or childish mimesis was a knee-jerk bodily reaction.[15] It is not, as Hans-Georg Gadamer says, that in the modern period "the concept of mimesis has lost its aesthetic force"; it is not that only in the premodern or childish form of mimesis in which the child's play of imitation was for the purpose of becoming "like that which is imitated" but to become "the object imitated" proper.[16] So, it must be the case that only in the ("modern") mediated mode (not moment) is mimesis aesthetic in the first place. In one version, mimesis is a representation and, therefore, possibly aesthetic. In the other, it is a conjuring forth or a manifestation of the thing itself (an embodiment). But even in that embodiment, the copy is iterative of the copied, a self-consciously different version of it.[17] One version does not precede the other; in some sense, all versions are equally original and radically new because of this process.

In his later work, Hansen comes closer to this understanding of the body's role in mimesis. For Hansen, the way in which the digital or virtual spaces allow for, encourage, or afford a drift from the "mimetic identification with the body image and toward creative play" gives such work its meaning.[18] Though in Hansen this becomes another sort of cyberutopianism, in fact it becomes clear that the experience neither begins nor stops with the body: "Decoupling identity from any analogical relation to the visible body, online self-invention effectively places everyone in the position previously reserved for certain raced subjects," or what Hansen calls a "radically unprecedented condition of selfhood."[19] Slavoj Žižek is right when he claims that the content of cyberspace is simply the self (id and ego) projected outside of the body and made manifest in the physical world rather than kept inside.[20] Study of such media simply make more tangible and evidentiary insights already accessible through conjecture and logic. But there is more to it than that. As the case of emoji will show, study of such media can better help us to find our position in the physical world in relation to and with/in our media.

Emoji: The Medium of Universal Expression?

One story told of media studies since at least McLuhan but on through Hansen is that print media (and its associated sign signification) reified the Cartesian mind-body duality. In this view, print media took us away from body and embodied mediation, while visual (from film to TV) and, more recently, digital media (from VR and AR to biomimetic prostheses) have brought us back to body and embodiment representing some originary, more natural moment. The preceding chapters expose the falsity of this historical narrative about media and its relation to body. Indeed, media stood in relation to body and embodiment through visualization of solid objects in space in chapter 2, sound similarity in chapter 3, becoming in chapter 4, and dwelling and building in chapter 5. Through the recent print-like scriptural form of emoji that is purportedly of the new digital visual regime and, therefore, more tightly connected to body, this final chapter examines the way emoji reveal both the always already embodied character of scripts and the myth of visual difference.

Emoji are not simply a fleeting fad in international youth culture but rather are, thus far, the most effective, if unintended, fruition of a long series of attempts to refine the complexities of spoken language into a universal pictographic script. At one time or another, various languages and scripts have been called "universal." Since at least the biblical dreams of the mythical Tower of Babel, linguists, governments, and philosophers (among others) pursued and "discovered" universal languages everywhere, in mathematics, science, music, laughter, tears, Latin, French, Arabic, English, the sinograph, Sanskrit, Esperanto, binary code, Blissymbolics, LoCoS, and now emoji. Perhaps the only real universal in this story about the desire to find universal scripts and languages is the continually renewed human struggle for better communication, for an improved "medium for language," a medium of meaning or of message transmission that is faster and clearer, logical, and pervasive—in sum, more immediate.

One history of emoji could start with the 1987 publication of a tome by the designer and semiotician Ōta Yukio titled *Pictogram Design: Pikutoguramu [emoji] dezain,* not as an absolute origin but as yet another significant marker of the multiple origins of emoji. The book itself is something of a coffee-table book of signs, from hieroglyphics to the (then cutting-edge) world of computer icons and international airport signage, but it also deals intensively with the idea of pictographic scripts.

Ōta's book is part of the rise in the usage of the Japanese word *emoji* (lit. "picture character") following the 1964 Tokyo Olympics, stemming from his efforts to create internationally legible signage for that mega-event. It was in 1964 that Ōta (who would later also design the "green running man" exit sign ubiquitous in Japanese and European public spaces) developed his LoCoS (Lovers' Communication System) pictorial script. Ōta's book was one obvious, significant source of inspiration for the designers of NTT DoCoMo's i-mode phone system (including the now famous Kurita Shigetaka),

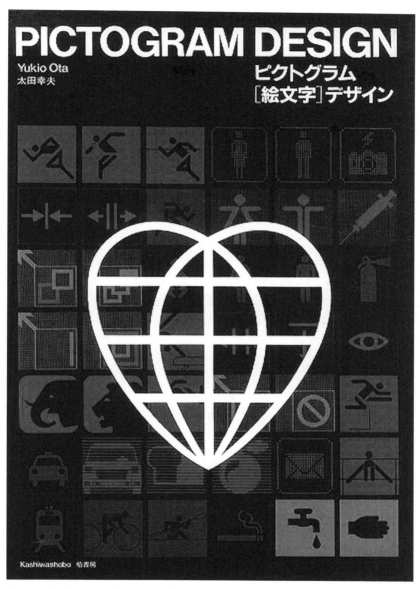

Figure 24. Cover of Ōta's book designed in conjunction with the September 4–16, 1987, exhibition curated by Kikutake Kiyonori, organized by the Nihon Design Committee, and displayed on the seventh floor of the Matsuya Ginza Department Store in Tokyo. Ōta Yukio, *Pictogram Design: Pikutoguramu [emoji] dezain* (Tokyo: Kashiwa Shobo, 1987).

who first released their set of 167 pictographic characters in 1998. One example of this influence is the NTT design team's choice to adopt a modified image of Gerd Arntz's "turban-wearing man," a design created in 1920s Vienna that had been reprinted in Ōta's 1987 book (see Figure 28). As both a sourcebook for the designers of the original emoji sets and as a history entwining what we would today call infographics and universal languages, *Pictogram Design* is a revealing point of departure.

The book is also something of a crystallization of the supposed value of the icon in modern life, far exceeding the realization of abstract visualizations within computing in the years immediately preceding Ōta's book. Looking back across the twentieth century for other forms of information display and its visual organization, Ōta most prominently and repeatedly cites Otto Neurath, a philosopher and sociologist with the Vienna Circle, a group known for promoting logical positivism and verificationism.[21] So, we should not be surprised to find that emoji's roots in the progressive, socialist educational apparatus continue to be echoed in the Silicon Valley utopianism surrounding them today. The claim that pictographs might best present complex information and arguments seems to reflect ancient educational calls for the reading of prayers through pictograms aimed at illiterate Japanese (see Figure 25). Like many technological developments in the history of new media (such as television), emoji began with (and perhaps will end with) a dream of universal humanism through education.

With the rise of socialism and machine design in the early twentieth century, a number of new, internationally minded projects created what seemed like real possibilities for mass education. The development of what is now known in infographic circles as the "Helvetica man," the ubiquitous pictogrammatic rendering of a human now most commonly associated with restroom signage, represents but one of these educational efforts. Combining the urge for widespread legibility and clarity, Neurath's International System of Typographic Picture Education (Isotype) provides perhaps the earliest attempt at a universal pictographic auxiliary language for the express purpose of educating the modern masses.[22] The idea of representing complex ideas pictographically remains with us today in the art of data visualization (the direct legacy of Isotypes), as well as in its "cute-ification," such as the recent depiction of "The Entire US Economy Depicted in Emoji."[23]

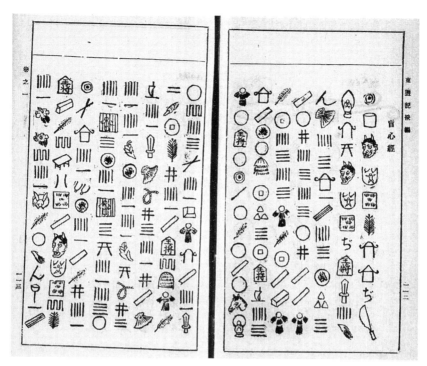

Figure 25. Early emoji? Image of a seventeenth-century rebus for prayer reading. Reproduced in Tachibana Kenkei, *Tōzaiyūki hokusōsadan* (Tokyo: Yūhōdō shoten, 1922). Courtesy of National Diet Library.

Touting the notion of signage as a language to its primarily Japanese audience, Ōta's book stages the very conflict between signage and language itself: *meaning* as controlled design in contrast to *meaning* by natural evolution. In a section titled "Why Pictograms?," the tension between static sign versus moving language becomes evident.[24] Ōta presents a critique of Isotypes by the graphic designer and artist Awazu Kiyoshi: "In the beginning Isotype tried to make language into 'a language to be seen with the eyes' from an educational aspect, but the problem of race rooted in it remained unsolved, and it was practically impossible to make it a global visual language."[25] Here, Ōta and Awazu raise the problem of Eurocentrism as a fundamental barrier to the global humanist goals behind Neurath's practice. Transcending the problems identified by an increased awareness of multiculturalism, another diagnosis Ōta gives for the failure of Neurath's method (rather than his theory itself) is that Isotypes are inflexible. Ultimately, *Pictogram Design* argues that Neurath strove for a mathematically definable language that would not need to change once it was composed. After a backpacking trip through Italy, during which he discovered the usefulness of signage for communication, Ōta became more optimistic about the possibilities than Awazu. Out of this optimism emerged Ōta's key innovation: he purposely constructed his LoCoS system and equipped it not only with a grammar but also with possibilities for future modification and growth.

In the most utopian claims about pictographs, the glyphs are all at once evocative of our cave-dwelling past and our globalized future: a better language, more direct than Japanese, more transparent than phonetic or even ideographic characters, and, simultaneously, more "Japanese" than Japanese and older than ancient hieroglyphics. According to the philosopher Tsurumi Shunsuke:

> As more and more people use things like Isotypes and LoCoS and mix them up, we draw closer to pictographs that everyone can use. The great thing about pictographs is that they are not so narrow as to benefit only Europeans alone, but are things that everyone can use equally. Another way in which they differ from language is that two- and three-year-old children can understand them right away. Even the elderly in their 70s and 80s can freely master pictographs.[26]

Tsurumi's appeal to the global reach of a pictographic script in 1991 cites the history of Neurath and Ōta, noting that, if it is to be successful, such scripts must not reside in a local or even regional culture but must remain withing the purview of all cultures and age groups.

Two films about global issues with which Ōta was involved display a kind of dedication to world education through "visual support." The 1979 film *Visualizing Global Interdependencies* followed up on Aaron Marcus's 1960 report of the same title.[27] Developed from a black-and-white slideshow presented at the University of Hawai'i's East-West Center, it features the transnational work of research fellows from India, Iran, the United States, and Japan and purportedly "developed a new visual language" (see Figure 26).[28]

The film reprises the Malthusian problems of population expansion, food systems, energy consumption, and environmental pollution

Figure 26. The *Visualizing Global Interdependencies* 1979 project depicts the four major concerns of population expansion, food, energy, and pollution. Image from Aaron Marcus, "New Ways to View World Problems," *East–West Perspectives* (Summer 1979): 16.

through use of Isotypes and emoji-like symbols. Despite its primary reliance on visual interfaces, it also uses verbal English terms such as *GNP, Calories, Consumption,* or *Metric Tons of Coal Equivalent* and relies on numbers to convey its arguments. Ōta would later draw on the pictographic lessons learned from this project to produce a different film with Alan Kitching (a developer of the Antics 2D-animation software system) for the United Nations University in 1984. The computer-animated *Sharing for Survival* (1984) made a more dynamic and cinematic film, giving a certain "flow," if not a previously lacking grammar, to the visual language. Like its predecessor, *Sharing for Survival* was intended to be partly educational. But it could also be seen as something of a flashy mission statement for the United Nations University. However, the voiceover narration by the famed British actor Peter Ustinov undercuts the notion that the animated images alone could convey the film's meaning. In his discussions of the film in *Pictogram Design,* Ōta maintains his focus on the notion that education and more direct communication can circumvent and supersede established and national languages.

To some extent, as we have seen, emoji were born from the rising internationalization in preparation for the 1964 Olympics. So consideration of the burgeoning theories around the rise of electronic age communication and information in the 1960s will help to understand those origins. In reflecting on the geopolitical state of the world in 1963, just a few years before the coining of the term *information society,* philosopher and critic Yoshimoto Takaaki wrote "The Copy and the Mirror" about how our political lives were even then always already mediated:

> All the events and achievements currently appearing in the world are merely mirrors that reflect the reality of events and achievements in which we dwell. And the mirror will also represent our situation.
>
> However, in this world, bizarre things sometimes exist along with reality. In one form, "knowledge" comes from somewhere in the world like a real "thing" and it lives in our brains. In this case, what conveys "knowledge" is literally the shipping, air mail, communication, or transportation networks. So there it is clear that circulating "knowledge" has become a fetish [*busshin*]. Among the classical left-wing of this country, Marx's phrase that "knowledge is merely an act of consciousness" has already ceased to exist. It is not simply that we lack this "act of consciousness"; we completely lack "conscious" human-beings.[29]

Yoshimoto makes plain that media (referred to here as information and communication infrastructures) do not connect with objective reality. Here he argues that the left had already been so "diffused and dispersed" over the past decades in Japan that revelation and transmission of knowledge itself would no longer reflect the economic and geostrategic realities of the postwar. Rather, he suggests that knowledge had simply become a widget traded using the information and communication infrastructure tools of the neoliberal state. Here the copying and circulation (representation or mirrors) of knowledge about the world alone would not suffice for its critique; rather, one needs to take stock of the media upon which such knowledge dwells in the world. In short, infrastructures themselves do not increase universalism or lead to higher consciousness. This clear statement of the structure of a media infrastructure system—that it manifests both types of mimesis (representation and mimicry)—is the crux of the argument in this book. And no truer a test for its idea could come than in the seemingly innocent and cute form of emoji.

A Technical History

In this vein, another history of emoji could begin in 1982 with the Sharp MZ-80K personal computer, which sold over one hundred thousand units worldwide and included sixty-eight "graphical symbols" (*gurafikku kigō,* such as a "nose" or "eyes") as characters on its keyboards and systems. Subsequently, the font designer Satō Yutaka's pictographic script (or font) on the emoji-history timeline included

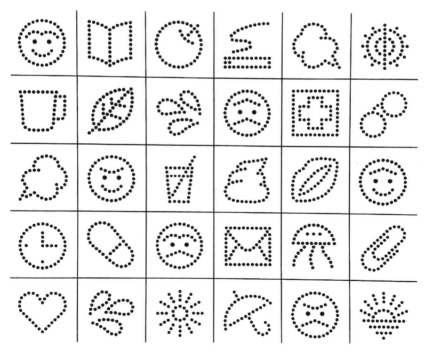

Figure 27. Pictographic font, honorable mention in the symbol division (*yakumono bumon*) at the eighth annual Ishii Mokichi Typeface Contest in 1984. Courtesy of Type-labo.jp.

early versions of a "heart," an "envelope," a "poop," or an "umbrella" (see Figure 27).[30]

Perhaps even more pertinent to this history, however, are pagers of the midnineties that came equipped with pictures as well as characters. In 1995, NTT DoCoMo sold a pager (in Japanese, a *pokeberu*, a "pocket bell") with a screen that was able to display a face with varying expressions. In a television commercial unveiling the product, a woman (played by Hazuki Riona) reading a book alone in a dark room receives a message from a man sitting in a park with another man. "I'm lonely" (*samishii*), reads the text on the screen of the device, white with a trim of purple and pink geometric designs. Next to the text of the message, a cartoonish face of a man with animated, upturned, plaintive eyebrows blinks, letting out a sigh of exasperation. Cut to the woman, contemplating the text and responding between this shot and the next cut. Then back to the man looking at his "manly" black and gray pager, the screen of which reads: "I'm really into you!" (*daisuki*), with a cute woman's cartoon face animated in a pucker and a rose floating behind her. The ad, in its brief twenty

Figure 28. *Top,* Gerd Arntz's designs for Otto Neurath's Isotypes reproduced in Ōta Yukio, *Pikutoguramu [emoji] dezain* (Tokyo: Kashiwa Shobo, 1987). *Bottom,* Biomimetic representational racial diversity depicted in a screengrab from a Google image search for "turban man emoji" after the skin tone additions were announced in 2015.

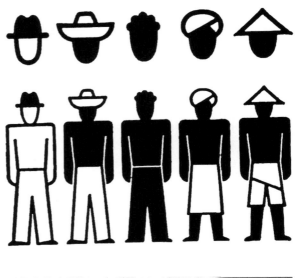

seconds, has all the salesmanship of the new form of writing it needs; seeing is believing: the new graphics present affect.[31] And this reading of emoji as conveyors of embodied affect holds through today in the common mistaking of a shared origin of *emoticon* and *emoji*.[32]

Perhaps driven by similar intentions as the midcentury icon designs for education, the designers of cell phone emoji borrowed the look for their contemporary digital pictograms directly from these keyboards, fonts, pagers, and even from Isotypes. To recognize the connection from early 1920s Isotypes to contemporary emoji, compare the cell phone emoji "turban man" to Gerd Arntz's Isotypes designs in Neurath's work. The DoCoMo designers who borrowed the forms of some emoji from Ōta's book took the basic appeal and the simple design of pictograms for specific marketing purposes (to open up a new, particularly "female" market for pagers), stripping away the original educational and internationalist intentions associated with the designs (see Figure 28). Identifying a particular historical or local origin of the script, then, gets us only so far. We must also judge claims to its "universality" from its function and design.

The Case for Particularism

It would be misleading to categorize all the discourse about emoji as "universalist" or "utopian" in orientation. If there is a real global revolution of emoji, however, it can be seen in the simple fact that a medium emanating from a specific moment of Japanese postwar internationalization (from echoes of early twentieth-century attempts toward global mass education in the midcentury efforts to build an international signage system at the Olympics) and from a narrow (particularly female) youth subculture circulating on Japanese mobile devices and cyberspaces became part of a global code for inscription. The movement of emoji from a local Japanese encoding system known as Shift-JIS to a global one (the pan-platform standard of Unicode) in such a short time is remarkable, if not unprecedented, and it was certainly not inevitable; Unicode's initial rejection of emoji in 2005 was reversed only in 2008 with corporate coaxing by Apple and Google, who sought to gain smartphone market share in Japan.

The very process of encoding the emoji characters, whether in Shift-JIS or in Unicode, has led to a number of problems and happy mistakes at the level of transcriptions and interface renderings—"slips" of signification within the media system that make any claims to the "universal" mythic at best. The many confusions between signs rendered across multiple platforms show that, in some important ways, cross-platform legibility might itself constitute an equivalent of the untranslatable: when, for instance, around 2010, a given code for an emoji on a DoCoMo phone might have been displayed as a "musical" note on an AU phone and as a "pile of poo" on a SoftBank iPhone.[33] Sociologist Inamasu Tatsuo writes that even despite such "difficulties concerning the compatibility between different devices and mobile phone companies," "the characters have already obtained the right of citizenship."[34] But this lack of stable trans-platform signifiers shows precisely not only how mediation matters but, moreover, how media history and, specifically, mediation history matter. It also reminds us of the fact that local cultural histories are often part of broader technological media histories.[35]

So, we need to move away from the technicist myths of "universality" to realize that emoji are, and always have been, strongly embedded in cultural conditions. Beyond the meek listing of ten national flags in the original sets (later remedied by the inclusion of most United Nation flags), the Unicode set of emoji remains highly skewed toward Japanese culture. Despite the famous addition of "taco" to the emoji syllabary and its paltry attempt at biomimetic "diversification" through six skin tones in 2015, there persists a disproportional representation of Japanese cultural icons, such as *sembei* (rice crackers), love hotels, *tengu* (mythological long-nosed ghostly creatures), Japanese driving learners' permit emblems, and curry rice. There are at least fifteen overt references to Japanese culture within the current Unicode emoji set (at least, if we trust the official name tags such as "*Japanese* castle" or "*Japanese* rice cracker"). But even some seemingly universal emoji, like the very popular "pile of poo," are based on highly specific Japanese cultural references. When code transcription is corporatized, standardized, and made part of a system on a device, it can result in a loss or, at the very least, in a transformation of meaning.[36] All "universal" aspirations and the respective discourses are limited not only by the practical realities of corporate image branding but also by linguistic realities wherein language is immediately localized—or even prelocalized—so that no image can be seen with fresh eyes.

Literary Usage and the Question of Universal Grammar

Grammar is inherently determined not by the design of emoji but by their usage. Consider an emoji novel, titled *Emoji Novel* (*Emoji shōsetsu*). It was written by a user of the pseudonym "Chicchikichī" and posted August 10, 2007, on the Eburisuta website for digital novel distribution. Filed under the category of *ren'ai* (love), the fifteen-page novel is presented completely in emoji (alternating between one and seven emoji per page), telling the story of a woman who works at a hospital and a man who gambles for a living. They go on a date together and consummate their love at a love hotel. The woman then gets in some kind of trouble (we only see the emoji for "SOS"), goes to the hospital, and has a baby; the novel ends with a celebration of the newborn's birth. Though the story is simple and short, there are instances when it becomes quite literary, if by "literary" we mean not merely the functional command of language but also the willingness to play with signification itself. In this regard, the love scene after a short fight and the later reconciliation is telling:

Figure 29. Four pages of Chicchikichī!'s 2007 emoji novel titled *Emoji Novel*. From the Eburisuta website for digital novel distribution.

Page Break

Page Break

Page Break

In just four pages, we are nearly given a complete narrative of a sexual encounter.[37] Reunited, the couple goes to a love hotel where they engage in acts not suitable for those under the age of eighteen, after which the woman is left in need of help. The insertion of the "blank space" of a 🔞 ("not for under eighteen" mark)—as a way of navigating a taboo subject—suggests precisely in a humorous way, but without actually showing us, what transcends the graphic signification we might expect from a love scene composed not of words but of pictures. By navigating around highly sexualized emoji such as the "eggplant" and the "peach," and by merely giving us a "blank space," the novel adheres to time-honored novel and film aesthetics that cut away or substitute the acts themselves with figurative expressions. What is lacking in the short staccato flashes of meaning in Chicchikichī!'s work is a clear grammar. Consider page 1:

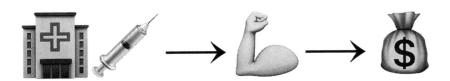

Figure 30. Page of Chicchikichī!'s 2007 emoji novel titled *Emoji Novel*. From the Eburisuta website for digital novel distribution.

Clearly, there is a woman. But is she at a hospital, receiving a shot to get strong—to then go on to spend money? Or is there something else going on? As in many modernist novels that teach their readers how to read them, the following page seems to instruct us how to interpret the first through a sort of parallel construction:

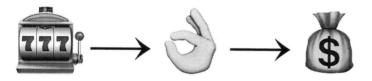

Figure 31. Page of Chicchikichī!'s 2007 emoji novel titled *Emoji Novel*. From the Eburisuta website for digital novel distribution.

Here, the man is gambling for money. This might lead us to reflect back to reconsider the woman's situation as well. Perhaps, we see now, the first page is meant as a comment on her employment and her means of making money. She administers medicine to cure people at a hospital for a living. In any case, the potential for confusion, I would argue, stems from the use of the arrows. They are obviously stand-ins for actions or verbs. The reader is forced to try to understand, not necessarily in a uniform method, the action that is supposed to take place here.

We can see a similar communicative tension when emoji stories on video (even prior to Animoji) try to animate emoji. Years before Hollywood produced *The Emoji Movie* (2017), numerous videos that animated emoji had already been posted online, such as the popular YouTube video "Game of Phones," a translation of the television series *Game of Thrones* into an all-emoji video. In such video experiments, a montage of otherwise static images (flashing between different emoji) often assumes the role of the "grammatical" arrows above.[38] Such use of cinematic grammar gestures toward the problems and gaps in the everyday usage of emoji as word-for-word substitutions. Such animating of emoji highlights not simply what functions emoji usually lack (grammar) but also what they tend to afford us (visual-verbal communication).

That is to say, the real revolution of emoji (if there was one at all) was the quick pervasiveness and penetration of the script across several platforms in a short span of time (not simply the ability to send pictures). Visual communication through pictorial symbols was at least theoretically possible on mobile phones through telemessaging, GIFs, and later *shamēru* (mobile phone photography as marketed by i-mode in 2000) long before the advent of emoji as a keyboard script input choice on platforms beyond the Japanese ones.[39] It follows then that either there is something unique about the pictogram script that gives cell phone emoji a special place and meaning among ideographic languages or there is nothing new under the sun since cave paintings.

A Genealogy of the "Poop" Emoji

A genealogy of one specific emoji can demonstrate the ways in which the script, even today, fails to attain the level of a "universal" or "transhistorical" signified, while continuously hinting at such a domain. The "pile of poo" (*unko* or *unchi māku*, "poop mark"), spotted almost everywhere in our digital media environment, might indicate some directions. Perhaps we should recognize that part of the popularity of the "pile of poo" emoji might be related to the global interest in the "poop" shape because of its characteristic swirl (the *makiguso* or *makifun*), even before it came to be labeled thus in Japan. Notably, the Japanese Wikipedia page for *unko māku* lists the engraving *The*

Perfumer, created by French craftsman Bernard Picart (1673–1733), as an origin for the shape of our pile today, though the equally authoritative 2006 packaging of a toilet calendar (by Yakult yogurt) recalls, as a kind of fun fact, a Japanese Edo-period version as one of the earliest examples.[40] But the premodern history of the shape of "swirly poop" does not quite explain its emoji anthropomorphization and the seemingly global fascination with it today.

To understand the meaning of the "pile of poo" at a deeper level, our discussion of universal humanism, media, mimesis, Japan, and emoji can benefit from a consideration of Gomi Tarō's most elegant work of Japanese literature, first published as *Minna unchi* in 1977. Following its translation into English as *Everyone Poops,* the book became a mainstay in children's world literature, perhaps as the result of its titular universal humanism.[41] Everybody poops, but how we express ourselves about it differs. Fundamentally, we humans all may seem to defecate, but the book goes beyond the human in its enumeration of who counts as "everyone." The educational (potty-training) book includes animals as its most basic set of candidates, only then building toward the human. In this sense, we can speak of a "universal animalism" if we include humans in the category of "animal" (as does the literal translation of the respective Japanese term *dōbutsu,* "animate things"). But maybe the notion that "everyone poops" is nothing but a commonplace fiction if it is expanded this broadly; maybe everyone only thinks that "everyone poops" or wants it to be the case that "everyone poops." Beyond the simple medical fact that many animals today (also some of the human variety) have to rely on colostomy bags or had their digestive tracts removed almost entirely, Gomi's book does not consider the possibility of a sentient machine—that is, a body without poop. In short, what about androids? Do they poop electric poop?

At one historical root of our globally popular "pile of poo" emoji, we encounter the robot. The "poop" emoji—at least in its playful form and usage—became part of the highly intertextual and self-referential world of Japanese popular culture after one significant appearance in Toriyama Akira's manga (and later television anime series) *Dr. Slump* (1980–84). The series revolves around the hapless Norimaki Senbei, otherwise known as Doctor Slump, and his invention, the android girl Arare (a.k.a. Arale).

Figure 32. Commercial star Ayami Nakajō plays the automaton Arare in a commercial for fashion brand GU in 2016. The character is identified by her cap and her main prop, poop on a stick.

Famously, Arare prods a pile of swirly poop with a stick asking it if it is lost, to which the faceless poop responds, "Go away; poop can't talk!" Further anthropomorphization (occasionally adding feet, eyes, and mouths) and chromatic shifts (from a dark brown to pink) happen when Arare and the shit she prods appear as minor characters in Toriyama's later and even more popular series *Dragon Ball* (1984–95). The stick became associated with the icon when the "poop" was marketed in the form of countless collectible goods such as poop-on-a-stick pillows, pens, and cell phone accessories. So, the vast international success of the *Dragon Ball* franchise might help to explain the adoption of the "poop" icon into the award-winning font dingbats in 1984, into pagers in 1996, and into Japanese cell phone emoji sets in 1998. We can then imagine the Unicode gatekeepers, through laziness or fun, approving all the famous Japanese characters as a set already time-tested and proven within the Japanese media ecology. But, since the "pile of poop" persistently remains in the top one hundred characters used, and since we can assume that most global emoji-users are not simply *Dragon Ball* fans, what could explain this emoji's popularity beyond its culture of origination?[42] I suggest that it is likely a kind of reverse mimesis. The remediation of the "poop mark" into digital environments betrays a truth some of us might rather not admit: globally, a primary site of cell phone use is the toilet.

What do we make out of this fertile mess? The "poop" character in our phones helps us to engage with our actual world, not simply to represent a universal condition; rather, it helps us to think about the poop on our phones. According to one study, as many as one-sixth of all cell phones today are covered with fecal matter and dangerous bacteria such as *E. coli*.[43] Emoji eloquently reaffirms the toilet not just as a site of texting but also as a site of reading. The "pile of poo" suggests what we probably already know about our new media—too many of us are spending far too long on the toilet with our new media gadgets. This mimicry might show us the true reason why the "poop" emoji is so popular globally, which is to say that the "poop" emoji is both a sign of our contemporary media consumption and a manifestation of its waste. Whether the global appeal of emoji stems from a kind of close or iconic representation of our collective lives or a universal life (we dance, we get sick, we are happy, we cry, we sweat, we poop) or whether they simply provide the necessary means for a new kind of contentless communication given the new media of texting cultures and social media on portable smartphones, part of the appeal, judging both from the character set composition and their usage, is simply the tight connection between the character set and the body.

What I want to suggest is that the "pile of poo" emoji is popular because of the way it not only conditions us to our newly remediated reality but also refers to that new reality in which both the fecal matter represented in our phone screens and the fecal matter actually on phones coalesce and become, if not indistinguishable, at least parallel. The "poop" emoji might not, therefore, be popular because poop is universal but because one particular use of the cell phone might be, if not universal, at least broadly popular. The "poop" character in our phones helps us engage with our daily situation of carrying this powerful medium with us. So the sign can be read not so much as a symbol or symptom of a real situation as an iconic mark or stain of the situation itself.

Mixed with jovial attitudes, the utopian rhetoric of universal language and free access around emoji suggests a free transmission of information—free from the need to translate and interpret and free from the cost of distribution, free from the sense that critical histori-cal cultural media studies would be necessary. Noting the prevalence of emoji, the discrepancies in transcriptions on different platforms, and the *hikikomori* phenomenon, Inamasu writes: "In this sense, 'universality' and the 'closed nature' entailed in pictogrammic com-munication as it is (even while advancing us towards isolation) is synchronizing with the composition of modern society developing under globalization."[44] Emoji are emblematic of the way in which our presentist, utopian images of new media function as harbingers of a rosy future of globalization or one-worldism and a mythical pre-linguistic past. Neurath's distinction between humanism, which brings high-level and complex information to a number of people, and popularization, which brings simplified, watered-down information to the greatest number of people, is important here; clearly emoji have skipped Neurath's first mode and jumped to the second. This is not inherent in the script; indeed, as Ōta's attention to verbal picto-graphs in his LoCoS script shows us, it is possible with the addition of new grammatical (particularly verbal) emoji that the script will become less rebus-like and more linguistic in its usage over time. But whether as a step back to cave paintings or one forward to a one-worldist paradise where miscommunication ceases, or both in a kind of postmodern global village, what is assumed in the varied responses and uses is that emoji are somehow clearly different in the way they signify, that they are ahistorical, acultural things in a way that differs from many other scripted languages that are ready to hand.

It is not that by using emoji we are now speaking a universalized Japanese language but that the medium itself has grown larger than the local, even as it still retains the mark of its origins. The scene of our mobile use is not so mobile but rather stuck in some very localizable sites. If the train is a common site for mobile life in Japan, driving while texting in the driving cultures may serve as a corollary outside Japan. But whether sitting on a Toto or an American Standard, understanding originally intended usages of emoji or not, the site of the toilet seems nearly universal. Emoji today are nearly universal in their prevalence and penetration but not in our usage. Different groups will use them differently. This is the closest to the promise of a being-in-common we might get. This is what the new real in practice looks like: a bunch of people on the cusp of becoming globalized just now prodding poop.

To give it one final prod, we need to return to thinking about the body proper. Using emoji to emote universal affect or represent a universal or particular human body has not been enough. We have not only started to think in emoji and see them, but also, with facial recognition on our phones and the advent of Memoji and Animoji, we have in some sense become emoji. This raises the question of what or who is being modified in the skin tone modifiers: Is it the emoji or is it us? Are emoji representing racial particulars or are we miming those presented by emoji?[45] White users of emoji have, according to several studies, a pronounced tendency to opt out of setting skin tone options because "proclaiming whiteness . . . felt uncomfortably close to displaying 'white pride,'" a fact that raised the question of whether such choice to opt out was itself the manifestation of a racial privilege unthinkable for some users of color.[46] Because only the tones but not the facial features had changed in 2015, one powerful though misdirected critique arose: "These new figures aren't emoji of color; they're just white emoji wearing masks."[47] In other words, the putatively racially neutral features of the early emoji sets were thought themselves to be white in their facial features. Regardless of whether they were white, Japanese, or neutral (universal or iconic), the fact that the birth of emoji skin tones enabled a new representationist critique of emoji itself points to the fact that the change in new media script had transformed how it could be discussed.

There are times when the material world is the ground for the form of cultural material in the world (representation) and times when it is not (mimicry). Emoji were, to a significant extent, made in Japan; the original emoji sets depicted the human body as strictly yellow in tone. Yet these two facts have little to do with one another in a causal way. It is true that Asian technologies hold a particularly fetishized place in the global imaginary; it is also true that many global technologies actually were made in Asia. The second fact embodied in material reality should not offset the first, also embodied in a material reality that is constructed and mediated through cultural material. The yellow's putative origins are as connected to the 1960s "Have a Nice Day" smiley (designed by Harvey Ross Ball and the brothers Bernard and Murray Spain) as they are to the development of that particular shade of chrome yellow.[48] In other words, the fact that the humanoid figures of the original emoji set were yellow is historically unrelated to the fact that emoji first appeared in a country whose people have long existed in the racist imaginary as having that skin tone.

An insistence to pay attention to Japanese media history is not to claim that the yellow skin of pre-2015 emoji must be read as Asian. Rather, this insistence (an insistence on the new real itself) is to argue that we cannot simply discount the kind of techno-orientalist reading of emoji that would do so. Of course, the historical argument about Ball's smiley face would have little bearing on a techno-orientalist critique of the original emoji set in terms of the yellow skin, because, indeed, the yellow emoji set once embedded in our media has to function in a world in which racism and techno-orientalism are part of lived reality. Ignoring the yellow tone of the originals, some argue that despite their 2015 racial diversification via skin tone modifiers, even yellow emoji "*continue* to technically center whiteness in the emoji set as an extension of American technoculture."[49] Other studies show the tendency toward whiteness is least profound in the American context and more pronounced, for instance, in Africa and Asia.[50] The point here is not to argue about whether users choose a mediated skin tone that matches their embodied one on the Fitzpatrick scale as an attempt to find some sort of representative or immediate connection between body and media but that users recognize their choice of skin tone will have effects on their meaning because their choice has to function in the world. After the advent of racial diversity modifiers in 2015, the default tone of emoji remains yellow; but to consider the tone neutral would be to ignore the demand for such skin tone modifiers in the first place.

Ultimately, the problem with emoji and race is not unlike the problem with CG and techno-orientalism with which this book began. We have already spoken of the simulation that CG can play with the human body and the importance of paying attention to the real bodies that will always underpin virtual bodies in CG cinema.[51] Yet it would be irrational from a formal or historical evidentiary standpoint to argue that emoji are yellow because Asian or Asian because yellow: humans (even severely jaundiced ones) are not chrome yellow; yellow comes from the transport of the smiley face and its supposed communication of affect into the new media world. And yet, once included in the writing systems on our phones that exist in the world with racism and techno-orientalism, it would be completely rational to read them in this way. To do so is just to acknowledge what it means to live with technology in the world, to experience the new real.

Conclusion
The Real Renewed
Rendering Techno-orientalism

This book has examined various histories of mediation to expose, develop, and project the ways in which media both represent and transform our world. If the entanglement of media and mimesis occurs within a singular modernity that has been largely (though not exclusively) defined by the West, then Japan is a useful place to see how well the concept works. Such a positioning of Japan as a pivotal test case has been problematic in media studies.[1] So we need to caution here that focus on Japanese media does not imply that Japan is the only place possible for tracking the relationship between media and mimesis. To argue otherwise would be to participate in a techno-orientalist stance that has been mentioned in previous chapters without prolonged discussion. This book has assumed that there is nothing essentially Japanese about these media and, in fact, has demonstrated that the specific uses and developments of media in Japan examined here are contingent on particular producers in specific moments and cultures of consumption. However, just because the book takes the lack of any inherent Japaneseness as a given does not necessarily mean that the book does not participate in the continuation of a cycle that ties Japan with media or technology. It does not, therefore, obviate the necessity for a direct consideration of techno-orientalism.

Media and mimesis are made visible within and imbricated in modes of technological fetishization that do not transcend and can contribute to techno-orientalist views of media. Indeed, even studying something else (a nontechnological object) would not get us beyond or outside the vortex of the techno-orientalist critique, because, even by avoiding discussion of technology, its presence could be read in the absence. This is to say, that (given the pervasive context of techno-orientalism) to speak of anything Japanese is potentially to step into the power dynamics at play in techno-orientalist critique. And in understanding this, the critique of techno-orientalism still cannot ipso facto transcend the operations or politics of techno-orientalism. Further, techno-orientalist criticism is a mode of understanding or knowing and, therefore, is itself a powerful technique applied to Asian-related material that will potentially reproduce some of the problematic power plays that it critiques about techno-orientalism.

Techno-orientalism is intimately tied to ideas about the "progress" of nations through world history, such as modernization theory and conceptualizations of the end of history. Its premise, that the future is "Asian," rests on a sense of history as geographically mappable, a notion visible in the work of Hegel or, more recently, Alexandre Kojève and Francis Fukuyama. The idea of the post–World War II decades as an "American Century," for instance, is part of a strange but enduring concept that world history began in Ur or Greece and progressed northwest, toward England via France and Germany. Just as America was the future for France at the time of the revolution, Japan (and to some extent China) became the future for the United States in the 1980s and 1990s.[2] But as a "latecomer" to (Western) modernity, Japan has also been seen as behind the times, a purportedly premodern, feudal, pagan culture that somehow still exists today as a high-tech, futuristic, postmodern wonderland.[3] This notion of Japan as in between or on a threshold—both spatially (on the margin of Asia) and temporally (fluxing between premodernity and postmodernity without ever quite arriving in modernity)—also fundamentally positions Japan as a Hegelian medium that helps negotiate the spatial and temporal domains between such binary concepts as modern and premodern, contemporary and future, East and West, etc. In this sense, Japan as a concept is itself a philosophical lever that might open a path to understanding as much as block it.

Views of Japan as holding such a hybrid position arise from a particular attitude toward "oriental" objects, especially technologies and media. The grand historical narrative suggests that, like Turkey and other supposedly belated outliers to a Western model of modernization, Japan's alternative modernity managed to hold on to its traditions while incorporating aspects of Western culture.[4] However, this displays a tendency in Western civilization theory to conceive of Japanese modernity as a kind of mimetic and, therefore, secondary and derivative modernity, a strange funhouse mirror distortion of Western modernity, which is presumed to be an original, undistorted, and evenly distributed example of social, scientific, economic, and political transition.

One way to resist this view of copycat modernity is to recognize that innovation always relies on creative borrowing, sampling, citation, repurposing, reusing, reprocessing, or rendering of available data. As modernism has taught us, we are all eternal copiers or incremental modifiers; there never has been an identifiable original.[5] In this way, modernity can be seen as an aesthetic discursive formation that has been constructed through the constant negotiation and the perpetual identifying and repositioning of new "others." Japan has long been front and center in this respect, both as an other (to the West) and as a self that finds other others (on continental Asia and in the West).

This suggests the power dynamics within modernity are always at least ambivalent—just as the colonial situation gives power to the colonist, it also confers (albeit limited and circumscribed) powers to the colonized via something like Homi Bhabha's "colonial mimicry" to resist and push back. This acknowledgment of multiple agencies under the general conditions of hegemony at least partially undoes any notion of a completely hegemonic center.[6] In her study of piracy as mimetic of the behavior of colonists, Barbara Fuchs's concept of "imperial mimesis" emphasizes sameness or identity over difference. In this sense, imperial mimesis might be another name for techno-orientalism, revealing not only the way fetishization of an Asian technology distorts the world and human relations within it but also the modes of wily innovation (like Bhabha's "sly civility") that can be produced in places that are thoroughly techno-orientalized like Akihabara. And imperial mimesis can be helpful for thinking about the historically key (yet strategically liminal) position of Japan in media studies. Fuchs conceives of imperial mimesis as crucially redefining mimesis in general to include "non-literary phenomena, . . . [and to designate] imitation of a model, whether by subjects, polities, or texts." To Fuchs's list of possible nonliterary mimetic phenomena, this book adds media as a "bridge" (as Fuchs puts it), the frame or system between the content of culture and the world in which the media exist.[7] So even as reverse orientalism (Occidentalism) and techno-orientalism are themselves forms of mimesis, as copies or (mis)representations, the media through which such behaviors are accomplished act as concrete bridges between constructed worlds and the given world.

A concrete example can be found in the discussion of computer graphics (CG) in chapter 1. Significantly, Azuma Hiroki and Saitō Tamaki, in their elaboration of cyberspace as a new medium, miss a particular aspect of CG: there is no such thing as pure digitization, just as there is no such thing as sign without referent. In fact, despite the feeling of a new digitized world in cyberspace, the digital realm is constantly pointing to and dependent on the realm outside it. One of the great "Japanese" film sagas conjures such digital bodies in our minds' eyes. The Hollywood *chambara* (swordplay) films known as the *Star Wars* saga have, in their twenty-first-century techno-orientalist prequels and spin-offs, created "completely digital" animated characters. Think, for instance, of Jar Jar Binks, the digital resurrection of Peter Cushing as Grand Moff Tarkin, or the return of a young Princess Leia decades after Carrie Fisher played the character. Jar Jar was seemingly created out of thin air, while Leia and Tarkin were created by using images of the actors captured on film at a given time. But in spite of this apparent difference, both types of imaging are grounded in the real world. The Jar Jar animation relied on the motion-captured embodied movements of actor Ahmed Best, and the portrayal was criticized for the racist stereotypes in the character's patterns of speech, which evoked Black minstrelsy figures such as Stepin Fetchit and Butterfly McQueen. This was not simply a case of audiences bringing their baggage into the reception of a cultural product but also of creators remediating their own cultural baggage into the production. Though no Jar Jar–shaped creature existed in the real world prior to his creation, the data from which his figure was rendered were very much of our world and, in that sense, not so dissimilar to the time-tripping computer-generated images of a young Carrie Fisher and death-defying ones of an aged Peter Cushing.[8] Though the desire to realize the impossible feat of creating something from nothing may seem to be limited to worlds of fantasy (like a techno-orientalist Hollywood appropriating plots and aesthetics from samurai films), it can be repeated with significant differences, of course, around almost any moment of cultural production, including those within Japan itself. For example, the digitized musical sensation Hatsune Miku stars in viral concert videos featuring thousands of live fans cheering, dancing, and singing along with a projected 3D hologram of the beloved pop icon, who is promoted as "completely digital."[9] But the completeness of the digitization is a myth sustained by magical technological thinking. In fact, Hatsune Miku's voice is simulated using Yamaha's VOCALOID software, which itself was rendered by mixing, stretching, and distorting diphthongs and tones that were originally sung by humans and recorded and stored in a voicebank.[10] Such examples, whether from Hollywood or Tokyo, suggest that no medium can overcome the structural limitations of signification that ground or embody even the most fictional, fantastic, and virtual simulacra in the real world. Creativity and imagination begin and end with the given world. It is magical thinking to suppose that something can be created from nothing.

And yet the spectacular desire to achieve the impossible creation of something from nothing persists. Today, social media seems to provide a potential space for such creation of identity. Our platforms in cyberspace seem to afford us freedom to be whoever we want to be in that world. And yet, as the anonymous spaces of chatrooms and bulletin boards of the mid-1990s to the mid-2000s gave way to named participation, such naming did not make the identities represented in cyberspace 2.0 any more real or make the former modes of participation any less real. In citizen's band (CB) radio, video gaming, and early social media, anonymous participation (enabled by handles, initials, pseudonyms, and fictional avatars) rendered in more stark relief the performative aspects of personality, identity, and mimicry already present in older social media conventions. With the rise in Japanese use of Facebook and Twitter in the aftermath of the catastrophic triple disasters of March 11, 2011—the Great East Japan Earthquake, the ensuing tsunami, and the nuclear meltdown it caused at Fukushima— named social networks have become, to take a metaphor from bygone communication structures, today's "bulletin boards" and "totem poles": they stand at the center of our global village, transposing our identities and associating them not with traditional families and filiation but with alternative bubbled communities of affiliation (LINE being the key social medium for this). The implicit message behind the widespread acceptance of these metaphors for new media, which draw on older forms of meaning dissemination, either cuts against the mainstream notion that new media are fundamentally new or reveals just how new they may be. That we understand new forms through metaphors that remediate them in terms of older ones betrays a glimpse of the new real that undergirds the sheen of marketing. New media have provided not more immediate connections but simply more intense mediation. Social media does not create something out of nothing; it stands as our exemplar of a world ecomimetically built on and echoing another world of social relations.

Techno-orientalism works in a similar way. As both an aesthetic mode of representation and a set of practices that transforms the world, it is but one manifestation of such magical thinking predicated on a mode of ignorance to connections between cultural products and their production in the world. The broader term *orientalism* is generally understood as an aesthetic cultivated from a simultaneous desire for and fear of the other. This aesthetic enables and perpetuates exploitation of historical inequalities or uneven distributions of power—i.e., the context and means of its production. One aspect of orientalism that is often missing from this standard narrative but is specifically relevant to Japan is the situation in which nonmetropole places were both demonized as derivative copiers in terms of degree of civilization and modernization and simultaneously associated with a technologized future that outstrips the center. Recognizing that images of uncontainable Asian technologies promote racism and fear of the Asian other while also critiquing desire for an unattainable Asian future, scholarship on techno-orientalism shows that, in some cases, the products of Asia have been seen paradoxically both as inferior, derivative copies and as desired technological innovations that the West itself might pilfer and copy. This technological fetishism is a reversal of a basic tendency of orientalism, in which the mimicry of the colonizer by the colonized creates an image of the other that is comfortably familiar yet different enough to remain separate.[11] In techno-orientalism, while this dynamic may continue to hold true as the non-Asian confronts familiar, yet different (putatively Asian) technology, it is also reversed as the non-Asian tries to copy, consume, and be transformed by the Asian technology. In short, mimesis, whether as representation or mimicry, is at the heart of techno-orientalism, but copying is not a unilateral, bottom-up phenomenon; it is at least a two-way street.

Studies of techno-orientalism have tended to be more concerned with one way more than the other, with identity critique more than with technology or media critique per se, and with North American cultural studies more than Asian studies.[12] In an effort to address the political, ethical, and moral wrongs endured through years of inequality, hegemony from elsewhere, and blatant racism against real human beings, and to think about the ways such wrongs manifest as violence to real bodies, such studies rightly focus on the representation of bodies: bodies of Asians, of cyborgs, and of transgender people, nations as bodies, bodies as others.[13] This book started from the premise that new media also provide a fertile ground for examining techno-orientalist tendencies. But it also shows that a broad definition of such media (extended to include the medium of the body, both those bodies represented by and those affected by these techno-orientalist representations) might draw this approach closer to identity critique than it might otherwise seem at first glance.

Examining the gadgets, networks, information flows, and media ecologies so integral to techno-orientalism's formation adds a new means of understanding techno-orientalism's root causes and pervasive tendrils.[14] Here it is important to repeat Ueno Toshiya's recognition that techno-orientalism is the result of the historical advent of information capitalism.[15] As a leader in the fields of communication and information technologies, Japan's entanglement in the wires of electronic informationization has deep roots. In 1967, futurologist Hayashi Yūjirō coined the phrase *information society* to describe an emerging state of computerized knowledge consumption.[16] Two years later, engineer Tonuma Kōichi mapped information flows as networks of pathways, resembling organic neural webs and imagining an early biotechnical view of the spread of electronic media. The Metabolist movement, which had earlier emerged from the same biotech sensibility, showed how information saturation was affecting daily life in the 1960s and continues to inform the global organic conception of the internet as a "web" today.[17] As a result of Japan's place, we might say techno-orientalism is at the heart of our contemporary understanding of media and our sense that new media reveal the possibility of making new worlds and making in the world.

Assuming that claims about the superiority or inferiority of media formats and cultural objects are themselves always culturally, historically, and socially inflected or premediated and, therefore, subjective, ideological arguments, it is clear that techno-orientalism (in relation to Japan) moves in at least two directions: on one hand, it is created by fears of a technological other, and on the other, it is evident in Japanese pride in the uniqueness and exceptionalism of the Japanese technological brand. Or to put it more broadly: "Stretching beyond Orientalism's premise of a hegemonic West's representational authority over the East, techno-orientalism's scope is much more expansive and bidirectional, its discourses mutually constituted by the flow of trade and capital across hemispheres."[18] In short, techno-orientalism is manifest by unequal power distribution, as well as in the production and circulation of things in a particular style.

Like the cultivation of colonial aesthetics explained by Karatani Kōjin, the exoticism of techno-orientalist style is a willful ignorance that brackets off other concerns to focus on one particular aspect, to cultivate a desire for or an interest in a Japanese or "Asian" technological object (often as a stand-in for the subject or person, as we have seen with the Madame Butterfly window).[19] What tends to be bracketed off in or ignored by techno-orientalism is a care for the actual cultural and geostrategic logics of Asia that have produced its circumstances for such presumably technological innovation or mediation. That is, exoticist consumers of techno-orientalist goods cultivate mystery and misunderstandings around the objects of their interest. And the twist is that this is equally true for many Japanese consumers of Japanese technological products as for many non-Japanese consumers.[20]

Such willful ignorance is not limited to those of patently orientalist inclinations but rather has become part of the lived realities of Japan. The work of orientalizing the other is not simply and unilaterally translated or transferred in Japan to elsewhere; it has become an active orientalizing of the self within Japanese culture. For example, the Japanese-language translations of those masterpieces of techno-orientalism *Neuromancer* and *Gulliver's Travels* do not translate the proper name of the nation "Japan" into a different space of alternative modernity, such as Turkey, India, Somalia, or Bolivia, but instead maintain the specific uniqueness of "Japan" for Japanese-language audiences. And "Japan" remains Japan in Japan, even in translations of the absurdist truism declared by Oscar Wilde's whimsical boy Vivian in "The Decay of Lying." Arguing that art should not be based on reality and, indeed, that nature copies art, Vivian takes the position that the presentation of Japanese people through Japanese art does not tell us a thing about Japanese people in reality; the country as seen through its art, he declares, does not exist.[21] In other words, Japanese translators and cosmopolitans have themselves become mediums channeling and re-creating the modern Western stereotypes about and desires for a virtual Japan that, if not quite Vivian's "pure invention," is at least partially reinvented through such musings. In this sense, "Japan" (the discursive formation) has been a new medium (or cyberspace) for channeling the other time of the future and the other space of fiction, even for the Japanese. Meanwhile, such an aesthetic works to erase Japan the place.

The techno-orientalist tendencies of literary fantasies from science fiction to aesthetic treatises are connected to their worldly offshoot, the tech industry. In other words, it is not only that the textual association of Japaneseness with technology or media can be read on the surface in the contents of culture but also that such fetishizing occurs around and through the technological products that emerge from that nation. In short, occasionally latent and periodically overt, techno-orientalism can be seen both in the Yoshiwara nightclub of Fritz Lang's *Metropolis* and in the nondescript black, hard plastic of a Nikon camera. This is not simply a case of aesthetic standards being applied differently to techno-orientalist cultural products than to technological and media machines. What seems common is the more subtle version wherein Japanese media are so normalized globally that they no longer signify as Japanese. The precision of a Seiko or Casio watch as transformative of time, the Sony Walkman as a producer of private space in public, and the crisp clarity of a Canon camera rendering visions of sports anew are all examples of discourses around Japanese technologies that have deep penetration beyond the Japanese market but tend no longer to redound back to Japan in terms of soft power.

Their techno-orientalist positioning in the market nevertheless is perpetuated. Globalization is not always about the homogenization of local cultures under the hegemonic capitalist, imperial, or franchise cultures like those of the United States; it can move in other directions that allow powerful innovations developed in nonhegemonic cultures to rise and gain market share (at times through transparently hiding their national or cultural origins and at times by overtly flouting the homogenizing paradigms of globalization).[22] Indeed, what is true for goods on the global market is doubly so for media: they are supposed to be transparent. Numerous examples of Japanese forms of seemingly transparent media silently adopted around the world include the development of the VHS format by Japan Victor Company (JVC), the success of 8chan and 4chan (copies of Japan's 2chan) as global platforms for broadcasting right-wing anger, and NTT DoCoMo's development of emoji.[23] The world has become so saturated with Japanese media innovations that people using Japanese media do not necessarily think about them as Japanese. As a result, "Japan" is often erased from Japanese media, due as much to the dominant norm of homogenization through globalization as to strategic marketing of "culturally odorless" products at historical moments when overtly Japanese products were viewed negatively, cultivating a quality of national ambiguity or statelessness (*mukokuseki*).[24] From the standpoint of ethics around essentialization, this is a net good (since nationalism of cultures has historically led to so much violence and racism). It may even be more accurate to a globalized world in which the geographical origin of technological goods and innovations has largely lost meaning (Nikon lenses are now made in Thailand). But such erasure of origin and identity that homogenization perpetrates is also obviously problematic, especially because (in its Asian versions) techno-orientalism is far from dead. Today the marker of Japanese style—as evidenced, for example, in the nondescript Uniqlo clothing (except perhaps for their T-shirt line that inserts kitsch over-the-top Japaneseness into the generic staples of global pop art)—is what Kōichi Iwabuchi calls "odorlessness" but with a catch: the odorlessness itself has become the aroma of the new aesthetic regime. In other words, the new globalization is not an erasure (even if it might have begun that way) but rather an assertion of a minimalist style and chic.

The aesthetics of erasure have become a hallmark of techno-orientalism as a style. That is, even as traces of Asia are erased, that erasure itself becomes an aesthetic to be prized. Witness the global success of minimalist brands from Murakami Haruki and David Mitchell novels to Huawei, TaoTronics, LG, and Samsung products; today, Japanese style does not have to be Japanese. Yet even as they homogenize and erase local cultural markers from products, marketers of Japanese exports and promoters of the pop cultural industry of video games and anime continue to cultivate a self-techno-orientalizing national image as technological and futuristic. While of course the dominant narrative of globalization as homogenizing is accurate, there are significant exceptions. Japanese products have "gone global" because of erasure, while others pose an overt challenge to homogenization under a global norm (Uniqlo T-shirts with images of Hokusai prints or video games steeped in the rich history of the Warring States period). Some cases combine both erasure and a challenge to homogenization: for instance, although Sony founder Akio Morita originally chose the company name in the 1950s as one that would not sound Japanese, he later insisted on the brand name "Walkman" for the groundbreaking device, despite the marketing advice of experts at the time, who argued that the name was oddly agrammatical in English.[25] In the first case, Morita homogenized to fit in; in the second case, he conformed to the global standard of English only in part. Similarly, the emoji character set still bears the marks of its Japanese origins in 1960s internationalization movements and 1990s pagers (*pokeberu*), even as the homogenizing Unicode has been slowly weeding out and contextualizing through augmentation culturally specific Japanese icons. The early awkwardness of the then still strange word *Walkman* or the continued presence of Himeji Castle and love hotels in the Unicode emoji set are exceptions to the rule of a homogenizing globalization. These are cases that at once can provoke warnings about threats to the apparent global hegemony of English-language civilization and stand as omens of the degradation as well as penetration of the Japanese language.[26] All of these mediated transformations of our daily experience mark the groundwork for the new real, which is defined by those everyday moments when media have so transformed reality itself that we can no longer understand the world without reference to our media.

The new real, then, is not simply a reverse mimesis or an instance of the content of cultural products changing the world. Rather, it marks how we live with and in media. Popular media remediate our usage of new media; at the same time, we behave in ways that mimic that mediated content. In moments of media shift, examples of hypermediation abound. When a medium mediates its own mediation ("homomediation" or "automediation"), we can see the emergence of the new real. It is not only that we copy the world and its mediated images and that that behavior is then itself mediated (ad nauseam) but also that our behaviors are always already thoroughly mediated. As we have seen throughout this book, the body is simply the clearest manifestation of how any mediation (even homo- or automediation) is somehow already premediated. Though the discussion of the "Haruhi" dancers in the previous chapter deals most explicitly with the question of the body, it has been implicit throughout this book. We began with the confusion of the animal body with the machine and human body as part of a Nipper–media nexus. Enami Nobukuni, Morioka Isao, and Rokudenashiko sought to control the mediation of their own bodies in increasingly biomimetical ways in order to stand out against a background. Miura Tamaki embodied the role of Madame Butterfly in a quest to fit into the background of the predefined role and creatively capitalize on her position through embrace of a schizoasthenic mimesis. Mimetic rivalry around *Gekkō kamen* showed how donning the medium of the mask repeated the work of media and related copycat violence to real bodies of youth. And the social relations ecomimetically constructed within a video game world revealed the limits of attempts to remake the world of social relations outside of the game—in which saving bodies can only be accomplished through giving up on media. The skin tone modifiers of emoji, too, remediate questions about a universal, human-embodied condition.

These microhistories of media reveal how media unceasingly fail to live up to their grandest hype. Despite claims that they can transport us across time and space, materialize figures before our eyes, conjure voices from the past or from our imagination, provide justice where there is none, make us violent or happy, create families or dissolve them, transcend linguistic limitations, and, thereby, connect us all, media highlight that our social disconnects lie beyond mediation. These multiple stories of mediation reveal that even though we may all have a body that shares features with other bodies, "the body" and its multiple mediations can never be the same for everyone in every instance. Therefore, we must question breathless utopian claims about media. And yet, we cannot help but see the world as different because of its inclusion of these media. We can no longer communicate without emoji; we conjure them in our speech even when no scripting is necessary. This behavior builds the new real, even as it necessarily always already feels a bit dated.

Acknowledgments

The foggiest notions of this book occurred to me during an Association for Japanese Literary Studies conference in 2008 at Princeton University, at which I presented a paper on Japanese cell phone novels and alternative history fiction. More than a decade of discussions, courses, research projects, presentations, and publications afforded me opportunities to clarify and refine the ideas. I am grateful to the many institutions and people who placed early bets on the nascent whim of this book.

I thank the various archives and institutions that provided access and affiliations: Meiji University, Waseda University, the National Diet Library, the Tokyo Photographic Art Museum, the JCII Camera Museum, the Yokohama Archives of History, the Johnson-Shaw Stereoscopic Museum, the Tsubouchi Memorial Theatre Museum Archives, Chiyoda-ku Library, and countless fan sites, blogs, and online communities provided key material support and information.

I thank various funding organizations: the Japan Foundation supported preliminary research in Tokyo; the Northeast Asia Council's Short-Term Research Travel Grant brought me back to Japan to continue research; Penn State's Institute for Arts and Humanities provided the time and space in which I first conceived of the present form of the book and began the arduous process of bringing parts together and presenting early ideas; and Penn State's Center for Humanities and Information gave me a chance to explore whether a related digital humanities project could fit into the book. The Department of Asian Studies at Penn State gave me the opportunity to direct our Global Summer Institute with Tina Chen and Joseph Jeon on the topic of Digital Asias, which helped me further consider the relation between analog and digital cultures and resulted in a special issue of *Verge: Studies in Global Asias,* published in 2021.

I thank my students who, over the years, have been sounding boards for many of the ideas here, in both my Japanese film and new media undergraduate classes and my Mimesis and New Media graduate seminar. In this regard, special thanks go to my colleague Brian Lennon for sharing his new media syllabus with me at that early stage.

Many colleagues gave sage advice and inspiration along the way: Shion Kono, Kukhee Choo, Yoshimi Shunya, Alex Zahlten, Tom Lamarre, Michael Bourdaghs, Alan Tansman, Christine Marran, Lea Pao, Bo An, Siting Jiang, James Kopf, Vasilije Ivanovic, Darwin Tsen, Sarah Townsend, Shuang Shen, Nergis Erturk, Christopher Castiglia, Michael Bérubé, Christian Haines, Yoshikuni Hiroki, Akira Lippit, and Steve Ridgely.

Though there is also a crowd of scholars too numerous to mention here who contributed in countless ways, a smaller subset of people whose deep engagement or off-hand remarks had profound effects on the specific directions taken here. I do my best to recall them all in the order in which their contributions can be read in the book, with certainty that there are names I have missed. Markus Nornes helped me think through the very first paragraph about film history and gave suggestions about photography. Andrea Bachner's symposium "The Global and the Primitive" encouraged me to push my thinking on early photography into the anthropological and three-dimensional. A conversation with Maki Fukuoka gave me perspective on Rokudenashiko's commitment to body scanning and printing as part of her embodied augmentation and modification practice. Mimi Long's invitation to speak at the Access Asia Forum at University of California, Irvine gave me the kick I needed to finish the chapter on records. I still cannot believe the tragic loss of my friend Sari Kawana, who gave me the brilliant advice to research Wilhelm Plage. Kerim Yasar kindly shared with me a draft of his work that dealt in part with the early record copyright precedent of *naniwa bushi* stylist Tōchūken Kumoemon. Hiromu Nagahara suggested a reading list on musicology that helped enrich my understanding of record culture in early twentieth-century Japan. Christopher Reed encouraged me to think more about the staging of Miura Tamaki's performances. Matthew Fraleigh helped me work through the Chinese on the dagger. Alisa Freedman not only encouraged my work on television through a conference panel that she organized but also included my piece on *Gekkō kamen* in a special issue of *Japan Forum* on children's culture.

Aaron Gerow's comments about Harimao challenged me to transform that early research into the television chapter published here. At the 2017 Replaying Japan conference, I was first able to sound my ideas about games, which benefited from those in attendance, including Rachael Hutchinson, Mimi Okabe, Martin Roth, and Hosoi Koichi. Subsequent revisions of early drafts of that unwieldy forty-thousand-word "video game chapter" benefited from the comments of Rachael Dumas and Paul Roquet. Elena Giannoulis's excellent conference on emoji at the Free University of Berlin helped me to articulate thoughts on scripting the world and resulted in a publication in the conference volume. In addition to reading through the manuscript in final stages with perceptive catches and suggestions, Seth Jacobowitz gave me the first public forum for presenting the main idea for the book in its entirety at the Kempf Fund Lecture Series in East Asian Languages and Literatures at Yale University.

Several other people also helped me through the final stages. Eric Hayot read theory-heavy drafts of the Introduction and Conclusion and offered suggestions that tightened the argument and smoothed the writing. Joe Jeon read the entire thing after it was accepted and gave truly spot-on constructive criticism, most of which I have been able to use to make the present volume more comprehensible. I thank Vincent Bruyere for reading in the late stages and highlighting some of my tendencies, as well as for introducing me to Damisch, Belting, and Bredekamp. Special thanks to Samuel Frederick for suffering through nearly the entirety immediately before submission to the press for review. I am truly fortunate to have such friends who are not only brilliant but also incredibly generous!

I would like to thank the University of Minnesota Press and especially Jason Weidemann, who saw potential in an early proposal, and Zenyse Miller, whose reassuring emails made the review process bearable. I would particularly like to thank the two excellent blind reviewers of the book, who generously revealed themselves afterward to open conversations and ultimately guarantee that what you hold in your hand is better than the draft they read. Accolades go to Ziggy Snow for judicious copyediting and Fred Kameny for the index.

Deep thanks go to Jens-Uwe Guettel, Benjamin Schreier, and Samuel Frederick of the Zeno's Paradoxical Writing Group, which read very early drafts that always seemed to be heading toward a finish line without quite arriving. Particular thanks go to Jennifer Boittin and

Maryam Frederick and the rest of the crew for moral support, angsty commiseration, and gustatory sustenance.

Thanks go to Benjamin D. Abel for auditory delights, for his unbridled curiosity, and for being my most cherished distraction during much-needed time away from the project. And to the person who listened to me drone on about this, who read drafts, suggested alternative angles, edited my sloppy writing, cracked me up when I needed to laugh, and burst my bubbles when they were floating too high, above all, I thank Jessamyn R. Abel, without whom none of this would exist.

Notes

Introduction

1. Martin Loiperdinger, "Lumiere's Arrival of the Train: Cinema's Founding Myth," trans. Bernd Elzer, *Moving Image* 4, no. 1 (July 26, 2004): 89–118.

2. Joseph L. Anderson and Donald Richie, *The Japanese Film: Art and Industry,* expanded ed. (Princeton, N.J.: Princeton University Press, 2018), 24; Eric Cazdyn, *The Flash of Capital: Film and Geopolitics in Japan* (Durham, N.C.: Duke University Press, 2002), 47; Aaron Andrew Gerow, *Visions of Japanese Modernity: Articulations of Cinema, Nation, and Spectatorship, 1895–1925* (Berkeley: University of California Press, 2010), 47; Komatsu Hiroshi, *Kigen no eiga: Eigashi no danmenzu* (Tokyo: Seidosha, 1991), 12; Tsukada Yoshinobu, *Nihon eigashi no kenkyu: Katsudo shashin torai zengo no jijo* (Tokyo: Gendai Shokan, 1980), 32. See also Tanaka Jun'ichiro, *Nihon eiga hattatsushi* (Tokyo: Chūō Kōronsha, 1975); Yoshida Yoshishige, *Eiga denrai: Shinematogurafu to Meiji no Nihon* (Tokyo: Iwanami Shoten, 1995).

3. See J. David Bolter and Richard Grusin, *Remediation: Understanding New Media* (Cambridge, Mass.: MIT Press, 1999).

4. See Bolter and Grusin, *Remediation.*

5. Yuriko Furuhata, *Cinema of Actuality: Japanese Avant-Garde Filmmaking in the Season of Image Politics* (Durham, N.C.: Duke University Press, 2013), 3.

6. Dorrit Cohn and Lewis S. Gleich, "Metalepsis and Mise en Abyme," *Narrative* 20, no. 1 (2012): 105–14; Lucien Dällenbach, *The Mirror in the Text* (Chicago: University of Chicago Press, 1989); Michel Foucault, *Discourse and Truth and Parrēsia,* ed. Henri-Paul Fruchaud, Daniele Lorenzini, and Nancy Luxon (Chicago: University of Chicago Press, 2019); Michel Foucault, *This Is Not a Pipe,* trans. James Harkness (Berkeley: University of California Press, 1983); Moshe Ron, "The Restricted Abyss: Nine Problems in the Theory of Mise en Abyme," *Poetics Today* 8, no. 2 (1987): 417.

7. David Croteau and William Hoynes, *Media/Society: Industries, Images, and Audiences* (Thousand Oaks, Calif.: Pine Forge Press, 2000); Dan Laughey, *Key Themes in Media Theory* (Maidenhead, U.K.: Open University Press, 2010); Marshall McLuhan, *The Gutenberg Galaxy: The Making of Typographic Man* (Toronto: University of Toronto Press, 2002); Joshua Meyrowitz, *No Sense of*

Place: The Impact of Electronic Media on Social Behavior (Oxford: Oxford University Press, 1985); Werner Wolf, Katharina Bantleon, and Jeff Thoss, eds., *Metareference across Media: Theory and Case Studies,* Studies in Intermediality 4 (Amsterdam: Rodopi, 2009).

8. Claude Elwood Shannon and Warren Weaver, *The Mathematical Theory of Communication* (Urbana: University of Illinois Press, 1998); Norbert Wiener, *The Human Use of Human Beings: Cybernetics and Society* (New York: Houghton Mifflin, 1950); Norbert Wiener, *Cybernetics, or Control and Communication in the Animal and the Machine* (Cambridge, Mass.: MIT Press, 2007).

9. See, for instance, James J. Gibson, *The Ecological Approach to Visual Perception* (New York: Psychology Press, 2014); John Guillory, "Genesis of the Media Concept," *Critical Inquiry* 36 (Winter 2010): 360.

10. Siegfried Zielinski, *Deep Time of the Media: Toward an Archaeology of Hearing and Seeing by Technical Means* (Cambridge, Mass.: MIT Press, 2006).

11. Thomas Lamarre, *The Anime Machine: A Media Theory of Animation* (Minneapolis: University of Minnesota Press, 2013).

12. Neil Postman, *Technopoly: The Surrender of Culture to Technology* (New York: Vintage, 1993), 18; Wendy Hui Kyong Chun, *Updating to Remain the Same: Habitual New Media* (Cambridge, Mass.: MIT Press, 2016); Giorgio Agamben, *State of Exception* (Chicago: University of Chicago Press, 2008).

13. For a clear summation of this line of inquiry, see Charles Acland, "Introduction: Residual Media," in *Residual Media,* ed. Charles R. Acland, xviii–xix (Minneapolis: University of Minnesota Press, 2007).

14. Marshall McLuhan and Quentin Fiore, *The Medium Is the Massage: An Inventory of Effects* (Berkeley, Calif.: Gingko Press, 2017).

15. Mitsuhiro Yoshimoto, "Hollywood, Americanism, and the Imperial Screen: Geopolitics of Image and Discourse after the End of the Cold War," *Inter-Asia Cultural Studies* 4, no. 3 (December 2003): 451–59; Mitsuhiro Yoshimoto, "National/International/Transnational: The Concept of Trans-Asian Cinema and the Cultural Politics of Film Criticism," in *Theorising National Cinema,* ed. Paul Willemen and Valentina Vitali, 254–61 (London: Bloomsbury Publishing, 2006); Mitsuhiro Yoshimoto, "The Difficulty of Being Radical: The Discipline of Film Studies and the Postcolonial World Order," *boundary 2* 18, no. 3 (1991): 242–57; Mitsuhiro Yoshimoto, "The University, Disciplines, National Identity: Why Is There No Film Studies in Japan?" *South Atlantic Quarterly* 99, no. 4 (October 1, 2000): 697–713.

16. Michel Foucault, "Of Other Spaces," trans. Jay Miskowiec, *Diacritics* 16, no. 1 (1986): 22–27; Ursula Heise, "Unnatural Ecologies: The Metaphor of the Environment in Media Theory," *Configurations* 10, no. 1 (Winter 2002): 149–68.

17. See Jonathan E. Abel and Joseph Jonghyun Jeon, "Unfolding Digital Asias," *Verge: Studies in Global Asia* 7, no. 2 (Fall 2021): vi–xxii.

18. David Morley and Kevin Robins, *Spaces of Identity: Global Media, Electronic Landscapes, and Cultural Boundaries* (New York: Routledge, 1995); David S. Roh, Betsy Huang, and Greta A. Niu, eds., *Techno-Orientalism: Imagin-*

ing Asia in Speculative Fiction, History, and Media (New Brunswick, N.J.: Rutgers University Press, 2015).

19. Arjun Appadurai, *Modernity at Large: Cultural Dimensions of Globalization* (Minneapolis: University of Minnesota Press, 1996), 35. See also Arjun Appadurai, "Disjuncture and Difference in the Global Cultural Economy," *Public Culture* 2, no. 2 (May 1, 1990): 9.

20. Gerow, *Visions of Japanese Modernity*, 47.

21. Steven Feld, "Pygmy POP: A Genealogy of Schizophonic Mimesis," *Yearbook for Traditional Music* 28 (1996): 1–35.

22. Zielinski, *Deep Time of the Media*; Friedrich A. Kittler, *Gramophone, Film, Typewriter* (Stanford, Calif.: Stanford University Press, 1999).

1. Welcome to the New Real!

1. John Guillory, "Genesis of the Media Concept," *Critical Inquiry* 36, no. 2 (2010): 357. See also the concept of media as the "middle term" in W. J. T. Mitchell and Mark B. N. Hansen, introduction to *Critical Terms for Media Studies,* ed. W. J. T. Mitchell and Mark B. N. Hansen (Chicago: University of Chicago Press, 2010), xix.

2. Guillory, "Genesis of the Media Concept," 348.

3. Paul de Man, *Blindness and Insight: Essays in the Rhetoric of Contemporary Criticism* (Minneapolis: University Minnesota Press, 1971); Kōjin Karatani, "Uses of Aesthetics: After Orientalism," trans. Sabu Kohso, *boundary 2* 25, no. 2 (1998): 150; Kōjin Karatani, "The Utility of Aesthetics," in *Nation and Aesthetics: On Kant and Freud* (New York: Oxford University Press, 2017), 79–92.

4. Slavoj Žižek, "Cyberspace, or The Unbearable Closure of Being," in *Endless Night: Cinema and Psychoanalysis, Parallel Histories,* ed. Janet Bergstrom, 96–125 (Berkeley: University of California Press, 1999); Slavoj Žižek, *The Plague of Fantasies* (New York: Verso, 1997); J. G. Ballard, "The Gioconda of the Twilight Noon," in *The Terminal Beach* (New York: Penguin Books, 1964), 201. See also Azuma Hiroki's and Slavoj Žižek's consideration of "cyberspace" in Takeshi Kadobayashi, "The Media Theory and Media Strategy of Azuma Hiroki," and Marilyn Ivy, "The InterCommunication Project: Theorizing Media in Japan's Lost Decades," in *Media Theory in Japan,* ed. Marc Steinberg and Alexander Zahlten, 80–100, 101–130 (Durham, N.C.: Duke University Press, 2017).

5. Slavoj Žižek, *The Abyss of Freedom* (Ann Arbor: University of Michigan Press, 1997), 63.

6. Azuma Hiroki, "Saibāsupēsu wa naze supēsu to yobareruka," *InterCommunication* 32, no. 9 (2000): 168. All the essays are reprinted as Azuma Hiroki, "Saibāsupēsu wa naze sō yobareruka (1997–2000)," in *Society: Jōhō kankyō ronshū—Azuma hiroki korekushon S* (Tokyo: Kōdansha, 2007), 207–375.

7. Following Richard Rorty's critique of the eyes and mirrors in relation to modern subject formation. Richard Rorty, *Philosophy and the Mirror of Nature* (Princeton, N.J.: Princeton University Press, 1979).

8. Bruce Sterling, *Mirrorshades: The Cyberpunk Anthology* (New York: Ace Books, 1988).

9. Samuel R. Delany and Takayuki Tatsumi, "Some Real Mothers: . . . The SFEye Interview," in *Silent Interviews: On Language, Race, Sex, Science Fiction, and Some Comics* (Middletown, Conn.: Wesleyan University Press, 2012), 171–72; "Some Real Mothers: An Interview," *Science Fiction Eye* 3, no. 1 (1988): 8.

10. Jacques Derrida, *Specters of Marx: The State of the Debt, the Work of Mourning, and the New International* (New York: Psychology Press, 1994). See also the Marxist response in Michael Sprinker, ed., *Ghostly Demarcations: A Symposium on Jacques Derrida's Spectres of Marx* (New York: Verso, 1999).

11. See Azuma Hiroki, *General Will 2.0: Rousseau, Freud, Google*, trans. John Person (New York: Vertical, 2014), and Azuma's blog on the subject of info-liberalism, "Jōhō jiyūron," *Hajou* (blog), October 2005, http://www.hajou.org/infoliberalism.

12. This is the blinder that Karatani and indeed Kant critique.

13. It is the issue that Marx took up in his work not so much to drop spirit but to ground it in material conditions.

14. Azuma, *Society*, 214.

15. Lev Manovich, "The Labor of Perception," Manovich, 1995, http://manovich.net/index.php/projects/the-labor-of-perception; Lev Manovich, "The Aesthetics of Virtual Worlds: Report from Los Angeles," *CTheory* (November 1995).

16. It is worth noting that Azuma's theory predates the widespread use of named social media (web 2.0) platforms such as Facebook and Twitter in Japan. From 1997 to 2000, when Azuma was working on the concept of cyberspace, Japanese internet use was still dominated by largely anonymous bulletin boards and chat rooms.

17. We could call it a Foucauldian web of power in knowing or a way in which "abstract force" accrues what Brian Massumi calls "ontopower." And this power is also deeply entangled with both the distributed form of the power of spectacle (Guy Debord) and that of labor exploitation (Marx). See Brian Massumi, *Ontopower: War, Powers, and the State of Perception* (Durham, N.C.: Duke University Press, 2015).

18. See Jacques Lacan, *The Seminar of Jacques Lacan*, book 20, *On Feminine Sexuality: The Limits of Love and Knowledge*, trans. Bruce Fink (New York: Norton, 1998), 72, 81. See also Jacques Lacan, "Geneva Lecture on the Symptom," trans. Russell Grigg, *Analysis* 1 (1989): 7–26.

19. Saitō Tamaki, *Media wa sonzai shinai* (Tokyo: NTT Shuppan, 2007), 21–22.

20. Lev Manovich, *The Language of New Media* (Cambridge, Mass.: MIT Press, 2002), 25.

21. Wendy Hui Kyong Chun, *Updating to Remain the Same: Habitual New Media* (Cambridge, Mass.: MIT Press, 2017), ix.

22. Wendy Hui Kyong Chun, "Introduction: Race and/as Technology; or, How to Do Things to Race," *Camera Obscura* 1, no. 24 (May 2009): 51.

23. See also Claude Elwood Shannon, *Claude E. Shannon: Collected Papers*, ed. Ernst Weber and Frederik Nebeker (New York: Wiley, 1993); Claude Elwood Shannon and Warren Weaver, *The Mathematical Theory of Communication* (Urbana: University of Illinois Press, 1962).

24. See Samuel Weber's particularly insightful *Mass Mediauras* for a summary explication of technê's relation with skill rather than technology per se. Samuel Weber, *Mass Mediauras: Form, Technics, Media* (Stanford, Calif.: Stanford University Press, 1996).

25. See Guillory, "Genesis of the Media Concept." Also Akira Mizuta Lippit, "Preface (Interface)," in *Media Theory in Japan,* ed. Marc Steinberg and Alexander Zahlten, xi–xv (Durham, N.C.: Duke University Press, 2017); Seth Jacobowitz, *Writing Technology in Meiji Japan: A Media History of Modern Japanese Literature and Visual Culture* (Cambridge, Mass.: Harvard University Asia Center, 2020).

26. See Lippit, "Preface (Interface)"; Marc Steinberg and Alexander Zahlten, introduction to *Media Theory in Japan,* ed. Marc Steinberg and Alexander Zahlten, 1–32 (Durham, N.C.: Duke University Press, 2017).

27. See Erich Auerbach, *Mimesis: The Representation of Reality in Western Literature* (Princeton, N.J.: Princeton University Press, 2013).

28. Guillory's account of mimesis and media is a victim of this forgetting of the other potential meanings within mimesis. See also Stephen Halliwell, *The Aesthetics of Mimesis: Ancient Texts and Modern Problems* (Princeton, N.J.: Princeton University Press, 2002).

29. Kōjin Karatani, *History and Repetition* (New York: Columbia University Press, 2012); Fredric Jameson, *A Singular Modernity: Essay on the Ontology of the Present* (New York: Verso, 2002).

30. See Atsuko Ueda, *Concealment of Politics, Politics of Concealment: The Production of "Literature" in Meiji Japan* (Stanford, Calif.: Stanford University Press, 2007).

31. Takahashi Yoshitaka, "Zeami no 'monomane' to Yōroppa-teki mimēshisu," *Kindai geijutsukan no seiritsu* (1965): 155–60; Takahashi Yoshitaka, "Zeami no 'monomane' to Yōroppa-teki mimēshisu," in *Takahashi Yoshitaka bungei riron chosaku-shūka* (Tokyo: Jinbun shoin, 1977), 157–62; Robert G. Sewell, "Mimeshisu to monomane: Arisutoteresu to Zeami no mohō no riron," trans. Yutaka Maekawa, *Hikaku Bungaku Kenkyu* 34 (1978): 252–58.

32. Yamaguchi Masao and Takashina Shūji, "Taidan: 'Mitate' to Nihon bunka," *Nihon no bigaku* 24 (1996): 4–23; Masao Yamaguchi, "The Poetics of Exhibition in Japanese Culture," in *Exhibiting Cultures: The Poetics and Politics of Museum Display,* ed. Ivan Karp and Steven D. Lavine, 57–67 (Washington, D.C.: Smithsonian Institution Press, 1991).

33. Hiromi Oda, "An Embodied Semantic Mechanism for Mimetic Words in Japanese" (PhD diss., Indiana University, 2000); Noriko Iwasaki, Peter Sells, and Kimi Akita, *The Grammar of Japanese Mimetics: Perspectives from Structure, Acquisition, and Translation* (New York: Taylor & Francis, 2016).

34. See Michael Lucken, *Imitation and Creativity in Japanese Arts: From Kishida Ryusei to Miyazaki Hayao* (New York: Columbia University Press, 2016); Raja Adal, *Beauty in the Age of Empire: Japan, Egypt, and the Global History of Aesthetic Education* (New York: Columbia University Press, 2019).

35. See Gyōfu Karuma, "CM: KDDI [Asano Tadanobu] au 'koitsu no namae oshiete,'" January 13, 2013, YouTube video, 0:30, https://www.youtube.com/watch?v=t8Ph5Wm6AL8.

36. Celia Lury, *Prosthetic Culture* (New York: Routledge, 2013); Karina Eileraas, *Between Image and Identity: Transnational Fantasy, Symbolic Violence, and Feminist Misrecognition* (New York: Lexington Books, 2007); Maurice O. Wallace and Shawn Michelle Smith, *Pictures and Progress: Early Photography and the Making of African American Identity* (Durham, N.C.: Duke University Press, 2012); Lynda Mannik, *Photography, Memory, and Refugee Identity: The Voyage of the SS Walnut, 1948* (Vancouver: University of British Columbia Press, 2013); Maiken Umbach and Scott Sulzener, *Photography, Migration, and Identity: A German-Jewish-American Story* (Cham, Switzerland: Springer, 2018); Peter Hamilton and Roger Hargreaves, *The Beautiful and the Damned: The Creation of Identity in Nineteenth Century Photography* (London: Lund Humphries, 2001).

37. Michel Foucault, "Of Other Spaces," trans. Jay Miskowiec, *Diacritics* 16, no. 1 (1986): 22–27.

38. Guillory, "Genesis of the Media Concept," 321–23, 346–47.

39. Halliwell, *Aesthetics of Mimesis,* 15.

40. Erich Auerbach, *Mimesis: The Representation of Reality in Western Literature* (Princeton, N.J.: Princeton University Press, 1953); Clement Greenberg, "Avant-Garde and Kitsch," *Partisan Review* 6, no. 5 (1939): 34–49; Luce Irigaray, *This Sex Which Is Not One* (Ithaca, N.Y.: Cornell University Press, 1985); Luce Irigaray, *Speculum of the Other Woman* (Ithaca, N.Y.: Cornell University Press, 1985); Richard Rorty, *Philosophy and the Mirror of Nature* (Princeton, N.J.: Princeton University Press, 2009). See also John D. Boyd, *The Function of Mimesis and Its Decline* (New York: Fordham University Press, 1980); Tom Cohen, *Anti-mimesis from Plato to Hitchcock* (New York: Cambridge University Press, 1994); Andrew Benjamin, *Art, Mimesis, and the Avant-Garde: Aspects of a Philosophy of Difference* (New York: Routledge, 2005).

41. Michael T. Taussig, *Mimesis and Alterity: A Particular History of the Senses* (New York: Psychology Press, 1993); Susan Buck-Morss, "Aesthetics and Anaesthetics: Walter Benjamin's Artwork Essay Reconsidered," *October* 62 (1992): 3–41; Susan Buck-Morss, *The Dialectics of Seeing: Walter Benjamin and the Arcades Project* (Cambridge, Mass.: MIT Press, 1991); Susan Buck-Morss, *The Origin of Negative Dialectics: Theodor W. Adorno, Walter Benjamin, and the Frankfurt Institute* (New York: Free Press, 1977); René Girard, *Violence and the Sacred* (London: A&C Black, 2005); René Girard, *A Theatre of Envy: William Shakespeare* (Leominster, U.K.: Gracewing Publishing, 2000); René Girard, *The Girard Reader* (New York: Crossroad, 1996); René Girard, *The Scapegoat* (Baltimore: Johns Hopkins University Press, 1989); René Girard, *To*

Double Business Bound: Essays on Literature, Mimesis, and Anthropology (Baltimore: Johns Hopkins University Press, 1988); Roger Caillois, *Man, Play, and Games* (Urbana: University of Illinois Press, 2001); Roger Caillois, "Mimicry and Legendary Psychasthenia," trans. John Shepley, *October* 31 (1984): 17–32; Tom Huhn, *Imitation and Society: The Persistence of Mimesis in the Aesthetics of Burke, Hogarth, and Kant* (University Park: Penn State University Press, 2010); Kendall L. Walton, *Mimesis as Make-Believe: On the Foundations of the Representational Arts* (Cambridge, Mass.: Harvard University Press, 1990).

42. Andrew E. Benjamin, *Art, Mimesis, and the Avant-Garde: Aspects of a Philosophy of Difference* (New York: Psychology Press, 1991), 13–25. See also Guillory, "Genesis of the Media Concept."

43. J. David Bolter and Richard Grusin, *Remediation: Understanding New Media* (Cambridge, Mass.: MIT Press, 1999), 273, 59.

44. Martin Jay, *Cultural Semantics: Keywords of Our Time* (Amherst: University of Massachusetts Press, 1998).

45. Weber, *Mass Mediauras*; Philippe Lacoue-Labarthe and Christopher Fynsk, *Typography: Mimesis, Philosophy, Politics* (Stanford, Calif.: Stanford University Press, 1998); Jacques Derrida, "Double Session," in *Dissemination* (London: Athlone Press, 1981), 173–366.

46. Here I draw on Lacan's useful distinction between "the real" and realities, imaginary, and symbolic domains. See seminars 3, 7, and 11 in Jacques Lacan, *The Psychoses, 1955–1956,* trans. Russell Grigg, *The Seminar of Jacques Lacan* (New York: W. W. Norton, 1997); Jacques Lacan, *The Ethics of Psychoanalysis, 1959–1960,* book 7 (New York: W. W. Norton, 1997); Jacques Lacan, *The Four Fundamental Concepts of Psycho-analysis* (New York: W. W. Norton, 1981). One might usefully compare Jean-François Lyotard's notion of truths as opposed to the truth here. See *The Postmodern Condition: A Report on Knowledge* (Minneapolis: University of Minnesota Press, 1984).

47. Timothy J. Welsh, *Mixed Realism: Videogames and the Violence of Fiction* (Minneapolis: University of Minnesota Press, 2016).

48. See Graham Harman, *The Quadruple Object* (New York: Zero Books, 2011); Graham Harman, *Object-Oriented Ontology: A New Theory of Everything* (New York: Penguin, 2018); Graham Harman, "Materialism Is Not the Solution: On Matter, Form, and Mimesis," *Nordic Journal of Aesthetics* 24, no. 47 (2015): 94–110; Graham Harman, "A New Sense of Mimesis," in *Aesthetics Equals Politics: New Discourses across Art, Architecture, and Philosophy,* ed. Mark Foster Gage, 49–61 (Cambridge, Mass.: MIT Press, 2019).

49. See J. David Bolter and Richard Grusin, *Remediation: Understanding New Media* (Cambridge, Mass.: MIT Press, 1999). See Saitō's comments on Matsuura Hisaaki in Saitō Tamaki, *Beautiful Fighting Girl,* trans. Keith Vincent and Dawn Lawson (Minneapolis: University of Minnesota Press, 2011), 196n1.

50. It is likely, for instance, that James Joyce was citing a Japanese Victor record when he wrote, "Thot's never the postal cleric, checking chinchin chat with nipponnippers!" in *Finnegans Wake* 485.36.

51. Lisa Gitelman, "How Users Define New Media: A History of the Amusement Phonograph," in *Rethinking Media Change: The Aesthetics of Transition*, ed. David Thorburn and Henry Jenkins (Cambridge, Mass.: MIT Press, 2004), 68.

52. We should note here Sianne Ngai's notion of cute as an aesthetic of consumption that "often seems to lead immediately to feelings of manipulation and betrayal" and precisely marks the consumer's powerlessness. Sianne Ngai, *Our Aesthetic Categories: Zany, Cute, Interesting* (Cambridge, Mass.: Harvard University Press, 2012), 86.

53. Michael T. Taussig, *Mimesis and Alterity: A Particular History of the Senses* (New York: Psychology Press, 1993), 219.

54. Taussig, *Mimesis and Alterity*, 220.

55. See Henry Jenkins, Sam Ford, and Joshua Green, *Spreadable Media: Creating Value and Meaning in a Networked Culture* (New York: NYU Press, 2013); Tony D. Sampson, *Virality: Contagion Theory in the Age of Networks* (Minneapolis: University of Minnesota Press, 2012). The copy of a copy is also known as a simulacrum. Gilles Deleuze, "Plato and the Simulacrum," trans. Rosalind Krauss, *October* 27 (1983): 45–56; Jean Baudrillard, *Simulacra and Simulation*, trans. Sheila Faria Glaser (Ann Arbor: University of Michigan Press, 1994); Brian Massumi, "Realer Than Real: The Simulacrum According to Deleuze and Guattari," *Copyright* 1 (1987): 90–97.

56. Azuma, *General Will 2.0*.

57. Translation modified from Saitō, *Beautiful Fighting Girl*, 156; Saitō Tamaki, *Sentō bishōjo no seishin bunseki* (Tokyo: Chikuma Shobō, 2006).

58. Michael Riffaterre, *Fictional Truth* (Baltimore: Johns Hopkins University Press, 1990).

59. Azuma Hiroki, *Gēmu-teki riarizumu no tanjō: Dōbutsukasuru posuto modan* 2 (Tokyo: Kōdansha, 2007).

60. Marshall McLuhan, *Understanding Media: The Extensions of Man* (Cambridge, Mass.: MIT Press, 1994), 305.

61. Greenberg, "Avant-Garde and Kitsch."

62. Timothy Morton, *Hyperobjects: Philosophy and Ecology after the End of the World* (Minneapolis: University of Minnesota Press, 2013).

63. See, for instance, "Bikutā koronbia no shinkyoku" (advertisement), *Yomiuri Shinbun*, August 23, 1908, morning edition, 4.

64. Michael Raine, "Adaptation as 'Transcultural Mimesis' in Japanese Cinema," in *The Oxford Handbook of Japanese Cinema*, ed. Daisuke Miyao (New York: Oxford University Press, 2014), 114. See also David Bordwell, *Ozu and the Poetics of Cinema* (Ann Arbor: University of Michigan Press, 1988), 67.

65. Tom Gunning, "Re-newing Old Technologies: Astonishment, Second Nature, and the Uncanny in Technology from the Previous Turn-of-the-Century," in *Rethinking Media Change: The Aesthetics of Transition*, ed. David Thorburn and Henry Jenkins, 61–80 (Cambridge, Mass.: MIT Press, 2004); *Dragnet Girl*, directed by Ozu Yasujirō (1933; New York: Criterion Collection, 2015), DVD.

66. Aaron Skabelund, *Empire of Dogs: Canines, Japan, and the Making of the Modern Imperial World* (Ithaca, N.Y.: Cornell University Press, 2011), 2.

67. Stuart Hall, "Encoding/Decoding," in *Media and Cultural Studies: Keyworks,* ed. Meenakshi Gigi Durham and Douglas M. Kellner, 163–73 (Hoboken, N.J.: John Wiley & Sons, 2009); Stuart Hall, *Encoding and Decoding in the Television Discourse* (Birmingham, U.K.: Centre for Contemporary Cultural Studies, 1973).

68. Rorty, *Philosophy and the Mirror of Nature.*

69. Derek Brewer, "Escape from the Mimetic Fallacy," in *Studies in Medieval English Romances: Some New Approaches,* ed. Derek Brewer, 1–11 (Woodbridge, U.K.: Boydell & Brewer Ltd., 1988).

70. Walter Benjamin, "On the Mimetic Faculty," in *Reflections* (New York: Schocken Books, 1986), 333–36. See also Walter Benjamin, "Doctrine of the Similar (1933)," trans. Knut Tarnowski, *New German Critique* 17 (1979): 65–69.

71. Nakai Masakazu, "Chikuonki no hari" (*Kyōto hinode shinbun,* June 5, 1933), in *Nakai Masakazu zenshū,* vol. 4 (Tokyo: Bijutsu shuppansha, 1981), available at *Aozora bunko,* https://www.aozora.gr.jp/cards/001166/card49713.html.

72. Adorno also remarks on this slippage as being present in the logo. Theodor W. Adorno, "The Curves of the Needle," *October* 55 (Winter 1990): 54.

73. Hatano Isoko, *Bikutā meiken monogatari: Nippā-chan* (Tokyo: Shōgakukan, 1952).

74. Komura Michizō, "Koinu no Nippā," with Hattori Junko and the Victor Children's Orchestra and with lyrics by Sakaguchi Jun, Japanese Victor, B-247 C-1222.

75. Streaming files of the record playing available at Jun'ichi, "Nippā no uta, mitsuke tatta w," zenmaijikake no ryū nishiki, https://ameblo.jp/969-dragon/entry-12396220242.html; Sakaguchi Jun, "Koinu no nippā," *Rekishi-teki ongen* (Kokuritsu Kokkaitoshokan), https://rekion.dl.ndl.go.jp/info:ndljp/pid/1332059.

76. Taussig, *Mimesis and Alterity,* 225.

77. Jane Bennett, *Vibrant Matter: A Political Ecology of Things* (Durham, N.C.: Duke University Press, 2010), 6.

78. See the Victor Online Store at https://victor-store.jp/. See also Ruth Edge and Leonard Petts, *The Collectors Guide to "His Master's Voice" Nipper Souvenirs* (London: EMI Group, 1997).

79. "Maitoshi Nigatsu yōka wa 'nippā no hi' to shite seitei," *Bikutāentateinmento puresurirīsu shōsai-mei,* January 15, 2015, https://www.jvcmusic.co.jp/company/press/2015/0206.html; "Nigatsu yōka wa 'nippā no hi': Bikutā inu nippā ga Nihon de kinenbi ni," *CDJournal nyūsu,* accessed October 14, 2020, https://www.cdjournal.com/main/news/yamazaki-aoi/64416; "Sūshinchū: Meiken nippā doggunrōru," Bikutā entateinmento, *Victor Entertainment,* accessed October 14, 2020, https://www.jvcmusic.co.jp/-/Discography/A025632/NZS-807.html.

80. Max Horkheimer and Theodor W. Adorno, *Dialectic of Enlightenment* (New York: Continuum, 1989), 93–110.

81. Ngai, *Our Aesthetic Categories.*

82. See especially books 3 and 10 of Plato, *Plato: Republic X*, trans. S. Halliwell (Oxford: Oxford University Press, 1988).

83. Adorno and Horkheimer, *Dialectic of Enlightenment*, 187.

84. Theodor W. Adorno, *The Culture Industry: Selected Essays on Mass Culture* (London: Routledge, 2020), 83.

85. Ruth Benedict, *The Chrysanthemum and the Sword: Patterns of Japanese Culture* (1946; New York: Meridian Books, 1967); Robert J. Smith, *Japanese Society: Tradition, Self, and the Social Order* (Cambridge: Cambridge University Press, 1983).

86. Yamazaki Masazumi, "Mimēshisu-ron: Maruyama Masao to haisen-go bungaku," *Gengo bunka-gaku kenkyū* 2 (2007): 46.

87. Literary critic Yamazaki Masazumi contrasts Maruyama's variety of wartime mimesis with another postwar mode of creative, life-sustaining mimesis. Masazumi argues that the postwar opened the possibility for a double layer structure in mimesis, wherein one layer dissolves the self and the other speaks it. He shows how mimesis as a form of self-preservation can result either in the suicidal tendencies of fascism or solipsism (as in the work of Dazai Osamu) or in the newly acquired survival skill of rejecting suicide via a kind of postwar egoism (as exemplified by Noma Hiroshi). Yamazaki, "Mimēshisu-ron," 51–56.

88. Masao Maruyama, "From Carnal Politics to Carnal Literature," in *Thought and Behavior in Modern Japanese Politics* (Oxford: Oxford University Press, 2008), 251.

89. Buck-Morss, "Aesthetics and Anaesthetics"; Buck-Morss, *Origin of Negative Dialectics*; Gertrud Koch, "Mimesis and Bilderverbot," *Screen* 34, no. 3 (October 1, 1993): 211–22; Andreas Huyssen, "Of Mice and Mimesis: Reading Spiegelman with Adorno," *New German Critique* 81 (2000): 65–82; Vittorio Gallese, "The Two Sides of Mimesis: Girard's Mimetic Theory, Embodied Simulation, and Social Identification," *Journal of Consciousness Studies* 16, no. 4 (January 1, 2009): 21–44.

90. See Buck-Morss, "Aesthetics and Anaesthetics," 17; Max Horkheimer and Theodor W. Adorno, *Dialectic of Enlightenment*, trans. John Cumming (New York: Herder and Herder, 1972), 180. Also discussed in Taussig, *Mimesis and Alterity*, 68.

91. Michele White, *The Body and the Screen: Theories of Internet Spectatorship* (Cambridge, Mass.: MIT Press, 2006); Katie Warfield, Crystal Abidin, and Carolina Cambre, *Mediated Interfaces: The Body on Social Media* (New York: Bloomsbury Academic, 2020); Gabriele Klein and Sandra Noeth, *Emerging Bodies: The Performance of Worldmaking in Dance and Choreography* (Bielefeld, Germany: Transcript Verlag, 2014); Kristin L. Arola and Anne Frances Wysocki, *Composing(Media) = Composing(Embodiment)* (Louisville: University Press of Colorado, 2012); Kenny K. N. Chow, *Animation, Embodiment, and Digital Media: Human Experience of Technological Liveliness* (Houndmills, U.K.: Palgrave Macmillan UK, 2013); Lisa Blackman, *Immaterial Bodies: Affect, Embodiment, Mediation* (Los Angeles: SAGE Publications, 2012).

2. Stereomimesis

1. Throughout this chapter, I use *stereography* to mean stereographic photography, *stereoscopy* to refer to looking through an apparatus to render three-dimensional images in the mind's eye, and *stereograph* to refer to the cardboard-mounted double image photographs taken from slightly differing vantage points.

2. I am in debt to collector and scholar Rob Oechsle, who has done a formidable job of gleaning much of Enami Nobukuni's life story from scant sources and photographic evidence and who, through his now defunct website at Enami .org and his Flickr account, has been a major disseminator of Enami's images. Unless otherwise attributed, all relevant information here about Enami stems from Oechsle's work. Rob Oechsle, "Searching for T. Enami," in *Old Japanese Photographs: Collectors' Data Guide,* ed. Terry Bennett, 70–78 (London: Bernard Quarritch, 2006).

3. Stephen Halliwell, *The Aesthetics of Mimesis: Ancient Texts and Modern Problems* (Princeton, N.J.: Princeton University Press, 2002), 5.

4. Horst Bredekamp comments: "Human beings have two conflicting drives: the urge to imitate the existing creation (natura naturata), and the incessant and curious urge to imitate the creativity of nature (natura naturans). Every new style evolves between these two forms of mimesis. That's the dialectic of the profitability of imitation and a loss of originality. Imitation always produces a loss of originality. Originality, for its part, produces a lack of style. And that defines the balance that keeps swinging back and forth throughout the history of humankind: style—innovation—style—innovation, the two principles of imitation." *The Technical Image: A History of Styles in Scientific Imagery,* ed. Horst Bredekamp, Birgit Schneider, and Vera Dünkel (Chicago: University of Chicago Press, 2019), 27.

5. Joseph Anderson and Barbara Fisher, "The Myth of Persistence of Vision," *Journal of the University Film Association* 30, no. 4 (1978): 3–8; Jonathan Crary, *Techniques of the Observer: On Vision and Modernity in the Nineteenth Century* (Cambridge, Mass.: MIT Press, 1992); Jonathan Crary, *Suspensions of Perception: Attention, Spectacle, and Modern Culture* (Cambridge, Mass.: MIT Press, 2001); Margarida Medeiros, Teresa Mendes Flores, and Joana Cunha Leal, *Photography and Cinema: 50 Years of Chris Markers La Jetée* (Newcastle upon Tyne, U.K.: Cambridge Scholars Publishing, 2015).

6. Kōjin Karatani, *Transcritique: On Kant and Marx* (Cambridge, Mass.: MIT Press, 2005); Kōjin Karatani, *History and Repetition* (New York: Columbia University Press, 2012).

7. Jacques Derrida, "Economimesis," trans. R. Klein, *Diacritics* 11, no. 2 (1981): 3–25.

8. Jacques Derrida, *Copy, Archive, Signature: A Conversation on Photography* (Stanford, Calif.: Stanford University Press, 2010), 7.

9. Derrida, *Copy, Archive, Signature,* 12.

10. Derrida, "Economimesis."

11. Eric Hayot, *On Literary Worlds* (Oxford: Oxford University Press, 2012), 58–67.

12. For more on ground and figure in terms of media, see Marshall McLuhan and Eric McLuhan, *Laws of Media: The New Science* (Toronto: University of Toronto Press, 1992).

13. *Anthony's Photographic Bulletin* 21 (1890): 286.

14. Terry Bennett, *Photography in Japan, 1853–1912* (Rutland, Vt.: Tuttle Publishing, 2012), 232.

15. *Association Belge de Photographie Bulletin* 32 (1905): 414.

16. In July 1905, Masuda Gi'ichi, president of the Jitsugyō no Nihon publishing company, negotiated with the military (*Rikugunshō bōei-shō*) for Enami Nobukuni (attached to the second army) to photograph the Russo–Japanese warfront, Manila, and Singapore. See Japan Center for Asian Historical Records record number C03026576500. The resulting photographs appeared in the Jitsugyō no Nihon's *Seirō shashin gachō* later that year.

17. See *National Geographic* vols. 40 (1921) and 42 (1922).

18. Japan Center for Asian Historical Records record number B09073034300.

19. Appendix to "Photographers in the Far East" (letter), folder Grosvenor, Gilbert H. Travels GHG Japan, Russia, Manchuria, Siberia 11–15.699F1, Box 66, National Geographic Archives, Washington, D.C. From this file, it seems Elizabeth Scidmore may also have had contact with Enami.

20. Bennett, *Photography in Japan*, 237.

21. Advertisement reproduced in Bennett, *Photography in Japan*, 233.

22. Crary, *Techniques of the Observer*, 124–25.

23. Yajima Masumi, "Hābāto Jōji Pontingu no utsushi shita: Nihon-shizen o daizai to shita shashin no kōsatsu," ed. Tōhokudaigaku kokusai bunka gakkai, *Kokusai bunka kenkyū* 1341, no. 0709 (2013): 117–30; Pierre Loti and Chantal Édel, *Japon: Fin de siècle—photographies de Felice Beato et Raimund von Stillfried* (Paris: Arthaud, 2000); Felice Beato, *Once upon a Time: Visions of Old Japan* (New York: Friendly Press, 1986); Luke Gartlan, *A Career of Japan: Baron Raimund von Stillfried and Early Yokohama Photography* (Leiden, The Netherlands: Brill, 2016); Iskander Mydin, "Historical Images, Changing Audiences," in *Anthropology and Photography, 1860–1920*, ed. Elizabeth Edwards, 249–52 (New Haven, Conn.: Yale University Press, 1992).

24. Jennifer Dalton, Nikki S. Lee, Anthony Goicolea, and David Henry Brown, "Look at Me: Self-Portrait Photography after Cindy Sherman," *PAJ: A Journal of Performance and Art* 22, no. 3 (2000): 47–56; Marvin Heiferman, "In Front of the Camera, Behind the Scene: Cindy Sherman's 'Untitled Film Stills,'" *MoMA* 25 (1997): 16–19; Biljana Scott, "Picturing Irony: The Subversive Power of Photography," *Visual Communication* 3, no. 1 (February 1, 2004): 31–59; Shimizu Akiko, *Lying Bodies: Survival and Subversion in the Field of Vision* (New York: Peter Lang, 2008); Susan Rubin Suleiman, *Subversive Intent: Gender, Politics, and the Avant-Garde* (Cambridge, Mass.: Harvard University

Press, 1990). See also Yasumasa Morimura, *To My Little Sister: For Cindy Sherman*, 1998, photo-silver dye bleach print, 31 × 55 in. (78.7 × 139.7 cm), International Center of Photography, https://www.icp.org/browse/archive/objects/to-my-little-sister-for-cindy-sherman.

25. Deborah Bright, *The Passionate Camera: Photography and Bodies of Desire* (New York: Psychology Press, 1998), 197; Laura Mulvey, *Fetishism and Curiosity: Cinema and the Mind's Eye* (New York: Macmillan International Higher Education, 2013), 97.

26. Daniel Novak, "Labors of Likeness: Photography and Labor in Capital," *Criticism: A Quarterly for Literature and the Arts* 49, no. 2 (Spring 2007): 125.

27. Jean Baudrillard, *Impossible Exchange* (London: Verso Books, 2012), 189.

28. Donna Jeanne Haraway, "Situated Knowledges: The Science Question in Feminism and the Privilege of Partial Perspective," in *Simians, Cyborgs, and Women: The Reinvention of Nature* (New York: Free Association Books, 1991), 189.

29. Slavoj Žižek, "Avatar: Return of the Natives," *New Statesman*, March 4, 2010.

30. The series of similar ads began in the *Asahi Shinbun*, October 11, 1902, issue on page 4. The version quoted from was carried on page 4 of the September 5, 1903, issue. William Reeves, Coin Controlled Apparatus, U.S. Patent 582,685, filed February 8, 1897, and issued May 18, 1897; William Reeves, "Coin Controlled Machine," Letters Patent No. 526,539 September 25, 1894.

31. Ogawa Kazumasa, *A Photographic Album of the Japan–China War: Nisshin sensō shashinchō* (Tokyo: Hakubundō, 1895); *Nisshin sensō jikki,* April 1896–99. See Kelly M. McCormick, "Ogawa Kazumasa and the Halftone Photograph: Japanese War Albums at the Turn of the Twentieth Century," *Technologies* 7, no. 2 (Spring 2017).

32. Takahashi Seori, *Kankaku no modan: Sakutaro, Jun'ichiro, Kenji, Ranpo* (Tokyo: Serika Shobo, 2003), 105. Digital copies of early books on photography such as *Seimikyoku hikkei* (1862) and *Shashinkyō zusetsu* (1867) are available the Open Dataset of the National Institute of Japanese Literature (Kokubunken dētasetto kan'i u~ebu etsuran) here: http://www2.dhii.jp/nijl_opendata/NIJL0197/049-0219/ and http://www2.dhii.jp/nijl_opendata/NIJL0192/049-0217/.

33. Enami took twelve of the twenty-four photos published in K. Ogawa, *Fuji-san* (1912); see digital copy on collector George C. Baxley's website: http://www.baxleystamps.com/litho/ogawa/ogawa_fuji_1912.shtml. Yamaguchi Masao, "The Poetics of Exhibition in Japanese Culture," in *Exhibiting Cultures: The Poetics and Politics of Museum Display,* ed. I. Karp and S. Lavine, 57–67 (Washington, D.C.: Smithsonian Institution, 1991).

34. See Urasaki Eishaku, *Nihon kindai bijutsu hattatsu-shi-Meiji-hen* (Tokyo: Tōkyō bijutsu, 1974), 314–18; Seiji M. Lippit, *Topographies of Japanese Modernism* (New York: Columbia University Press, 2002), 142. See the list of Panorama Halls at "Panorama," Misemono kōgyō nenpyō, http://blog.livedoor.jp/misemono/archives/52115993.html. See also Richard Okada, "'Landscape' and the Nation-State: A Reading of *Nihon fukei ron,*" in *New Directions in the Study of Meiji*

Japan, ed. Helen Hardacre and Adam Lewis Kern (New York: Brill Japanese Studies Library, 1997), 102.

35. Mentioned in Kamoi Takeshi, "Jittai shashin no hanashi," *Kōgyō kagaku zasshi* 4 (1910): 400.

36. Bernd Poch, "Das Kaiserpanorama: Das Medium, seine Vorgänger und seine Verbreitung in Nordwestdeutschland," http://www.massenmedien.de/kaiserpanorama/emden/emden.htm.

37. "Kimura kōseikan honten nichirosensō sōgan shashin dai hanbai," *Asahi Shinbun,* April 3, 1904.

38. Hosoma also sees the likelihood of divergent evolution. Hosoma Hiromichi, *Asakusa jūnikai: Tō no nagame to kindai no manazashi* (Tokyo: Seidosha, 2011), 167.

39. Crary, *Suspensions of Perception,* 163.

40. Hosoma, *Asakusa jūnikai,* 157, 161.

41. Alfred North Whitehead, *Process and Reality* (New York: Simon and Schuster, 2010); James Jerome Gibson, *The Ecological Approach to Visual Perception* (New York: Psychology Press, 1986); Mark B. N. Hansen, *Feed-Forward: On the Future of Twenty-First-Century Media* (Chicago: University of Chicago Press, 2015); Katherine Hayles, *Unthought: The Power of the Cognitive Nonconscious* (Chicago: University of Chicago Press, 2017).

42. Hosoma, *Asakusa jūnikai,* 158.

43. Hosoma, 158.

44. See "Dainippon ryōunkaku no zu," special materials no. 89200828, April 10, 1890; 89200829, September 30, 1890; 15200106, October 7, 1890; 89200827, December 1890, Edo Tokyo Hakubutsukan. Also "Dainippon ryōunkaku no zu," 1890, bunko no. 10 08073 0014, Waseda library, http://www.wul.waseda ac.jp/kotenseki/html/bunko10/bunko10_08073_0014/index.html; facsimile in Kitagawa Chikashi, *Sensōji bunka* (5) (Tōkyō: Sensōji shiryō hensanjo, 1963), available at the Meiji Taisho 1868–1926 Showcase, http://showcase.meijitaisho .net/entry/ryounkaku_02.php.

45. See also "Kanarazu Ryōunkaku ni nobore," special materials no. 88977119, Edo Tokyo Hakubutsukan. "Ryōunkaku tōkaku kiji," *Kōdan zasshi* (22) February 7, 1891, and Utagawa Kunisada III, "Ryōunkaku-ki e-sugoroku," special materials no. 87102202, November 1890, Edo Tokyo Hakubutsukan.

46. Lippit, *Topographies of Japanese Modernism,* 52.

47. Elaine Gerbert, introduction to Ranpo Edogawa, *The Strange Tale of Panorama Island,* trans. Elaine Gerbert (Honolulu: University of Hawai'i Press, 2013), x.

48. Brian Massumi, "Panoscopie: La photographie panoramique de Luc Courchesne," *CVPhoto* 60 (2003): 22–26. English translation available at Brian Massumi, "PANOSCOPIA: The Panoramic Photography of Luc Courchesne," accessed July 28, 2011, http://www.brianmassumi.com/english/essays.html.

49. Edogawa Ranpō, "The Man Traveling with the Brocade Portrait" ["Oshie to tabi suru otoko" (1929)], trans. Michael Tangeman, in *Modanizumu: Modern-*

ist Fiction from Japan, 1913–1938, ed. William Jefferson Tyler, 376–93 (Honolulu: University of Hawai'i Press, 2008).

50. The affordances here are not the static ones of the cinema associated with male flaneur gaze but more akin to those of the female transportive media of the flaneuse's diorama as described in Anne Friedberg, *Window Shopping: Cinema and the Postmodern* (Berkeley: University of California Press, 1994). Thus the viewing affordances of the tower and vending machine present the distributed power over a consumer society described in Debord.

51. Lippit, *Topographies of Japanese Modernism,* 142.

52. Ranpō, "Man Traveling with the Brocade Portrait," 386.

53. Ai Maeda, "The Panorama of Enlightenment," trans. Henry D. Smith, *Text and the City: Essays on Japanese Modernity* (Durham, N.C.: Duke University Press, 2004), 83.

54. Timon Screech, *The Lens Within the Heart: The Western Scientific Gaze and Popular Imagery in Later Edo Japan* (New York: Routledge, 2018), 120–27.

55. Hosoma, *Asakusa jūnikai,* 163.

56. Crary, *Techniques of the Observer,* 124–25; Ray Zone, *Stereoscopic Cinema and the Origins of 3-D Film, 1838–1952* (Lexington: University Press of Kentucky, 2014), 75.

57. Crary, *Suspensions of Perception,* 139.

58. Hosoma, *Asakusa jūnikai,* 158.

59. Hosoma, 160.

60. For instance, the Gaumont Stereodrome, the Richard Taxiphote, the Caldwell Sweetheart viewer, the Ica Multiplast, and the Becker tabletop viewers mentioned in Anne Wilkes Tucker et al., eds., *The History of Japanese Photography* (New Haven, Conn.: Yale University Press, 2003), 335.

61. Susan Sontag, *On Photography* (New York: Farrar, Straus and Giroux, 2011), 31.

62. "Tokkyo shōkai no zanshin hatsumei kikai Tōkyō Nihonbashi," *Yomiuri Shinbun,* October 22, 1903.

63. Crary also mentions the connection to peeping. See *Suspensions of Perception,* 136.

64. Crary, *Techniques of the Observer,* 9.

65. Mark B. N. Hansen, *New Philosophy for New Media* (Cambridge, Mass.: MIT Press, 2004), 37–38.

66. Walter Benjamin, "Imperial Panorama: A Tour of German Inflation," in *Reflections: Essays, Aphorisms, Autobiographica; Writings,* trans. Edmund Jephcott (New York: Schocken Books, 1978), 75.

67. The Arita machine now on display at the Nihon kamera hakubutsukan (Japanese Camera Museum) plays the children's song "Moshi moshi kameyo," suggesting that at least one variety of the machine was intended for a younger audience than the 1905 models displaying photos of the war. Sugiyama Kazuo, *Pachinko tanjo: Shinema no seiki no taishu goraku* (Osaka: Sogensha, 2008), 134. It is unclear if this is the same machine displayed in a 2012 exhibit at the museum

that was listed as having appeared in 1897. See also the design for a similar model with an organ in Hosoma, *Asakusa jūnikai,* 158, fig. 7-2.

68. Hosoma, *Asakusa jūnikai,* 156.

69. Sugiyama, *Pachinko tanjo,* 137–38. See also John Plunkett, "Selling Stereoscopy, 1890–1915: Penny Arcades, Automatic Machines, and American Salesmen," *Early Popular Visual Culture* 6, no. 3 (November 1, 2008): 240.

70. Sugiyama, *Pachinko tanjo,* 132–33.

71. "Arita seisakusho jidō panorama-kyō jidō omikuji-ki jidō tsujiura yasu dan-ki hoka" (advertisement), *Asahi Shinbun,* February 20, 1914. Similar ads appeared in the March 15, June 4, and November 1 issues of *Jitsugyō no Nihon* magazine. See also Sugiyama, *Pachinko tanjo,* 134; Aruki Nasu, "Taishō jidai no jidō hanbaiki," *Aruki Nasu no nikki-chō,* accessed April 2018, http://sutoratosu111 .blog.fc2.com/blog-entry-32.html.

72. Advertisement reproduced in Hosoma, *Asakusa jūnikai,* 190; Sugiyama, *Pachinko tanjo,* 132–37.

73. "The real consumer has become a consumer of illusions. The commodity is this materialized illusion and the spectacle is its general expression." Guy Debord, *Society of Spectacle,* trans. Ken Knabb (Berkeley, Calif.: Bureau of Public Secrets, 2014), 19.

74. Maeda, "Panorama of Enlightenment," 77–89; Henri Lefebvre, *The Production of Space* (New York: Wiley, 1992), 46–65.

75. Baudrillard, *Impossible Exchange,* 181–87.

76. See Oliver Wendell Holmes, "The Age of Photography," *Atlantic,* June 1859, 738–48, available online retitled as Oliver Wendell Holmes, "The Stereoscope and the Stereograph," *Atlantic,* June 1859, https://www.theatlantic.com/ magazine/archive/1859/06/the-stereoscope-and-the-stereograph/303361/.

77. Crary, *Techniques of the Observer,* 30, 35, 50n54. See also Daniel L. Collins, "Anamorphosis and the Eccentric Observer: Inverted Perspective and Construction of the Gaze," *Leonardo* 25, no. 1 (1992): 73–82.

78. Indeed, late nineteenth-century mathematical discourse also used *rittai* to refer to the objects of solid geometry. Fujisawa Rikitaro, "Sanjutsu kyōkasho," in *Gekan* (Tokyo: Dainihon tosho, 1896). I thank Steve Ridgley for this point.

79. Wilhelm Max Wundt, *Lectures on Human and Animal Psychology* (New York: MacMillan, 1896), 202.

80. Uiruherumu Bunto, *Jinrui oyobi dōbutsu shinrigaku kougi,* trans. Terauchi Ei (Tokyo: Shūeidō, 1902).

81. Crary, *Techniques of the Observer,* 120–25. Ultimately the long-valued myth of the "persistence of vision" residing in the eyes for the apprehension of movement in film continues on at a remove in the brain that has to make singular sense of double images in something like a persistence of image for the apprehension of space.

82. Edogawa Rampo, "Horrors of Film," trans. Seth Jacobowitz, in *The Edogawa Rampo Reader* (Tokyo: Kurodahan Press, 2008); Roland Barthes, *Camera Lucida: Reflections on Photography* (New York: Macmillan, 1981), 96.

83. Derrida, *Copy, Archive, Signature*.

84. The "click" of stereoscopic apprehension is well described in Thomas Banchoff et al., *3D: Double Vision*, ed. Britt Salvesen (Los Angeles: Prestel, 2018); and Susan R. Barry, *Fixing My Gaze: A Scientist's Journey into Seeing in Three Dimensions* (New York: Basic Books, 2009).

85. Susan Sontag, *On Photography* (New York: Farrar, Straus and Giroux, 2011), 98.

86. Crary, *Techniques of the Observer*, 125.

87. See Crary, 132–37.

88. See Figure 8. For convergence in stereography, see Otagi Michifusa, "Sutereo ni kansuru moro mondai," *Shashin kōgyō*, August 1953, 92–94. For convergence and polarized lenses for viewing film, see Ōtomo Shōji, "Rittai eiga: 'Tōtarusukōpu,'" *73 Nihon SF besuto shūsei* 2 (1973): 250–53.

89. Ishikawa Kenji, *3D rittai eizō ga yattekuru: Terebi eiga no 3 D fukyū wa kō naru!* (Tokyo: Ōmu-sha, 2010).

90. Edogawa Rampo, *The Edogawa Rampo Reader*, trans. Seth Jacobowitz (Tokyo: Kurodahan Press, 2008).

91. Hagiwara Sakutaro, "Boku no shashinki," *Asahi kamera* 28, no. 4 (October 1939): 701.

92. Jun Tanaka, "Urban Poetics and Photography: Methodology and Some Case Studies" (paper presented at For the New Urban Poetics, Korea University, Seoul, South Korea, April 12, 2008). Jun Tanaka places Hagiwara on par with Benjamin.

93. Hagiwara Sakutaro, "Panorama-kan nite," in *Hagiwara Sakutaro zenshū*, vol. 2 (Tokyo: Chikuma shobō, 1976), 271–74.

94. According to the count by Tsukada Shinya et al., "Kindai shijin Hagiwara Sakutarō no satsuei shita shashin ga toraeta fūkei yōso ni kansuru kentō," *Randosukēpu kenkyū: Onrain ronbun-shū* 5 (2012): 91. The remaining stereoscopic photos capture a variety of buildings, waterways, and landscapes.

95. Kumagai Kensuke, "Hagiwara Sakutarō 'Aoneko-igo' to kyōshū-'nosutarudjiya' no rekishi-sei," *Jinbun kenkyū* 193 (2017): 22; Izawa Kōtarō, "'Kyōshū' no kyori," in *'Geijutsu shashin' to sono jidai* (Tokyo: Chikuma shobō, 1986), 179–95; Izawa Kōtarō, "Kyōshū no gen fūkei," in *Nihonshashinshi o aruku* (Tokyo: Chikuma gakugei bunko, 1999), 198–213; Tanaka Jun, "Toshi no shigaku—Hagiwara Sakutarō no sutereo shashin," *Toshi no shigaku* (2007): 349–70.

96. Hagiwara Sakutaro, *Teihon Aoneko: Jijo, Hagiwara Sakutaro zenshū*, vol. 2 (Tokyo: Chikuma shobō, 1976), 582–95.

97. See, for instance, Thomas Lamarre's discussion of Oshii Mamoru's *Avalon*. Thomas Lamarre, *The Anime Machine: A Media Theory of Animation* (Minneapolis: University of Minnesota Press, 2013), 125.

98. Hagiwara Yōko, "Chichi no makuramoto," in *Bungei dokuhon Hagiwara Sakutarō* (Tokyo: Kawade shobō, 1976), 147.

99. Hagiwara Yōko, "Chichi no makuramoto," 148.

100. Bernard Stiegler, *Technics and Time: Disorientation* (Stanford, Calif.: Stanford University Press, 1998), 15.

101. Rampo, *Strange Tale of Panorama Island,* 78.

102. "Restrictions on Photography in the Precincts of Kotoku-in," Kotoku-in, April 1, 2015, http://kotoku-in.jp/en-site/#post-10.

103. See Rob Oechsle's post as Okinawa Soba (Rob), "The Daibutsu at Kamakura, Japan," Flickr, https://www.flickr.com/photos/okinawa-soba/albums/72157604804207290/. See also *Daibutsu of Kamakura,* Miriam and Ira D. Wallach Division of Art, Prints, and Photographs: Photography Collection, New York Public Library, https://digitalcollections.nypl.org/items/510d47d9-c50b-a3d9-e040-e00a18064a99.

104. Preceded by the wooden statue, which had been destroyed in 1248 with its housings destroyed in storms in 1334, 1369, and 1498, the current statue has sat on its platform for some seven hundred years, even enduring serious damage to its base in the earthquake of 1923.

105. *Daibutsu of Kamakura.*

106. David L. Bourell, Joseph J. Beaman Jr., Ming C. Leu, and David W. Rosen, "A Brief History of Additive Manufacturing and the 2009 Roadmap for Additive Manufacturing: Looking Back and Looking Ahead," *RapidTech 2009: Proceedings of the US–TURKEY Workshop on Rapid Technologies.*

107. Morioka Isao, "Rittai shashinzō no hatsumei: Chōkoku sokkuri ni dekiru," *Kodomo no kagaku* 8, no. 3 (1928): 86–89; Morioka Isao, "Rittai shashinzō no hanashi," *Kaizō* 10, no. 7 (July 1928): 83; Morioka Isao, "Rittai shashinzō no hanashi," *Shashin bunka,* January 1928, 86–88; Uemura Taku, Okada Tetsurō, Morioka Isao, and Suzuki Takashi, "Supekutoru shashin: Shashin-yō kenchiku, Rittai shashin-zō," in *Kōjō shashin-jutsu (saishin shashin kagaku taikei),* vol. 9, ed. Nakamura Michitarō, 1–19 (Tokyo: Seibundō shinkōsha, 1936); Matsuoka Yuzuru, "Dagu no rittai shashin-zō," *Bungeishunjū,* December 1932, 12–14. Early news articles are posted on the guide to the company at the Rittaishashinzō company website, "Kaisha anai," Rittaishashinzō kabushiki kaisha, http://www.rittai.co.jp/annai.html. "Sunbun mo chigawanu shōzō rittai shashin no hatsumei kore koso sekai-tekina o tegara to origami o tsuke rareta Morioka-shi," *Tokyo Asahi Shinbun,* September 27, 1927; "Rittai no zō katachi o shashin de utsusu hatsumei Tōyōdai tetsugaku shusshin seinen ga kansei," *Yomiuri Shinbun,* August 27, 1927.

108. See a list of celebrity statues at the Rittaishashinzō company's website, "VIP sakuhinshū"Rittaishashinzō kabushiki kaisha," http://www.rittai.co.jp/sakuhin/VIP.html. There are other statues visible on Nikon's website, which contracted with Morioka from 1936 to 1946 to further develop his techniques: "Nikon chan'neru > shira rezaru Nikon no rekishi > sutereo shashin chōzō-hō," Kabushikigaisha Nikon, accessed 2014, http://www.nikon.co.jp:80/channel/recollections/10/.

109. In a similar line of argumentation, Hans Belting recounts that a "Christo-mimesis" "was not . . . the business of the painter or of images." Hans Belting, *Likeness and Presence: A History of the Image before the Era of Art* (Chicago: University of Chicago Press, 1994), 138, 150.

110. Morioka Isao, Photographic Method of Reproducing Original Objects, U.S. Patent US1719483A, filed September 21, 1927, and issued July 2, 1929.

111. Morioka Isao, "Rittai shashinzō no hatsumei: Chōkoku sokkuri ni dekiru," *Kodomo no kagaku*, September 1928, 89; "Rittaishashinzō, Shiseidō rittaishashinzō-bu," *Yomiuri Shinbun*, evening ed., October 12, 1933. Sven Saaler buys this utopian rhetoric about labor-saving in situating the technology in the economic downturn of the late 1920s. See Sven Saaler, *Men in Metal: A Topography of Public Bronze Statuary in Modern Japan* (Leiden, the Netherlands: Brill, 2020), 203.

112. Morioka Isao, "Rittai shashin-zō," in *Supekutoru shashin: Shashin-yō kenchiku, Kōjō shashin-jutsu (saishin shashin kagaku taikei)*, vol. 9, ed. Nakamura Michitarō (Tokyo: Seibundō shinkōsha, 1936), 6.

113. Matsuoka Yuzuru, "Dagu no rittai shashin-zō," *Bungeishunjū* (December 1932): 13–14.

114. See Jonathan Crary, "Spectacle, Attention, Counter-Memory," *October* 50 (1989): 97–107.

115. Jean Baudrillard, *Simulacra and Simulation* (Ann Arbor: University of Michigan Press, 1994).

116. Saaler, *Men in Metal*.

117. See Jayson Makoto Chun, *A Nation of a Hundred Million Idiots? A Social History of Japanese Television, 1953–1973* (New York: Routledge, 2006); Simon Partner, *Assembled in Japan: Electrical Goods and the Making of the Japanese Consumer* (Berkeley: University of California Press, 2000), 173–75.

118. Hal Foster et al., *The Return of the Real: The Avant-Garde at the End of the Century* (Cambridge, Mass.: MIT Press, 1996), 128.

119. See also Rokudenashiko, *What Is Obscenity? The Story of a Good for Nothing Artist and Her Pussy*, trans. Anne Ishii, ed. Anne Ishii and Graham Kolbeins (Tokyo: Koyama Press, 2016); Rokudenashiko, *Waisetsu tte nan desu ka?* (Tokyo: Kinyōbi, 2015).

120. Crary, "Spectacle, Attention, Counter-Memory," 98.

121. *Rittai eiga wa (eiga kankyaku no) sōzōryoku o kyohisuru*. Shimuzu and Ogi cited in Nakamura Hideyuki, "19531 D-toshi, Nihon 'rittai eiga' gensetsu to eiga kankyaku," in *Kankyaku e no apurōchi*, ed. Hideaki Fujiki, vol. 14 of *Nihon eigashi sōsho* (Tokyo: Shinwasha, 2011), 75.

122. Lamarre, *Anime Machine*, 125.

123. "Restaurant Sushi Singularity," Open Meals, http://www.open-meals.com/sushisingularity/index.html.

3. Schizoasthenic Media

1. Otomo Katsuhiro, *Kanojo no omoide* (Tokyo: Kōdansha, 1990), 19.

2. Michel Chion, *Audiovision: Sound on Screen* (New York: Columbia University Press, 1994), 129.

3. Steven Feld, "Pygmy POP: A Genealogy of Schizophonic Mimesis," *Yearbook for Traditional Music* 28 (1996): 13.

4. See Luce Irigaray, *Speculum of the Other Woman*, trans. Gillian C. Gill (Ithaca, N.Y.: Cornell University Press, 1985), 257.

5. Catherine Munroe Hotes, "Wagorō Arai: His World of Silhouette Animation," *Nishikata Film Review* (blog), September 8, 2014, http://nishikataeiga .blogspot.com/2014/09/wagoro-arai-his-world-of-silhouette.html.

6. "Kage'e eiga 'Chōchōfujin no gensō' kan joshi dōjō no shin sakkyoku de kaigai e purāge-shi e tsuraate 'utsushi,'" *Asahi Shinbun*, March 29, 1940.

7. Y. Nagai and K. Kobatake, *Japanese Popular Music: A Collection of the Popular Music of Japan Rendered in to the Staff Notation* (Osaka: S. Miki & Co, 1891); Rudolf Dittrich, *Six Japanese Popular Songs Collected and Arranged for the Pianoforte* (Leipzig, Germany: Breitkopf & Härtel, 1894).

8. "DaisyField.com Archive of Japanese Traditional Music," DaisyField.com, http://daisyfield.com/music/htm/-genres/japan.htm; Hara Kunio, "Puccini's Use of Japanese Melodies in Madama Butterfly" (master's thesis, University of Cincinnati, 2003).

9. Itō Nobuo, *Chosakuken jiken hyakuwa: Sokumen kara mita chosakuken hattatsushi* (Tokyo: Chosakuken Shiryō Kyōkai, 1976); Luo Li, *Intellectual Property Protection of Traditional Cultural Expressions: Folklore in China* (Cham, Switzerland: Springer Science & Business, 2014); Jessica Christine Lai, *Indigenous Cultural Heritage and Intellectual Property Rights: Learning from the New Zealand Experience?* (Cham, Switzerland: Springer Science & Business Media, 2014); Joseph Charles Hickerson, *Copyright and Folksong* (Washington, D.C.: Archive, 1975). See also Stephen M. Best, *The Fugitive's Properties: Law and the Poetics of Possession* (Chicago: University of Chicago Press, 2010).

10. Miura Tamaki, "Putchiini ni shōtai sarete," in *Ochōfujin*, ed. Yoshimoto Akimitsu, 87–97 (Tokyo: Tosho sentā, 1997).

11. Arthur Groos, "Return of the Native: Japan in Madama Butterfly/Madama Butterfly in Japan," *Cambridge Opera Journal* 1, no. 2 (July 1989): 170; also cited in "Puccini Wants a Book for an American Opera," *New York Times*, January 20, 1907; Arthur Groos, "Cio-Cio-San and Sadayakko: Japanese Music-Theater in *Madama Butterfly*," *Monumenta Nipponica* 54, no. 1 (1999): 41–73.

12. Mayama Seika, *Tōchūken Kumoemon Mayama Seika senshū*, vol. 4 (Tokyo: Dainihon yūbenkai kōdansha, 1947); Kerim Yasar, *Electrified Voices: How the Telephone, Phonograph, and Radio Shaped Modern Japan, 1868–1945* (New York: Columbia University Press, 2018), 91–109; Nobuo Itō, *Chosakuken jiken hyakuwa: Sokumen kara mita chosakuken hattatsushi* (Tokyo: Chosakuken Shiryō Kyōkai, 1976), 197. See also Otani Takushi, "Tōchūken Kumoemon jiken," *Jōhō kanri* 56, no. 8 (2013): 552–55.

13. R. Murray Schafer, *The New Soundscape* (New York: Associated Music Publishers, 1969). See also R. Murray Schafer, *The Soundscape: Our Sonic Environment and the Tuning of the World* (New York: Knopf, 1977).

14. David Saunders, *Authorship and Copyright* (New York: Routledge, 1992), 171.

15. For a list of the Japanese records, see Kunio Hara, "The Death of Tamaki Miura: Performing *Madama Butterfly* during the Allied Occupation of Japan," *Music and Politics* 11, no. 1 (Winter 2017), https://doi.org/10.17613/px11-vk55. For the U.S. records, see *Discography of American Historical Recordings*, s.v. "Miura, Tamaki," https://adp.library.ucsb.edu/index.php/talent/detail/28303/Miura_Tamaki_vocalist_soprano_vocal.

16. Watanabe Hamako, *Nagasaki no Ochōsan,* lyrics by Ko Fujiura, composed by Nobuyuki Takeoka, arranged by Takio Niki, Nippon Columbia, 30348 A222, September 1939.

17. "About 'Jizuki-Uta," Daisyfield Archive of Japanese Traditional Music, DaisyField.com, http://daisyfield.com/music/htm/japan/Jizuki-Uta.htm.

18. A relatively complete discography of Miura's work is available in Tanabe Hisayuki, *Kōshō Miura Tamaki* (Tokyo: Kindai bungeisha, 1995), 452–55. See also the limited discography in Kunio Hara, "The Death of Tamaki Miura: Performing *Madama Butterfly* during the Allied Occupation of Japan," *Music and Politics* 11, no. 1 (Winter 2017): 1–26.

19. Hara, "Death of Tamaki Miura"; Puccini, "Un Bel Di Vedremo" (*Hareta hi no*) and "Con Onor Muore" (*Misao ni shinuru wa*), Chōchōfujin, Bikutā kangengakudan Bikutā rekodo 4149-A 4149-B (released June 1930), http://dl.ndl.go.jp/info:ndljp/pid/1321734.

20. Though preceded by Columbia records A49260 and A49265 released in November of 1917 featuring "Un bel dì, vedremo" and "Vogliatemi bene," it was Miura's version of "Con onor muore" on Nipponophone 5178, July 1922, that went viral. By one account on May 13, 1922, Miura had already laid down twenty different songs on twenty different records. "Miura tamaki no rekōdo fukikomi mi chōkan ongaku," *Yomiuri Shinbun,* May 13, 1922; "Record Dealers Reap Harvest on Miura Songs: Phonograph Companies Sell 80,000 Selections of Noted Singer," *Japan Times,* August 5, 1922; also mentioned in Hara, "Death of Tamaki Miura," 11.

21. Puccini, "Un Bel Di Vedremo."

22. Tanabe Hisayuki, *Kōshō Miura Tamaki* (Tokyo: Kindai bungeisha, 1995), 269–70.

23. Recorded on November 18, 1935, for sale beginning in January 1936, Columbia (Koromupia) record #35480A celebrated lyrics translated by Miura with a score edited by Okuyama Sadakichi. Those lyrics are transcribed in *Miura Tamaki zenshū* [pamphlet] (Tokyo: Nippon Columbia, 1995), 43.

24. Noboru Miyata, "The History and Present State of the Japanese Copyright Clearance System," *ABD 2000* 31 (2): 5–6, available on the Asia-Pacific Cultural Centre for UNESCO site at http://www.accu.or.jp/appreb/09/pdf31-2/5_6ABD31-2.pdf.

25. See Tōru Mitsui, "Copyright and Music in Japan: A Forced Grafting and Its Consequences," *Music and Copyright,* ed. Simon Frith (Edinburgh: Edinburgh University Press, 1993), 137.

26. "Ochōfujin no haikei o satsuei ni," *Asahi Shinbun*, April 2, 1932.

27. "Shin eiga-hyō: Kikyōna misemono to shite tsūyō no nue-teki eiga: *Ochō-fujin*," *Yomiuri Shinbun*, March 28, 1933.

28. "Shin eiga-hyō: 'Ochōfujin' (Paramaunto eiga) fuman to kenen, daga, yo-kumo kore made Nihon-ka shita engi," *Asahi Shinbun*, March 22, 1933. See also Nakamura Midori, "1930-nendai Shanhai ni okeru Hariuddo eiga 'Madamu bata-furai' no juyō," *Bunka ronshū* 42, no. 3 (2013): 1.

29. *Asahi Shinbun*, February 27, 1933, morning edition.

30. See Ralph S. Brown, "The Widening Gyre: Are Derivative Works Getting Out of Hand?," *Cardozo Arts & Entertainment Law Journal* 3, no. 1 (1984): 12. See also Carol A. Ellingson, "The Copyright Exception for Derivative Works and the Scope of Utilization," *Indiana Law Journal* 56, no. 1 (1980–1981): 14.

31. "Rajio: Rajiorebyū 'Ochōfujin no gensō' Shōchiku gakugeki-bu ga enshutsu suru, rebyūka sareta kageki," *Asahi Shinbun*, February 17, 1933; "Shibai 'Ochōfu-jin no gensō' Shōchiku," *Yomiuri Shinbun*, March 27, 1933.

32. "Tōkyō odori to *Ochōfujin no gensō* Shōchiku-za no shōjokageki o miru," *Asahi Shinbun*, April 15, 1933; "Gurabia: Shōchiku shōjo kageki kōen, Ochōfujin no gensō," *Fujo-kai* 47, no. 5 (May 1933): 44–45.

33. "Ochōfujin no gensō' wa gensaku o hyōsetsu shingai: Mirano no churudei gakufu kaisha Shōchiku Kido jūyaku o uttau," *Kōbe Yūshin nippō*, October 8, 1933. The article also mentions that a song "Berlin no musume" (probably Georg Kai-ser's 1918 "Das Frauenoper") was also involved in the suit.

34. This was but one in a stream of suits and requests for fees increasingly lev-ied by Plage's Tokyo office over the course of the year. By the summer of 1932, the Plage office was working full tilt to obtain fees from the entire Japanese culture industry at large. He asked for a monthly fee of 600 yen in July 1932 from Nippon hōsō kyōkai (NHK, Japan Broadcasting Corporation), the national broadcaster, for copyright royalties for broadcasting the records of European composers and musicians, raising the fee the following summer to 1,500 yen. The cost ratio of playing Japanese music as opposed to foreign music was 6:15 yen, effectively halting the airing of foreign music on NHK between 1933 and 1934. Revisions to Japanese copyright law in 1934 enhanced the rights of phonograph record pro-ducers but did little to stop Plage from levying fees on performance. He contin-ued to pursue copyright fees for the performance of European music, charging a fee of 5 yen per performance and between 1 and 1.5 yen per song, making it diffi-cult for producers of such events to earn a profit. Sumio Iijima, "Musical Copy-rights in Japan," *Bulletin of the Copyright Society of the U.S.A.* 23 (1975): 401–3. See also Kawabata Shigeru, "The Japanese Record Industry," *Popular Music* 10, no. 3 (October 1991): 343; Ōie Shigeo, *Purāge senpū* (Tokyo: Reibunsha, 1974); Itō Nobuo, *Chosakken jiken to chosakken hanrei: Sokumen yori mita chosakken hattatsu-shi* (Tokyo: Monbushō, 1968), 36–41.

35. In August 1931, the Takarazuka Kageki Revue produced *Concise Madame Butterfly* (*Shukusatsu Chōchō-san*). See Arthur Groos, "Introduction: The Taka-

razuka Concise Madame Butterfly," *Asia-Pacific Journal: Japan Focus* 4, no. 14 (July 15, 2016): art. no. 7.

36. Ōie Shigeo, *Purāge senpu* (Tokyo: Reibunsha, 1974), 7–9; Ōie Shigeo, *Nippon chosakuken monogatari: Purāge hakase no tekihatsuroku* (Tokyo: Seizansha, 1999), 62–63; Itō Nobuo, *Chosakuken jiken hyakuwa: Sokumen kara mita chosakuken hattatsushi* (Tokyo: Chosakuken Shiryō Kyōkai, 1976), 123–24; "Purāge senpū ni 'kikyaku' no bōfū-rin! Kido-shi ni gaika agaru," *Asahi Shinbun,* December 29, 1936; "Chosaku kenpō o meguru Purāge mondai," *Gekkan gakufu* 26, no. 2 (1937): 90–91.

37. See coverage in Ōie, *Purāge senpu*; Ōie, *Nippon chosakuken monogatari*; Itō, *Chosakuken jiken hyakuwa.* See also Yamashita Hiroaki, "'Purāge senpū' no hanashi," *Hōritsu shinbun,* July 3 and 5, 1937; "Plage's Copyright Case Is Rejected by Tokyo Court: Failed to Register Claims, Says Ruling of Long Pending Suit," *Japan Times,* January 7, 1937.

38. "Hōkō o kaete sairai, Purāge no 'tsumuji kaze,' Shōchiku kageki o osou 'ochōfujin' 'omoide' ni soshō baishō: Kido Shōchiku senmu-dan," *Asahi Shinbun,* March 16, 1937.

39. Ōie, *Purāge Senpū,* 22; Ōie, *Nippon chosakuken monogatari,* 50; Yamada Kōsaku, "Sakkyoku hōsōka no hihan," *Yomiuri Shinbun,* June 16, 1932; "Yamada Koscak Leaves for Germany," *Japan Times,* May 6, 1937.

40. Ōie, *Purāge senpū,* 26. See also Sumio, "Musical Copyrights in Japan," 402.

41. "Copyright Body Formed; Group Has 28 Members," *Japan Times,* July 17, 1935.

42. "Purāge no tegami: Berunu jōyaku dattai no hitsuyō," *Yomiuri Shinbun,* September 24, 1936.

43. Christopher Heath and Kung-Chung Liu, eds., *Copyright Law and the Information Society in Asia* (New York: Oxford University Press, 2007).

44. Kunishio Kōichirō, "Chikuonki 'Rekōdo' no ensō to chosakuken," *Keisatsu kenkyū,* December 1937.

45. See Best, *Fugitive's Properties.*

46. Sumio, "Musical Copyrights in Japan," 403.

47. Christopher Heath, "Intellectual Property and Anti-trust," in *History of Law in Japan since 1868,* ed. Wilhelm Röhl (London: Brill, 2005), 506; Yoshimura Tamotsu, "Chūkai gyōmu-hō no ritsuansha: Kunishio Kōichirō," in *Nihon chosakken-shi* (Tokyo: Daiichishobō, 1993), 187–209; Koji Okumura, "Collective Management of Copyright and Neighbouring Rights in Japan," in *Collective Management of Copyright and Related Rights* (Alphen aan den Rijn, the Netherlands: Kluwer Law International, 2010), 384–85.

48. Mitsui, "Copyright and Music in Japan," 138.

49. Wilhelm Plage, "More about Copyright," *Japan Times,* April 5, 1940.

50. "Police Plague Plage on Copyright Law Suspended Suspected Violation," *Japan Times,* March 29, 1940.

51. Sumio, "Musical Copyrights in Japan," 403; "Chosakuken ni kansuru

chūkaigyōmu ni kansuru hōritsu" [April 5, 1939], *Nihon shuppan nenkan* (Tokyo: Kyōdo Shuppansha, 1943), 1,094.

52. "Police to Probe Dr. Plage on Copyright Law," *Japan Times*, March 25, 1940.

53. Irigaray, *Speculum of the Other Woman*, 251.

54. Kurumatani Hiroshi, "Nihon ga unda daiikkyū no sekai hito: Yūmei sugiru Miura Tamaki fujin," *Shokumin* 12, no. 12 (1933): 140–43. See also the editorial comment in the May 19, 1920, *Japan Times*.

55. See Tanabe Hisayuki, "Jitensha tsūgaku," in *Kōshō Miura Tamaki* (Tokyo: Kindai bungeisha, 1995), 39–44; Hiroshi Makoto, "Various Stages of the Japanese Conception of Beauty: Madame Tamaki," *Japan Times*, May 19, 1929; "Nippon Day by Day: Recollections by Miura," *Japan Times*, January 7, 1936. Also mentioned in the pamphlet from her June 1936 performance at the Kabuki-za, available at "'Chōchōfujin' Kabukiza (1936.6)," *Zōsho mokuroku* (blog), September 28, 2011, https://blog.goo.ne.jp/1971913/c/fb93b294f6765425392ab8aeeddc5e88.

56. "Orufoisu ensō-sha Yoshikawa ya ma, shibata tamaki, Miyawaki sen san jō shashin," *Bijutsu shinpō*, August 1903, 2–11; "Tragedy of a Singer," *Japan Times*, June 1, 1932.

57. Hara, "Death of Tamaki Miura," 26.

58. Brian Burke-Gaffney, *Starcrossed: A Biography of Madame Butterfly* (Manchester, U.K.: EastBridge, 2004); Jan van Rij, *Madame Butterfly: Japonisme, Puccini, & the Search for the Real Cho-Cho-San* (San Francisco: Stone Bridge Press, 2001); Kusudo Yoshiaki and Noda Kazuko, *Mō hitori no chōchōfujin: Nagasaki Gurabā-tei no on'na shujin tsuru* (Tokyo: Mainichi shinbunsha, 1997).

59. "A Japanese 'Madama Butterfly,'" *Times* (London), June 1, 1915.

60. "Kōkashu o eta sakkyokka Bu-shi wa fujin o yorokobi mukau," *Asahi Shinbun*, April 25, 1920, morning edition, 9. See also "Madame Miura Meets Puccini," *Japan Times*, April 27, 1920.

61. Tamaki, "Putchiini ni shōtai sarete," 87–89 (emphasis added).

62. See Ayako Kano, "Japanese Theater and Imperialism," *US Japan Women's Journal* 12 (1997): 17; Margherita Long, *This Perversion Called Love: Reading Tanizaki, Feminist Theory, and Freud* (Stanford, Calif.: Stanford University Press, 2009) 3–4; Ueno Chizuko, "In the Feminine Guise: A Trap of Reverse Orientalism," *U.S.-Japan Women's Journal* 13 (1997): 3–25; Ueno Chizuko, "In the Feminine Guise: A Trap of Reverse Orientalism; Collapse of 'Japanese Mothers,'" in *Contemporary Japanese Thought* (New York: Columbia University Press, 2005), 225–62.

63. Y. Soga, "The Orient in Hawaii," *Japan Times*, October 20, 1929. For similar anecdotes, see Mari Yoshihara, "The Flight of the Japanese Butterfly: Orientalism, Nationalism, and Performances of Japanese Womanhood," *American Quarterly* 56, no. 4 (2004): 984; Robert C. Lancefield, "Hearing Orientality in (White) America, 1900–1930" (PhD diss., Wesleyan University, 2004), 203.

64. "Madame Tamaki Miura, Japan's pioneer opera singer, spoke in English over the radio on Wednesday which was relayed across the seas. The title of her

talk was 'From my Native Country: Nippon.'" "Miura Talks to the World," *Japan Times,* November 23, 1935. Edward C. Moore, *Forty Years of Opera in Chicago* (New York: Horace Liveright, 1930), 302.

65. Tanabe Hisayuki, "Miura Tamaki denki shiryō kō: Tamaki no chosaku to Setouchi Harumi no *Ochōfujin,*" *Tokoha Gakuen Tanki Daigaku kiyō* 14, no. 31–45 (1982): 41. See also Itō Nobuo, *Chosakuken jiken hyakuwa: Sokumen kara mita chosakuken hattatsushi* (Tokyo: Chosakuken Shiryō Kyōkai, 1976), 157.

66. Hisayuki Tanabe, *Kōshō Miura Tamaki=Madame Tamaki Miura* (Tokyo: Kindai Bungeisha, 1995), 387.

67. Hara, "Death of Tamaki Miura."

68. See Hara.

69. See Hara.

70. "Miura Sings for Slums," *Japan Times,* December 18, 1935; "Tamaki Miura in Peru," *New York Times,* October 26, 1919.

71. *Japan Times,* April 15, 1936; "Singers Confer on Organization of 1940 Chorus," *Japan Times,* June 3, 1938.

72. *Japan Times,* April 6, 1923; *Japan Times,* September 10, 1932; "To Give Recital," *Japan Times,* August 16, 1936.

73. "Threatening Letter Received by Miura," *Japan Times,* September 12, 1922.

74. "Tamaki Miura Gets Letter Threatening Her Life If She Continues Concerts in Japan; Singer Wants to Return to Safety in the USA," *Japan Times,* June 21, 1932, 1.

75. *Japan Times,* September 3, 1932; Sonoike Kin'naru, "Mosukuwa deatta Miura Tamaki fujin" (first published in *Gekkan Gakufu,* March 1933), in *Sovueto engeki no inshō* (Tokyo: Kensetsu-sha, 1933), 130–38.

76. "Tamaki Miura to Present Tea Set to Mussolini," *Japan Times,* October 4, 1932; "Madame Miura to Sing Butterfly in Japanese," *Japan Times,* January 13, 1937; *Japan Times,* November 7, 1937; "Miura Tamaki Will Sing at the Italian German Japanese Friendship Society's Musicale in the Gunjin Kaikan on Nov 17," *Japan Times,* November 22, 1937; *Japan Times,* December 4, 1937.

77. *Japan Times,* April 23, 1915; December 10, 1937; September 19, 1940.

78. *Japan Times,* December 6, 1935.

79. "Ochōfujin mo 'Purāge-ka,'" *Asahi Shinbun,* June 19, 1937, 11.

80. *Ibaraki no geinō-shi,* ed. Ibaraki bunka dantai rengō (Mito, Japan: Ibaraki-ken kyōiku iinkai, 1977), 286.

81. Quotation translated in "Soprano Composes Music for Film," *Japan Times,* March 31, 1940.

82. "Wadai no kagee eiga: 'Ochōfujin no gensō' Asahi eiga chikaku kōkai: Miura Tamaki, Nichigeki e," *Asahi Shinbun,* April 18, 1940, 3. See also Itō Nobuo, *Chosakken jiken to chosakken hanrei: Sokumen yori mita chosakken hattatsu-shi* (Tokyo: Monbushō, 1968), 41.

83. Ōie Shigeo, *Purēge senpu* (Tokyo: Reibunsha, 1974), 28; "Purāge shin-senpū: 'Ochōfujin' no jōen enki," *Asahi Shinbun,* May 2, 1940, 2; "Manshū-san no purāge senpū kan joshi no ochōfujin jōen o enki," *Yomiuri Shinbun,* May 2,

1940, 2; "'Chōchōfujin' wa chūshi," *Yomiuri Shinbun,* May 2, 1940, evening ed., 3; "Copyright Suit Postpones Opera on Eve of Premiere as Plage Scores," *Japan Times,* May 3, 1940.

84. Takebayashi Kenshichi, "Saikin wadai o tenbō su: 'Ochōfujin' to Purāge senpū," *Eiga Asahi* (July 1940): 95–96. Takebayashi Kenshichi had long been a nom de plume of Naoki Sanjugo, who had been dead six years, so this was likely written by his compatriot Yokomitsu Riichi.

85. "More about Copyright: Letter from Wilhelm Plage," *Japan Times,* April 5, 1940.

86. See Philip Towle, Margaret Kosuge, and Yoichi Kibata, *Japanese Prisoners of War* (New York: A&C Black, 2000), 131–32. See Hans Erik Pringsheim, "Copyright Law to Guard Authors: Government Agent," *Japan Times,* March 24, 1940, 1; Wilhelm Plage, "More about Copyright," *Japan Times,* April 5, 1940; Klaus Pringsheim, "Out of Tune," *Japan Times,* April 7, 1940.

87. Miura Tamaki, *Miura Tamaki: Ochō fujin,* ed. Akimitsu Yoshimoto (Tokyo: Nihon Tosho Sentā, 1997), 95.

88. John Luther Long, "Madame Butterfly," *Century Magazine,* January 1898, 375.

89. Arthur Groos, "Return of the Native: Japan in Madama Butterfly/Madama Butterfly in Japan," *Cambridge Opera Journal* 1, no. 2 (July 1989): 170.

90. Groos, "Return of the Native," 170.

91. See Irigaray, *Speculum of the Other Woman,* 255.

92. Moriguchi Tari and Hayashi Itoko, *Bunkateki jūtaku no kenkyū* (Tokyo: Arusu, 1922), 221.

93. See Marshall McLuhan's phrase "windows on the world" and "Not many ages ago, glass windows were unknown luxuries. With light control by glass came also a means of controlling the regularity of domestic routine, and steady application to crafts and trade without regard to cold or rain. The world was put in a frame." Marshall McLuhan, *Understanding Media* (Cambridge, Mass.: MIT Press, 1964), 204, 128. See Friedrich Kittler on windows from Leon Battista Alberti's "finestra aperta" to MS Windows in Friedrich Kittler, *Optical Media* (Cambridge, Mass.: Polity Press, 2009), 56–83. Consider the importance of the train window or Alberti's "open window" to Thomas Lamarre's understanding of the anime machine in Thomas Lamarre, *The Anime Machine: A Media Theory of Animation* (Minneapolis: University of Minnesota Press, 2009), xv, 32. Anne Friedberg, *The Virtual Window: From Alberti to Microsoft* (Cambridge, Mass.: MIT Press, 2006); Leon Battista Alberti, *Leon Battista Alberti: On Painting* (New York: Cambridge University Press, 2013); Helen M. Greenwald, "Picturing Cio-Cio-San: House, Screen, and Ceremony in Puccini's Madama Butterfly," *Cambridge Opera Journal* 12, no. 3 (2000): 237–59.

94. See Stacy Spies, *Metuchen* (Mount Pleasant, S.C.: Arcadia Publishing, 2000).

95. Antoinett Rehmann Perrett, "Simplicity in Suburban Home," *House and Garden* 27 (June 1915): 416–18.

96. Melissa Eriko Poulsen, "Writing Madame Butterfly's Child," *Amerasia Journal* 43, no. 2 (2017): 162.

97. Félix Régamey, *The Chrysantheme Papers: The Pink Notebook of Madame Chrysantheme and Other Documents of French Japonisme,* trans. Christopher Reed (Honolulu: University of Hawai'i Press, 2010).

98. On pierced walls of the cave, see Irigaray, *Speculum of the Other Woman,* 263.

99. "'Madam Butterfly' *Opera* [1906]," nos. 43.98.37 and 41.420.215, Byron Company Collection, Museum of the City of New York.

100. For information on the collection of cards, see Leopoldo Metlicovitz, "Envelope for the Series Madama Butterfly," and especially "Pinkerton and Butterfly behind a Screen" (Milan: G. Ricordi & Co., 1904), accession nos. 2012.8388.1 and 2012.8388.2, Leonard A. Lauder collection, Museum of Fine Arts, Boston.

101. Mordaunt Hall, "A Charming Cho Cho San," *New York Times,* December 26, 1932.

102. See Whitney Grace, "Lengthening Shadows," in *Lotte Reiniger: Pioneer of Film Animation* (Jefferson, N.C.: McFarland, 2017), 18–28.

103. Karl Marx, *Grundisse: Foundations of the Critique of Political Economy* (New York: Penguin, 1973), 690–712; Eric Lott, *Love and Theft: Blackface Minstrelsy and the American Working Class* (New York: Oxford University Press, 1993); Walter Benn Michaels, "The Myth of 'Cultural Appropriation': Even Our Own Stories Don't Belong to Us," *Chronicle of Higher Education* 63, no. 40 (July 2, 2017): https://www.chronicle.com/article/the-myth-of-cultural-appropriation/. See also Rosemary J. Coombe, *The Cultural Life of Intellectual Properties: Authorship, Appropriation, and the Law* (Durham, N.C.: Duke University Press, 1998).

104. Fukuzawa Yukichi was among the first in Japan to recognize the key role of copyright measures in the flourishing of the medium of books. Peter Francis Kornicki, *The Book in Japan: A Cultural History from the Beginnings to the Nineteenth Century* (Honolulu: University of Hawai'i Press, 2001), 181, 242, 245–46; Fukuzawa Yukichi quoted in Kawakita Nobuo, "Fukuzawa Yukichi no shoki no chosakuken kakuritsu undō," *Kindai Nihon kenkyū* 5 (1988): 28–29. See also Kurata Yoshihiro, *Chosakken shiwa* (Tokyo: Senrisha, 1980), 10; Fukuzawa Yukichi, *Fukuzawa Yukichi zenshū,* vol. 19 (Tokyo: Iwanamishoten, 1971), 449; Yoshimura Tamotsu, *Hakkutsu Nihon chosakukenshi* (Tokyo: Daiichi Shobō, 1993).

105. For a sequel covering subsequent Trouble's future life, see the Sessue Hayakawa film *His Birthright,* directed by William Worthington (1918; Moraga, Calif.: Silent Hall of Fame Enterprises, 2015), DVD.

106. Michael Taussig, *Mimesis and Alterity* (New York: Routledge, 1993), xiii.

107. See Yasar, *Electrified Voices.*

108. Kawabata Shigeru, "The Japanese Record Industry," *Popular Music* 10, no. 3 (October 1991): 327–45; Heath, "Intellectual Property and Anti-trust," 505–6; Thomas Elsaesser and Malte Hagener, "Cinema as Ear: Acoustics and Space," in *Film Theory: An Introduction through the Senses* (New York: Routledge, 2010), 157.

109. Collective administration of copyright is regulated by the Act on Management Business of Copyright and Neighbouring Rights (act no. 131 of November 29, 2000; hereafter Copyright Management Act). It replaced the Act on the Intermediary Business Concerning Copyright (1939). The Copyright Law from 1939 to 2000 aimed to break up monopolies and end the exploitation of users and creators by industry and JASRAC. Hisao Shiomi and Peter Ganea, "Copyright Contract Law," in *Japanese Copyright Law: Writings in Honour of Gerhard Schricker,* ed. Peter Ganea, Christopher Heath, and Hiroshi Saitō (The Hague: Kluwer Law International, 2005), 89. Questions of intermediaries and copyright have returned to the fore with new media of the internet. See Paul Ganley, "Google Book Search: Fair Use, Fair Dealing, and the Case for Intermediary Copying," SSRN, January 24, 2006, https://dx.doi.org/10.2139/ssrn.875384. YouTube has also removed nearly thirty thousand copyrighted files after receiving complaints of copyright infringement from the Japanese Society for Rights of Authors, Composers, and Publishers. Viacom International Inc. et al. v. YouTube Inc., YouTube LLC., and Google Inc. (Civ. 2103, 3582, S.D.N.Y. 2010); Matthew Rimmer, *Digital Copyright and the Consumer Revolution* (Northampton, Mass.: Edward Elgar Publishing, 2007), 254.

110. Nishimura Ayano and Siio Itiro, "Contexinger: Nichijō no kontekusuto o torikomi utau Volcaloid," *Jōhōshorigakkai kenkyū hōkoku* 38, no. 9 (2013): 1–6.

4. Copycat Rivalries

1. Namekawa Michio, *Terebi to kodomo* (Tokyo: Maki shobō, 1961), 18; Shimotsuki Jūkurō, "Issei o fūbi shita terebi bangumi '*Gekkō kamen,*'" in *Omoide wa terebihīrō to tomoni: Boku-ra ga sodatta 1960-nendai* (Tokyo: Bungei-sha, 2006), 60. A sample English-subtitled version of *Gekkō kamen* was sent to the United States to see if the series could be sold there and occasionally is posted to the web today. "'Gekkō kamen' mo mihonban, chikaku yushutsu," *Asahi,* May 3, 1959, Tokyo morning ed.; Osaki Teizō, *Showa kodomo bumu* (Tokyo: Gakushu kenkyusha, 2010); "'Chisai Gekko kamen': Tsui muchu de tobi oriru," *Yomiuri Shinbun,* June 19, 1959, morning ed.; "Gekko kamen gokko de gakudo kega: Yane kara ochi," *Yomiuri Shinbun,* June 19, 1959, morning ed., 11.

2. See, for instance, "Asatte wa shichigosan ryūkō-fuku wa terebi no ninkisha," *Yomiuri Shinbun,* November 13, 1958, evening ed.

3. Ochi Masanori, "Taikenteki terebi-ron," *Jiyū* 6 (1978): 145–51.

4. Simon Partner, *Assembled in Japan: Electrical Goods and the Making of the Japanese Consumer* (Berkeley: University of California Press, 2000).

5. See, for instance, Ōya Sōichi quoted in Jayson Makoto Chun, *"A Nation of a Hundred Million Idiots"? A Social History of Japanese Television, 1953–1973* (New York: Routledge, 2007), 3.

6. Paul Dumouchel, "Indifference and Envy: Girard and the Anthropological Analysis of Modern Economy," in *The Ambivalence of Scarcity and Other Essays* (East Lansing: Michigan State University Press, 2014), 149–60; George

Erving, "René Girard and the Legacy of Alexandre Kojeve," *Contagion: Journal of Violence, Mimesis, and Culture* 10, no. 1 (2003): 111–25.

7. René Girard, "Innovation and Repetition," *SubStance* 19, no. 2/3 (1990): 7–20.

8. Joel Hodge, "Superheroes, Scapegoats, and Saviors: The Problem of Evil and the Need for Redemption," in *Violence, Desire, and the Sacred,* vol. 3, *Mimesis, Movies, and Media,* ed. Scott Cowdell, Chris Fleming, and Joel Hodge (New York: Bloomsbury, 2016), 66.

9. René Girard, *Violence and the Sacred* (London: A&C Black, 2005); René Girard, *Things Hidden since the Foundation of the World,* trans. Jean-Michel Oughourlian and Guy Lefort (Stanford, Calif.: Stanford University Press, 1987).

10. René Girard, *A Theatre of Envy: William Shakespeare* (Leominster, U.K.: Gracewing Publishing, 2000); René Girard, *Myth and Ritual in Shakespeare: A Midsummer Night's Dream* (Stanford, Calif.: Stanford University Press, 1973); René Girard, *To Double Business Bound: Essays on Literature, Mimesis, and Anthropology* (Baltimore: Johns Hopkins University Press, 1988); René Girard, *Oedipus Unbound: Selected Writings on Rivalry and Desire,* ed. Mark Rogin Anspach (Stanford, Calif.: Stanford University Press, 2004); René Girard, *Mimesis and Theory: Essays on Literature and Criticism, 1953–2005,* ed. Robert Doran (Stanford, Calif.: Stanford University Press, 2008).

11. See Michael Lucken, *Imitation and Creativity in Japanese Arts: From Kishida Ryusei to Miyazaki Hayao* (New York: Columbia University Press, 2016), chap. 2.

12. Hagiwara Sakutarō, "Mohōsha ni yotte haradatashiku sareru," in *Hagiwara Sakutarō zenshū,* vol. 4 (Tokyo: Chikuma shobō, 1975), 210–11.

13. See Lucken, *Imitation and Creativity in Japanese Arts.*

14. Richard H. Okada, *Figures of Resistance: Language, Poetry, and Narrating in "The Tale of the Genji" and Other Mid-Heian Texts* (Durham, N.C.: Duke University Press, 1991).

15. Rein Raud, "Chinese Calligraphic Models in Heian Japan: Copying Practices and Stylistic Transmission," in *The Culture of Copying in Japan: Critical and Historical Perspectives,* ed. Rupert Cox, 143–55 (New York: Routledge, 2007).

16. Steven T. Brown, *Theatricalities of Power: The Cultural Politics of Noh* (Stanford, Calif.: Stanford University Press, 2001), 21.

17. Zeami, "A Mirror Held to the Flower (Kakyō)" and "The Aesthetics of Ambiguity: The Artistic Theories of Zeami," in *On the Art of the No Drama: The Major Treatises of Zeami,* ed. Yamazaki Masakazu and J. Thomas Rimer (Princeton, N.J.: Princeton University Press, 1984), 158, xxix–xlv; Mark J. Nearman, "Kakyō: Zeami's Fundamental Principles of Acting," *Monumenta Nipponica* 37, no. 3 (1982): 333–42; "Kakyō: Zeami's Fundamental Principles of Acting (Part Two)," *Monumenta Nipponica* 37, no. 4 (1982): 459–96; "Kakyō: Zeami's Fundamental Principles of Acting. Part Three," *Monumenta Nipponica* 38, no. 1 (1983): 49–71.

18. Aristotle, *The Poetics of Aristotle,* trans. Preston H. Epps, II:6 (Chapel Hill: University of North Carolina Press, 2010), 11.1448b4–17.

19. Abe Kōbō, "Monomane ni tsuite: Hitotsu no kigeki eiga-ron," *Eiga geijutsu* (December 1957): 24.

20. Abe, "Monomane ni tsuite," 25.

21. Abe quotes Karl Marx, *Grundrisse: Foundations of the Critique of Political Economy* (New York: Penguin, 2005), 110.

22. Peter Cotes and Thelma Niklaus, *The Little Fellow* (New York: Philosophical Library, 1965), 7.

23. Ōoka Shōhei, "Monomane geijutsu mō kekkō," *Geijutsu shinchō* 10, no. 5 (May 1959): 114–21.

24. Ōoka, "Monomane geijutsu mō kekkō," 118.

25. Ōoka, 115.

26. Takahashi Yoshitaka, "Zeami no 'monomane' to Yōroppa-teki mimēshisu," in *Takahashi Yoshitaka bungei riron chosaku-shū-ka* (Tokyo: Jinbunshoin, 1977), 158.

27. Takahashi, "Zeami no 'monomane,'" 161.

28. Takahashi, 161.

29. Takahashi, 162.

30. Paraphrasing Wolfgang Palaver, *René Girard's Mimetic Theory* (East Lansing: Michigan State University Press, 2013), 149. See also Girard, *Violence and the Sacred*, 166–68; *Things Hidden*, 35; *Theatre of Envy*, 61–62.

31. Mamoru Sasaki, *Neon Sain to Gekko Kamen: Senkosha Kobayashi Toshio No Shigoto* (Tokyo: Chikuma Shobo, 2005).

32. "Taun (Terebi): *Gekkō kamen* yomigaeru? Yume yo mōichido no ichi tenkei," *Shūkan shinchō* 7, no. 30 (July 1962): 19.

33. Sasaki Mamoru, *Sengo hīrō no shōzō: "Kane no naru oka" kara "Urutoraman" e* (Tokyo: Iwanami Shoten, 2003), 122, 148–49.

34. Thomas V. Morris, "What's behind the Mask?," in *Superheroes and Philosophy: Truth, Justice, and the Socratic Way,* ed. Thomas V. Morris, Matt Morris, and William Irwin, 250–67 (Chicago: Open Court Publishing, 2005).

35. Joel Hodge, "Superheroes, Scapegoats, and Saviors: The Problem of Evil and the Need for Redemption," in *Violence, Desire, and the Sacred*, vol. 3, *Mimesis, Movies, and Media,* ed. Scott Cowdell, Chris Fleming, and Joel Hodge (New York: Bloomsbury, 2015), 62.

36. Sasaki, *Neon Sain to Gekko Kamen,* 109–10.

37. Tzvetan Todorov, *The Fantastic: A Structural Approach to a Literary Genre* (Ithaca, N.Y.: Cornell University Press, 1975), 63 (emphasis added).

38. Takahashi Yasuo, "Gekkō kamen wa daredeshō? Terebi eiga 'Gekkō kamen'-ron moshikuwa seigi-ron," *Sapporodaigaku sōgō ronsō* 9 (March 2000): 238.

39. Kawauchi Kōhan (a.k.a. Yasunori), *Gekko kamen: Kawauchikōhan gekkō kamen* (Tokyo: Nanōsha, 1958), 1, 275–76.

40. Kōhan Kawauchi, *Ofukurosanyo* (Tokyo: Magajinhausu, 2007), 42–45.

41. Cited in Sasaki, *Neon Sain to Gekko Kamen,* 108.

42. Maria Burnett, *Open Secret: Illegal Detention and Torture by the Joint Anti-*

terrorism Task Force in Uganda (New York: Human Rights Watch, 2009); Carlos Gamerro, *An Open Secret* (South Royalton, Vt.: Steerforth Press, 2011).

43. Eric P. Nash, *Manga Kamishibai: The Art of Japanese Paper Theater* (New York: Harry N. Abrams, 2009).

44. Although this scene of filmic superimposition following Gekkō Kamen's presumed demise is absent from the October 1958 manga version, the feeling remains in the title of the episode, which remains "Justice Does Not Die [*Seigi wa shinazu*]." Kuwata Jirō and Kōhan Kawauchi, *Gekkō Kamen: Kanzenban seigi no shō* (Tokyo: Manga Shoppu, 2009), 62–76.

45. Frantz Fanon, *Black Skin, White Masks* (New York: Penguin Books, 2020).

46. Terada Seiichi, *Hanzai shinri kōwa* (Tokyo: Shinri-gaku kenkyūkai, 1918).

47. Terada, *Hanzai shinri kōwa*, 386–95.

48. Aaron Andrew Gerow, *Visions of Japanese Modernity: Articulations of Cinema, Nation, and Spectatorship, 1895–1925* (Berkeley: University of California Press, 2010), 53–64.

49. "Bōryoku bamen no tsuihō o hatajirushi ni," *Yomiuri Shinbun,* July 3, 1960, evening ed.; Hidaka Ichirō, *Nihon no hōsō no Ayumi* (Tokyo: Ningen no kagakusha, 1991), 184.

50. "Shin bangumi o happyō terebi kara bōryoku bamen tsuihō," *Yomiuri Shinbun,* June 22, 1960; "Bōryoku bamen no tsuihō o hatajirushi ni," *Yomiuri Shinbun,* July 3, 1960, evening ed.

51. Bruce Suttmeier, "Assassination on the Small Screen: Images and Writing in Oe Kenzaburo," *Mosaic: An Interdisciplinary Critical Journal* 41, no. 2 (June 2008): 75–91.

52. Shimizu Ikitarō, "Terebijon jidai," *Shisō* 9 (November 1958): 359.

53. Shimizu writes, "The more advanced the media, the more likely it is to be conservative or reactive." Quoted in Yokoyama Shigeru, "Datsu terebi jidai no tōrai: Shimizu Ikutarō no ronjita terebi to shakai, han seiki-go no saihō," *NHK hōsō bunka kenkyūjo nenpō* (Tokyo: Nippon Hōsō Kyōkai 2008), 203. See also Shun'ya Yoshimi, "From Street Corner to Living Room: Domestication of TV Culture and National Time/Narrative," trans. Jodie Beck, *Mechademia* 9 (2014): 126–42; Aaron Gerow, "From Film to Television: Early Theories of Television in Japan," in *Media Theory in Japan,* ed. Marc Steinberg and Alexander Zahlten, 33–51 (Durham, N.C.: Duke University Press, 2018).

54. Namekawa Michio, *Terebi to kodomo* (Tokyo: Maki shoten, 1961).

55. Namekawa, *Terebi to kodomo*, 18, 144, 154.

56. Namekawa, 51.

57. Namekawa, 280.

58. Namekawa, 48, 110.

59. Namekawa, 240. See also *Yomigaeru Shōwa kodomo shinbun: Shōwa 21-nen—Shōwa 37-nen-hen* (Tokyo: Shōwa kodomo shinbun hensan iinkai Nihon-bungeisha, 2007), 131.

60. Namekawa, *Terebi to kodomo,* 194.

61. Roger Caillois, *Man, Play, and Games,* trans. Meyer Barash (Chicago: University of Illinois Press, 1961), 120.

62. "Kodomo no asobi: Chīsai 'gekkō kamen' tsui muchū de tobioriru," *Yomiuri Shinbun,* June 15, 1959, 9.

63. Hamaya Hiroshi, *Hito to mono 9* (Tokyo: Mujirushi, 2018), 80–81.

64. See "Takeda yakuhin gekkō kamen arinamin CM 4," *Senkōsha fotonikuru Tokuten eizō 3 CM sakuhin-shū* (Tokyo: Senkōsha, 2015), DVD.

65. See "CM3 Takeda yakuhin gekkō kamen arinamin" and "CM 4; Takeda yakuhin panbitan CM," *Nobuhiro-sha fotonikuru (zuroku)* (Tokyo: Bikutā Entateinmento, 2015), DVD.

66. There were at least four different giveaway tie-in cardboard masks with cellophane for sunglasses that circulated during the run of the show. These can occasionally be found on sale today at https://page.auctions.yahoo.co.jp under searches for "Gekkō kamen Takeda yakuhin kōgyō."

67. "PanVitan Perē: Takeda Yakuhin kōgyō," *Yomiuri Shinbun,* March 24, 1959, evening ed.

68. Hanada Kiyoteru, "Kamen no hyōjō," *Gunzō* (March 1949): 1–9; Susan Jolliffe Napier, *Escape from the Wasteland: Romanticism and Realism in the Fiction of Mishima Yukio and Oe Kenzaburo* (Cambridge, Mass.: Harvard University Press Asia Center, 1995), 230; Noriko Mizuta Lippit, *Reality and Fiction in Modern Japanese Literature* (White Plains, N.Y.: M. E. Sharpe, 1980), 181–83.

69. Hanada, "Kamen no hyōjō," 4–5.

70. Paraphrasing Wolfgang Palaver, *René Girard's Mimetic Theory* (East Lansing: Michigan State University Press, 2013), 149.

71. Tanigawa Ken'ichi, *Tanigawa ken'ichi zenshū,* vol. 12 (Tokyo: Fusanbō intānashonaru, 2006), 97.

72. Matsumoto Toshio, "Kamen kō," in *Genshi no bigaku* (Tokyo: Firumu Ātosha, 1976), 259.

73. Matsumoto, "Kamen kō," 259.

74. Matsumoto, 254. See Atsuko Sakaki, "Scratch the Surface, Film the Face: Obsession with the Depth and Seduction of the Surface in Abe Kōbō's *The Face of Another,*" *Japan Forum* 17, no. 3 (November 1, 2005): 386n14.

75. Matsumoto, "Kamen kō," 262.

76. Agnes Horvath, *Modernism and Charisma* (New York: Palgrave Springer, 2013), 16.

77. See Thomas Lamarre, *The Anime Ecology: A Genealogy of Television, Animation, and Game Media* (Minneapolis: University of Minnesota Press, 2018), 41, 42. See also Kurosawa Kiyoshi's *Kairo* (2001) and Hideo Nakata's *Ringu* (1998).

78. Lamarre, *Anime Ecology,* 245.

79. Leo Ching, "Empire's Afterlife: The 'South' of Japan and 'Asian' Heroes in Popular Culture," *Global South* 5, no. 1 (September 2, 2011): 85–100; Leo Ching, "Champion of Justice: How Asian Heroes Saved Japanese Imperialism," *PMLA* 126, no. 3 (May 2011): 644–50; Higuchi Naofumi, *"Gekkō kamen" o tsu-*

kutta otokotachi, Heibonsha shinsho, vol. 435 (Tokyo: Heibonsha, 2008), 35–71. See discussion of "liveness" in Lamarre, *Anime Ecology.* This format could be a precursor to the V-cinema discussed in Alexander Zahlten, *The End of Japanese Cinema: Industrial Genres, National Times, and Media Ecologies* (Durham, N.C.: Duke University Press, 2017).

80. "Terebi no 'kiken-sei' PR wo," *Yomiuri Shinbun,* October 12, 1962.

81. Similar images of the tower in mid-construction can be seen in the opening credits of the 2005 nostalgia film *Always: Sunset on Third Street (Ōruweizu: San-chōme no Yūhi)* directed by Yamazaki Takashi.

82. "Gekkō kamen de wa arimasen," *Yomiuri Shinbun,* November 12, 1959, evening ed.

83. "'Gekkō kamen daiyaku tsukamaru: Tonai to Nagoya de akadenwa arashi," *Yomiuri Shinbun,* May 21, 1959; "Young TV 'Cop' Turns Out to Be Crook in Real Life," *Japan Times,* May 22, 1959.

84. "Nichiyō no asa, ginkō ni gōtō: Ikebukuro ni 'Gekkō kamen': Shukuchoku ni kamitsukare tōsō," *Yomiuri Shinbun,* September 20, 1959, evening ed.

85. See Gekkō Kamen in Jonathan E. Abel, "Masked Justice: Allegories of the Superhero in Cold War Japan," *Japan Forum* 26, no. 2 (2014): 187–208; "Miike ryūketsu kaihi," *Chūnichi nyūsu* (Tokyo: Chunichieigasha, July 29, 1960), 341:1, available at http://chunichieigasha.co.jp/video/4706/.

86. "Osorubeki rōtein: Sore o umidashita no wa nani ka eiga ya terebi o mohō," *Asahi Shinbun,* February 20, 1963, evening ed.

87. Martin Heidegger, *Introduction to Metaphysics* (New Haven, Conn.: Yale University Press, 2014), 38.

88. See Yasunaga Eitarō, "Enoki Misako: Ippuippu-sei o mamoru Gekkō kamen," *Gendai no me* 16, no. 10 (October 1975): 274–81.

89. Ozu Yasujirō's *Ohayo* (1960).

90. Hanada Kiyoteru, "Seigi no mikata; Gekkō Kamen!! Oshima Nagisa-ron," *Eiga hyōron* (September 1960): 16–19.

91. Hanada, "Kamen no hyōjō."

92. Steve Clark Ridgeley, *Japanese Counterculture: The Antiestablishment Art of Terayama Shuji* (Minneapolis: University of Minnesota Press, 2010).

93. Terayama Shūji, "Chisai kyozo 13: Gekkō Kamen," *Shukan Asahi Janaru* (April 6, 1973): 51–53.

94. Kaneko Masaru, *Gekkō Kamen no keizaigaku: Saraba musekinin shakai yo* (Tokyo: Asahi bunko, 2004).

95. Terashima Jitsurō, "Nōryoku no ressun: Akadō suzunosuke to Gekkō Kamen: Toikake to shite no sengonihon," *Sekai* (January 2010): 41–43.

96. "'Gekko kamen' de seiji katsudo no dansei byoshi," *Shakai nyusu,* March 16, 2006.

97. See Tsujiyama Kiyoshi, *Tsujiyama Kiyoshi: Shōhizei hantaitō,* accessed August 31, 2012, https://geocities.co.jp/Milkyway-Vega/6529/kiyosi.html.

98. Akatsuka Yukio, "'Mohō hanzai' to wadai-ka," *Ushio* 237, no. 2 (1979): 182.

99. For the terrorist spectacles, consider at least the Japanese Red Army

incidents of Asama-Sansō (Asama sansō jiken) and Lod Airport of 1972, the Morinaga Glico Incidents (Guriko, Morinaga jiken, 1984–85), the 1995 Aum Shinrikyō sarin gas attacks on the Tokyo subway, and the copycat hijacking of All Nippon Airways Flight 857 in 1995. Lone-wolf incidents include Miyazaki Tsutomu in mid-1980s, the killing spree in Akihabara (Akihabara Tōrima Jiken) of 2008, and the arson attack on anime studio Kyoto in 2019.

100. Miyabe Miyuki, *Mohōhan,* vol. 5 (Tokyo: Shinchōsha, 2005); Miyabe Miyuki, *Puppet Master,* trans. Ginny Tapley Takemori (Tokyo: Creek & River Co., 2014–2016).

5. Interpassive Ecomimesis

1. Robert Pfaller, *Interpassivity: The Aesthetics of Delegated Enjoyment* (Edinburgh: Edinburgh University Press, 2017).

2. Jordan Pruett, "On Feeling Productive: Videogames and Superfluous Labor," *Theory & Event* 22, no. 2 (2019): 402–16.

3. Pfaller, *Interpassivity,* 12.

4. Pfaller, 18–19.

5. Yoshioka Hiroshi, "Taidan: Mycom gēmu sōseiki o oete," in *Gēmuka suru sekai: Konpyūta gēmu no kigōron,* ed. Nihon Kigō Gakkai Taikai, Sōsho semiotoposu 8 (Tokyo: Shin'yōsha, 2013), 49.

6. Keiko McDonald, "Family, Education, and Postmodern Society: Yoshimitsu Morita's *The Family Game,*" *East-West Film Journal* 4, no. 1 (December 1989): 63; Keiko I. McDonald, *Reading a Japanese Film: Cinema in Context* (Honolulu: University of Hawai'i Press, 2005), 146; Aaron Gerow, "Playing with Postmodernism: Morita Yoshimitsu's *Family Game,*" in *Japanese Cinema: Texts and Contexts,* ed. Alastair Phillips and Julian Stringer (New York: Routledge, 2007), 247; Ian Buruma, "Humor in Japanese Cinema," *East-West Film Journal* 2, no. 1 (December 1987): 26–32; Satō Tadao, "Tokyo on Film," *East-West Film Journal* 2, no. 2 (June 1988): 1–12.

7. See also "Ko-shoku ichimi shichimi," *Asahi Shinbun,* November 20 1981; "Mune tsuka reta `ko-shoku no sabishisa' hitotoki," *Asahi Shinbun,* December 20, 1981; Wada Shigeaki, Kyū Eikan, and Hasegawa Keitarō, "Ima ko-shoku no jidai'dakara (jōhō nan demo sōdan-shitsu)," *Chūō kōron* 98, no. 5 (May 1983).

8. Uemura Masayuki, Hosoi Kōichi, and Nakamura Akinori, *Famikon to sono jidai: Terebi gēmu no tanjō* (Tokyo: NTT Shuppan, 2013), 110–11.

9. It is likely not simply random that hockey is the game featured in the film. As Picard mentions, hockey was one of the earliest video games on a console in Japan, beginning in 1973 with Taito's clone *Pro Hockey.* See Martin Picard, "The Foundation of Geemu: A Brief History of Early Japanese Video Games," *Game Studies* 13, no. 2 (December 2013), http://gamestudies.org/1302/articles/picard.

10. Ryu Nihon no, "CM aisu hokkē – famikon disuku shisutemu," June 30, 2021, YouTube video, 0:29, https://www.youtube.com/watch?v=qha_J_oPoZo. Also at Kinjo Game Channel, "1987 Nintendo (NES) ICE HOCKEY Commercial

Message," January 25, 2022, YouTube video, 0:30, https://www.youtube.com/watch?v=-UOOYY41Y70.

11. Marshall McLuhan, *Understanding Media: The Extensions of Man* (Cambridge, Mass.: MIT Press, 1994).

12. Gil Friend, "Ecomimesis: Copying Ecosystems for Fun and Profit," *New Bottom Line* 5, no. 4 (February 14, 1996), https://natlogic.com/resources/publications/new-bottom-line/vol5/4-ecomimesis-copying-ecosystems-fun-profit/.

13. Timothy Morton, *Ecology without Nature: Rethinking Environmental Aesthetics* (Cambridge, Mass.: Harvard University Press, 2007).

14. Alenda Y. Chang, "Games as Environmental Texts," *Qui Parle* 19, no. 2 (2011): 63.

15. Timothy Morton, *Dark Ecology: For a Logic of Future Coexistence* (New York: Columbia University Press, 2016).

16. For a graphic representation of the double helix structure, see Takano Yashuhiro, "Murakami Haruki 'Sekai no owari to hādoboirudo wandārando,'" *Bungaku sakuhin o yomu* (blog), 2006, http://www005.upp.so-net.ne.jp/Kaede02/sakuhin2/sekai_hard.html.

17. Murakami Haruki, *Murakami haruki zen sakuhin, 1979—1989: Sekai no owari to hādoboirudowandārando* (Tokyo: Kōdansha, 1990), 519. Translation modified from and emphasis added to Murakami Haruki, *Hard-Boiled Wonderland and the End of the World,* trans. Alfred Birnbaum (New York: Vintage, 1993), 353.

18. See also Haruki Murakami, *Pinball, 1973,* trans. Alfred Birnbaum (Tokyo: Kodansha, 1985), 12.

19. Karin Wenz, "Death," in *The Routledge Companion to Video Game Studies,* ed. Mark J. P. Wolf and Bernard Perron (New York: Routledge, 2014), 311.

20. Betsuyaku Minoru, "'Nerima OL satsujin jiken': Ochikochi-hō o sōshitsu shita hanzai-sha," *Chūō kōron* 98, no. 12 (November 1983): 267–73; Betsuyaku Minoru, "Tokushū = eiga eizō kara bungaku e: Miru koto no ochikochi-hō," *Kaie: Atarashī bungaku no techō* 4 (April 1979); Betsuyaku Minoru, "Chūkei no sōshitsu [The Loss of a Middle Ground]," in *Uma ni notta Tange Sazen* (Tokyo: Libroport, 1986), 10–13; Betsuyaku Minoru, "'Chūkei' toshite no Ajia," *Tokushū Higeki kigeki: Watashi no naka no Ajia* 43, no. 3 (1990): 14–16; Betsuyaku Minoru, "Atetsuke hanzai no kozu' bosei," in *"Bosei" no hanran: Heisei hanzai jikenbo* (Tokyo: Chūō kōron shinsha, 2002), 76–77. See John Whittier Treat, *Writing Ground Zero: Japanese Literature and the Atomic Bomb* (Chicago: University of Chicago Press, 1995), 64.

21. See Kasai Kiyoshi, "Hyōron shakai ryōiki no shōshitsu to 'sekai' no kōzō (Tokushū posuto-raitonoberu no jidai e)," *Shōsetsu tripper: Janru o asobu 'torippa,* March 2005, 35–43; Kasai Kiyoshi, *Tantei shōsetsu wa 'sekai' to sōgū shita* (Tokyo: Nan'undō, 2008), 65; Kasai Kiyoshi, "Sekaikei to reigai jōtai," in *Shakai wa sonzai shinai: Sekaikei bunkaron,* ed. Genkai shōsetsu Kenkyūjo, 21–62 (Tokyo: Nan'undō, 2009).

22. Maejima Satoshi, *Sekai-kei to wa nani ka: Posuto-Evua no otaku-shi* (Tokyo: Seikai-sha, 2014); Azuma Hiroki, *Nipponteki sōzō-ryoku no mirai: Kūru japanorojī no kanōsei* (Tokyo: Nippon hōsō shuppankyōkai, 2010); Tamaki Saitō, *Beautiful Fighting Girl* (Minneapolis: University of Minnesota Press, 2011).

23. Uno Tsunehiro, *Zero-nendai no sōzō-ryoku* (Tokyo: Hayakawa shobō, 2008); Christopher Howard, "The Ethics of Sekai-Kei: Reading Hiroki Azuma with Slavoj Žižek," *Science Fiction Film and Television* 7, no. 3 (November 8, 2014): 365–86.

24. Famiutsu ekkusu bokkusu henshū-bu, ed., *Shutainzu gēto kōshiki shiryōshū* (Tokyo: Entāburein, 2010), 120. All of the Science Adventure series games share the odd semicolon with *Steins;Gate: Chaos;Head, Robotics;Notes, Chaos;Child*. The semicolon evokes something like the geeky language of leetspeak, thereby creating a culture of those in the know and those outside it. Here the semicolon evokes the world of coding in which the symbol often is used as a "statement separator" or a mark for separate axes in a multidimensional array. So the mark is there less as a semantic marker than as a symbol evoking the world of computing and, by proxy, science.

25. Famiutsu ekkusu bokkusu henshū-bu, *Shutainzu gēto kōshiki shiryōshū*, 12–113. See also "Steins;Gate roke-chi tansaku," *Studio Rei* (blog), http://studio-ray.jp/blog/?p=674; "Seichi junrei: Shutainzugēto-hen," *Hippocampus* (blog), http://blog.livedoor.jp/peko_74-imas/archives/2926767.html; and especially the geotagged map on "'Shutainzugēto' butai tanbō (seichi junrei) matome," *Sōda, seichi ni ikou* (blog), http://blog.livedoor.jp/seichijunrei/archives/cat_50049220.html.

26. See Otanews and Torabo websites at http://otanews.livedoor.biz/archives/ and http://nlab.itmedia.co.jp/nl/articles/.

27. Matsubara Tatsuya and Hayashi Naotaka, "Namida no 'fōntorigāshisutemu' tanjō hiwago e Mon 'kami gē' to wadai futtō! Ekkusubokkusu 360 'Shutainzu gēto' chō ronguintabyū keisai," *Dengeki onrain*, http://dengekionline.com/elem/000/000/212/212275/index-3.html. See a similar use of *trigger* in Kazuhito Shiratori, Masao Hase, and Hoshino Junichi, "Kankyō jōhō o han'ei saseta kontekusuto awuea na gēmu," *Shadan hōjin Jōhōshori gakkai kenkyū hōkoku IPSJ SIG Technical Reports* 18 (2007): 17–23.

28. J. David Bolter and Richard Grusin, *Remediation: Understanding New Media* (Cambridge, Mass.: MIT Press, 1999).

29. This frequency analysis was based on a text extraction of the entire corpus of the Xbox edition.

30. Ueno Chizuko, "Kaisetsu," in Etō Jun, *Seijuku to sōshitsu "haha" no hōkai* (Tokyo: Kōdansha bungeibunko, 1993). See also Ann Sherif, "The Politics of Loss: On Eto Jun," *positions: east asia cultures critique* 10, no. 1 (2002): 111–39.

31. Asada Akira, "Infantile Capitalism and Japan's Postmodernism," *South Atlantic Quarterly* 87 (1988): 629–34; Anne Allison, *Permitted and Prohibited Desires: Mothers, Comics, and Censorship in Japan* (Berkeley: University of Cali-

fornia Press, 2000); Niwa Akiko and Tomiko Yoda, "The Formation of the Myth of Motherhood in Japan," *U.S.-Japan Women's Journal*, English Supplement, no. 4 (1993): 70–82; Tomiko Yoda, "The Rise and Fall of Maternal Society: Gender, Labor, and Capital in Contemporary Japan," *South Atlantic Quarterly* 99, no. 4 (October 1, 2000): 865–902; Uno Tsunehiro, *Bosei no disutopia* (Tokyo: Shūeisha, 2017); Ōtsuka Eiji, *Shōjo Minzokugaku: Seikimatsu no shinwa o tsumugumi konomatsuei* (Tokyo: Kobunsha, 1989); Ōtsuka Eiji, "Enjo kōsai to rekishi kara no tōsō," *Ronza* (July 1997): 30–35; Ōtsuka Eiji, *Etō Jun to shōjo feminismteki sengo subculture bungakuron* (Tokyo: Chikuma Shobō, 1998).

32. See also the discussion of family in Rachael Hutchinson, *Japanese Culture through Videogames* (New York: Routledge, 2019).

33. See YouTube interviews of Bose (a.k.a. Koshima Makaoto) and Itoi Shigesato, "M1+2 Event (subtitled)," Starmen.Net Youtube, June 7, 2007, YouTube video, 9:45, https://www.youtube.com/watch?v=lKpaKlatg5M; see also "Mother - Famicom (1989), Game Boy Advance (2003)," Hardcore Gaming 101, http://hg101.kontek.net/mother/mother1.htm.

34. "Shutage ren'ai ron: Chichi to musume, Soshite musume o ubau yoso no otoko," *Itagome: Otomege Reviews,* May 8, 2017, http://itagome.jugem.jp/?eid=245.

35. "Netabare: Amane-ka kakei-zu," Shutainzu gēto, http://zugtierlaster56.rssing.com/chan-26939252/latest.php.

36. See the collection of tweets archived by @muneyakecirno under the title "*Steins;Gate* no rabomen o kazoku, SERN o shakai to okikaeru to," January 11, 2010, at https://togetter.com/li/3031.

37. Uno Tsunehiro, "Reipu fantajī no seiritsu jōken—shōjo gensō o meguru yasuhiko yoshikazu-ron," *Yuriika = Eureka* 27, no. 11 (September 2007): 106–10.

38. Uno, *Zero-nendai no sōzō-ryoku,* 271.

39. Okawada Akira, "Gēmu risuto," in *Sabukaruchā sensō: "Sekaikei" kara "sekai naisen" e,* ed. Genkai Shōsetsu Kenkyūkai, 372–76 (Tokyo: Nan'undō, 2010).

40. See Tsuchimoto Ariko, "Kakū no bishōjo ni takusa reta kyōdō gensō!," in *Otaku no hon* (Tokyo: JICC Shuppankyoku, 1989), 103–15; Ueno Chizuko, "Rorikon to ya oi-zoku ni mirai wa aru ka!?," in *Otaku no hon* (Tokyo: JICC Shuppankyoku, 1989), 130–34; Betsuyaku Minoru, "Atetsuke hanzai no kōzu' bosei,'" in *"Bosei" no hanran: Heisei hanzai jikenbo* (Tokyo: Chūō Kōron Shinsha, 2002), 76–77; Kasai Kiyoshi, "Hyōron shakai ryōiki no shoshitsu to 'sekai' no kōzō (tokushu posutoraitonoberu no jidai e)," *Shosetsu tripper: Janru o asobu 'torippa* (2005): 35–43; Kurose Yōhei, "Kyarakutā ga, mite iru: Anime hyōgenron josetsu," *NHK bukkusu bekkan Shisō chizu,* ed. Azuma Hiroki and Kitada Akihiro, 1 (April 2008): 459–60.

41. Maejima pointedly asks "whether sekai-kei is in a co-dependent relationship with criticism." Maejima Satoshi and Nishijima Daisuke, *Sekaikei to wa nani ka* (Tokyo: Sofutobank bunko, 2014), 198.

42. Dani Cavallaro, *Anime and the Visual Novel: Narrative Structure, Design, and Play at the Crossroads of Animation and Computer Games* (Jefferson, N.C.: McFarland, 2010).

43. Azuma Hiroki, *Gēmu-teki riarizumu no tanjō: Dōbutsu-ka suru posuto modan 2* (Tokyo: Kōdansha, 2007), 271.

44. Viktor Shklovsky, "Art as Technique," in *Russian Formalist Criticism*, ed. L. T. Lemon and M. Reis, 3–57 (Lincoln: University of Nebraska Press, 1965).

45. Azuma, *Gēmu-teki riarizumu no tanjō*, 181.

46. See Jesper Juul, "A Clash between Game and Narrative," and "The Player and the Game," at www.jesperjuul.net/.

47. Lubomír Doležel, *Heterocosmica: Fiction and Possible Worlds* (Baltimore: Johns Hopkins University Press, 1998), 21.

48. Nick Montfort, *Twisty Little Passages: An Approach to Interactive Fiction* (Cambridge, Mass.: MIT Press, 2005), vii. The game itself is a parody of the post-Tamagotchi wave *Shīman* (1999), the virtual pet game that featured a talking carp-like fish with a human head and included a microphone in its original sales package.

49. Montfort, *Twisty Little Passages*, 3–4.

50. N. Katherine Hayles, *Electronic Literature: New Horizons for the Literary* (South Bend, Ind.: University of Notre Dame, 2008), 8.

51. Slavoj Žižek, "Is It Possible to Traverse the Fantasy in Cyberspace?," in *The Žižek Reader* (London: Blackwell-Wiley, 1999), 102–24.

52. Pfaller, *Interpassivity*, 3.

53. Pfaller, 4.

54. Azuma, *Gēmu-teki riarizumu no tanjō*.

55. See Espen J. Aarseth, *Cybertext: Perspectives on Ergodic Literature* (Baltimore: Johns Hopkins University Press, 1997); Montfort, *Twisty Little Passages*.

56. Brian Ruh, "The Comfort and Disquiet of Transmedia Horror in Higurashi: When They Cry (Higurashi No Naku Koro Ni)," *Refractory: A Journal of Entertainment Media* (June 22, 2014), http://refractory.unimelb.edu.au/2014/06/22/higurashi-brian-ruh/. See also Adachi Kayu, "Shiten ga ninau messēji: 'Higurashi no naku koroni' ni miru noberugēmu no monogatari kōsei-hō," *Animēshon kenkyū* 12, no. 1 (2011): 19–29.

57. Pfaller, *Interpassivity*, 7–8.

58. Azuma, *Gēmu-teki riarizumu no tanjō*, 275.

59. "(Sawa gēmu) 'shutainzu gēto' 'rūpu' ga unda aratana mirai-sa yawaka," *Asahi Shinbun*, July 11, 2011.

60. Bolter and Grusin, *Remediation*, 27.

61. Bolter and Grusin, 94.

62. Nikita Sharma, "Your Favorite Cell Phone Might Be Harming Your Health," *Disseminate Knowledge: International Journal of Research in Management Science and Technology* 2, no. 2 (2014): 96.

63. See Picard, "Foundation of Geemu," n11. See "Machi kōjō sekai e tobu:

Toranjisutarajio eigyō man no tatakai," in *Purojekuto ekkusu: Chōsenshatachi* (Tokyo: NHK entāpuraizu, 2001).

64. *Steins;Gate* is negative too but brings the contradiction into our very understanding of the plot.

65. From my review of 1980s and 1990s advertisements in the following magazines: SoftBank's *Oh!PC* and *Oh!HC*; Kōgakusha's *I/O*; Shogakukan's *Popukomu*; Nikkei-sha's *Nikkei Pasokon*; and Denpa shinbun-sha's *Denshi kōsaku magajin* and *Gekkan maikon*.

66. The Super Famicom Link and Mario advertisement appeared on the back cover of *Weekly Famikon tsūshin*, no. 180 7(2), May 29, 1992.

67. Fujita Akiko, "Dōga saito de ninki no 'gēmu jikkyō' hōritsu-teki ni ki o tsukerubeki ten wa?," Bengoshi dottokomu nyūsu, January 17, 2014, https://www.bengo4.com/internet/n_1115/.

68. Chōrō, "Tokuni imi wanai: *Steins;geito* o jikkyō purei part 9," Niconico dōga, June 13, 2015, http://www.nicovideo.jp/watch/sm26476884. See also Richard S. Chang, "You Say Gigawatt, I Say Jigowatt," *Wheels* (blog), *New York Times*, April 8, 2008, https://wheels.blogs.nytimes.com/2008/04/08/you-say-gigawatt-i-say-jigowatt/.

69. Comment at 9:51 of Masa Haruko (mairisu-yō), "[Jikkyō] imasara hitonihakikenai shutainzu gēto part 3," Niconico dōga, November 11, 2015, http://www.nicovideo.jp/watch/sm27564206.

70. Manji, "Shutainzu gēto demo-ban han'i nomi jimi jikkyō part 18," Niconico dōga, March 14, 2010, http://www.nicovideo.jp/watch/sm10025268.

71. See the discussion of "*neta*-like communication" as the seed of discourse in Suzuki Kensuke, *Bōsō suru intānetto: Netto shakai ni nani ga okite iru ka* (Tokyo: Isuto puresu, 2002). See also Azuma's notion of "contentless communication" in Azuma, *Gēmu-teki riarizumu no tanjō*, as well as the discussion in Ōtsuka Eiji and Azuma Hiroki, *Riaru no yukue: Otaku wa dō ikiru ka* (Tokyo: Kōdansha, 2008).

72. Ion, "imai asami no SSG," Niconico dōga, November 8, 2014, http://www.nicovideo.jp/watch/sm24874001.

73. Toshiya Ueno, "Techno-Orientalism and Media-Tribalism: On Japanese Animation and Rave Culture," *Third Text* 13, no. 47 (1999): 95–106.

74. "Disaster Prevention Information," Guide for Residents, Tokyo Metropolitan Government, https://www.metro.tokyo.lg.jp/english/guide/bosai/index.html.

75. Toshifumi Nakabayashi, "Revival from the Great East Japan Earthquake by Fukushima Game Jam" (Game Developers Conference GDC14, San Francisco, March 2014), https://www.gdcvault.com/play/1020803/Revival-from-the-Great-East; Shin Kiyoshi, "Localizing Global Game Jam: Designing Game Development for Collaborative Learning in the Social Context," in *Advances in Computer Entertainment*, ed. Anton Nijholt, 117–32 (New York: Springer, 2012).

76. P. Bowles and L. T. Woods, *Japan after the Economic Miracle: In Search of New Directions* (New York: Springer Science & Business Media, 2012); Parissa

Haghirian, *Routledge Handbook of Japanese Business and Management* (New York: Routledge, 2016); M. Itoh, *The Japanese Economy Reconsidered* (New York: Palgrave Macmillan, 2000); Joe Peek and Eric S. Rosengren, "Unnatural Selection: Perverse Incentives and the Misallocation of Credit in Japan," *American Economic Review* 95, no. 4 (2005): 1144–66; J. Mark Ramseyer, "Legal Rules in Repeated Deals: Banking in the Shadow of Defection in Japan," *Journal of Legal Studies* 20, no. 1 (1991): 91–117; Kazuo Ueda, "Causes of Japan's Banking Problems in the 1990s," in *Crisis and Change in the Japanese Financial System*, ed. Takeo Hoshi and Hugh Patrick, 59–81 (New York: Springer US, 2000).

77. Kevin R. Brine and Mary Poovey, *Finance in America: An Unfinished Story* (Chicago: University of Chicago Press, 2017); N. Katherine Hayles, *How We Became Posthuman: Virtual Bodies in Cybernetics, Literature, and Informatics* (Chicago: University of Chicago Press, 1999); N. Katherine Hayles, *Unthought: The Power of the Cognitive Nonconscious* (Chicago: University of Chicago Press, 2017).

78. Yoshioka Hiroshi, "'Maikongēmu sōsei-ki' o oete," in *Gēmukasuru sekai: Konpyūta gēmu no kigōron*, ed. Nihon kigō gakkai, Sōsho semiotoposu, 48–49 (Tokyo: Shin'yōsha, 2013).

79. Uno, *Zero-nendai no sōzō-ryoku*, 19, 96, 116.

80. See "Shinyōgēmu" (Credit Game), InterCommunication Center, 2001, http://www.ntticc.or.jp/en/feature/2001/Credit_Game/Events/event02.html, http://www.ntticc.or.jp/en/feature/2001/Credit_Game/Works/creditgame_a.html, http://www.ntticc.or.jp/ja/feature/2001/Credit_Game/Works/creditgame_b_j.html.

6. Mediated Expressions

1. John Brownlee, "Anime Flash Mob Dances in Akihambra," *Wired*, April 12, 2007, https://www.wired.com/2007/04/anime-flash-mob/.

2. Hamano Satoshi, "Suzumiya haruhi no seisei-ryoku: Kyarakutā-teki karada no mimēshisu," *Yuriika*, July 2011, 597.

3. Toshiya Ueno, "Techno-Orientalism and Media-Tribalism: On Japanese Animation and Rave Culture," *Third Text* 13, no. 47 (1999): 95–106.

4. Azuma Hiroki, *General Will 2.0: Rousseau, Freud, Google*, trans. John Person (New York: Vertical, 2014).

5. Bernadette Wegenstein, "Body," in *Critical Terms for Media Studies*, ed. W. J. T. Mitchell and Mark B. N. Hansen (Chicago: University of Chicago Press, 2010), 19.

6. Wegenstein, "Body," 33; Jussi Parikka, *Insect Media: An Archaeology of Animals and Technology* (Minneapolis: University of Minnesota Press, 2010).

7. Mark Hansen, *Embodying Technesis: Technology beyond Writing* (Ann Arbor: University of Michigan Press, 2000), 51. See N. Katherine Hayles, *How We Became Posthuman: Virtual Bodies in Cybernetics, Literature, and Informatics* (Chicago: University of Chicago Press, 2008); Nicholas Mirzoeff, *Bodyscape: Art, Modernity, and the Ideal Figure* (New York: Routledge, 2018); Marshall

McLuhan, *Understanding Media: The Extensions of Man* (Cambridge, Mass.: MIT Press, 1994).

8. Walter Benjamin, "Doctrine of the Similar (1933)," trans. Knut Tarnowski, *New German Critique* 17 (1979): 65; Walter Benjamin, "On the Mimetic Faculty," in *Reflections* (New York: Schocken Books, 1986), 333.

9. Karen Barad, *Meeting the Universe Halfway: Quantum Physics and the Entanglement of Matter and Meaning* (Durham, N.C.: Duke University Press, 2007), ix. See also Tim Ingold, *Making: Anthropology, Archaeology, Art, and Architecture* (New York: Routledge, 2013), 132.

10. Hansen, *Embodying Technesis*, 52.

11. Hansen, 190.

12. Hansen, 190.

13. Saitō Tamaki, *Media wa sonzai shinai* (Tokyo: NTT Shuppan, 2007), 77.

14. Pierre Bourdieu, *Outline of a Theory of Practice* (Cambridge: Cambridge University Press, 1977), 218n44.

15. Susan Buck-Morss, *The Dialectics of Seeing: Walter Benjamin and the Arcades Project* (Cambridge, Mass.: MIT Press, 1991), 263. And later she writes that Benjamin's conceptualization of mimesis is an "inventive reception" (264).

16. Hans-Georg Gadamer, *Truth and Method,* trans. Joel Weinsheimer and Donald G. Marshall (New York: Bloomsbury Publishing, 2004), 115.

17. Gadamer, *Truth and Method,* 133.

18. Mark B. N. Hansen, *Bodies in Code: Interfaces with Digital Media* (New York: Routledge, 2012), 102.

19. Hansen, *Bodies in Code,* 145.

20. Slavoj Žižek, "Ideology Is the Original Augmented Reality," *Nautilus,* November 2, 2017, http://nautil.us/issue/54/the-unspoken/ideology-is-the -original-augmented-reality; Slavoj Žižek, *Incontinence of the Void: Economico-Philosophical Spandrels* (Cambridge, Mass.: MIT Press, 2019).

21. And the group had a profound influence on the early Wittgenstein, who adopts a similar picture theory of language in his *Tractatus Logico-Philosophicus* (1922). Thomas E. Uebel, *Rediscovering the Forgotten Vienna Circle: Austrian Studies on Otto Neurath and the Vienna Circle* (Dordrecht, the Netherlands: Springer Science & Business Media, 2012), 90. See also Ray Monk, *How to Read Wittgenstein* (London: Granta Books, 2019), 41.

22. Otto Neurath, *Empiricism and Sociology,* with Robert S. Cohen (New York: Springer Science & Business Media, 2012), 224.

23. Squarely Rooted, "PRESENTING: The Entire US Economy Depicted in Emoji," *Business Insider,* October 17, 2014, http://www.businessinsider.com/ the-economy-in-emoji-2014-10.

24. Ōta Yukio, *Pikutoguramu [emoji] dezain* (Tokyo: Kashiwa Shobo, 1987), 79–90.

25. Ōta, *Pikutoguramu [emoji] dezain,* 95.

26. Tsurumi Shunsukei, *Kotoba wa hirogaru* (Tokyo: Fukuinkanshoten, 1991), 412.

27. A summary of the work was published in Aaron Marcus, "New Ways to View World Problems," *East West Perspectives* (Summer 1979): 15–22. See also Aaron Marcus, "Visualizing Global Interdependencies," *Graphic Design (Japan)* 79 (1960): 57–62, video available at AMandAssociates, "Visualizing Global Interdependencies," July 21, 2011, YouTube video, 14:53, https://www.youtube.com/watch?v=tc8Skq4HVwc.

28. Marcus, "New Ways to View World Problems," 15.

29. Yoshimoto Takaaki, "Mōsha to kagami," in *Yoshimoto Takaaki zenshū,* vol. 13 (Tokyo: Keisō shobo, 1969), 144.

30. See Yutaka Satoh, "Ōbunshotai," Type-Lab, accessed August 22, 2018, http://www.type-labo.jp/Ohbun.html.

31. Zaruemon channel 02, "1995-nen-goro no CM hadzuki riona Dokomo no pokeberu berumī," September 1, 2015, YouTube video, 0:16, https://www.youtube.com/watch?v=uoeRqp3Lcx4.

32. Though they seem to share a common root, *emoticon* is an English compound truncation from *emotion* and *icon,* whereas *emoji* is a Japanese expression composed of *e* ("picture") and *moji* ("characters"). Emoji, therefore, have no necessary or inherent connection to emotions. See, for instance, the mistranslation of *emoji* as *emoticon* in Matsuda Misa, "Discourses of Keitai in Japan," in *Personal, Portable, Pedestrian: Mobile Phones in Japanese Life,* ed. Mizuko Itō, Daisuke Okabe, and Misa Matsuda (Cambridge, Mass.: MIT Press, 2005), 35.

33. See Nakamura 001, "Dokomo kara jīmeru ni mēru o okuru to 'onpu' no emoji ga 'unko' ni naru," *Tsuyobi de susume* (blog), November 26, 2010, http://nakamura001.hatenablog.com/entry/20101126/1290736227.

34. Inamasu Tatsuo, "'Emoji' no tsukawarekata (tokushū keitai sekai): Keitai hyōgen," *Kokubungaku: Kaishaku to kyōzai no kenkyū* 53, no. 5 (2008): 109.

35. See Inamasu, "'Emoji' no tsukawarekata."

36. See Koichi Yasuoka, "Pictographs in Mobile Phones and Their Character Codes," *Journal of Information Processing and Management* 50, no. 2 (2007): 67–73.

37. Chicchikichī, "Emoji shōsetsu," *Muka shōsetsu nara Eburisuta* (blog), August 10, 2007, https://estar.jp/_novel_view?w=2637775.

38. See "Oneohtrix Point Never - Boring Angel," Oneohtrix Point Never, December 23, 2013, YouTube video, 4:17, https://www.youtube.com/watch?v=qmlJveN9IkI. See Cara Rose DeFabio, "Game of Phones," April 2, 2014, YouTube video, 1:44, https://www.youtube.com/watch?v=loSYKT4FgGU.

39. See Aaron Marcus, "User Interface Design and Culture," in *Usability and Internationalization of Information Technology,* ed. Nuray Aykin, 51–78 (Mahwah, N.J.: Lawrence Erlbaum Associates, 2005).

40. See Wikipedia, s.v. "うんこマーク," accessed August 22, 2018, https://ja.wikipedia.org/wiki/うんこマーク. The Yakult packaging is further discussed in "Kogane no rasen wa doko kara kita no ka: Maki guso no kigen [washiki]," *Dodome iro no hakubutsukan iyageriumu neo* (blog), http://iyagerium.blog90.fc2.com/blog-entry-85.html.

41. Gomi Taro, *Minna unchi* (Tokyo: Fukuonkan Shoten, 1977); Gomi Taro, *Everyone Poops,* trans. Amanda M. Stinchecum (La Jolla, Calif.: Paw Prints, 2008).

42. See Mona Chalabi, "The 100 Most-Used Emojis," *FiveThirtyEight* (blog), June 5, 2014, https://fivethirtyeight.com/features/the-100-most-used-emojis.

43. Sora Song, "Study: 1 in 6 Cell Phones Contaminated with Fecal Matter," *TIME,* October 17, 2011, http://healthland.time.com/2011/10/17/study-1-in-6 -cell-phones-contaminated-with-fecal-matter/.

44. Inamasu, "'Emoji' no tsukawarekata," 111.

45. Andrew McGill, "Why White People Don't Use White Emoji," *Atlantic,* May 9, 2016.

46. Jason Reed, "The Problem with Emoji Skin Tones That No One Talks About," *Daily Dot,* November 23, 2018, https://www.dailydot.com/irl/skin-tone -emoji/.

47. Paige Tutt, "Apple's New Diverse Emoji Are Even More Problematic than Before," *Washington Post,* April 10, 2015.

48. See Marcel Danesi, *The Semiotics of Emoji: The Rise of Visual Language in the Age of the Internet* (New York: Bloomsbury Publishing, 2016); Sabine Doran, *The Culture of Yellow, or The Visual Politics of Late Modernity* (New York: A&C Black, 2013).

49. Miriam E. Sweeney and Kelsea Whaley, "Technically White: Emoji Skin-Tone Modifiers As American Technoculture," *First Monday* 24, no. 7 (2019): https://journals.uic.edu/ojs/index.php/fm/article/download/10060/8048 (emphasis added).

50. Alexander Robertson, Walid Magdy, and Sharon Goldwater, "Self-Representation on Twitter Using Emoji Skin Color Modifiers," *Proceedings of the International AAAI Conference on Web and Social Media* (March 28, 2018): 680–83; Alexander Robertson, Walid Magdy, and Sharon Goldwater, "Emoji Skin Tone Modifiers: Analyzing Variation in Usage on Social Media," *ACM Transactions on Social Computing* 3, no. 2 (April 19, 2020): 1–25.

51. See Jane Hu, "Ang Lee's Tears: Digital Global Melodrama in *The Wedding Banquet, Hulk,* and *Gemini Man,*" *Verge: Studies in Global Asias* 7, no. 2 (2021): 151–76. See also Gertrud Koch, "The Human Body as Generic Form: On Anthropomorphism in Media" (Animate panel, Terms of Media II: Actions Conference, Brown University, October 10, 2015).

Conclusion

1. See the work of Yoshimoto Mitsuhiro critiquing just such usage in film studies: Mitsuhiro Yoshimoto, "The Difficulty of Being Radical: The Discipline of Film Studies and the Postcolonial World Order," *boundary 2* 18, no. 3 (1991): 242–57; Mitsuhiro Yoshimoto, "Questions of Japanese Cinema: Disciplinary Boundaries and the Invention of the Scholarly Object," in *Learning Places: The Afterlives of Area Studies,* ed. Masao Miyoshi and H. D. Harootunian, 368–400 (Durham, N.C.: Duke University Press, 2002).

2. Christopher Bush, *The Floating World: Japoniste Aesthetics and Global Modernity* (New York: Columbia University Press, forthcoming).

3. Karatani Kōjin, "One Spirit, Two Nineteenth Centuries," in *Postmodernism and Japan,* ed. Harry Harootunian and Masao Miyoshi, 259–72 (Durham, N.C.: Duke University Press, 1987).

4. See Arjun Appadurai, *Modernity At Large: Cultural Dimensions of Globalization* (Minneapolis: University of Minnesota Press, 1996); Andrew Wachtel, *Alternative Modernities* (Durham, N.C.: Duke University Press, 2001); Bruce M. Knauft, *Critically Modern: Alternatives, Alterities, Anthropologies* (Bloomington: Indiana University Press, 2002); Fredric Jameson, *A Singular Modernity: Essay on the Ontology of the Present* (London: Verso, 2002); Thomas Lamarre and Kang Nae-hui, ed., *Impacts of Modernities,* vol. 3 of *Traces: A Multilingual Series of Cultural Theory and Translation* (Hong Kong: Hong Kong University Press, 2004); Peter Osborne, "Modernism as Translation," in *Philosophy in Cultural Theory* (London: Routledge, 2013), 67–76.

5. Even Pound's injunction to "make it new" presumes an ontological "it" that is remade in the process. Ezra Pound, *Make It New: Essays* (New Haven, Conn.: Yale University Press, 1971).

6. Ricardo Roque, "Mimesis and Colonialism: Emerging Perspectives on a Shared History," *History Compass* 13, no. 4 (April 2015): 201–11.

7. Barbara Fuchs, *Mimesis and Empire: The New World, Islam, and European Identities* (Cambridge: Cambridge University Press, 2003), 4; see also 118 for her use of "imperial mimesis."

8. Gertrud Koch, "The Human Body as Generic Form: On Anthropomorphism in Media" (Animate panel at Terms of Media II: Actions Conference, Brown University, October 10, 2015).

9. Matthew Hawkins, "Game Character More Real Than Actual Human, Says PBS," NBC News, April 4, 2012, https://www.nbcnews.com/tech/tech-news/game-character-more-real-actual-human-says-pbs-flna654235.

10. Sandra Annett, "What Can a Vocaloid Do? The Kyara as Body without Organs," *Mechademia: Second Arc* 10 (2015): 163–77; Cole Masaitis, "The Vocaloid Phenomenon of Vocal Synthesis and Sample Concatenation" (master's thesis, University of Mary Washington, 2017). See discussion in Takahashi Yoshitaka, "Zeami no 'monomane' to Yōroppa-teki mimēshisu," in *Takahashi Yoshitaka bungei riron chosaku-shū-ka* (Tokyo: Jinbunshoin, 1977), 161.

11. See Maruyama Masao, *Gendai seiji no shisō to kōdō* (Tokyo: Miraisha, 2006); Komori Yōichi, *Posutokoroniaru = Postcolonial* (Tokyo: Iwanami Shoten, 2001); Homi K. Bhabha, *The Location of Culture* (New York: Routledge, 1994).

12. Waldemar Zacharasiewicz, *Imagology Revisited* (Amsterdam: Rodopi, 2010).

13. David Morley and Kevin Robins, *Spaces of Identity: Global Media, Electronic Landscapes, and Cultural Boundaries* (New York: Routledge, 1995), 147–73; Eve Bennett, "Techno-Butterfly," *Science Fiction Film & Television* 5, no. 1 (January 1, 2012): 23–46; Christopher Fan, "Techno-Orientalism with

Chinese Characteristics: Maureen F. McHugh's *China Mountain Zhang*," *Journal of Transnational American Studies* 6, no. 1 (2015), https://doi.org/10.5070/T861019585; Ken McLeod, "Afro-Samurai: Techno-Orientalism and Contemporary Hip Hop," *Popular Music* 32, no. 2 (May 2013): 259–75; Greta Aiyu Niu, "Techno-Orientalism, Nanotechnology, Posthumans, and Post-Posthumans in Neal Stephenson's and Linda Nagata's Science Fiction," *MELUS* 33, no. 4 (2008): 73–96; Takeo Rivera, "Do Asians Dream of Electric Shrieks? Techno-Orientalism and Erotohistoriographic Masochism in Eidos Montreal's *Deus Ex: Human Revolution*," *Amerasia Journal* 40, no. 2 (January 2014): 67–87; May Telmissany and Stephanie Tara Schwartz, *Counterpoints: Edward Said's Legacy* (Newcastle upon Tyne, U.K.: Cambridge Scholars Publishing, 2010); Wester Wagenaar, "Wacky Japan: A New Face of Orientalism," *Asia in Focus: A Nordic Journal on Asia by Early Career Researchers* 3 (2016): 46–54.

14. Some of this work of transfer from body to media and back has begun in Japanese studies in the work of scholars like Yoshimoto Mitsuhiro on film, Thomas Lamarre on anime, or Ian Condry on rap music.

15. Ueno Toshiya, "Japanimation and Technoorientalism," in *The Uncanny: Experiments in Cyborg Culture,* ed. Bruce Grenville (Vancouver: Arsenal Pulp Press, 2001). See also Ueno Toshiya, "Rizumu dansu mimeshisu," *Urban Tribal Studies* 3, no. 10 (July 2000): 228–41.

16. Hayashi Yūjirō, "Jōhō shakai to atarashii kachi taikei," *Chochiku Jihō* 74 (1967): 20–25; Hayashi Yūjirō, *Jōhōka Shakai* (Tokyo: Kōdansha Gendai Shinsho, 1969).

17. Tonuma Koichi, "Human Settlement Pattern in Japan," *Ekistics* 25, no. 148 (1968): 187–92; Yuriko Furuhata, *Cinema of Actuality: Japanese Avant-Garde Filmmaking in the Season of Image Politics* (Durham, N.C.: Duke University Press, 2013); Rem Koolhaas and Hans Ulrich Obrist, *Project Japan: Metabolism Talks,* ed. Kayoko Ota and James Westcott (London: Taschen, 2011).

18. David S. Roh, Betsy Huang, and Greta A. Niu, *Techno-Orientalism: Imagining Asia in Speculative Fiction, History, and Media* (New Brunswick, N.J.: Rutgers University Press, 2015), 3.

19. Drawing on Kant, Karatani calls this willful ignorance a "bracketing" of concern. See Karatani Kōjin, "Uses of Aesthetics: After Orientalism," trans. Sabu Kohso, *boundary 2* 25, no. 2 (1998): 145–60; Karatani Kōjin, *Teihon Karatani Kōjin shū: Nēshon to bigaku 4* (Tokyo: Iwanami Shoten, 2004); Karatani Kōjin, *Nation and Aesthetics: On Kant and Freud,* trans. Jonathan E. Abel, Hiroki Yoshikuni, and Darwin H. Tsen (New York: Oxford University Press, 2017).

20. See Kikuchi Yuko, *Japanese Modernisation and Mingei Theory: Cultural Nationalism and Oriental Orientalism* (New York: Routledge Curzon, 2004).

21. Oscar Wilde, "The Decay of Lying," in *Oscar Wilde: The Major Works* (Oxford: Oxford University Press, 2000), 235–36; Osukā Wairudo, *Osukā Wairudo zenshū 4-sho,* trans. Nishimura Kōji (Tokyo: Ōdzuchi-sha, 1981). See also Rinko Miho, "Osukā Wairudo no 'yuibishugi' saikō e no oboegaki: 'The Decay of Lying' ni okeru japonisumu," *Rīdingu* 26 (September 30, 2005): 92–100.

22. Marc Steinberg, *The Platform Economy: How Japan Transformed the Consumer Internet* (Minneapolis: University of Minnesota Press, 2019), 180–205.

23. Steinberg, *Platform Economy*, 193–95.

24. On odorlessness, see Iwabuchi Koichi, *Recentering Globalization: Popular Culture and Japanese Transnationalism* (Durham, N.C.: Duke University Press, 2002), 24–30. On mukokuseki, see Ōtsuka Eiji, *Kasō genjitsu hihyō: Shōhi shakai wa owaranai* (Tokyo: Shin'yōsha, 1992), 151; Ōtsuka Eiji, "Komikku sekai sehai," *Sapio* 8 (1993): 10–12.

25. Paul Du Gay, Stuart Hall, Linda Janes, Anders Koed Madsen, Hugh Mackay, and Keith Negus, *Doing Cultural Studies: The Story of the Sony Walkman* (Los Angeles: SAGE Publications, 2013), 42–74.

26. Mizumura Minae, *The Fall of Language in the Age of English* (New York: Columbia University Press, 2015).

Index

Page numbers in italic refer to illustrations.

Jonathan E. Abel is associate professor of Asian studies and comparative literature at the Pennsylvania State University. He is author of *Redacted: The Archives of Censorship in Transwar Japan.*